# SECURITIES VALUATION

# SECURITIES VALUATION

*Applications of Financial Modeling*

Thomas S. Y. Ho
Sang Bin Lee

New York   Oxford
OXFORD UNIVERSITY PRESS
2005

Oxford University Press

Oxford   New York
Auckland   Bangkok   Buenos Aires   Cape Town   Chennai
Dar es Salaam   Delhi   Hong Kong   Istanbul   Karachi   Kolkata
Kuala Lumpur   Madrid   Melbourne   Mexico City   Mumbai   Nairobi
São Paulo   Shanghai   Taipei   Tokyo   Toronto

Published by Oxford University Press, Inc.
198 Madison Avenue, New York, New York 10016
www.oup.com

Oxford is a registered trademark of Oxford University Press

**Library of Congress Cataloging-in-Publication Data**

Ho, Thomas S. Y.
   Securities valuation : applications of financial modeling / by Thomas S. Y. Ho and Sang
   Bin Lee.
      p. cm.
   Includes index.
   ISBN-13: 978-0-19-517274-4 (alk. paper) — ISBN-13: 978-0-19-517275-1 (pbk. : alk. paper)
   ISBN 0-19-517274-4 (alk. paper) — ISBN 0-19-517275-2 (pbk. : alk. paper)
      1. Investments—Mathematical models.   2. Securities—Valuation—Mathematical models.
      3. Finance—Mathematical models.   4. Investments—Case studies.   I. Yi, Sang-bin.
      II. Title.
   HG4515.2.H6 2005
   323.63'2—dc22                                                      2004063588

Printing number: 9 8 7 6 5 4 3 2 1

Printed in the United States of America
on acid-free paper

# Contents

*Preface*    x

## 1. Introduction    1

1.1  Diversification    1

1.2  Capital Asset Pricing Model (CAPM)    5

1.3  Beta: The Systematic Risk    7

1.4  The Stock Model—Dividend Discount Model    9

1.5  An Application of the Capital Asset Pricing Model in Investment Services    11

*Excel Model Exercises*    11

    E1.1  Diversification    11

        Case: Managing the Risk of a Pension Fund    12

    E1.2  CAPM    15

        Case: Quarterly Earnings Report of an Energy Storage Operator    16

    E1.3  Dividend Discount Model    22

        Case: Valuation of a Real Estate Investment Trust (REIT)    23

*Notes*    26

*Bibliography*    27

## 2. Equity Options    29

2.1  Description of an Option    29

2.2  Institutional Framework    30

2.3  Put-Call Parity    31

2.4  The Main Insight of the Black-Scholes Model    33

2.5  Valuation Methods    40

2.6  Relationships of Risk-Neutral and Market Binomial Lattices    45

2.7  Option Behavior and the Sensitivity Analysis    46

2.8  Applications of Option Models    48

*Excel Model Exercises*    51

    E2.1  Cox-Ross-Rubinstein Option Pricing Model    51

        Case: Private Wealth Management—Designing a Structured Product    52

E2.2  The Put-Call Parity     64
      Case: Proprietary Trading Desk     65
E2.3  The Black-Scholes Option Pricing Model     70
      Case: Use of Put Options in Hedging     71
E2.4  The Relationship of Risk-Neutral and Market
Binomial Lattices     80
      Case: Asset Allocation and the Expected Returns
of an Option     80

*Notes*     83
*Bibliography*     83

## 3. Exotic Options     85

3.1  Options with Alternative Payoffs at Expiration     85
3.2  Options with Boundary Conditions     87
3.3  Options with the Early Exercise Feature (American) and the
Bellman Optimization     90
3.4  Compound Options     95
*Excel Model Exercises*     97
    E3.1  American Stock Option     97
        Case: Valuing Employee Stock Options     97
    E3.2  Compound Option     104
        Case: Project Financing and the Compound Option     105
    E3.3  Digital Option     110
        Case: IPO Incentive Option and Executive Option
Design     111
    E3.4  Greeks (Delta, Gamma, Theta, Vega, Rho, Omega):
A Binomial Lattice Versus a Closed-Form Solution     115
        Case: Valuing an Equity-Structured Product from
a Term Sheet     116
*Bibliography*     121

## 4. Bond Mathematics, Treasury Securities, and Swaps     123

4.1  Bond Mathematics     123
4.2  Bonds and Bond Markets     125
4.3  Swap Markets     127
4.4  Economics of the Yield Curve     128
4.5  The Bond Model     132
4.6  Forward Prices and Forward Rates     135
4.7  Duration and Convexity     140
4.8  Applications of the Bond Analytics     147

*Excel Model Exercises*    149

E4.1 Effective Duration    149

Case: Interest Rate Bet Using Effective Duration    151

E4.2 Par Yield Curve, Spot Yield Curve, Discount Function, and Forward Prices    155

Case: The Law of One Price and Marking a Bond Position    156

E4.3 Dollar Duration    160

Case: Transfer Pricing and Hedging at a Treasury Desk    165

E4.4 Swap Model    168

Case: A Hedging Program Designed by an Asset Liability Committee    169

*Notes*    173

*Bibliography*    173

## 5. Bond Options    175

5.1 Interest Rate Movements: Historical Experiences    175

5.2 Equilibrium Models    180

5.3 Arbitrage-Free Models    183

5.4 Key Rate Duration and Dynamic Hedging    189

*Excel Model Exercises*    193

E5.1 Cox-Ingersoll-Ross Model    193

Case: Building a Model by Knowing Your Clients    194

E5.2 Vasicek Model    198

Case: Defined Benefits and Asset Management    199

E5.3 Ho-Lee Model    203

Case: Using an Arbitrage-Free Model to Determine Profit Release    203

E5.4 The Black Model of the Bond Option    208

Case: Proprietary Trading Desk    209

E5.5 Swaption Model    212

Case: Marking to Market an Illiquid Derivative Position    213

*Notes*    217

*Bibliography*    217

## 6. Corporate Bonds: Investment Grade    219

6.1 Describing a Corporate Bond    219

6.2 Valuation of a Bond    224

6.3 Option-Adjusted Spread    229

6.4 Valuation of Callable Bonds    233

6.5  Valuation of Sinking Fund Bonds      236
    *Excel Model Exercises*      241
        E6.1  Callable Bonds      241
            Case: Funding Working Capital with Debt      241
        E6.2  Sinking Fund Bonds      246
            Case: Securitization and the Asset-Backed
            Securities      246
    *Note*      251
    *Bibliography*      251

## 7. Corporate Bonds: High-Yield Bonds      252

7.1  An Example of a High-Yield Bond      252
7.2  Institutional Framework of Bankruptcy and Bankruptcy
    Proceedings      255
7.3  The Fisher Model      258
7.4  An Actuarial Model      259
7.5  Historical Experience and Estimation of the Parameters
    of Default Models      260
7.6  The Reduced-Form Models      264
7.7  The Structural Models      266
7.8  Valuation of a Debt Package Using a Compound Option Model      269
    *Excel Model Exercises*      273
        E7.1  Credit Default Swap      273
            Case: Credit Derivatives, Insurance Premiums,
            and Callable Bonds      274
        E7.2  Ho-Singer Model      278
            Case: Reorganization and Debt Restructuring      280
    *Note*      284
    *Bibliography*      284

## 8. Other Bonds: Convertible Bonds, MBS, CMO      287

8.1  Description of a Convertible Bond      287
8.2  Call Provision and Forced Conversion      289
8.3  Credit Risk      293
8.4  Mortgage-Backed Securities (Pass-Through Certificates)      293
8.5  Prepayment Model and Valuation      295
8.6  Collateralized Mortgage Obligations (CMOs)      301
8.7  Other Bonds      305
    *Excel Model Exercises*      307
        E8.1  Convertible Bonds      307
            Case: Hedging a Convertible Bond Issue      308

E8.2  Mortgage-Backed Securities (Level Payments, PSA,
IO & PO)    310

Case: Pricing a Guaranteed Investment Contract
and the Profit Spread    311

*Bibliography*    315

*Index*    316

# Preface

$S$*ecurities Valuation* is a textbook on valuing securities, which include equity, government securities, equity and bond options, corporate bonds, mortgage-backed securities, CMOs, and other securities. The textbook is written for the undergraduates and graduate classes in finance and mathematical finance, but it differs from other standard textbooks in a number of ways to meet the changing needs in the classroom.

Today, students need to better appreciate the use of financial theory in the real world. Standard "from theory to practice" finance textbooks tend to take the approach of describing the institutional details, providing a range of practical applications of financial theories, and listing the financial mathematical tools used in practice. We believe that this approach is limited and falls far short of what is needed by the students. Finance should be taught as a skill in solving practical problems. The emphasis should be on the *thinking process*. In practicing, or even drilling, this thinking process in classrooms we can better prepare our students for careers in finance. This book is written to enhance students' capability in applying this process to solve practical problems.

The process should begin with identifying the business problem. Then the problem should be systematically analyzed by making an appropriate list of assumptions and formulating the financial model. The model should then be used to derive the solutions, applying the quantitative skills. Finally, the solutions should be tested for their applicability to the business problem. This financial modeling process is simply a disciplined approach to solving the business problem. "The model" may be a specific mathematical formulation like the Black-Scholes model or a concept like a business model, which often means "a business idea of making money."

This process is repeated in the eight chapters of this book. Each chapter begins with a problem in valuation, then formulates the problem, and finally provides the solutions. We then summarize the specific models related to the theory at the end of each chapter. For each model, we clearly state their assumptions, input data, and output solutions. The model is illustrated by a numerical example, which is implemented by an Excel model.

To underscore the importance of the thinking process, after each model is presented, we present a "case." The case is a hypothetical real-life situation that raises practical issues relevant to the model. From the case, students are encouraged to first identify the business problem, then formulate the problems in terms of the models, and finally provide the solutions. These cases deal with many practical important issues in day-to-day financial businesses. Many of them are drawn from the authors' work experience over the past twenty years. They pose open-ended questions and are intended to challenge the students to think deeply about many financial issues that at first glance may seem simple and straightforward. Further, these cases enable the students to learn to state their assumptions in solving a business problem and to appreciate the limitations of their model solutions.

We hope that these cases can deliver the important message: financial models are essential tools in modern finance not because they are perfect, but because the managers know their limitations and are skilled in interpreting the model results. This book provides twenty-six such cases, using or discussing the valuation models under different practical situations. The skills of applying the model to provide answers are then further reinforced by the end-of-chapter exercises. Excel models are provided for these exercises.

*Securities Valuation* is not just a stand-alone textbook. It is an integral part of a series of finance textbooks, and the series is supported by the companion website. Every course is confined by the number of lectures in one semester. We believe the students should also appreciate the course material in a much broader context of finance. The broader context is provided in *The Oxford Guide to Financial Modeling*, which presents an overview of financial modeling in finance. Using the *Oxford Guide* as a reference, students can understand how the valuation models can be used for balance sheet items, accounting corporate finance, and much more.

Further, to enable the students to apply the models in practice, we provide a companion website, www.thomasho.com, where more than 130 financial models are free to all visitors. These Excel models open the "black box," enabling students to study the algorithms. The Excel models are simple to use in that students input the data and the outputs are provided in a simple format. The design encourages students to use these models extensively to appreciate both the power and limitations of financial modeling. Finally, many solutions to the exercises are provided by the Excel models, which are saved as files in the website, and the numerical examples given in this book are based on those Excel models. The people, companies, and episodes described in the cases and exercises are all fictitious. Any resemblance to people or incidents in the real world is purely coincidental.

## HOW TO USE THE BOOK

The book is designed for both MBA and undergraduate finance and mathematical finance courses at the introductory and intermediate levels. The flexibility of the book allows professors to select the relevant portions that they think are appropriate for their courses. The courses that this book can be used for are usually given the names "Options and Futures," "Derivatives," "Financial Engineering," and "Fixed-Income Securities." Furthermore, the book can be used as a supplementary book for other textbooks in the securities valuation area.

The cases can be used for classroom discussions. They can be topics for term papers or questions for take-home exams. Students should use the cases to relate the theories to practical situations. Further, students should use the Excel models to provide solutions to the problems and therefore get hands-on experience in using the financial models.

The book material can be covered in one semester. These chapters contain the standard materials for the standard classes in securities valuation. We also include some of the models that are often omitted in a standard curriculum for lack of class time. We can do so because the Excel models are available to the students, enabling the professors to focus on the applications of the models and not just the derivation of the models.

At the end of each chapter, we provide several sections reviewing the materials of the chapter. Each section contains a brief description of one of the models covered in the chapter, the model assumptions, and its applications. A case related to the model is given to provide the students a context for the application of the model. In this way, students can appreciate modeling beyond the mathematical derivations.

Excel models are available at www.thomasho.com. For example, in Chapter 2 we provide a set of exercises on the Cox-Ross-Rubinstein option pricing model, and the Excel implementation of the model is available at the website. Numerical examples and exercises, with answers, based on the models are also provided at the website. The Excel models enable students to value a broad range of securities, which would otherwise be difficult to do. By using the Excel models, the exercises lead students to explore some of the implications of the models and their validity in the real world by comparing the model prices with the quoted prices.

## ACKNOWLEDGMENTS

We would like to thank Blessing Mudavanhu and Yuan Su of Market Risk Management, AIG, for their research assistance. We are grateful to the research team at Hanyang University, Korea, for providing invaluable assistance in research and in the preparation of the book. We are especially thankful for the help of Yoon Seok Choi, Hanki Seong, and Mi Sook Park. We thank the staff of Oxford University Press for their active support of this project. Finally, we want to thank our families for their support.

# 1

# Introduction

Central to many financial problems is the valuation of the shares of a firm. How do we value a privately held firm when there is no trading of its shares? What are the determinants of the value of a publicly traded firm? How do we analyze the value of a firm?

One approach is to determine the stock value by calculating the present value of the expected cash flows to the shareholders of the firm. This chapter will describe a model that determines the appropriate discount rate of such a cash flow. The discount rate can incorporate the risk premium of holding the stock.

## 1.1 DIVERSIFICATION

H. M. Markowitz was the first to show that not all risky assets require a risk premium even if we are all risk-averse.[1] He applied the diversification theory to portfolio management. *Diversification* is defined as the lowering of risks by holding multiple risky assets. That is, a portfolio of risky assets may have less risk than an individual risky asset.

Consider a simple example. Suppose that an individual has $100. He takes a gamble flipping a coin. He can double his bet if it lands on heads, or lose it all if it lands on tails. The two outcomes, head and tail, have an equal probability. If he bets all $100 on one flip of the coin, the expected outcome would be $100, but the standard deviation is $100. If he spreads the risks to two flips, betting $50 each time, the outcomes and the probabilities are given below:

|  | Head/Head | Head/Tail | Tail/Tail |
|---|---|---|---|
| Probability | 0.25 | 0.5 | 0.25 |
| Outcome | $200 | $100 | 0 |

The expected outcome is $100 = 0.25 \times \$200 + 0.5 \times \$100 + 0.25 \times \$0$. The standard deviation is

$$\$70.71 = \sqrt{0.25 \times (\$200 - \$100)^2 + 0.5 \times (\$100 - \$100)^2 + 0.25 \times (\$0 - \$100)^2}.$$

The expected outcome is $100, but the standard deviation is reduced to $70.71 from $100 by spreading the risks over two flips. The individual can spread the risks further by 100 flips of the coin with a $1.00 bet on each. In this case, the standard deviation, which is the square root of the number of flips times the standard deviation of the payoff of each flip, becomes almost negligible: $10 (= \sqrt{100} \times 1$). The reason for this is that 100 flips of the coin are independent of each other, and each flip of the coin has the same standard deviation. If we apply this logic to the two-flips example, we have $70.71 (= \sqrt{2} \times \$50$), which is the same as above. Intuitively, with many bets made at the same time, the number of heads is approximately the same as the number of tails, and therefore the gains and the losses tend to balance each other, resulting in minimal risks. Not all diversification can lead to eliminating all risks. The crucial assumption made in this example is that there is no correlation between the outcome of one flip of a coin and another.

The assertion that a portfolio of risky assets may have less risk than any individual risky asset is also used in practice. Imagine that a casino has numerous slot machines. The risk of winning at a slot machine is exciting to the gambler, a source of enjoyment. But the returns to the casino owner in playing against these gamblers are basically risk-free. The risks to each gambler are diversified in aggregate for the casino owner. From the casino owner's perspective, slot machines have no risk and no risk premium. The casino does not require a risk premium to discount the revenues from each slot machine, even though the gambling profit for each machine is uncertain.

We now extend this idea to portfolio management. Let us consider a security—a stock. The stock price can take on a range of values with assigned probabilities at the end of a time horizon, say one year. This is called the probability distribution. We will use this probability distribution to specify the risks and returns of a stock, and then to derive a strategy to minimize the portfolio risk while maximizing the portfolio returns. Two common distributions that financial research often uses are normal distribution and lognormal distribution. Since they represent the stock returns, we no longer assume that these distributions are uncorrelated. Stock returns in general are positively correlated with each other.[2]

Normal distribution is symmetrical and lognormal distribution is asymmetrical. These distributions are defined by the mean and standard deviations. The mean shifts the distributions to higher or lower values. The standard deviations change the dispersion of the distributions. (See figure 1.1.)

Stock returns are defined as the proportional change in price over a time horizon (say one year), minus 1.

$$\text{Stock returns} = \frac{S(T)}{S(0)} - 1$$

where $S(T)$ is the stock price at the end of the period and $S(0)$ is the stock price at the initial date. We assume that there are no dividends or other returns during this holding

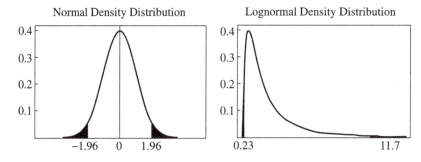

**Figure 1.1** Normal and lognormal distributions with a mean and a standard deviation. The means and standard deviations of the two distributions are (0,1) and (0.5,1) respectively. The probability that a normally distributed variable falls beyond 1.96 or less than −1.96 is 2.5% each. The probability that a lognormally distributed variable has a value more than 11.7 or less than 0.23 is 5% each. Since the normal distribution is symmetric, the left shaded area is the same shape as the right shaded area. This is not the case for the lognormal distribution.

period. Stock prices are often modeled as lognormal because the lognormal distribution does not allow negative stock prices, whereas the normal distribution does allow the possibility. For cases where the outcomes are fairly symmetrical, normal distributions are used because they have many desirable properties. We will be clear about which distribution we use in our description of risks.

Risks or uncertainties are central to financial research. For this reason, these probability distributions are used extensively in this book. Whenever a variable (say the returns of a stock) is assigned as a distribution, it represents a range of outcomes with their assigned probabilities, and the variable is not just one number but many possible numbers. The distribution can be reduced to one number when we take the expectation of the distribution or the standard deviation of the distribution.

Markowitz began his analysis with the perfect capital market assumptions. The investor has a specific investment horizon, say one year. At the end of the period, the investor calculates the worth of the portfolio and decides his level of happiness with the gain/loss via the utility. Assume that there are many securities in a perfect capital market.

Under these assumptions, the investor would construct a mean variance analysis. He would try to construct a portfolio and calculate its expected returns and standard deviation. The optimal portfolio would be the one that gives the highest expected returns for a risk level that is acceptable to the given risk tolerance.

The Markowitz model provides a prescriptive solution to the investment problem. In this case, we are told how to construct the optimal portfolio for ourselves. Markowitz's approach is called a normative theory or a prescriptive theory. His message is clear. An individual stock has a lot of risk. A better approach to investment is to take a portfolio approach. The importance of the portfolio approach is diversification. Therefore not all the risk of an individual stock is relevant to investment. Some of the individual stock risk can be diversified away, but some cannot. As we noted earlier, in the presence of correlations, stock risks can no longer be entirely eliminated by diversification.

Suppose we hold a portfolio of stocks whose returns are independent of each other; when one stock rises, no one can infer how the other stocks will behave. If we spread our investments across these stocks by investing $1/n$ in each of the $n$ stocks, and if there are many stocks, then the risks cancel out each other. The resulting portfolio has no risks. However, stock returns are not all independent of each other, and therefore a portfolio can never be designed such that the risks are all diversified away. The risk of stock returns can be minimized by carefully selecting stocks. Part of stock risks can be diversified, and therefore the appropriate discount rate or the required rate of return of the stock should be based on the risk that cannot be diversified. The risk that cannot be diversified away is called *systematic risk* or *market risk*. The risk that can be diversified away is called the *residual (or unsystematic) risk*. (See figure 1.2.)

What are the implications of diversification? Diversification is a way of reducing risk by forming a portfolio of individual stocks. Therefore, we can see that an individual stock has two types of risk, depending on whether the stock belongs to a portfolio or stands alone. When the stock stands alone, we can measure its risk by the standard deviation. However, when the stock is a part of a portfolio, we can measure the risk of the stock by how much the stock contributes to the portfolio risk. The portfolio risk is less than the summation over the risk of the individual stocks in the portfolio. The reason for this is the diversification effect. To quantify how much the stock contributes to the portfolio risk, we use a covariance between the stock's returns and the portfolio returns rather than a standard deviation.

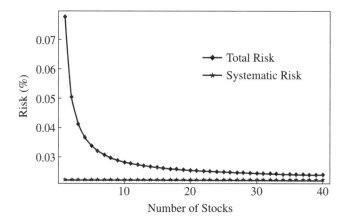

**Figure 1.2**  Effects of portfolio size on average portfolio risk for daily stock returns. We randomly sample 40 stocks from November 11, 2002, to February 5, 2003. The firms included in the sample are CVS Corp., Adobe System, Delphi Corp., Moody's Corp., Ford Motor Co., and Apollo Group. The data source is http://finance.yahoo.com. The x-axis and y-axis represent the number of stocks and the daily volatility of the portfolio respectively. The figure shows that the protfolio risk decreases with the number of stocks in the portfolio. But the portfolio risk cannot be eliminated completely. The minimum level of the portfolio risk is call the market risk. This figure shows that as we put 30 stocks or more in the portfolio, the portfolio risk (0.024787%) is very close to the market risk (0.0223695%). This means that we can diversify away most of individual stock risk by forming a portfolio of 30 stocks.

To explain why the covariance is an appropriate measure when the stock is part of a portfolio, we use a simple example of two stocks, A and B. Stock A and stock B have $\sigma_A$ and $\sigma_B$ for their stand-alone risk. When we form a portfolio with them, we have the portfolio risk $\sqrt{\omega_A^2\sigma_A^2 + 2\omega_A\omega_B\sigma_{A,B} + \omega_B^2\sigma_B^2}$, where $\sigma_{A,B}$ is a covariance between stock A and stock B and $\omega_A(\omega_B)$ is a weight of stock A (stock B). We manipulate the portfolio risk as follows to see that the covariance is a proper measure.

$$\sigma_P^2 = \omega_A^2\sigma_A^2 + 2\omega_A\omega_B\sigma_{A,B} + \omega_B^2\sigma_B^2$$
$$= \omega_A^2\sigma_A^2 + \omega_A\omega_B\sigma_{A,B} + \omega_A\omega_B\sigma_{A,B} + \omega_B^2\sigma_B^2$$
$$= \omega_A(\omega_A\sigma_A^2 + \omega_B\sigma_{A,B}) + \omega_B(\omega_A\sigma_{A,B} + \omega_B\sigma_B^2)$$
$$= \omega_A \times \sigma_{A,P} + \omega_B \times \sigma_{B,P}$$

When we manipulate the above equation, we substitute $\sigma_{A,P}(\sigma_{B,P})$ for $\omega_A\sigma_A^2 + \omega_B\sigma_{A,B}$ $(\omega_A\sigma_{A,B} + \omega_B\sigma_B^2)$.[3] We see that the covariance between stock A (stock B) and the portfolio constitutes the portfolio risk. Therefore, stock A's risk when it is part of the portfolio can be measured by the covariance, which is a marginal increase of the portfolio risk due to stock A. When we marginally increase stock A's weight, we see that the portfolio risk increases by $\sigma_{A,P}$.

The most important implication of diversification is that the risk of a stock to the investor should not be the standard deviation of the stock returns. The risk premium assigned to the stock is therefore not related to the standard deviation, but it should be related to the marginal increase of the risk to the portfolio when we add the stock. In other words, the risk premium assigned to a stock is related to the marginal increase in the risk the stock contributes to the portfolio.

## 1.2 CAPITAL ASSET PRICING MODEL (CAPM)

The Markowitz theory generally applies to any portfolio of risky assets: slot machines, real estate, commodities, anything risky. The normative approach of Markowitz's method almost provides a prescription for constructing an optimal portfolio of risky assets. To construct an optimal portfolio of stocks, we need to know the variances and covariances, and their expected returns, of the stocks. Using an optimization algorithm, we can find the optimal portfolio that provides the highest expected returns for a given level of risk. A collection of the optimal portfolios constitutes the *efficient frontier*. Once we have an efficient frontier, the next question would be which point on the efficient frontier will be selected as an optimal portfolio of risky assets and what will be an equilibrium price of a risky asset if investors behave optimally to maximize their expectation, given their risk preference. In other words, what would be the relationship between the risk and the expected return of risky assets in the mean-variance world? The *Capital Asset Pricing model* (CAPM) is proposed to answer the above question.

Sharpe continues this line of argument to provide a positive theory, CAPM.[4] He takes the next steps from where Markowitz left off, adding two assumptions to the perfect capital market assumptions. First, he assumes that all investors have the same one-period horizon, and borrow and lend at the same risk-free rate. Second, all market participants have the same information at the same time. This way, no one has private information or better information. They have homogeneous expectations in that they all agree with the forecasts of risks and expected returns of the risky assets.

Given these assumptions, Sharpe argues that in Markowitz's world, everyone should use all the stocks traded in the market and go through the optimization process as Markowitz would envision. All the investors would maximize the returns for their optimal level of risk. In equilibrium, when all the trades are completed, there will be a special set of portfolios deserving more attention—the *efficient portfolios* of risky assets, those with the highest returns for each level of risk.

If we put all the expected returns and the standard deviations of all the portfolios on a diagram plotting the risk and return trade-off, we will see that the locus of the efficient frontier is a curve (see figure 1.3). Now, use a ruler and draw a straight line between the risk-free rate and the tangent point on the efficient frontier of risky assets. This line, called the *capital market line*, is optimal for everyone, even better than the efficient frontier of risky assets. This means that along the capital market line, the portfolio achieves a higher return for the same risks. A point on this capital market line can be reached by holding a combination of the tangent portfolio and the risk-free asset. The higher the proportion invested in the tangent portfolio, the closer the point is to the tangent portfolio. The lower the proportion invested in the tangent portfolio, the closer the point is to the risk-free asset. That means everyone should hold the tangent portfolio on the efficient frontier of risky assets and the risk-free rate.

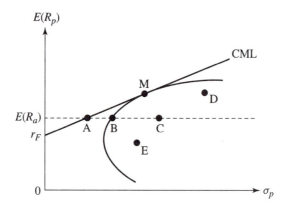

**Figure 1.3** Capital market line. The efficient frontier is the portfolio of stocks that offers the highest expected returns for a given risk level. The capital market line (CML) is the line tangent to the efficient frontier from the risk-free asset. The capital market line, which should represent the optimal portfolio for all risk-averse investors, is a combination of the market portfolio and the risk-free asset. Portfolio A is efficient, whereas portfolio B is not efficient even though it is on the minimum variance set of risky assets. Portfolio C also is not efficient, because it has more risk than portfolio A even though they yield the same expected return. Portfolios D and E are not efficient, because they are inside the efficient frontier.

To illustrate, consider the following numerical example. Suppose we have five stocks and calculate their historical returns and standard deviations from their historical returns. The results are presented below.

| Stock | A | B | C | D | E |
|---|---|---|---|---|---|
| Returns (%) | 10 | 10 | 10 | 12 | 8 |
| Standard deviation | 0.3 | 0.4 | 0.6 | 0.8 | 0.5 |

Let us assume that the historical returns are appropriate estimates of the expected returns of the stock; then we can plot these numbers with returns on the y-axis and the standard deviations on the x-axis. These plots show the feasible set of the risk and returns trade-off.

A risk-averse investor would hold the tangent portfolio and a large position in risk-free investments. A less risk-averse investor would hold a larger tangent portfolio and less risk-free investments. An even less risk-averse investor would borrow at the risk-free rate to invest in the tangent portfolio—buying the tangent portfolio at the margin. This result, often referred to as the *Separation Theorem*, refers to the theoretical result that investors' portfolios differ only by the proportion of their holdings in the risk-free asset and the tangent portfolio. In a way, this result is very counterintuitive. It seems to suggest that everyone holds the same portfolio of stocks, differing only in the allocation of their risk-free investments and the tangent portfolio. However, the result is not as surprising as it might at first appear. After all, we assume that everyone is the same except for their risk aversion, and therefore there is no reason for the theory to predict many different optimal portfolios. Risk aversion decides on the trade-off of the tangent portfolio's higher expected returns and corresponding higher risk in relation to the risk-free rate.

If everyone holds the tangent portfolio, then that portfolio must be the actual observed portfolio in the stock market—a portfolio consists of all the stocks in the market, with the portfolio weight of each stock being the proportion of its capitalization (the stock price times the number of shares outstanding) to the value of the market. This portfolio is a *market portfolio*. Since CAPM is an equilibrium model where the market demand for a risky asset should be equal to the market supply of the risky asset, we should impose the market-clearing condition to derive CAPM. We know that every investor holds the same portfolio of risky assets, the tangent portfolio, regardless of the degree of risk preference. Since the market demand for a risky asset should be equal to the market supply of the risky asset and every investor holds the identical portfolio of risky assets, the identical portfolio should be the market portfolio. Otherwise, we cannot have the market-clearing condition.

Now, every investor holds the market portfolio. To measure the risk of an individual stock in the market portfolio, we should calculate the covariance between the individual stock and the market portfolio. The variance of the market portfolio is given in equation (1.1), where $\sigma_M^2$ is the variance of the market portfolio and $N$ is the total number of stocks in the market portfolio.

$$\sigma_M^2 = \omega_1 \operatorname{cov}(\tilde{R}_1, \tilde{R}_M) + \omega_2 \operatorname{cov}(\tilde{R}_2, \tilde{R}_M) + \cdots + \omega_N \operatorname{cov}(\tilde{R}_N, \tilde{R}_M) \qquad (1.1)$$

If we divide the both sides of equation (1.1) by $\sigma_M^2$, we have

$$1 = \omega_1 \frac{\operatorname{cov}(\tilde{R}_1, \tilde{R}_M)}{\sigma_M^2} + \omega_2 \frac{\operatorname{cov}(\tilde{R}_2, \tilde{R}_M)}{\sigma_M^2} + \cdots + \omega_N \frac{\operatorname{cov}(\tilde{R}_N, \tilde{R}_M)}{\sigma_M^2}$$

$$= \omega_1 \beta_1 + \omega_2 \beta_2 + \cdots + \omega_N \beta_N$$

where $\beta_i = \frac{\operatorname{cov}(\tilde{R}_i, \tilde{R}_M)}{\sigma_M^2}$, $i = 1, \cdots, N$

Dividing by $\sigma_M^2$ is a kind of normalization. Since the covariance is a measure of the systematic risk, $\beta$ is also the measure of the systematic risk, because it is the covariance divided by the same number for all the risky assets, $\sigma_M^2$. In particular, when the risky asset is the market portfolio itself, then $\beta$, according to the definition, is 1.

Now we can calculate the expected return of a stock and its systematic risk, which is $\beta$. The relationship between the expected return and $\beta$ is linear, simply a mathematical derivation.[5] It is called the *security market line*.

To the extent that all individuals hold similar views on the market and there are no fundamental differences among individuals, CAPM is an approximation to the real world. The weight of the theory can be verified empirically.

## 1.3   BETA: THE SYSTEMATIC RISK

We now extend this thought process another step further. We have not done any empirical tests, nor do we have any evidence to support any part of the theory. We are just following the argument to its logical conclusion.

First let us introduce the definition of *index fund*. Index funds are stock portfolios available to any investor. They are constructed to mimic the market portfolios, such as Standard and Poor's 500 (S&P). These portfolios have returns similar to the market portfolio, and investors can invest in an index fund as if they were buying a stock. They do not have to select many stocks and manage them.

Consider a particular stock. Its uncertain returns can be broken into two parts: one moves in step with the market and the other is totally unrelated to the market. Under the CAPM assumptions, there is only one factor in the capital market—the market portfolio risk. Only this risk factor is systematic; all other risks become diversifiable. Then any stock can be thought of as a portfolio of an index fund, risk-free rate, and a noise term. To isolate the noises from the rest of the portfolio, we can use a line of best fit to the scattered plots of the stock returns and the market returns. The slope of this line specifies the sensitivity of the stock returns to the market portfolio returns. (See figure 1.4.)

If we assume the risk premium of the market to be $\pi (= E[R_M] - r_f)$, then the risk premium of the stock must be $\beta \times \pi$. Therefore, the expected return of the stock is linearly related to the systematic risk of the stock, $\beta$. The plot of the expected returns of risky assets against the risky assets' $\beta$s is called the security market line. Then the required expected return of the risky asset is given by the Capital Asset Pricing model:

$$E[R_i] = r_f + \beta_i(E[R_M] - r_f) \tag{1.2}$$

This result yields a number of important insights on the pricing of securities. Consider an asset that has positive returns when the market falls and has negative returns when the market rises. There are few stocks like this, if any. Such a stock would have a negative $\beta$. The stock would have an expected return less than the risk-free rate, even though the stock is risky. An investor would wish to hold such a stock even though the stock has an

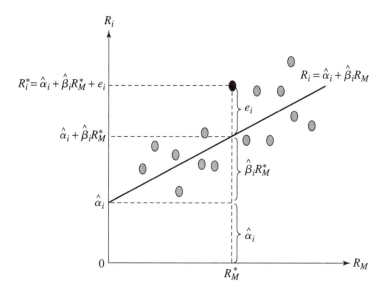

**Figure 1.4** Line of best fit to determine $\beta$. A scatter plot of the observed (monthly) returns of a stock and the market portfolio over a period of time, say five years. Market returns are on the x-axis and the stock returns on the y-axis. The $\beta$ of the stock is the slope of the line that best fits the scattered points. The $\beta$ determines the risk premium of the stock according to the Capital Asset Pricing model.

Expected Return %

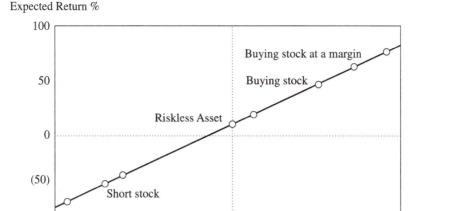

**Figure 1.5** Security market line: Relationship between expected return and $\beta$. When a stock is part of a portfolio, the individual stock risk can be defined as an additional risk that the stock adds to the portfolio risk. We can quantify the additional risk as a covariance of the stock with the portfolio, which is referred to as $\beta$ risk. When the covariance of the stock with the portfolio is positive, we have positive $\beta$, and vice versa. The $\beta$ of the risk-free asset is 0, and for the asset with positive (negative) $\beta$, the expected rate of return is above (below) the risk-free rate of return.

expected return less than the risk-free rate because it can lower the portfolio risk. The model is consistent with the arbitrage argument. Suppose we set up a trust where we have a small portfolio of stocks. We then issue shares of the portfolio. This construct is identical to setting up a mutual fund as a closed-end fund. The $\beta$ of the share is the same as the portfolio $\beta$. According to the CAPM, the expected return for the stock with the portfolio $\beta$ is exactly the expected return of the portfolio.

The importance of the CAPM in finance is that it provides a systematic way to calculate the required rate of return on risky assets. The market reaches its equilibrium when the required rate of return equals the expected rate of return. For this reason, the CAPM can also be used to calculate the required rate of return on risky assets. This required rate of return is based on the market valuation.

The general methodology in valuing a risky asset is to follow the valuation procedure as we would a recipe in a cookbook. First, we estimate the expected cash flows of risky assets for the investors. Second, we estimate the $\beta$ of the risky assets. Third, we apply the CAPM to determine the required rate of return on the asset. Finally, we use the required rate of return to discount the expected cash flows in order to determine the present value, which is the value of the asset. (See figure 1.5.)

## 1.4   THE STOCK MODEL—DIVIDEND DISCOUNT MODEL

This section derives a valuation model of a stock. To simplify the exposition, let us assume that the stock pays steady dividends, and the value of the stock is the present value of all the dividends that we can receive from the stock. Of course, in principle, a firm can retain all the earnings all the time and reinvest them without paying any dividends. The stock would still be valuable even though the firm pays no dividends. In this case, we can still assume that at some time the firm will distribute its value.

In this case, the stock price is the present value of all the future dividends. Let us further suppose that the stock's dividends grow at a constant rate $g$.

$$div(n + 1) = div(n)(1 + g) \tag{1.3}$$

Let us assume that the required rate of return is $R_{req}$. Then the stock price is

$$S = \frac{div(1)}{(1 + R_{req})} + \frac{div(1)(1 + g)}{(1 + R_{req})^2} + \frac{div(1)(1 + g)^2}{(1 + R_{req})^3} + \cdots \tag{1.4}$$

This equation can be simplified to

$$S = \frac{div(1)}{(R_{req} - g)} \tag{1.5}$$

The required rate of return of a stock must equal the expected rate of return at market equilibrium. Given the risk of the stock, if the market requires the stock to provide a rate of return of at least $R_{req}$, which is greater than the expected return, then the stock price would fall because the stock is not expected to provide the return needed. When the price is sufficiently low and the expected rate rises to equal the required rate of return, we have reached equilibrium. Since the required rate of return of the stock can be specified by the CAPM, we therefore have a valuation model for a stock.

In general, dividends do not grow at a constant rate. Often, forecasts of dividends are provided for the next several years. This is accomplished by using the forecasts of the future earnings and a constant dividend payout ratio to determine the dividends. We then assume that at some future date, the dividends will grow at a constant rate. Then the model can be written as

$$S = PV \text{(forecast dividends over } T \text{ periods)} + \frac{div(T + 1)}{(R_{req} - g)(1 + R_{req})^T} \tag{1.6}$$

PV (forecast dividends over $T$ periods) is the present value of the projected dividends over a projected horizon of $T$ years. The projected horizon is usually decided by analysts depending on the availability of information on the dividends, goodness of the forecast, and other information on the firms and the markets. This discount rate, used to determine the present value of the projected dividends, is the required rate of return of the equity or the expected return of equity, which is $R_{req}$.

For example, when div(1) = \$2.00, the growth rate $(g)$ for next three years = 18%, the growth rate $(g)$ from the fourth year = 6%, and the required rate of return $(R_{req})$ = 16%,

$$PV \text{(forecast dividends over 3 periods)} = \frac{2}{1.16} + \frac{2 \times 1.18}{1.16^2} + \frac{2 \times 1.18^2}{1.16^3} = 5.262$$

$$S(3) = \frac{div(4)}{R_{req} - g} = \frac{2 \times 1.18^2 \times 1.06}{0.16 - 0.06} = 29.519$$

$$S(0) = 5.262 + \frac{29.519}{1.16^3} = 24.174$$

## 1.5  AN APPLICATION OF THE CAPITAL ASSET PRICING MODEL IN INVESTMENT SERVICES

The CAPM has broad applications to investment services. We provide one simple example here. According to the CAPM, the most efficient portfolio is the market portfolio. Market portfolios are often taken to be Standard and Poor's 500 (S&P) market index or some other broad-based index. Mutual funds are constructed to replicate these market indices. There are many closed-end funds that replicate these broad-based indices. These funds seek to minimize the management fees and hence to minimize the transaction costs. At the same time their returns should closely match the broad-based indices that often have many stocks. (S&P has 500 stocks.)

Exchange-traded funds are traded like a stock on the exchange. Investors can buy the market portfolio by just buying these stocks. (SPY stands for the Standard and Poor's Stock index and QQQ stands for the NASDAQ index.) As a result of the CAPM, these funds are made available to investors so that they can optimize their own portfolios.

# EXCEL MODEL EXERCISES

## E1.1  DIVERSIFICATION

### Definition

Diversification is defined as the lowering of risks by holding multiple risky assets. That is, a portfolio of risky assets may have less risk than an individual risky asset.

### Description of the Model

Suppose we hold a portfolio of stocks whose returns are independent of each other. When one stock rises, no one can infer how the other stocks will behave. If we spread our investments across these stocks by investing $1/n$ in each of the $n$ stocks, then the risks diversified, resulting a much smaller risk as compared to holding only one stock.

### Numerical Example

Suppose that an individual has $100. He takes a gamble flipping a coin. He can double his bet if it lands on heads, or lose it at all if it lands on tails. The two outcomes, heads and tails, have an equal probability. The expected outcome and the standard deviation when he flips the coin twice are 100 and 70.7107, respectively. If he flips the coin one hundred

| Numerical example 1 | | | | |
|---|---|---|---|---|
| **Inputs** | | | | |
| | | | | |
| Initial wealth (w) | 100 | | | |
| The number of trials (n) | 2 | n ≤ 10 | | |
| Probability of landing on head (p) | 0.5 | 0 ≤ p ≤ 1 | | |
| | | | | |
| **Outputs** | | | | |
| | | | | |
| The number of heads (k) | 0 ≤ k ≤ n | 0 | 1 | 2 |
| Payoff | | 0 | 100 | 200 |
| Probability of k heads = $_nC_k \, p^k(1-p)^{n-k}$ | | 0.25 | 0.5 | 0.25 |
| Expected payoff | 100 | 0 | 50 | 50 |
| Expected squared payoff | 15000 | 0 | 5000 | 10000 |
| Variance | 5000 | | | |
| Standard deviation | 70.71068 | | | |
| | | | | |
| Numerical example 2 | | | | |
| **Inputs** | | | | |
| | | | | |
| The number of trials | 100 | | | |
| Probability of landing on head (p) | 0.5 | | | |
| | | | | |
| **Outputs** | | | | |
| | | | | |
| Expected payoff | 100 | | | |
| Standard deviation | 10 | | | |
| | | | | |
| **Interim Calculations** | | | | |
| | | | | |
| Expected payoff | 2wp | | | |
| Standard deviation | $2w \sqrt{p(1-p)}/\sqrt{n}$ | | | |

Figure E1.1

times with a $1 bet on each flip, the expected outcome and the standard deviation when he flips the coin one hundred times are 100 and 10, respectively. See figure E1.1.

## Application

The most important implication of diversification is that the risk of a stock to the investor should not be the standard deviation of the stock return. The risk premium assigned to the stock is therefore not related to the standard deviation, but it should be related to the marginal increase of the risk of the portfolio when we add the stock.

## Case: Managing the Risk of a Pension Fund

Sal Modigliani closed his eyes and sighed. In his hand was the morning paper with the news headline: "Greenspan Favors Entitlement Cuts." Alan Greenspan was the chairman of the Federal Reserve Bank, and he suggested that the government should scale back social security, but no politician in the election year supported Greenspan's idea. "This is no rocket science. I know so," Sal muttered. Julia Leung, his quantitative assistant, listened.

Sal was a senior vice president of a pension plan, overlooking $80 billion investments. The shareholders of the plan set the benefits and the contributions to the plans. The plan invested the funds contributed so that the funds later provided financial support to the retirees. "When people these days start working at age thirty, retire at fifty-five, and expect to live well till eighty-five, retirement funds have to grow from trees." Sal sighed again, shaking his head. "Well Sal, these politicians think that you can in fact grow the returns from trees," said Julia. "To make that math work, we need plenty more than the 3% real return that we can get these days. They want 7% without risks. How is it possible?"

"Sal, everyone knows that it is not possible. Do not lose sleep over what you cannot do. We know buying bonds, even inflation-indexed bonds, will not solve the problem. We have to take risk, diversified risk. Right?" "Well, that is why we already have over 50% in equity, 20% in fixed income, and the rest in inflation-linked securities." "Is that all we are doing now?"

"No, we then allocate our investments in different active management programs. In these programs, we have managers actively manage a portion of the portfolios, active in alternative investments like hedge funds and other investments to get higher returns. We have to make sure the returns of these programs are not correlated to diversify the risks further."

"I see, this way, the marginal contribution of risk of each program is lowered by diversification. You are betting that the risks of the active management can be diversified. How much risk do you allocate to active management?" Sal explained: "At the moment, the board has approved that we can even exceed 20% of our investments in these active programs. The rest of the investments are in passive asset-liability benchmark portfolios."

"It is ironic that we in fact have to take risks to lower the risk of not meeting the funding requirement," Julia became somewhat philosophical about these investment policies. "Back to work, Julia. Enough thinking for the day." Sal raised his voice and got up.

*"Taking more risks to lower risks? Is that possible? Diversification?" Julia was thinking as she followed Sal to his office. "What is the problem that we are trying to solve anyway? What assumptions are we using to come up with these investment strategies?"*

## Exercises and Answers

1. Select forty stocks randomly from http://finance.yahoo.com. Calculate the daily standard deviation of the portfolio with equal weights to see how the standard deviation decreases on average when we add more stocks to the portfolio. First start with one stock and then add one by one until we have a portfolio of forty stocks. What are the systematic risk and the unsystematic risk of the portfolio? When we add one more stock to the portfolio, what is the marginal decrease in the portfolio risk on average by adding one more stock? Show that the systematic risk of the portfolio is related to the average covariance of the stocks that belong to the portfolio.

    *Answer:* The portfolio risk $(\overline{\sigma}_p^2)$ is $\frac{1}{k}\overline{\sigma}_i^2 + \frac{k-1}{k}\overline{\sigma}_{ij}$ where $\overline{\sigma}_i^2$ is the average of the variances, $\overline{\sigma}_{ij}$ is the average of the covariances, and $k$ is the number of stocks in the portfolio.

When the number of stocks goes to infinity, the portfolio risk converges to the average of the covariances.

The average risk of the portfolio with thirty-nine stocks is 6.1993%, and the average risk of the portfolio with forty stocks is 6.1902%. Therefore the marginal decrease is 0.0091%. The market risk is 5.8382%. The difference between 6.1902% and 5.8382% is the unsystematic risk. See figure E1.2.

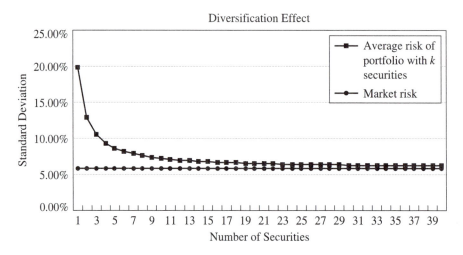

Figure E1.2

| Outputs | | | |
|---|---|---|---|
| $\rho_{AB}$ | | 0.5 | -1 |
| $\sigma_P$ | | 0.175 | 0.05 |

Figure E1.3

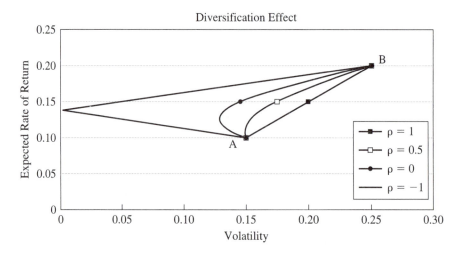

Figure E1.4

2. Assume that we have two stocks called stock A and stock B. The expected rates of return are 10% and 20%, respectively. The corresponding standard deviations of the two stocks are 15% and 25%, respectively. When the correlation coefficient between them is 0.5, what is the standard deviation of the portfolio with equal weights? Repeat the same question when the correlation coefficient is between $-1$ and $+1$.
*Answer:* See figures E1.3 and E1.4.

## Further Exercises

1. The following variance-covariance matrix of three stocks is given. For example, stock A's standard deviation is 6%, and the covariance between stock A and stock B is 0.32%. How would you buy two stocks that would have no portfolio risk?

$$\begin{bmatrix} 0.0036 & 0.0032 & -0.0048 \\ 0.0032 & 0.0049 & 0.0050 \\ -0.0048 & 0.0050 & 0.0064 \end{bmatrix}$$

*Answer:* The correlation coefficient between asset A and asset C is minus 1. Therefore, the portfolio risk of two stocks can be zero. The weight of stock A is 4/7 and the weight of stock C is 3/7, because $(4/7) \times 6\% - (3/7) \times 8\% = 0$.

2. We have the following variance-covariance matrix of two stocks. What is the risk of stock A when we hold only stock A? When we have stock A and stock B with equal proportions, what is the risk of the portfolio?

$$\begin{bmatrix} 0.0036 & 0.0021 \\ 0.0021 & 0.0049 \end{bmatrix}$$

*Answer:* The risk of stock A is 0.06, and the risk of stock B is 0.07. The portfolio risk is 5.635%.

# E1.2    CAPM

## Definitions

The risk-free rate $(r_f)$ is the one-period risk-free rate. The expected rate of return on a market portfolio (stock $i$) is $E[R_M](E[R_i])$. The measure of systematic risk of stock $i$ is $\beta_i$. $\beta_i$ is the sensitivity of the rate of return on a stock with respect to the market portfolio's rate of return. For example, assume that $\beta_i$ is 0.4 and the market portfolio return increases by 10%. Then, the stock's rate of return increases by 4%.

## Description of the Model

The Capital Asset Pricing model (CAPM) explains what the relationship would be between the risk and the expected return of risky assets in the mean-variance world. The CAPM provides a systematic way to calculate the required rate of return on risky assets. The market reaches its equilibrium when the required rate of return equals the expected rate of return on risky assets. For this reason, the CAPM can also be used to calculate the required rate of return.

| Inputs | | | |
|---|---|---|---|
| Risk-free rate ($r_f$) | 0.05 | | |
| $E[R_M]$ | 0.15 | | |
| $\beta_i$ | 1.2 | | |
| Outputs | | | |
| $E[R_i]$ | 0.17 | $= r_f + (E[R_M] - r_f)\beta_i$ | |

**Figure E1.5**

## Numerical Example

Suppose the risk-free rate of return is 5%. The expected rate of return on the market portfolio is 15%. The beta of a stock is 1.2. Calculate the equilibrium rate of return of the stock. See figure E1.5.

## Application

According to the CAPM, the most efficient portfolio is the market portfolio. Market portfolios are often taken to be Standard and Poor's 500 (S&P) market index or other broad-based indices. Mutual funds are constructed to replicate these market indices. There are many closed-end funds that replicate these broad-based indices. These funds seek to minimize the management fees and hence minimize the transaction costs. At the same time their returns should closely match the broad-based indices that often have many stocks. S&P has 500 stocks.

## Case: Quarterly Earnings Report of an Energy Storage Operator

Gloria Bohemia, the president of Energy Resources, Ltd., took a sip of water and nodded to Swanihili Narayana, the director of investor relations. Swanihili leaned toward the microphone of the conference call and announced: "Gentlemen, that is all Gloria would say about our quarterly financial results. Let's take a five-minute break, and she will be delighted to take any questions from you," and she switched off the conference call carefully. "Who is on the call, do you know?" Gloria asked. "The three sell-side firms that follow us. Then we have the usual suspects in the pension fund world. I think we need to watch out for two hedge funds from Texas." "Hedge funds?" "Yes. They are getting active on our stock." Five minutes passed.

"Gloria, congrats on the earnings. This is Davio Salimano of Salimano Hedge Funds. Given the beating on the energy sector last quarter, how did Energy weather it so well?" "Davio, Energy is a storage operator. We do not trade any derivatives. Therefore the liquidity of the market does not affect us. We do not do explorations. We just buy natural gas from the Texas basin in the summer. Pump the gas into the reservoir up here in Illinois. We then pump the gas back out in winter when the demands go up. Our profit depends mainly on the demand for gas. The producers cannot adjust supply to the seasonal demand, and we carry the excess supply for them over the seasons."

"Gloria, we did some work on your stock beta. Your stock does not correlate well to our energy sector. Why is that?" "Davio, I really cannot comment on your research. I think it depends a lot on what you mean by 'energy sector.' Not all energy stocks are the same, as I just explained."

"Gloria, you are now giving $1 dividend per share. The stock closed yesterday at $20. What is your forecast of revenue growth?" "We believe our revenue ties to the demand closely. Our region is growing steadily at 2% by volume annually, and the industry kind of assumes 3% inflation in our business."

"Gloria, this is Jimmy Lam of Bull Bear Hedge Fund of Texas. I am concerned with your reputation risk. What if you cannot deliver the gas under contract?" "We do have enough reserve to ensure supply even in an extended cold winter. Further, we have contracts for gas delivery under certain stress scenarios."

"How about operational risks? How much of the gas you store cannot be retrieved?" "5%. We lose about 5% in storing the gas. We monitor that part of the operation all the time." "Can I go through some of your financial numbers again?" " Sure, let me put Maria on the phone now. As you know Maria is our CFO." Gloria stretched her arms and said to herself: "Hedge funds—they may be buying or selling. They surely are asking."

*Gloria's mind wandered: "How will the hedge funds price our stock? How would the reputation risk and operational risk come into the equations?"*

## Exercises and Answers

1. The Capital Asset Pricing model is concerned with how to price stocks by determining the expected rate of return of stocks. To this end, we need the Separation Theorem and market equilibrium. What assumptions do we need to derive the Separation Theorem? Under the Separation Theorem, all the investors hold the same risky portfolio in a combination with the risk-free asset.
   *Answer:* We assume that every investor has the same risk-free lending or borrowing rate and every investor has the same information about the expected return (the variance and the covariance of the stocks). Then every investor has the same efficient portfolio and the same tangent portfolio. Since every investor has the same information about the stocks, they should have the same efficient frontier. Furthermore, since they have the same risk-free rate, a straight line from the risk-free rate in the y-axis should touch the same point on the efficient frontier. The same point on the efficient frontier is called the tangent portfolio. Since every investor holds the same tangent portfolio, we can say that every investor's portfolio of risky assets is the same.
2. We can measure the individual stock's risk in two ways depending on whether we hold the stock on its own or we hold the stock as a part of a portfolio. In the former case, we measure the stock risk by the standard deviation of the stock's rates of return. However, in the latter case, we measure the stock risk by the covariance between the stock's rates of return and the portfolio's rates of return. Can you explain why we have two seemingly inconsistent risk measurers for the same individual stock?
   *Answer:* Because of the diversification effect, we have two risk measures. To quantify how much the stock contributes to the portfolio risk, we use a covariance between the stock's returns and the portfolio's returns rather than a standard deviation.
   To explain why the covariance is an appropriate measure when the stock belongs to the portfolio, we use a simple example of two stocks called stock A and stock B. Stock A and stock B have $\sigma_A$ and $\sigma_B$ for their stand-alone risk. When we form a portfolio

with stock A and stock B, we have the portfolio risk as $\sqrt{\omega_A^2 \sigma_A^2 + 2\omega_A \omega_B \sigma_{A.B} + \omega_B^2 \sigma_B^2}$, where $\sigma_{A.B}$ is a covariance between stock A and stock B and $\omega_A (\omega_B)$ is a weight of the stock A (stock B). We manipulate the portfolio risk as follows to see that the covariance is a proper measure.

$$\sigma_P^2 = \omega_A^2 \sigma_A^2 + 2\omega_A \omega_B \sigma_{A.B} + \omega_B^2 \sigma_B^2$$

$$= \omega_A^2 \sigma_A^2 + \omega_A \omega_B \sigma_{A.B} + \omega_A \omega_B \sigma_{A.B} + \omega_B^2 \sigma_B^2$$

$$= \omega_A (\omega_A \sigma_A^2 + \omega_B \sigma_{A.B}) + \omega_B (\omega_A \sigma_{A.B} + \omega_B \sigma_B^2)$$

$$= \omega_A \times \sigma_{A.P} + \omega_B \times \sigma_{B.P}$$

When we manipulate the above equation, we substitute $\sigma_{A.P} (\sigma_{B.P})$ for $\omega_A \sigma_A^2 + \omega_B \sigma_{A.B} (\omega_A \sigma_{A.B} + \omega_B \sigma_B^2)$—where $\sigma_{A.P} = Cov(\tilde{R}_A, \tilde{R}_P) = Cov(\tilde{R}_A, \omega_A \tilde{R}_A + \omega_B \tilde{R}_B) = Cov(\tilde{R}_A, \omega_A \tilde{R}_A) + Cov(\tilde{R}_A, \omega_B \tilde{R}_B) = \omega_A \times Cov(\tilde{R}_A, \tilde{R}_A) + \omega_B \times Cov(\tilde{R}_A, \tilde{R}_B) = \omega_A \times \sigma_A^2 + \omega_B \times \sigma_{A.B}$. We see that the covariance between stock A (stock B) and the portfolio constitutes the portfolio risk. Therefore, stock A's risk when belonging to the portfolio can be measured by the covariance, which is a marginal increase of the portfolio risk due to stock A. When we marginally increase the stock A's weight, we see that the portfolio risk increases by $\sigma_{A.P}$.

3. We assume the following probability distribution of risky assets X and Y for each economic state next year. The risk-free rate of return is 2.5%. See table E1.1.

(a) Calculate the means and the standard deviations for the two risky assets.
   *Answer:* See figure E1.6.

(b) Based on the means and the standard deviations, is it possible for a highly risk-averse investor to choose asset X rather than asset Y? Note that the highly risk-averse investor has an indifference curve whose slope is very steep.
   *Answer:* The efficient frontier consisting of the risk-free asset and the asset X has a higher slope than the efficient frontier consisting of the risk-free asset and the asset Y. Note that the efficient frontier consisting of a risky asset and a risk-free asset is a straight line connecting the risk-free asset to the risky asset. The slopes are 1.76778 ($= (5 - 2.5)/1.4142$) and 1.59101 ($= (7 - 2.5)/2.8284$), respectively.

**Table E1.1**

| State (i) | Probability $X_i$ | $X_i$ (%) | Probability $Y_i$ | $Y_i$ (%) |
|-----------|-------------------|-----------|-------------------|-----------|
| Horrid    | 0.2               | 3.0       | 0.2               | 3.0       |
| Bad       | 0.2               | 4.0       | 0.2               | 5.0       |
| Average   | 0.2               | 5.0       | 0.2               | 7.0       |
| Good      | 0.2               | 6.0       | 0.2               | 9.0       |
| Great     | 0.2               | 7.0       | 0.2               | 11.0      |

|              | $X_i$    | $Y_i$    |
|--------------|----------|----------|
| std($R_i$)   | 0.014142 | 0.028284 |
| E($R_i$)     | 0.05     | 0.07     |
| Slope of CML | 1.7678   | 1.5910   |

**Figure E1.6**

(c) Since asset Y dominates asset X in each economic state in the sense that asset Y's return is higher than asset X's return in all states of the world, an investor should choose asset Y regardless of the degree of his risk aversion. How do you reconcile this observation with answer (b)?

*Answer:* Answer (b) is based on the mean-variance analysis, which is correct only under specific assumptions.

4. Choose six stocks from http://finance.yahoo.com and calculate the expected return and the variance-covariance matrix. Assume that the market portfolio consists of six stocks and the weights are equal for simplicity. Calculate the betas of the six stocks. Plot the expected returns and the betas in the x- and y-axis respectively. Can you see that six points constitute a straight line? We assume that the risk-free rate is 5%. Originally, to empirically test the CAPM, the researchers have tried to see whether the relationship between the beta and the expected rate of return is linear or the intercept of the security market line is the risk-free rate. Can you explain why the above hypotheses are not legitimate to test the CAPM?

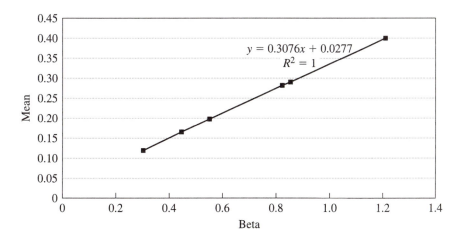

Figure E1.7

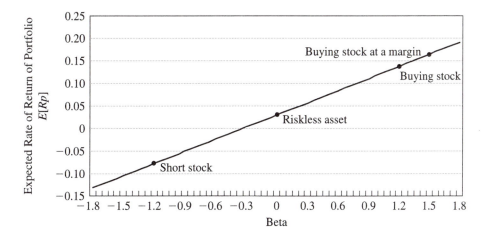

Figure E1.8

*Answer:* Research has shown that when the market portfolio is on the efficient frontier, we have a linear relationship between the expected return and $\beta$ risk. See figure E1.7.

5. Show that borrowing at the risk-free rate to buy a stock has a higher expected return and beta than not borrowing to own the stock. Also show that shorting a stock has lower expected return and beta as compared to buying a stock.

*Answer:* See figure E1.8.

| Outputs | | |
|---|---|---|
| **CML** | | |
| $E(R_i)$ | 0.28160 | $= r_f + \sigma_i (E[R_M] - r_f)/\sigma_M$ |
| | | |
| **SML** | | |
| $E(R_i)$ | 0.18457 | $= r_f + (E[R_M] - r_f)\beta_i$ |

**Figure E1.9**

(a)

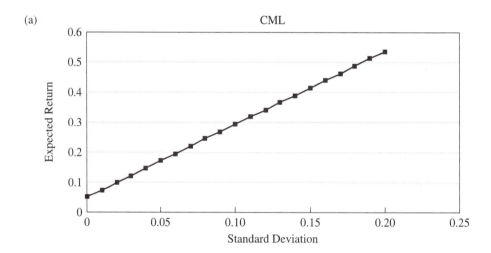

**Figure E1.10**

(b)

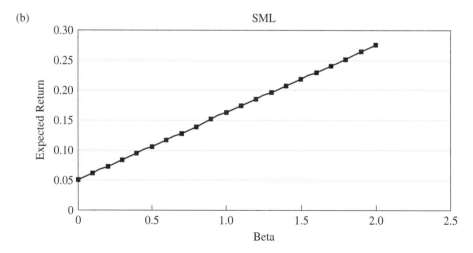

Table E1.2

| State | Probability | $\tilde{R}_A$ | $\tilde{R}_M$ |
|-------|-------------|------|------|
| I | 0.2 | 0.3 | 0.18 |
| II | 0.4 | 0.1 | 0.15 |
| III | 0.3 | 0.25 | 0.10 |
| IV | 0.1 | −0.05 | −0.10 |

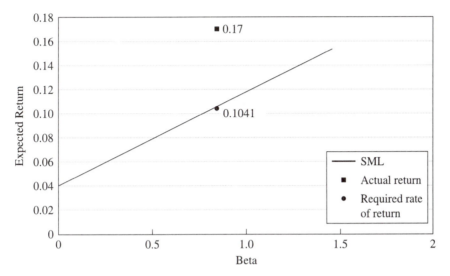

Figure E1.11

6. Choose one stock from http://finance.yahoo.com. Draw a capital market line and a security market line.
   *Answer:* We select IBM and S&P 500 monthly data for a period from January 1996 to December 2000. See figures E1.9 and E1.10.
7. The rates of return of stock A and the market portfolio can be predicted as in table E1.2. The risk-free rate of return is 4%.
   (a) Determine the capital market line.
      *Answer:* $E[R_A] = r_f + ((E[R_M] - r_f)/\sigma_M)\sigma_A = 0.04 + 0.9792\sigma_A$.
   (b) Derive the security market line and draw the diagram.
      *Answer:* $E[R_A] = r_f + (E[R_M] - r_f)\beta_A = 0.04 + 0.076\beta_A$. See figure E1.11.
   (c) Calculate the beta and the required rate of return of stock A.
      *Answer:* The beta is 0.8433 and the required rate of return is 0.1041
   (d) Determine whether stock A is undervalued or overvalued.
      *Answer:* The stock A's actual return is 17%. However, the required rate of return is 10.41%. Therefore, it is undervalued.

## Further Exercises

1. Suppose the risk-free rate of return is 7%. The rate of return on the market portfolio is 20%. The beta of a stock is 1.2. Calculate the equilibrium rate of return of the

stock. If the stock pays $10 dividend annually, what is the stock price? If the market price of the stock is $50, do you want to long or short the stock?

*Answer:* The required rate of return is 22.6%. The equilibrium stock price is 44.2478. Therefore, we short the stock.

2. Suppose that the stock's beta is 1.4 and the equilibrium rate of return is 12%. If the market portfolio return changes from 10% to 15%, what is the stock's expected rate of return?

*Answer:* The risk-free rate is 5%. The new required rate of return is 19%.

## E1.3  DIVIDEND DISCOUNT MODEL

### Definition

The value of the stock is the present value of all the dividends that we can receive from the stock.

### Description of the Model

The value of a security depends on the future cash flows from the security and the risk level involved in the cash flows. For example, if the future cash flows are risk-free, we can discount the future cash flow at the risk-free rate. However, if the future cash flows are risky, we should use a risk-adjusted rate of return as a discount rate. We know that the more risky the future cash flows are, the higher the discount rate becomes, because the present value of the more risky cash flows should be less. Since we will receive the future dividends by holding a stock, we can discount the future dividends at an appropriate discount rate. We can use the Capital Asset Pricing model to determine such a discount rate.

### Numerical Example

Suppose the dividend next year is $2. The dividend growth rate for the next three years is 18%, and the growth rate from the fourth year onward is 6%. The required rate of return is assumed to be 16%. Calculate the stock price. For simplicity, we assume an annual dividend payment. See figure E1.12.

| Inputs | |
| --- | --- |
| Cost of equity | 0.16 |
| Growth rate for the next 3 years | 0.18 |
| Growth rate from year 4 | 0.06 |
| $DPS_1$ | 2 |
| **Outputs** | |
| Stock price | 24.1736029 |

Figure E1.12

The present value of the dividends we will receive over the next three years is 5.262.

$$PV(\text{dividends over three years}) = \frac{2}{1.16} + \frac{2 \times 1.18}{1.16^2} + \frac{2 \times 1.18^2}{1.16^3} = 5.262$$

Since the dividends from the fourth year onwards grow at 6%, the dividend at the fourth year is $2 \times 1.18^2 \times 1.06$, and the present value of the dividends from the fourth year as of the third year is 29.519.

$$S(3) = \frac{div(4)}{R_{reg} - g} = \frac{2 \times 1.18^2 \times 1.06}{0.16 - 0.06} = 29.519$$

Therefore, the stock price is the sum of two values.

$$S(0) = 5.262 + \frac{29.519}{1.16^3} = 24.174$$

## Application

Stock valuation is based on the notion that dividends will be paid from the future earnings. The ratio of the dividend to the earning is called the payout ratio, and the plowback ratio is 1 minus the payout ratio. Since part of the earnings is retained for future investments and the future investments generate more dividends in the future, we can discount the future dividends to calculate the stock price.

## Case: Valuation of a Real Estate Investment Trust (REIT)

Excellent Mortgage, Inc., is organized for tax purposes as a real estate investment trust (REIT). The firm must pay much of its earnings as dividends to the shareholders. The firm's capital has to be mainly paid-in equity investments and not retained earnings. The firm does not pay the federal and state income taxes on the corporate level. The firm is a single-family residential mortgage lender that originates and acquires a broad range of mortgages. Further, Excellent buys a significant portion of their mortgages via internet nationally. The mortgage portfolio has reached $8 billion.

Greg Jose is the CEO of the company. His first appointment of the day is a junior stock analyst, Alec Takahashi, who has been assigned to cover his stock, which is traded on the Big Board. "Good morning Mr. Jose" said Alec as he shook hands with Greg. "Call me Greg, please. What can I do for you today?"

"Well, Mr. Jose—I mean Greg—I would like to learn more about your firm." "Well, which version do you want? The long one or the short one—they are both good. Excellent remains an excellent company." "Well, start with the short version."

"OK. We have our excellent salespeople contacting high net worth individuals out there, anywhere in the country. We lend them mortgages, backed by their fancy real estates. We can lend them $30 million if they have real estate value over $50 million. Of course we have excellent credit analysts in evaluating our credit risk exposure to these mortgagors. We also have an excellent capital market team. These people use our mortgages as collateral to raise funds. Then we use the funds to buy more mortgages. Do you follow now?"

"What is the business model? I mean how do you make money" asked Alec. "We have an excellent business model. This is how it works. We lend our mortgages out charging x% interests. We make sure that the interest rates exceed our funding costs, enough to cover all our operating costs and net our shareholders an excellent profit." "But, would you not be exposed to a lot of interest rate risk when you leverage to buy your mortgages." "Not at all, Alec. We have an excellent quant here who makes sure that our interest rate exposure is close to zero. I mean zilch. He uses interest rate swaps to do that."

"That is good, sir . . . I mean Mr. Jose . . . sorry, I mean Greg. But if your business model is so excellent, why is your P/E so low." "What do you mean so low?" "Well, your stock is now trading at a P/E of 10, while the average P/E in S&P is closer to 20." "Alec, we are a REIT." "Can you explain that?" "Alec, we cannot evaluate a REIT like a Microsoft. We cannot use our retained earnings to grow, and we pay all our earnings as dividends. If we want to grow, we need more equity capital. To get more equity capital, we have to sell shares. If the market requires 10% returns on the investment for our type of business, you get P/E to be 10. Bang, 10. That is all." "Greg, I see now. Have an excellent day."

*Alec was closing the door behind him. "Actually I do not see it at all." Alec whispered to himself. "What am I going to write in my analyst report? I just cannot say Excellent is excellent, can I?"*

## Exercises and Answers

1. The next-year dividend and earning per share are $5 and $7, respectively. The required rate of return is 15%. The rate of return on equity (ROE) is 20%. The ROE is the ratio of earnings per share to book equity per share. The dividend growth rate is the plowback ratio multiplied by the return on equity. If we invest 60% of the earnings and the rate of return on equity is 20%, the book equity per share will increase by 0.6 × 0.2, or 12%. Therefore, earnings and dividends per share will also increase by 12%. See figure E1.13.

   (a) Calculate the stock price using the dividend discount model.

   *Answer:* The dividend per share is $5, the earning per share is $7, the growth rate is 2/35 (= plowback ratio × ROE = (2/7) × 0.2), and therefore the stock price is 53.8462 (= 5/(0.15 − 2/35)).

| Inputs | | | |
|---|---|---|---|
| Cost of equity | 0.15 | | |
| EPS at year 1 | 7 | | |
| DPS at year 1 | 5 | | |
| ROE | 0.2 | | |
| **Outputs** | | | |
| Stock price | 53.8461538 | | |
| Present value of growth opportunity | 7.17948718 | $= NPV_1/(K_e\text{-}g)$ | |
| | 7.17948718 | $= DPS_1/(K_e\text{-}g)\text{-}EPS_1/K_e$ | |

Figure E1.13

(b) The stock price can be defined by $P_0 = (EPS_1/r) + PVGO$, where r is a required rate of return and PVGO is the present value of growth opportunities. Calculate the present value of growth opportunities. To do that, first calculate the present value at year 1 when we invest $EPS_1 - Dividend_1$ at year 1 and receive a perpetual cash flow of $(EPS_1 - Dividend_1) \times ROE$ from year 2 on. Then calculate the present value at year 2 and so on. Once we calculate the present value at each period, discount them at a required rate of return to calculate the PVGO. For simplicity, we assume that the new projects have the same risk as the existing projects.

*Answer:* If we invest the plowback amount at year 1, $2 (= \$7 - \$5)$, we receive the perpetual cash flows, \$0.4 $(= \$2 \times 0.2)$, from year 2. The net present value of the perpetual cash flows as of year 1 is 0.666667 $(= \$0.4/0.15 - \$2)$.

If we invest the plowback amount at year 2, \$2.11429 $(= \$7 \times \frac{37}{35} - \$5 \times \frac{37}{35})$, we receive the perpetual cash flows, \$0.422857 $(= \$2.11429 \times 0.2)$, from year 3. The net present value of the perpetual cash flows as of year 2 is 0.704758 $(= \frac{\$0.422857}{0.15} - \$2.11429)$. If we continue the same procedure, we can see that the net present value of the perpetual cash flows grows at 5.71429%. Therefore, the present value of the growth opportunity is 7.17949 $(= \frac{0.666667}{0.15 - 0.0571429})$.

(a)

| Growth Rate | Stock Value |
|---|---|
| 0.00% | $12.5000 |
| 1.00% | $13.3333 |
| 2.00% | $14.2857 |
| 3.00% | $15.3846 |
| 4.00% | $16.6667 |
| 5.00% | $18.1818 |
| 6.00% | $20.0000 |
| 7.00% | $22.2222 |
| 8.00% | $25.0000 |
| 9.00% | $28.5714 |
| 10.00% | $33.3333 |

(b)

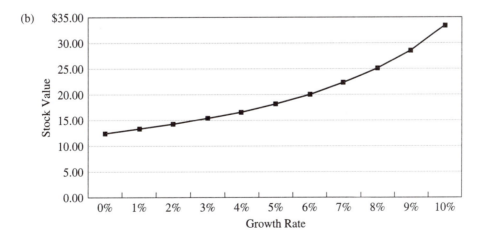

Figure E1.14

(c) Another way to calculate the PVGO is to calculate the stock price using the dividend discount model. Since $EPS_1/r$ is the present value of the future earnings when there is no growth in the earnings, the PVGO is the difference between the stock price and the present value of perpetual cash flows when there is no growth in the company.

*Answer:* The stock price with the PVGO is $5/(0.15 - 2/35)$ and the stock price without the PVGO is $7/0.15$. Therefore the PVGO is the difference between them, which is 7.17949.

2. It is known that the dividend discount model is sensitive to growth rate. To see this sensitivity, we assume the same data as the numerical example except for the second-period growth rate. For simplicity, we assume that the dividend growth rate is 10% from this year on. Draw a diagram to see how the stock price responds when we change the growth rate. Note that the growth rate should be less than the required rate of return.

*Answer:* The stock value changes from $12.50 to $33.33 when the growth rate goes from 0.0% to 10.0%, which means that the stock price significantly depends on the dividend growth rate. See figure E1.14.

## Further Exercises

1. Suppose the dividend this year is $5. The dividend growth rate for the next five years is 10%, and the growth rate from the sixth year onward is 6%. The required rate of return is assumed to be 16%. Calculate the stock price. For simplicity, we assume an annual dividend payment.

*Answer:* The stock price is 62.0176555.

2. The next-year dividend and earning per share are $6 and $8, respectively. The required rate of return is 20%. The rate of return on equity (ROE) is 30%. Calculate the stock price and the present value of growth opportunities.

*Answer:* The stock price is $48 and the present value of growth opportunity is $8.

3. Suppose the next-year earning per share is $8. The dividend payout ratio and the rate of return on equity are predicted below. The required rate of return is assumed to be 10%. Calculate the stock price and the present value of growth opportunities. See table E1.3.

*Answer:* The stock price is $153 and the present value of growth opportunity is $73.

Table E1.3

|  | Year 1 | Year 2 | Year 3 | From Year 4 |
|---|---|---|---|---|
| Dividend Payout Ratio | 0.4 | 0.5 | 0.6 | 0.8 |
| ROE | 0.5 | 0.4 | 0.3 | 0.2 |

## Notes

1. For this work, Harry Markowitz received the Nobel Prize in economics in 1990.

2. A random variable $Y$ is defined to be normally distributed if its density is given by $f(y; \mu, \sigma^2) = \frac{1}{\sqrt{2\pi\sigma^2}} \exp\{\frac{-(y-\mu)^2}{2\sigma^2}\}$. The mean and variance of $Y$ are $\mu$ and $\sigma^2$, respectively. Let $X$ be a positive random variable and let a new random variable $Y$ be defined as $Y = \log_e X$. If $Y$ has a normal distribution, then $X$ is said to have a lognormal distribution. The density of a lognormal

distribution is $f(x; \mu, \sigma^2) = \frac{1}{x\sqrt{2\pi\sigma^2}} \exp\{-\frac{1}{2\sigma^2}(\log_e x - \mu)^2\}$ where $-\infty < \mu < \infty$ and $\sigma > 0$. The mean and variance of $X$ are $e^{\mu + \frac{1}{2}\sigma^2}$ and $e^{2\mu + 2\sigma^2} - e^{2\mu + \sigma^2}$, respectively. Intuitively, the random variable $X$ is lognormally distributed if $\log_e X$ is normally distributed.

3. The average risk of a portfolio made up of $k$ securities out of the market portfolio is

$$\overline{\sigma}^2 = \frac{1}{k}\overline{\sigma}_i^2 + \frac{k-1}{k}\overline{\sigma}_{ij}.$$

where $\overline{\sigma}_i^2$ = the average of variance of all the individual stocks which comprise the market portfolio, and $\overline{\sigma}_{ij}$ = the average of covariance of all the individual stocks which comprise the market portfolio.

Here we assume that the market portfolio consists of 40 different stocks. To understand how we derive the formula, we illustrate that the formula holds when the market portfolio consists of four stocks and we select three stocks out of four stocks to form the portfolio. Assume that the market portfolio consists of four stocks which are A, B, C, and D. We choose 3 stocks from the market portfolio and invest 1/3 in each stock. The number of the three-stock-portfolios is $\binom{4}{3}$ and the average risk of those portfolios is

$$\overline{\sigma}_k^2 = \frac{\sigma_{ABC}^2 + \sigma_{BCD}^2 + \sigma_{CDA}^2 + \sigma_{DAB}^2}{4} \quad \text{when } k = 3$$

where

$$\sigma_{ABC}^2 = \frac{1}{9} \cdot \sigma_A^2 + \frac{1}{9} \cdot \sigma_B^2 + \frac{1}{9} \cdot \sigma_C^2 + \frac{2}{9} \cdot (\sigma_{AB} + \sigma_{BC} + \sigma_{CA})$$

$$\sigma_{BCD}^2 = \frac{1}{9} \cdot \sigma_B^2 + \frac{1}{9} \cdot \sigma_C^2 + \frac{1}{9} \cdot \sigma_D^2 + \frac{2}{9} \cdot (\sigma_{BC} + \sigma_{CD} + \sigma_{DA})$$

$$\sigma_{CDA}^2 = \frac{1}{9} \cdot \sigma_C^2 + \frac{1}{9} \cdot \sigma_D^2 + \frac{1}{9} \cdot \sigma_A^2 + \frac{2}{9} \cdot (\sigma_{CD} + \sigma_{DA} + \sigma_{AC})$$

$$\sigma_{DAB}^2 = \frac{1}{9} \cdot \sigma_D^2 + \frac{1}{9} \cdot \sigma_A^2 + \frac{1}{9} \cdot \sigma_B^2 + \frac{2}{9} \cdot (\sigma_{DA} + \sigma_{AB} + \sigma_{DB})$$

Therefore,

$$\overline{\sigma}_k^2 = \frac{1}{3} \cdot \frac{(\sigma_A^2 + \sigma_B^2 + \sigma_C^2 + \sigma_D^2)}{4} + \frac{2}{3} \cdot \frac{2(\sigma_{AB} + \sigma_{AC} + \sigma_{AD} + \sigma_{BC} + \sigma_{BD} + \sigma_{CD})}{12}$$

$$= \frac{1}{3} \cdot \overline{\sigma}_i^2 + \frac{2}{3} \cdot \overline{\sigma}_{ij}$$

4.
$$\sigma_{A,P} = Cov(\tilde{R}_A, \tilde{R}_P) = Cov(\tilde{R}_A, \omega_A\tilde{R}_A + \omega_B\tilde{R}_B) = Cov(\tilde{R}_A, \omega_A\tilde{R}_A) + Cov(\tilde{R}_A, \omega_B\tilde{R}_B)$$

$$= \omega_A \times Cov(\tilde{R}_A, \tilde{R}_A) + \omega_B \times Cov(\tilde{R}_A, \tilde{R}_B) = \omega_A \times \sigma_A^2 + \omega_B \times \sigma_{A,B}$$

5. William Sharpe, a professor at Stanford University, extended Markowitz's diversification theory to a market equilibrium theory. In 1990 he received the Nobel Prize in economics for this theory.

## Bibliography

Black, F., M. Jensen, and M. Scholes. 1972. *The Capital Asset Pricing Model: Some Empirical Tests, Studies in the Theory of Capital Markets*. New York: Praeger.

Elton, E. J., M. J. Gruber, S. J. Brown, and W. Goetzmann. 2003. *Modern Portfolio Theory and Investment Analysis*, 6th ed. New York: John Wiley and Sons.

Fama, E. F. 1970. Efficient capital markets: A review of theory and empirical work. *Journal of Finance*, 25, no. 5, 383–417.

Fama, E. F. 1991. Efficient capital markets: II. *Journal of Finance*, 46, no. 5, 1575–1617.

Haugen, R. A. 2000. *Modern Investment Theory*, 5th ed. Englewood Cliffs, NJ: Prentice-Hall.

Markowitz, H. M. 1952. Portfolio selection. *Journal of Finance*, 7, no. 1, 77–91.

Modigliani, F., and M. Miller. 1958. The cost of capital, corporation finance and the theory of investment. *American Economic Review*, 48, 267–297.

Modigliani, F., and M. Miller. 1963. Corporate income taxes and the cost of capital: A correction. *American Economic Review*, 53, no. 3, 433–443.

Mossin, J. 1966. Equilibrium in a capital asset market. *Econometrica*, 34, no. 4, 768–783.

Roll, R. 1977. A critique of the asset pricing theory's tests: Part 1. On past and potential testability of the theory. *Journal of Financial Economics*, 4, no. 2, 129–176.

Sharpe, W. F. 1964. Capital asset prices: A theory of market equilibrium under conditions of risk. *Journal of Finance*, 19, no. 3, 425–442.

# 2

# Equity Options

O ption pricing is an important subject. Stock options are traded on the exchanges. Many financial contracts contain options that cannot be detached and traded separately. These options are called *embedded options*. Many financial contracts have contingency features such that the holder has the right to pay for an installment of the cost at a future date as a more complex form of an option.

For these reasons, investors and corporations alike are interested in a methodology for valuing options. But what approach can we use to determine their worth? How can we determine the appropriate required expected returns or discount rate? What is the appropriate risk premium for holding an option? If we use the Capital Asset Pricing model to value an option, how do we determine the $\beta$ of an option when $\beta$ may change over time, depending on the stock price level?

Unfortunately, methodologies like the Capital Asset Pricing model are too imprecise to determine the value of options, since the estimation of the $\beta$ can have significant errors. A new approach is needed to value an option.

## 2.1 DESCRIPTION OF AN OPTION

A *European call option* on a stock gives the holder the right to buy the underlying stock at a fixed price at a specified time. For example, a holder of a Microsoft call option can buy Microsoft at a fixed price, the strike price of $60 on the expiration day (say March 30 of this year). On the expiration date, if Microsoft is trading at $70, the call option holder would exercise the call option, buying the Microsoft stock for $60, $10 below the market. However, if the Microsoft stock trades at $50 on the expiration date, the holder would simply let the option expire, because the investor would not buy the Microsoft stock at a price $10 higher than the price traded in the market. The holder therefore has the option to exercise his right whenever it is to his advantage.

Obviously, an investor would consider buying a call option when he thinks that the stock will rise in value—for example, the Microsoft stock rising to $70 by the end of March. However, if he thinks that the Microsoft price will fall to $50, then he needs to consider another security, a put option. A *European put option* on a stock gives the holder the right to sell (not buy) the underlying stock at the strike price on the expiration date. In this case, if the Microsoft stock trades at $50 at the expiration, the put option would be worth $10. But if Microsoft stock trades at $60, the put option would expire worthless.

In what ways are options different from stocks? Given that a security is called an "option," we may think that the central difference between a stock and an option is that options give the holder the right—not the obligation—to do something. There is a choice built into the terms and conditions of the option security. This choice is a feature of an option, but it is not the central matter. After all, why wouldn't a rational investor exercise a call option when the stock price is above the strike price at expiration? Conversely, why would the rational investor want to buy that stock at a price higher than the market price by exercising a call option when the stock price is below the strike price? These same questions can be raised for the put options.

A rational investor always follows an optimal exercise rule at expiration to maximize his returns. Therefore, in pricing an option, under the rational behavior of the holder of the option, we can think of an option as a security that pays the stock price net of the strike price whenever the stock price is above the strike price at expiration, and otherwise pays nothing. A payment rule, based on the prevailing stock price, for the option holder is specified on the expiration date. This rule is important in defining the option.

In order to discuss how these payoff rules affect the option prices, we need to review option terminologies. An option security is usually called an option contract. Option prices are often called *option premiums*. We say a buyer holds the contract while the seller writes the contract. Time to expiration is the length of time to the expiration date. *Nearby contracts* refer to options with a short time to expiration. The risk of the underlying stock price returns is measured by the standard deviation of the returns, called the *stock volatility*. The intrinsic value is the value of the option if the option were to be exercised immediately. The *intrinsic value* of a call option is the underlying stock price net of the strike price if the netting is positive. Otherwise it is 0. For a put option, the intrinsic value is the strike price net of the underlying stock price, if the difference is positive. Otherwise it is 0. An option is said to be *at the money* if the underlying stock is trading around the strike price; it is *in the money* if the intrinsic value is positive; and it is *out of the money* when the intrinsic value is 0.

The *payoff diagram* is defined as the payment to the option holder on the expiration date. For the call option, the payoff is given by

$$C_T = Max\,[S_T - X, 0] \tag{2.1}$$

where $C_T$ is the call price or the payoff to the call option on the expiration date, $T$; $S_T$ is the underlying stock price on the expiration date, $T$; and $X$ is the strike price.

For the put option, the payoff is given by

$$P_T = Max\,[X - S_T, 0] \tag{2.2}$$

where $P_T$ is the put option price at the expiration date.

Equations (2.1) and (2.2) are called *terminal conditions of the options* because they specify the payout at the expiration date. Call and put stock options have particularly simple payout specifications.

Call options provide the upside return but protect the downside risk, losing, at most, the initial investment should the stock price fall. Similarly, the put option offers the upside return when the stock price falls and downside protection when the stock price rises.

## 2.2   INSTITUTIONAL FRAMEWORK

Exchange-traded stock options are contracts between two parties. There are as many holders of the contracts as there are sellers. The number of contracts sold (and bought) for a particular security is called the *open interest*. Options can be traded on stock, forwards and futures, commodities, and other financial securities. In the United States,

**Table 2.**1  The Market Closing
Microsoft Option Prices for 2/4/2002
for Strike 60 at 62.66

| Month | Call | Put |
|-------|------|-----|
| March | 3.4 | 0.7 |
| April | 4.4 | 1.7 |
| July | 5.4 | 2.7 |

On February 4, 2002, Microsoft was trading
at 62.66. For the strike price, 60, the call and
put premiums are given. Since the call options are in the money, the call premiums are
larger than the intrinsic value. The differences
between the call premiums and the intrinsic
value are the time values. As time to maturity
increases, the time value increases.

the exchange-traded options are American options, referring to the feature that the
option holder can exercise the option at any time before the expiration date.

Exchange-traded options on stocks such as the NASDAQ-100 Index Tracking Stock,
Microsoft, Cisco Systems, and Citigroup are traded on the American Stock Exchange;[1]
index options such as the Dow Jones Industrial Average Call and Put, on the Chicago
Board of Trade.[2] There are also over-the-counter options customized for specific needs.
For example, on February 4, 2002, Microsoft was trading at 62.66. Table 2.1 gives the
call option and put option prices for the strike price, 60, for each expiration date.

In table 2.1, the intrinsic values of the March call and put contracts are 2.66 (=
$Max[62.66 - 60, 0]$) and 0. The prices show that the market trades the call option
at a price exceeding the intrinsic price by 0.84 (= 3.40–2.66) for the possible higher
returns when the Microsoft price rises (of course weighing the possible loss of the entire
premium of 3.40 if the price falls instead). For the put option, the market assigns 0.70
for the probability that Microsoft falls below 60 by the end of March.

The time to expiration of these exchange-traded stock options is typically less than
a year. The exchange-traded options with longer expiration are called *LEAPs* (long-
term equity anticipation securities). For example, on February 4, 2002, the call and put
options of Microsoft LEAPs expiring in January 2003 are reported to be traded at 11.60
and 6.50, respectively. We can see that the premiums of both call and put options increase
with the time to expiration compared with the option prices in table 2.1, reflecting the
higher likelihood of these options expiring with higher expected returns as the time of
expiration lengthens.

## 2.3  PUT-CALL PARITY

A European call option, a European put option with the same strike price and expiration
date, and the underlying stock are not independent of each other. In fact, any one of them
can be replicated by the other two securities: the call option is a combination of the stock
and the put option, and the put option is a portfolio of the stock and call option. This
relationship is called the *put-call parity*, first proposed by Stoll (1969).

Let $C$ and $P$ be the prices of the call and put options, respectively. The options are
European and have the same strike price, $X$, and the same underlying stock, $S$. Let the

continuously compounding risk-free rate be $r$ and the time to expiration $T$. Then the following relationship must hold.

$$C - P = S - PV(X) \qquad (2.3)$$

where $PV(X)$ is equal to $e^{-rT}X$, discounting the strike price at the risk-free rate.

In order to demonstrate that the put-call parity is correct, we need to consider the payoffs, at expiration of a portfolio, of holding the call option and shorting the put option. The payoff of the portfolio is given by

$$Y = Max\,[S_T - X, 0] - Max\,[X - S_T, 0] \qquad (2.4)$$

Now consider the case when the stock price exceeds the strike price at expiration. In this case, at expiration, $Max\,[S_T - X, 0] = S_T - X$ while $Max\,[X - S_T, 0] = 0$. Therefore, the payout of the portfolio is $Y = S_T - X$.

When the stock price is below the strike price at expiration, the payout $Y$ is also equal to $S_T - X$. This means that the portfolio holding a long position in a call option and writing a put option with the same exercise price and maturity date has the same value as holding the underlying stock and owing the strike price in cash, for all the possible values of the stock price at the expiration date.

The put-call parity can be explained graphically. Consider a portfolio consisting of a long call and a short put (see figure 2.1).

The stock price is 62.66, and the strike price of the call and the put is 60. The present value of the exercise price is 59.96. The call premium is 3.4 and the put premium is 0.7. Since the put-call parity can be expressed such that (long a call + short a put) is equal to (long a stock + risk-free borrowing), the cash flow at maturity of longing the call and shorting the put is equal to that of longing the stock combined with risk-free borrowing.

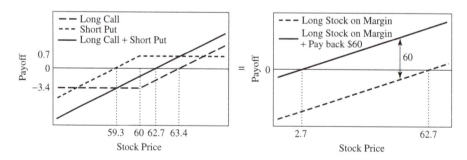

**Figure 2.1** Put-call parity. The stock price is 62.66, and the strike price of the call and the put options is 60. The present value of the exercise price is 59.96. The call premium is 3.4 and the put premium is 0.7. The left panel shows the profile of a portfolio consisting of longing a call and shorting a put. Since the profile shows the cash flow at time T, the —— line indicates the cash flow of the call at maturity against various stock prices at maturity. The – – line can be represented in a similar way. The combined cash flow is a 45° straight line, which crosses the horizontal line originating at 0 when the stock price is 62.7. The right panel shows the profile of a portfolio of longing a stock and shorting a risk-free asset (i.e., borrowing). The - - - line in the right panel indicates the profile of longing the stock when we have bought the stock at 62.66 by borrowing 59.96. Since the principal amount with interest should be paid back at maturity, the dotted line shifts downward by 60.

The left panel in figure 2.1 represents the cash flow at maturity when we have a portfolio that consists of longing a call and shorting a put. The right panel in figure 2.1 indicates the cash flow at maturity when we long a stock by borrowing the present value of an exercise price.

The put-call parity can be explained intuitively. We have mentioned that call options offer the upside returns while protecting the downside risk, and shorting the put options means that we are exposed to the downside risk with a truncated upside. When we combine the two positions, we have both upside gain and downside risks of a stock without any protection. This means that we have the risk of a stock.

The simplicity of the put-call parity result often disguises its important implications. First, any analysis of the call option, including its pricing, can extend directly to the put option. Consider the numerical example of the Microsoft March contracts. The traded options allow holders to exercise the options early, while the put-call parity does not allow options to have such a feature. We will ignore the value of early exercise until we revisit this issue later. Since the stock, the put, and the call are 62.66, 0.70, and 3.40, respectively, we have

$$S + P - C = 62.66 + 0.70 - 3.40 = 59.96$$

The value 59.96 is the present value of the exercise price 60, where the discount rate will be the short-term funding costs for the arbitrage trading over the period from February 4 until the expiration date. This formula must take the bid-ask spreads (the price difference between the highest bid price and the lowest ask price) set by the market makers and other transaction costs into account, and in practice, the arbitrage-free models can be approximately correct only within a band around the theoretical price. Within such a band, an arbitrage position cannot be profitable because of all the transactions cost in implementing the trade. In most cases, these bands are quite narrow.

This numerical example illustrates that the prices of the put option, the call option, and the stock must be aligned according to the put-call parity; otherwise, arbitrage opportunities would occur. The alignment should be within the bid-ask spread or within the cost of an arbitrage.

Second, the put-call parity prescribes a straightforward *static hedging strategy*. Suppose an investor is holding an illiquid call option. He would not want to be exposed to the market risk. Using the put-call parity, he can sell both the underlying stock and the corresponding put option, and invest the proceeds at a risk-free rate of return. The net position would result in a risk-free position. This hedge position is static in the sense that the position does not have to be revised until the expiration date, when the entire position can be liquidated.

## 2.4   THE MAIN INSIGHT OF THE BLACK-SCHOLES MODEL

Prior to 1973 there had been many attempts to value options. The general approach was to use a risk and return framework, applying the discounted cash flow method. First, we determine the expected return of the underlying stock. Then we determine the expected payoff of the option at the expiration date. As a result, the option price is the present value of the expected payoff. However, determining the appropriate discount rate is difficult when we use this approach.

This methodology can be applied to primary securities such as stocks, as seen in the dividend discount model. However, because by definition the value of derivative securities depends on the underlying securities and the underlying securities' prices are changing on a real-time basis, the continual change of risks inherent in derivative securities prohibits a rigorous valuation model from determining the appropriate discount rate.

To overcome this difficulty, Black and Scholes devised a way to neutralize the risk inherent in options. Since this risk is driven by the stock, we can eliminate the risks of the option by taking the opposite position in the stock. There should be a specific ratio between the stock and option positions such that the risks of the stock and the option exactly cancel each other. This argument's main issue concerns a search for the combination such that the portfolio has no risks. This combination is referred to as "the *hedge ratio*" or the Greek letter delta ($\Delta$) in the current literature.

## Construction of a Binomial Lattice of Stock Prices

The model specifies the rules for trading a security, the behavior of the investors, and a trading mechanism—the arbitrage mechanism. Now we proceed to describe a basic model that enables us to value securities.

We assume a discrete time model where all trading occurs at regular intervals. All investors make their decisions at the same time, including revising their portfolio and adjusting for their expectations. The market clears at these time intervals at one price for each security. Let the times of trading be denoted by $n$. For clarity of exposition, we assume that each time interval is one year. In practice, depending on the purpose of the modeling, the time interval can be daily for most instruments.

This section formulates the model that describes the uncertainties. The model is described by flipping a coin: head (up state) and tail (down state) are the "outcomes," with their corresponding probabilities. We will assume that the probability of the up state is $q$, and of the down state, $(1 - q)$.

The flip of a coin can be considered an event with two possible outcomes. After each event, an outcome is determined, and each successive event has another two possible outcomes. All of the possible future outcomes can be illustrated in a "tree" that maps all the possible paths of a random walk. We say the tree is "recombining" if an up state followed by a down state equals a down state followed by an up state.

Forcing the tree to recombine reduces the number of nodes. If the tree does not recombine, each node will have another two outcomes after each period. In $N$ periods, there will be $2^N$ nodes at time $N$. That is, the number of states at any time $N$ grows exponentially with the number of periods $N$. However, in a binomial lattice (*a recombining tree*), the number of states is only $(N + 1)$. There are significantly fewer states to manage in a binomial lattice model. By forcing the tree to recombine, we have constructed a binomial lattice.

This binomial lattice is a random walk. At any time $n$, there are $(n + 1)$ possible states of the world. Each state is denoted by $i$. We refer to the $i$th state at time $n$ as the node $(n, i)$. At the initial node, we can calculate the probability of reaching any node $(n, i)$ for a particular $n$, a probability distribution that is called *binomial distribution*. We get a distribution of the likelihood of the position of the point. Given the probability

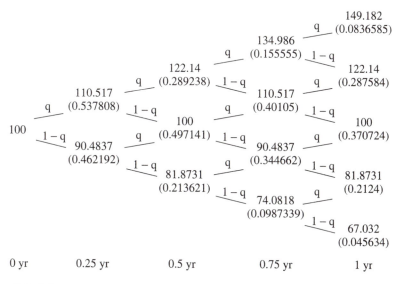

**Figure 2.2** A binomial stock price process. The value of the stock price is denoted at each node with the probability of arriving at the node, which is in parentheses. The continuously compounding risk-free rate of return ($r$) is 5% and the volatility is 20%. The initial stock price is 100, the time to maturity ($T$) is one year, and $m$ is equal to 4. The parameters are $u = \exp\{\sigma\sqrt{1/m}\} = 1.10517$, $d = 1/u = 0.904837$, and $p = (\exp[\frac{r}{m}] - d)/(u - d) = 0.537808$.

distributions and the outcomes, expected values and standard deviations of future uncertain outcomes can be calculated.

For example, let the price of a stock be $S$. In the up state, the price becomes $S_u$, and in the down state, $S_d$. Consider only one step. The expected price is

$$E[S] = qS_u + (1 - q)S_d \qquad (2.5)$$

and the standard deviation $\sigma$ is

$$\sigma^2 = q(S_u - E[S])^2 + (1 - q)(S_d - E[S])^2. \qquad (2.6)$$

Consider an example of a binomial process of a stock price. To this end, we assume that the stock price follows a multiplicative binomial process. During a time period, the stock goes up or down. The initial stock price is 100 and the time to maturity is one year. The continuously compounding risk-free rate of return, $r$, is 5%. The stock volatility is 20%. Figure 2.2 shows a binomial stock price process.

The expected values and standard deviations of the stock price at each period are given in table 2.2. As time passes, the expected value and the standard deviation increase.

**Table 2.2** The Mean and Volatility of the Binomial Stock Price Process

| Time (year) | 0 | 0.25 | 0.5 | 0.75 | 1 |
|---|---|---|---|---|---|
| Expected value | 100 | 101.258 | 102.532 | 103.821 | 105.127 |
| Standard deviation | 0 | 9.988 | 14.3376 | 17.824 | 20.8911 |

As time passes by, the volatility increases because we expect more uncertainty at later periods.

The reason for the increasing expected value is due to the upward probability, which is greater than 0.5. The reason for the increasing volatility is that the difference between the highest and the lowest stock price is increasing as we go further in the future, which is an inherent property of the binomial process.

Note that since the rate of return is measured by the continuously compounding rate, the expected annual return over one year is 5.127% ($= \exp(0.05) - 1$), which is greater than 5%.

The binomial lattice in modeling risk has a number of interesting properties. This process is a Markov process. That is, at each node, the possible outcomes are independent of how the price arrives at that node. The Markov property is frequently used in finance, and many financial models have the Markov property. The formal definition of the *Markov property* is that the conditional distribution of $\tilde{S}(T)$, given information up until $t$ (where $t < T$), depends only on $S(t)$. Even though the formal definition of Markov is a little bit unfriendly, the intuition behind Markov is straightforward. If we assume that stock prices have the Markov property, we simply say that we need only today's stock price to guess tomorrow's stock price. We do not have to collect past prices, because information contained in the price history is already incorporated into today's stock price. In this case, $t$ is today and $T$ is tomorrow. The amount of information we can extract to predict tomorrow's stock price is the same regardless of whether we collect the price history or only look at today's stock price.

The Markov property is related to the efficient market hypothesis, which says that stock prices instantaneously reflect information. As long as stock prices instantaneously reflect information under the efficient market hypothesis, we cannot squeeze more information from the price history, and we can only use today's price to predict tomorrow's price.

## The Dynamic Hedging Argument

Section 2.3 demonstrated how we can replicate a call option using a put option and the underlying stock. This section will show that we can replicate the call option using the underlying stock and the risk-free investment only at each node on the binomial lattice tree. Different from the put-call parity, this hedging requires a continual revision of our portfolio of stock and risk-free position at each node. This continual revision of a portfolio is called *dynamic hedging*.

Let us give a numerical example to intuitively explain the seemingly complex idea. Let us assume that there are three securities in a one-period and two-states setting. Security A at time 0 is $55, and its value at time 1 is $75 when the weather at time 1 is sunny and $35 when the weather at time 1 is rainy. We further assume that the sunny weather and the rainy weather are mutually exclusive—only one of them will occur at time period 1. Security B's value is $35 when the weather at time 1 is sunny and $75 when the weather at time 1 is rainy. Note that the payoffs of securities A and B directly offset each other in their outcomes. (See figure 2.3.)

Finally, the risk-free rate of return over one period is 10%, which means that the price of the risk-free asset at time 0 is $100 when its value at time 1 is $110, regardless of the weather at that time. Let this risk-free asset be called security C. The problem we are facing now is how much we should pay to buy stock B at time period 0.

Our first observation is that stock A and stock B are risky assets because their cash flow at time 1 depends on the weather at time 1. Security C is a risk-free asset because

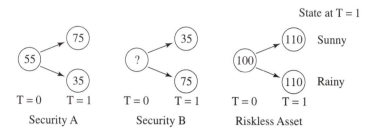

State at T = 1

**Figure 2.3** The portfolio outcomes. The price of security A goes to 75 when the weather is sunny at time 1 and to 35 when it is rainy at time 1. The price of security B goes to 35 when it is sunny at time 1 and to 75 when it is rainy at time 1. The risk-free rate of one period is 10%. When we form a portfolio by combining one share of security A with one share of security B, we will have a risk-free portfolio, even though we put together risky securities. This is a basic idea behind option pricing.

its cash flow is the same regardless of the weather. However, if you add one share of security A to one share of security B, it is equal to the share of security C, which is risk-free ($75 + $35 = $110). The portfolio value at time 1 is $110, regardless of the weather at time 1. Since the portfolio of security A and security B is risk-free, its value at time 0 is 100 when we apply the law of one price. Therefore, the price of one share of security A and one share of security B must equal 100 (since the portfolio value is the sum of its components). This argument leads us to conclude that the price of security B at time period 0 is $45 (= $100 − $55).

Let us continue with this example. If the price of security B happens to be $50 and not $45, what will happen? Since security B's price is greater than $45, we have an arbitrage opportunity. We sell one share of security B and one share of security A. This sale provides $105. Now we buy security C for $100, leaving us a cash inflow of $5. What is nice for the arbitrageur is that the cash flow at time 1 is always 0, regardless of the sunny or rainy weather. The payout of security C, $110, can be used to meet the uncertain obligated payments of securities A and B. Arbitrage trading will continue until the selling pressures of A and B lead to falls in their prices until we reach a new price level where there is no arbitrage opportunity. Similarly, if security B is trading below 45 (say 40), we will buy securities A and B and sell security C.

Interestingly, we have priced security B without making any assumptions about the probability of having the sunny or rainy weather at time 1. Furthermore, we do not need to know the expected rate of return of security A. Not having to know the likelihood of sunny or rainy weather at time 1 is surprising, because, using the discounted cash flow method, we need to know the probabilities to determine the expected value and the risks. However, when we use an arbitrage argument, probability distribution is irrelevant for pricing purposes.

## Derivation of the Black-Scholes (Discrete Time) Model

The Black-Scholes option pricing model is derived in a continuous time framework by solving a stochastic differential equation. Here, we provide the model, often called the Cox-Ross-Rubinstein model (1979) or the Rendleman-Bartter model (1979), in discrete time. The discrete time model is more intuitive to explain and may offer a flexible approach to valuing a broad range of securities.

Before we begin developing the pricing model, we will state the assumptions of the model:

1. The stock follows a multiplicative binomial process. During a time period, its price goes up to $uS$ or down to $dS$, where $d < e^r < u$.
2. The stock volatility is constant. Stock risk is the only source of risk for the purpose of valuing the options.
3. The continuously compounding risk-free interest rate is constant at $r$. In this section, we will automatically assume a flat yield curve with all the forward rates being the same.
4. The market is perfect, with no frictions such as transaction costs, and the market is efficient, the prices fully reflecting all available market information. There are no short selling constraints.
5. The call option has a strike price $X$ and time to expiration $n$.

First we derive the binomial option pricing model in a simple one-period case. We begin by assuming a binomial stock process. The second step determines the payoff one period hence, which is the maturity date in this example. Once the stock process is given, we can easily calculate the payoff by the boundary condition of the option. We construct a *levered portfolio* consisting of the stock and the bond B to duplicate the option payoff at the maturity date. We call the duplicating portfolio the levered portfolio because we buy the stock on margin. Since the option has the same cash flows as the levered portfolio, the option value at this period should be equal to the cost of constructing the levered portfolio to avoid any arbitrage opportunities. Alternatively, we can create a risk-free portfolio to price the option. We now elaborate the method in four steps.

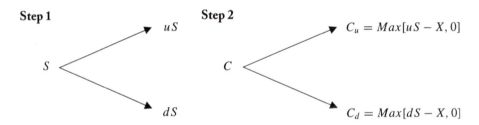

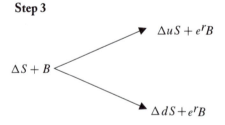

In step 1, we construct a binomial lattice of the stock, where $u$ and $d$ are defined by the volatility of the stock and $r$ is the continuously compounding risk-free rate as specified in figure 2.2. In step 2, we consider one period before the expiration of the option. At the expiration date, we know the payoffs of the options, as specified in equations (2.1) and (2.2).

In step 3, we construct a levered portfolio by holding $\Delta$ shares of stock and a risk-free asset $B$ to duplicate the cash flow of the European call option.

$$\Delta u S + e^r B = C_u$$

$$\Delta d S + e^r B = C_d$$

By solving the two equations, we get

$$\Delta = \frac{C_u - C_d}{uS - dS} > 0 \tag{2.7}$$

Substituting $\frac{C_u - C_d}{uS - dS}$ for $\Delta$ in equation (2.7), we get $B = \frac{C_d u - C_u d}{e^r (u - d)}$.

Since we know $B$ and $\Delta$, we can solve for $C$ by substituting $\Delta S + B = C$ in the equation. We have $C = \frac{pC_u + (1-p)C_d}{e^r}$, where $p = \frac{e^r - d}{u - d}$, $1 - p = \frac{u - e^r}{u - d}$.

Note that we have not used the subjective view of the expected return of the stock or the subjective view of the probability of the stock's outcomes. $p$ is defined by the stock lattice and is called the risk-neutral probability, which we will discuss further later. The formulas are applied to each node of the option lattice. As long as we know the payoff of the option at the expiration date, we can apply the formulas recursively and solve for all the option prices at all the nodes in the lattice.

To provide a clearer explanation of this dynamic hedging, we can derive the same binomial option pricing model by constructing an alternative hedging using a risk-free hedging portfolio.

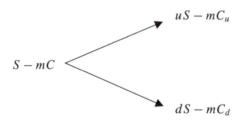

In step 3', a risk-free hedge portfolio of longing one share of $S$ and shorting $m$ shares of $C$ should be risk-free by construction; the cash flow at the up state should be the same as the cash flow at the down state.

$$uS - mC_u = dS - mC_d \tag{2.8}$$

Simplifying the above equation, we get $m = \frac{uS - dS}{C_u - C_d} = \frac{1}{\Delta}$

Substituting $\frac{uS - dS}{C_u - C_d}$ into $m$ in equation (2.8) and using the fact that the risk-fee cash flow should be discounted at the risk-free rate, we have

$$S - mC = \frac{uS - mC_u}{e^r} = \frac{dS - mC_d}{e^r}$$

Simplifying the above expressions, we have the same binomial option pricing model.

$$C = \frac{pC_u + (1-p)C_d}{e^r}, \quad p = \frac{e^r - d}{u - d}, 1 - p = \frac{u - e^r}{u - d}$$

Note that $p$ can be interpreted as a probability because it is less than 1 and greater than 0. Therefore, the expression for $C$ can be interpreted as the present value of the expected payoff of the option. If we extend this construction of the option value recursively from one period to two periods and to $n$ periods, as we will explain further in the following section, the expression for the option value is given below.

$$C = \frac{1}{e^{r \cdot n}} \sum_{i=0}^{n} \binom{n}{i} p^i (1-p)^{n-i} Max\left[0, u^i d^{n-i} S - X\right]$$

where $\binom{n}{i} = \frac{n!}{(n-i)!i!}$ is the binomial factor. This is the discrete time option pricing model. $Max\left[0, u^i d^{n-i} S - X\right]$ is the terminal condition of the European call option for each state $i$, and $e^{-r \cdot n}$ is the present value factor, using the risk-free rate. The main insight of the Black-Scholes model is that the option price $C$ can be interpreted as the discounted expected value of the payoff of the option at expiration under the risk-neutral probability $p$. For this reason, if we construct the stock lattice according to figure 2.2, which is based on the risk-neutral probability, and determine the option prices on that lattice, we can derive the option price according to the option pricing model. We will discuss the specific valuation methodologies next, using these insights.

## 2.5   VALUATION METHODS

### Backward Substitution Valuation Method

The idea of the pricing methodology is intuitive. The binomial lattice enables us to itemize all the relevant information for valuing the option at each node. Each node specifies the state and time of the world, as in figure 2.2. First, the price of the option is specified at the terminal date by the payoff rule of the option. Take a node one period before the terminal date. At that time and state, we know the risk-neutral expected value of the option. In other words, we know the perfect hedge, using the stock and bond to replicate the option. The cost of the replicating portfolio is the option price, where we also have proved that the price is, in fact, the expected risk-neutral value of the option discounted back at the risk-free rate. Using this argument, we can determine all the option prices for all the states of the world at the time one period from the terminal date.

Let us consider the time two periods from the terminal date. We can repeat the same argument. This time, since we know all the option prices at the time 1 period from the terminal date, we can calculate the expected risk-neutral values. Then we discount back at the risk-free rate to determine the option prices for all the states of the world for two periods from the terminal date.

We can determine the option price recursively, always one period back at each iteration. In repeating the process, we will arrive at the initial date, and the price of the option at that point is the price of the option at present, the price that we seek to determine. This procedure of pricing the option is called *backward substitutions*. (See figure 2.4.)

Consider a numerical example, using the lattice depicted in figure 2.2. Consider a call option expiring at the end of year 1 with a strike price of 100 (at the money). The results are shown in figure 2.5.

$$C_{uu} = Max\,[S_{uu} - X, 0]$$

$$C_u = \frac{pC_{uu} + (1-p)C_{ud}}{e^r}$$

$$C_{ud} = Max\,[S_{ud} - X, 0]$$

$$C = \frac{pC_u + (1-p)C_d}{e^r}$$

$$C_d = \frac{pC_{ud} + (1-p)C_{dd}}{e^r}$$

$$C_{dd} = Max\,[S_{dd} - X, 0]$$

$$u = \exp\left\{\sigma\sqrt{\frac{1}{m}}\right\}, d = \frac{1}{u}, p = \frac{\exp[\frac{r}{m}] - d}{u - d}$$

**Figure 2.4** Payoffs of the option at the nodes in a binomial lattice. Stock prices are assumed to go up and down by the factors $u$ and $d$, respectively. The European call option on the stock matures at period 2 with strike price $X$. At period 2, the option has an intrinsic value. At period 1, the option value is the expected value discounted by the risk-free rate. To calculate the expected value, we use the risk-neutral probabilities, $p$, rather than actual probabilities. Under risk-neutral probabilities, all the securities have the same rate of return, which is the risk-free rate regardless of the risk level they might assume. $\sigma$ is the stock volatility. $u$ and $d$ are the upward movement and downward movement factors. $r$ is the continuously compounding risk-free interest rate. $p$ is risk-neutral probability. $m$ is the number of subperiods partitioned in a period. Since $r$ and $\sigma$ are measured for one period, we have to adjust accordingly when we divide one period into $m$ subperiods.

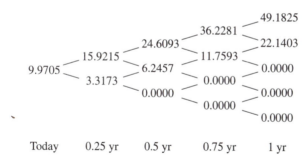

| Today | 0.25 yr | 0.5 yr | 0.75 yr | 1 yr |

**Figure 2.5** A risk-neutral binomial lattice for the option price. Given the same binomial stock price process as in figure 2.2, we calculate the binomial call option price process. The continuously compounding risk-free rate and the initial stock price are the same as in figure 2.2 and are adjusted accordingly by partitioning the one period into four subperiods. The parameters are $u = \exp\{\sigma\sqrt{1/m}\} = 1.10517, d = 1/u = 0.904837, S = 100, \sigma = 0.2, r = 0.05, T = 1$, and $p = (\exp[\frac{r}{m}] - d)/(u - d) = 0.537808, 1 - p = 0.462192$. At maturity, the call option prices are the intrinsic values. When rolled back by one subperiod, the call option price is the expected value discounted by the one-subperiod risk-free interest rate. For example, at 0.75 year and the highest node, the expected value is $49.182580 \times 0.5378 + 22.1403 \times 0.462192$. If we discount the expected value by the one-subperiod risk-free rate, which is 1.01258, we have 36.2281, which is the call option value at the node. The option values at the other nodes will be calculated in a similar manner. If we roll back to the initial period, we have 9.97052 as the current call option price.

## Risk-Neutral Valuation Approach—Closed-Form Solution

Now consider the risk-neutral option lattice. This lattice is based on the risk-neutral stock lattice by assuming that the stock has a risk-free return, as if all market participants were risk-neutral. We can make this assumption because in the dynamic hedging argument, we never use any notion of risk aversion or risk premiums. Arbitrage arguments are preference-free.

We repeatedly apply this arbitrage argument at each node of the lattice. If we know the exact payout on the expiration date for each stock price, we should know the option price one step before the expiration date that would ensure the portfolio return is the risk-free rate. If we know the values of the option at the nodes one step before the expiration for all the stock values, then we can calculate the option price for each stock price two steps before the expiration. If we continue that thought process, we can determine the option price.

Therefore, in this procedure, any investor would agree on the option price, independent of his risk aversion. The pricing is preference-free. If the valuation is preference-free, then we can assume that the stock price movement is determined by the risk-neutral market participant. That means we can assume that everyone is risk-neutral and all risky assets, both the underlying stock and its options, have risk-free expected returns.

Since the stock movement is assumed to be following a random walk with risk-neutral probabilities, the stock price at the terminal date is

$$S_{n,i} = Su^i d^{n-i}$$

where $n = $ discrete time and $i = $ the number of upward movements.

Given these stock terminal values, we can determine the option payoff at the terminal date. And, in turn, given the value of the option at each node at the terminal date, we can calculate the expected value using the risk-neutral probabilities $p$. The expected value is

$$\text{risk-neutral expected call option payoff} = \sum_{i=0}^{n} Max\left[Su^i d^{n-i} - X, 0\right] \binom{n}{i} p^i (1-p)^{n-i}$$

The price of the option, being the present value of the expected value discounted at the risk-free rate, is therefore

Cox-Ross-Rubinstein model

$$C = e^{-r \cdot n} \sum_{i=0}^{n} Max\left[Su^i d^{n-i} - X, 0\right] \binom{n}{i} p^i (1-p)^{n-i} \tag{2.9}$$

where $r$ is the risk-free rate for the one-period step size. (See table 2.3.)

The Black-Scholes model is usually expressed in a form where the step size converges to 0. In the limit, equation (2.9) becomes

Black-Scholes model

$$C = SN(d_1) - Xe^{-rT}N(d_2) \tag{2.10}$$

**Table 2.3** Option Payoffs and Corresponding Binomial Probabilities in the
Cox-Ross-Rubinstein Model

| (1) *Number of Upward Movements* | 0 | 1 | 2 | 3 | 4 | *Sum* |
|---|---|---|---|---|---|---|
| (2) Payoffs Max[$S$-$X$, 0] | 0.0000 | 0.0000 | 0.0000 | 22.1403 | 49.1825 | — |
| (3) Binomial coefficients | 1 | 4 | 6 | 4 | 1 | 16 |
| (4) Binomial probabilities | 0.0456 | 0.0531 | 0.0618 | 0.0719 | 0.0837 | — |
| (3) × (4) | 0.0456 | 0.2124 | 0.3707 | 0.2876 | 0.0837 | 1.0000 |
| (5) Expected payoffs (2) × (3) × (4) | 0.0000 | 0.0000 | 0.0000 | 6.3672 | 4.1145 | 10.4817 |

Call option value can be obtained by calculating the expected value at maturity (year 1) and discounting the expected value by the risk-free rate over four subperiods. 10.4817 is the expected value at year 1. The call option value, 9.97052, can be obtained by discounting 10.4817 with $\exp\{\frac{r}{m} \cdot 4\} = 1.01258^4 = 1.05127$. The sum of the probabilities is one. The sum of all the binomial coefficients equals the total number of paths, which is 16 ($= 2^4$).

where

$$d_1 = \frac{\ln(S/X) + (r + \sigma^2/2)T}{\sigma\sqrt{T}}, \qquad d_2 = d_1 - \sigma\sqrt{T}$$

$N(\cdot)$ is the cumulative normal distribution

The interpretation of the Black-Scholes model is the same as that for discrete time. The option value is the expected value of the option payoff discounted at the risk-free rate. The expected option payoff is determined by a stock process that follows a lognormal distribution, with a drift at the risk-free rate and a constant volatility.

## Pathwise Methodology

We can view the lattice from another perspective. A lattice is a representation of many possible scenarios. In fact, there are $2^N$ scenarios, exhausting all the possibilities of the price paths of the stock if the terminal discrete period is $N$. We can then analyze the behavior of an option, scenario by scenario. A path on a lattice (a scenario) is a vector of events starting from the initial state. A path is denoted by $(+, -, +, \ldots)$, where "+" means the stock moves up and "−" means that the stock moves down. We analyze a scenario in order to understand what happens when a stock takes a specific path in the lattice. It does not matter whether the path is taken in the risk-neutral lattice or the true lattice,[3] because the node values are the same regardless of the lattice. Once the path is specified in the stock lattice, the paths are also specified in the option lattices. In other words, while there are four lattices, a scenario path is well defined in all the lattices (as will be further explained in section 2.6).

A *pathwise value* is the present value of the cash flow based on the risk-neutral lattice discounted over each period at the risk-free rate. The probability assigned to each pathwise value is the probability calculated using the risk-neutral probability: $p^i(1 - p)^{N-i}$, where $p$ is the risk-neutral probability, $N$ is the final period, and $i$ is the number of up states for that scenario.

## Numerical Example of the Pathwise Values

Table 2.4 shows that the mean value of the pathwise values is the same as that determined by the backward substitution approach. The pathwise value is the risk-adjusted present value of the payoffs along each scenario.

The option price is the mean of the pathwise values of the risk-neutral lattice. That means the value of an option is the mean of the present values of the option cash flows for all the scenarios. When we pay for an option, we are in fact paying for the mean of all possible outcomes. We have constructed the pathwise values from the risk-neutral lattice.

The pathwise approach enables the approximate construction of any option as a combination of options. This can be achieved by seeking a combination of options that have the same pathwise values. Consider a special case of a portfolio of options whose pathwise values are all 0. In this case, if we follow one particular scenario over time, we will have cash inflows and outflows. When the cash flows of the portfolio of options along a scenario are invested (or borrowed) at the risk-free rate, at any future date and state of the world the terminal value is always 0 under each scenario because the pathwise value is 0. Therefore, if we can construct a portfolio of options such that the portfolio has the same pathwise values as those of another option, then the portfolio of options is equivalent to that particular option in the sense that the terminal values in all the scenarios are the same, allowing for borrowing and investing at the risk-free rate. Furthermore, if the pathwise values are constant, then the security is equivalent to cash or the risk-free asset.

**Table 2.4** European Option Pricing by Pathwise Valuation

| Scenarios | (1) Payoffs | (2) Probabilities | (3) Discount | (1) × (2) × (3) |
|-----------|-------------|-------------------|--------------|------------------|
| {0, 0, 0, 0} | 0.00000 | 0.0456 | 0.95123 | 0.00000 |
| {0, 0, 0, 1} | 0.00000 | 0.0531 | 0.95123 | 0.00000 |
| {0, 0, 1, 0} | 0.00000 | 0.0531 | 0.95123 | 0.00000 |
| {0, 0, 1, 1} | 0.00000 | 0.0618 | 0.95123 | 0.00000 |
| {0, 1, 0, 0} | 0.00000 | 0.0531 | 0.95123 | 0.00000 |
| {0, 1, 0, 1} | 0.00000 | 0.0618 | 0.95123 | 0.00000 |
| {0, 1, 1, 0} | 0.00000 | 0.0618 | 0.95123 | 0.00000 |
| {0, 1, 1, 1} | 22.14028 | 0.0719 | 0.95123 | 1.51416 |
| {1, 0, 0, 0} | 0.00000 | 0.0531 | 0.95123 | 0.00000 |
| {1, 0, 0, 1} | 0.00000 | 0.0618 | 0.95123 | 0.00000 |
| {1, 0, 1, 0} | 0.00000 | 0.0618 | 0.95123 | 0.00000 |
| {1, 0, 1, 1} | 22.14028 | 0.0719 | 0.95123 | 1.51416 |
| {1, 1, 0, 0} | 0.00000 | 0.0618 | 0.95123 | 0.00000 |
| {1, 1, 0, 1} | 22.14028 | 0.0719 | 0.95123 | 1.51416 |
| {1, 1, 1, 0} | 22.14028 | 0.0719 | 0.95123 | 1.51416 |
| {1, 1, 1, 1} | 49.18247 | 0.0837 | 0.95123 | 3.91387 |
| Sum |  | 1.0000 |  | 9.97052 |

The scenarios consist of ones or zeros that represent the upward movements and downward movements, respectively. The payoffs are the call option value at maturity when we follow the corresponding scenarios. If we multiply the payoffs by the corresponding probabilities and discount them with the appropriate discount factors, we have the pathwise value for each path. If we sum up the pathwise values, we have the call option price, 9.97052, which is the same as the two previous methods (figure 2.5 and table 2.3).

## 2.6   RELATIONSHIPS OF RISK-NEUTRAL AND MARKET BINOMIAL LATTICES

It is important to remember that when we are using the risk-neutral probabilities, the expected values or distributions of values are not the true distributions. This interplay between the market lattice and the risk-neutral lattice is always a source of confusion. To avoid this confusion, we introduce two separate lattices: the market lattice and the risk-neutral lattice. The prices of all securities at each node in the market lattice should be the same as those of the corresponding node in the risk-neutral lattice. The two lattices differ in the probabilities assigned to the model.

In much of financial research, we concentrate on the pricing, and not the market distributions of the values. After all, this is the most important feature of the relative valuation approach, which says that we do not need to know the expected return or the required return of the underlying stock, and that we can price the option relative to the stock.

For this reason, we often ignore the market lattice and use the risk-neutral lattice's probabilities. Here we need to introduce the lattices. (See figure 2.6.) Given the underlying security (for example, a stock), we can determine its expected returns and volatilities, and the market probability, $q$. These parameters will enable us to construct the risk-averse binomial lattice in figure 2.6.

From the risk-averse binomial model, we can construct the risk-neutral binomial lattice of the stock using the risk-free rate of drift, $r$, and the risk-neutral probability, $p$. On the risk-neutral binomial lattice, we can determine the lattice for the option at each node, given the terminal conditions. From the risk-neutral binomial lattice of the option,

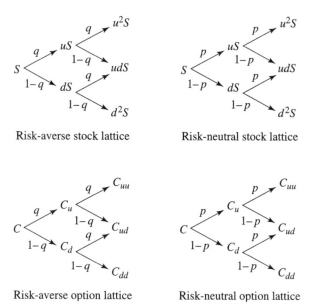

Risk-averse stock lattice          Risk-neutral stock lattice

Risk-averse option lattice          Risk-neutral option lattice

**Figure 2.6**  Risk-averse vs. risk-neutral lattices. The only difference between the actual world and the risk-neutral world is the specification of the probability; $q$ is the actual probability and $p$ is the risk-neutral probability.

we can now derive the risk-averse binomial lattice of the option by the transformation of the risk-neutral probability $p$ to the market probability $q$.

The four lattices are the risk-averse stock lattice, risk-neutral stock lattice, risk-averse option lattice, and risk-neutral option lattice. A node $(n, i)$ represents the same instant of time and state. For this reason, the stock prices of each node in the true lattice and in the risk-neutral lattice are the same. They are the same because in the construction, we only change the probabilities from market to risk-neutral. The outcomes remain the same for each node. Similarly, the option prices at each node on the risk-averse option lattice and on the risk-neutral option lattice are the same.

The difference between the risk-averse lattice and the risk-neutral lattice is the probabilities. The risk-averse lattice uses the market probabilities that assure the expected returns, and volatilities allow for risk premiums.

## 2.7   OPTION BEHAVIOR AND THE SENSITIVITY ANALYSIS

Five key variables affect option prices—the underlying price, the volatility (standard deviation of returns), the risk-free rate, the exercise price, and the time to maturity. How each variable affects an option price when the other four variables are constant is called the *comparative statics*. They are often called the "Greeks." Understanding the comparative statics is important for investors who wish to gain more insight into how option strategies should be formulated when responding to a rapidly changing market environment. (See figures 2.7 and 2.8.)

*Delta* is defined as the sensitivity of the option price to the stock price; $\Delta$ indicates a small change.

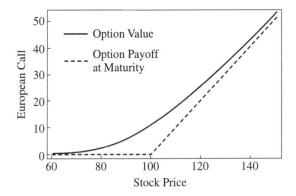

**Figure 2.7** Simulation of the European call option value for a range of stock prices. The stock price is between $60 and $150. The exercise price is $100. The stock volatility (standard deviation) is 0.5. The continuously compounding risk-free rate is 10%. The time to maturity is 0.25 year. We have partitioned 0.25 year into 20 subperiods to generate a smooth European call option profile by a binomial option pricing model. The European call option value converges to the 45° line originating from the present value of the exercise price when the stock price goes up. It implies that the higher the stock price goes, the more similar the two price movements will be. The solid line indicates the option value and the broken line indicates the payoff at maturity.

$$Delta = \frac{\Delta C}{\Delta S} \tag{2.11}$$

Delta also measures the number of stocks we need to short to hedge a call option. The hedge ratio enables traders or other market professionals to hedge any option position at the evaluation time. Or they can use the hedge ratio to determine the number of options to be used to hedge a stock position. We need to add "at the evaluation time" to emphasize that the replicating portfolio has to be continually revised. This strategy is called dynamic hedging. (See figure 2.9.)

*Gamma* is the ratio of the change of delta to the change in the stock price. It measures the extent to which the option price does not move in step with the underlying stock price. An important aspect of an option is that the option returns have high potential positive returns with the downside loss protected. Such a payout must lead to the option price not moving in step with the underlying stock price. An option with a large gamma would suggest that the option has significant downside protection relative to the potential positive returns.

$$Gamma = \frac{\Delta Delta}{\Delta S} \tag{2.12}$$

*Vega* is the sensitivity of the option price to a small change in volatility. It occurs in an option because of the gamma in the option: the higher the volatility of the stock, the more the gamma of the option will stand to gain, because the holder will have both an accelerated gain and a protected downside. For this reason, the option value will rise with increase in volatility.

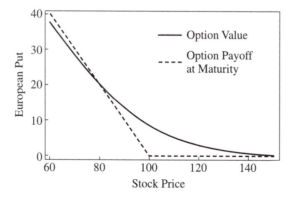

**Figure 2.8** Simulation of the European put option value for a range of stock prices. The stock price is between $60 and $150. The exercise price is $100. The stock volatility is 0.5. The continuously compounding risk-free rate is 10%. The time to maturity is 0.25 year. We have partitioned 0.25 year into 20 subperiods to generate a smooth European put option profile by a binomial option pricing model. The European put option value converges to the 45° line originating from the present value of the exercise price when the stock price goes down. It implies that the lower the stock price, the more similar the two price movements will be. The stock and the options would move in step. The solid line indicates the option value, and the dotted line indicates the payoff at maturity.

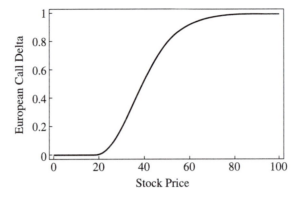

**Figure 2.9** Delta surface. The stock price is between $0 and $100. The exercise price is $45. The stock volatility (standard deviation) is 0.3. The continuously compounding risk-free rate is 10%. The time to maturity is one year. We have partitioned one year into 50 subperiods to generate a smooth European call option delta profile by the binomial option pricing. Delta is a measure that shows how the European call option changes given a unit change of the underlying stock price. As the stock price goes up, delta converges to 1, which implies that the amount of price change is the same regardless of the stock or the European call option. Therefore, deep-in-the-money options behave as if they were stocks.

$$Vega = \frac{\Delta C}{\Delta \sigma} \tag{2.13}$$

*Theta* is the time decay, which is the change in the option price over a short period of time, assuming the other variables (including the stock price) do not change. As time to maturity decreases, the opportunity of benefiting from the downside protection or gain on the upside return decreases. Therefore, the option value decays.

$$Theta = \frac{\Delta C}{\Delta t} \tag{2.14}$$

## 2.8  APPLICATIONS OF OPTION MODELS

### Option Trading

The basic idea of using an option is to provide protection on the downside risk. If the investor believes the stock price will rise, buying a call option will enable the holder to realize higher returns if the stock rises. However, the holder always has the maximum loss of only the initial investment, because an investor cannot lose more than he pays for an asset. Similarly, if the investor believes the stock will fall, he can buy a put option.

A *covered call* refers to writing a call option while holding the underlying stock. The investor (or corporation) receives the premium, often treated as income to the firm. When the stock price falls below the strike price at expiration, the covered call position will have only the stock position. If the stock price rises above the strike price at expiration, the option holder will exercise the option, and the investor (or corporation) will receive the strike price, losing the position in the stock. When comparing a covered call position against holding the stock alone, the investor is capping the upside of the stock position to the strike price while still bearing all the downside risk of the stock. In return, the investor (or corporation) receives the premiums up front as income.

Options offer effective ways to implement different investment strategies. Equivalent strategies using only stocks and bonds can be prohibitively expensive in terms of the transaction costs. One popular use of a put option is as "insurance." If we are concerned with the stock portfolio losing significant value when the market falls, put options can be bought to protect the downside of the portfolio.

We must remember that time decay, gamma (curvature to the price risk), and vega (sensitivity to the volatility risk) are interrelated for a particular option. An option with high gamma may also have high vega risk. Therefore a portfolio of options may be needed to satisfy the requirements of an option strategy.

## An Option Strategy: A Straddle

There are many option strategies. We will discuss one particular strategy to illustrate how the financial model is used to analyze the effectiveness of an option strategy. If the investor thinks that the market will move significantly, but is unsure of which direction, he can buy the volatility. In this case, the investor buys a call and a put with the same strike price. This position is called a straddle. A straddle enables the holder to profit from a significant upward or downward move of the stock, or an increase in the stock's volatility. However, if the stock does not move significantly, the position will lose value in the time decay. Therefore, if we plot the value of the straddle against the stock price level, the straddle performance profile is a u-shape with the minimum point at the current stock price.

Figure 2.10 shows that the delta of the straddle is 0 at the current stock price; thus the price of the straddle reaches its lowest value at the current price, and the value increases if the stock price either increases or decreases significantly. When the stock price is high, the call option is significantly in-the-money and the put option is significantly out-of-the-money. For this reason, the delta of the straddle is the same as that of the deep-in-the-money call option; that is, delta equals 1. Conversely, when the stock price is low, the put option is deep-in-the-money and the call option is out-of-the-money, and the delta becomes $-1$.

As expected, the gamma of the straddle is highest at the current stock price. After all, the purpose of the straddle is to capture the accelerated increase in value as the stock price increases or decreases. As we explained before, the vega and gamma are similar because they both capture the value of the option in relation to the stock volatility. Figure 2.10 shows that the straddle vega and straddle gamma behave very similarly.

## Implied Volatility

The stock volatility is often estimated from the historical stock returns. The volatility is the standard deviation of the time series of the stock returns. However, such a measure of the risk of the stock is dependent on historical experience and is not forward-looking. If we believe that the stock has a higher risk in the future than that in the past, then this approach may not be correct.

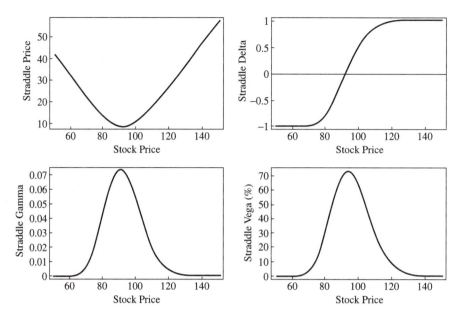

**Figure 2.10** Profile delta, gamma, and vega of the straddle over a range of stock prices. The straddle consists of longing one call and one put with the same strike price. The purpose of the straddle is to capture the accelerated increase in value as the stock price deviates from the current price level, regardless of the direction. The stock price range is from 50 to 150. The stock volatility is 12%. The maturity is one year. The continuously compounding risk-free rate is 8%. We have partitioned one period into 50 subperiods for accuracy purposes. The delta of the straddle is 0 at the current stock price, which means that the straddle price reaches its lowest value at the current stock price, and the straddle price increases if the stock price either increases or decreases significantly. When the stock price is high, the call option is significantly in-the-money and the put option is significantly out-of-the-money. Since the delta of a deep-in-the-money call option converges to 1 and that of a significantly out-of-the-money put option is almost 0, the delta of the straddle is the same as that of the deep-in-the-money call option, which is 1. Exactly the reverse interpretation holds when the stock price is low. As expected, the gamma of the straddle is highest at the current stock price.

A stock option offers an alternative approach to measuring the stock volatility on a forward-looking basis. We can use the Black-Scholes model to determine the volatility as an input to the model such that model option price equals the observed option price. This volatility measure is called the *implied volatility*.

Consider a stock that has different options, put and call with different strike prices and expiration dates. The prices of these options should be determined by the volatility of the stock. Therefore, we can use the Black-Scholes model to determine the stock volatility that best fits the observed option prices. Using the best-fitted volatility to determine the model prices of the option, we can determine the deviation of the observed prices from the model prices. In this approach we do not rely on the historical estimation of the stock volatility but use the stock's implied volatility, derived from the market observed option prices. When we use this approach, we say that we have calibrated the model to the observed prices. This calibration procedure is a practical method of using financial models that do not depend on historical experience.

# EXCEL MODEL EXERCISES

## E2.1   COX-ROSS-RUBINSTEIN OPTION PRICING MODEL

### Definitions

The initial spot yield curve is expressed in a continuously compounding rate. The discount function is determined from the initial spot yield curve. The one-period forward rate is then derived. The underlying stock volatility could be assumed to be time-dependent. Specifically, we can assume that the stock volatility changes over time, even though the volatility is constant in the numerical example. The downward movement size is the inverse of the upward movement size. Hence, we can determine the upward (or downward) movement size as long as we know the downward (or upward) movement size. The risk-neutral probability of the upward movement can be determined by the upward movement size, the downward movement size, and the risk-free interest rate.

### Description of the Model

The model prices the call and put equity options based on the assumptions of the perfect capital market, arbitrage-free at any instant of time. Using the binomial lattice framework, the model can determine the price of an option, relaxing many of the Black-Scholes model assumptions.

Specifically, the Cox-Ross-Rubinstein model can deal with

- any shape of the yield curve
- dividend-paying stock
- time-dependent stock volatility so that it can incorporate the term structure of volatility of a stock
- American call and put options

### Numerical Example

Consider a European call option on a stock. We assume that the underlying stock price is 100, with strike price 100 expiring in one year. The stock does not pay dividends. The yield curve is flat at 5%. The term structure of volatility of the underlying stock is flat at 20%. The number of subperiods is six. The model shows that the price of the European call option is 10.1256. See figures E2.1 and E2.2.

We calculate the difference between the European call option prices, using the Cox-Ross-Rubinstein model and the Black-Scholes model, to see how accurately the Cox-Ross-Rubinstein model approximates the Black-Scholes model as we divide one year into many subperiods. As we can see, the difference becomes negligible when the number of subdivisions approaches twenty.

### Application

The Cox-Ross-Rubinstein equity option pricing model can be used broadly in practice because it can value American options and options on dividend-paying stocks.

(a)

| Inputs | | | | |
|---|---|---|---|---|
| Stock price ($) | S | 100 | | |
| Strike price ($) | X | 100 | | |
| Stock volatility | $\sigma_S$ | 0.2 | | |
| Time to expiration (year) | T | 1 | | |
| Risk-free rate | r | 0.05 | | |
| Dividend yield | d | N/A | | |
| The number of periods | n | 6 | dt = T/n | |
| | | | | |
| Upward movement | u | 1.0851 | = exp($\sigma\sqrt{dt}$) | |
| Downward movement | d | 0.9216 | = 1/u | |
| Risk-neutral probability of u | p | 0.5308 | = (exp(rdt)-d)/(u-d) | |
| **Outputs** | | | | |
| | | Call | Put | |
| European option price | | 10.1256 | 5.2485 | |

(b)

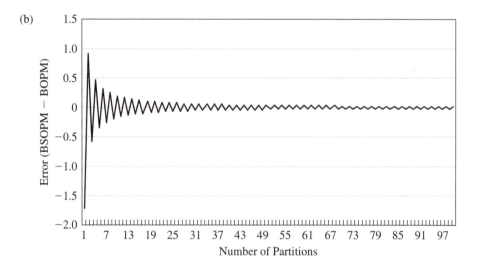

Figure E2.1

## Case: Private Wealth Management— Designing a Structured Product

Ahmed Khan is the vice president of Amina Mansoor Securities Company (AMS) in charge of the Private Wealth Management group. His clients are individuals with high net worth that exceeds $20 million. His group provides them asset management services, execution of trades, and market research as well as assistance in tax, estate, and trust planning. Most important of all, he has to understand his clients' needs and provide solutions. In building a relationship with each client, providing each client a personalized solution, he can then build a client base for the firm for many services that the firm provides.

He has a broad range of clients. Many of them are business owners and they often have special needs. A case in point, today, he met with a new client who asked for "principal preservation" investment. He would like to invest $2 million with AMS. He

**Stock lattice**

| Time | 0 | 1 | 2 | 3 | 4 | 5 | 6 | State |
|---|---|---|---|---|---|---|---|---|
| | | | | | | | 163.215 | 6 |
| | | | | | | 150.418 | 138.624 | 5 |
| | | | | | 138.624 | 127.756 | 117.739 | 4 |
| | | | | 127.756 | 117.739 | 108.508 | 100.000 | 3 |
| | | | 117.739 | 108.508 | 100.000 | 92.159 | 84.934 | 2 |
| | | 108.508 | 100.000 | 92.159 | 84.934 | 78.274 | 72.137 | 1 |
| | 100.00 | 92.159 | 84.934 | 78.274 | 72.137 | 66.481 | 61.269 | 0 |

**Call option lattice**

| 0 | 1 | 2 | 3 | 4 | 5 | 6 |
|---|---|---|---|---|---|---|
| | | | | | | 63.214965 |
| | | | | | 51.247930 | 38.624497 |
| | | | | 40.277352 | 28.585483 | 17.738905 |
| | | | 30.224621 | 19.391759 | 9.337430 | 0.000000 |
| | | 21.723634 | 12.494533 | 4.915050 | 0.000000 | 0.000000 |
| | 15.055460 | 7.780762 | 2.587191 | 0.000000 | 0.000000 | 0.000000 |
| 10.125573 | 4.729344 | 1.361849 | 0.000000 | 0.000000 | 0.000000 | 0.000000 |

**Figure E2.2**

would like to take the stock market risk in the next ten years. But he wanted his $2 million to be safe. Typically, other investors of principal preservation would want a payoff at the end of the tenth year of at least $2 million. However, this client says that he needs $1 million in five years and another $1 million in ten years. What should he do?

After giving it some thought, he decided that the client's portfolio should consist of a five-year zero-coupon bond, a ten-year zero-coupon bond, and a call option on the S&P index expiring in ten years. This way, the portfolio satisfies the client requirements. However, he has to decide on the strike price of the call option, and he decided to use the at-the-money option. To arrange for a ten-year stock option could be quite expensive, and so he decided to use a dynamic hedging strategy. He needed to calculate the hedge ratios of the trade.

Ahmed called Mary Kim, the quantitative analyst at the equity derivative group. "Mary, I need a favor." "Yes, Ahmed, shoot." "My client in essence needs a ten-year at-the-money call option on a hypothetical S&P index that pays no dividends." "Ahmed, your marketing people are wonderful, poetic but not precise. What are you talking about—S&P with no dividends?!" "I need an underlying asset that has the volatility of the S&P, and the asset pays no dividends." "Do you want the historical volatility or the implied volatility?" "How do we get the long-dated implied volatility for the S&P? Aren't the exchange-traded options short-dated?" "We make a market of long-dated S&P options here. We would be able to sell you something."

"Mary. You people are great. Can you price the product for me based on a $1 million S&P notional amount? Remember, no dividends." "OK. I will work out the price by checking how much it will cost us to hedge the position. At the moment, our book is quite thin on these options, and we do not have any offsetting positions. We probably need to dynamic hedge this position for a while to neutralize the risks."

Ahmed now turned his attention to determining the investment amount of the option. It would be $2 million net of the two zero-coupon bonds. "Should I buy Treasuries or other bonds with higher yields? I had better check with the fixed-income people."

*Meanwhile Ahmed started thinking about writing up the proposal to his client. "I need to show him that the investment is appropriate. How can I explain to him the risk and return of the investments? How should I start?"*

## Exercises and Answers

1. Given the numerical example, calculate the hedging ratios. Confirm that a hedge portfolio duplicates the call option value at each node. Also show that the hedge portfolio is a self-financing portfolio.

   *Answer:* The hedge ratio represents how much the call option price changes for a small change of the stock price. For example, if the hedge ratio is 0.5, then for a small change of the stock price like $0.2, the option price changes by $0.1. Therefore, if we hold a portfolio of buying two options and selling one stock, the portfolio value will be unchanged for a small change of the stock price. On a binomial lattice, the hedge ratio can be determined by the ratio of the option volatility to the stock volatility. The volatility on a binomial lattice is one-half of the difference between the up-state price and the down-state price. For example, the hedge ratio at the initial node is 0.6316, because the stock volatility is 8.175 (= (108.51 − 92.16) × 0.5), the call option volatility is 5.165 (= (15.06 − 4.73) × 0.5), and the ratio is 0.6316 (= 5.165/8.175); see figure E2.3. Once we know the hedge ratio, we can determine how many stocks

**Hedge ratio (Δ)**

| | | | | | |
|---|---|---|---|---|---|
| 0.63164085 | 0.78600524 | 0.92113674 | 1 | 1 | 1 |
| | 0.42604416 | 0.6060247 | 0.81609939 | 1 | 1 |
| | | 0.18632953 | 0.32622792 | 0.57116366 | 1 |
| | | | 9.2311E-16 | 1.6162E-15 | 2.8297E-15 |
| | | | | 0 | 0 |
| | | | | | 0 |

**Risk-free asset (B)**

| | | | | | |
|---|---|---|---|---|---|
| -53.038512 | -70.23205 | -86.729997 | -97.530991 | -98.347145 | -99.170129 |
| | -34.534663 | -52.821709 | -76.058421 | -98.347145 | -99.170129 |
| | | -14.463806 | -27.477804 | -52.201316 | -99.170129 |
| | | | -6.604E-14 | -1.255E-13 | -2.383E-13 |
| | | | | 0 | 0 |
| | | | | | 0 |

**Levered portfolio (ΔS + B = C)**

| | | | | | | |
|---|---|---|---|---|---|---|
| 10.125573 | 15.055460 | 21.723634 | 30.224621 | 40.277352 | 51.247930 | 63.214965 |
| | 4.729344 | 7.780762 | 12.494533 | 19.391759 | 28.585483 | 38.624497 |
| | | 1.361849 | 2.587191 | 4.915050 | 9.337430 | 17.738905 |
| | | | 0.000000 | 0.000000 | 0.000000 | 0.000000 |
| | | | | 0.000000 | 0.000000 | 0.000000 |
| | | | | | 0.000000 | 0.000000 |
| | | | | | | 0.000000 |

Compare this lattice with call option lattice.

**Figure E2.3**

we should buy to duplicate the call option. At time 0, we long 0.6316 shares of the stock and borrow $53.04 at the risk-free rate to end up at $10.126 cash flow, which is the call option value. At time 1 and state 1, we should long 0.7860 shares of the stock and borrow $70.23 at the risk-free rate to match the call option value. The other nodes can be interpreted in a similar way.

Once we establish the hedge position at time 0, we can go up to state 1 or go down to state 0 at time 1, depending on which state will occur at time 1. Let us assume that state 1 occurs at time 1. At this state, we need to long 0.7860 shares of the stock and borrow $70.23 at the risk-free rate. Since the portfolio at time 0 is buying 0.6316 shares of the stock and borrowing $53.04 at the risk-free rate, time 0, we should buy 0.1544 more shares of the stock (= 0.7860 − 0.6316) and borrow 16.7497 more (= 70.232 − 53.038 × exp(0.05/6)). The cash outflow from longing the stock (= 0.1544 × 108.508 = 16.7497) is identical to the cash inflow for the additional borrowing; see figure E2.4. Therefore, this portfolio can be called self-financing. We can easily check whether this self-financing still holds if the down state occurs at time 1.

2. Repeat question 1, using a risk-free portfolio to duplicate the call option.
   *Answer:* We denote the number of the stocks to buy as "a" and the number of the call options to short as "m"; see figure E2.5. When we formulate a portfolio of longing "a" stocks and shorting "m × a" call options, the portfolio generates a one-period risk-free rate of return. For example, at the initial node, we buy one stock and sell 1.58317817 call options, which costs 83.9694145. This portfolio will be worth 84.6720834 regardless of which state we arrive at period 1. That is why this portfolio is called a risk-free portfolio.

3. Why do we use a risk-free rate of return to calculate a seemingly risky asset like an option? Why do we not use risk preference of investors to evaluate options?
   *Answer:* To evaluate risky assets like derivatives, we should calculate how risky the cash flow from derivatives is, which is not simple, or nearly impossible, if the risk involved in the risky asset is changing on a real-time basis. To cope with this problem, we create a risk-free portfolio consisting of risky assets. Recall that constructing a portfolio with two assets that are perfectly negatively correlated leads us to hold a risk-free asset. Therefore, if we have the correct hedging ratios, we can create a risk-free asset. Once we have the risk-free asset, we should discount the cash flow from the risk-free portfolio. That is why we need the risk-free rates of return rather than risk-adjusted rate of return. By the same logic, we do not need the risk preference on the part of investors to evaluate derivatives like options.

4. Show that all the risky assets generate risk-free rates of return regardless of how risky they are in a risk-neutral world. For example, the rate of return on a stock is uncertain in a real world. However, the rate of return on a stock in a risk-neutral world is always the risk-free rate.
   *Answer:* The expected rate of return on the stock is always the risk-free rate, because we calculate the expected return with a risk-neutral probability. If we calculate the expected rate of return using a market probability, we should use the risk-adjusted rate of return, which depends on a time-varying risk. In a risk-neutral world, every risky asset yields a risk-free rate of return. However, in a real world, risky assets yield their expected returns, which are proportional to their risk level. In the Excel sheet, the initial stock price is 100, and it grows at the risk-free rate of return of 5%. See figures E2.6 and E2.7.

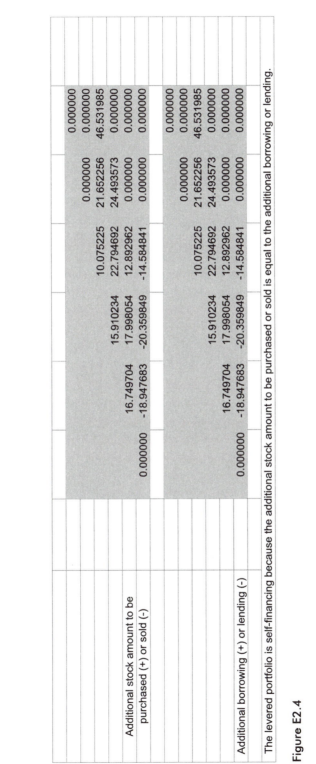

Additional stock amount to be purchased (+) or sold (-)

Additional borrowing (+) or lending (-)

The levered portfolio is self-financing because the additional stock amount to be purchased or sold is equal to the additional borrowing or lending.

**Figure E2.4**

| | | | | | | |
|---|---|---|---|---|---|---|
| | | | | 1 | 1 | 1 |
| | | | 1.08561516 | 1.22534095 | 1.75081168 | 3.534E+14 |
| | | 1.27225614 | 1.65009776 | 3.06534153 | 6.1874E+14 | N/A |
| m = 1/Δ | 1.58317817 | 2.34717453 | 5.36683575 | 1.0833E+15 | N/A | N/A |

| | | | | | | |
|---|---|---|---|---|---|---|
| | | | | 0.88274618 | 0.88274618 | 0.88274618 |
| | | | 0.90680549 | 0.92379209 | 0.94989746 | 1.03933569 |
| | | 0.94761154 | 0.979574 | 1.02215698 | 1.11839886 | N/A |
| The number of stocks to buy (a) | 1 | 1.04457502 | 1.09991335 | 1.20347644 | N/A | N/A |

| | | | | | | | |
|---|---|---|---|---|---|---|---|
| | | | | 86.0951104 | 86.8155674 | 87.5420532 | 88.2746185 |
| | | | 85.3806322 | 86.0951104 | 86.8155674 | 87.5420532 | 88.2746185 |
| | | 84.6720834 | 85.3806322 | 86.0951104 | 86.8155674 | 87.5420532 | 88.2746185 |
| (S - mC)a | 83.9694145 | 84.6720834 | 85.3806322 | 86.0951104 | 86.8155674 | 87.5420532 | 88.2746185 |
| | | | | | N/A | N/A | N/A |

Figure E2.5

## Step 4 — Calculation of Probabilities of Arriving at Each Node on the Binomial Lattice

(a)

**Binomial coefficients**

| | Step 0 | Step 1 | Step 2 | Step 3 | Step 4 | Step 5 | Step 6 |
|---|---|---|---|---|---|---|---|
| | 1 | 1 | 1 | 1 | 1 | 1 | 1 |
| | | 1 | 2 | 3 | 4 | 5 | 6 |
| | | | 1 | 3 | 6 | 10 | 15 |
| | | | | 1 | 4 | 10 | 20 |
| | | | | | 1 | 5 | 15 |
| | | | | | | 1 | 6 |
| | | | | | | | 1 |

**$p^i(1-p)^{(n-i)}$**

| | Step 0 | Step 1 | Step 2 | Step 3 | Step 4 | Step 5 | Step 6 |
|---|---|---|---|---|---|---|---|
| | 1.0000 | 0.5308 | 0.2817 | 0.1495 | 0.0794 | 0.0421 | 0.0224 |
| | | 0.4692 | 0.2491 | 0.1322 | 0.0702 | 0.0372 | 0.0198 |
| | | | 0.2202 | 0.1169 | 0.0620 | 0.0329 | 0.0175 |
| | | | | 0.1033 | 0.0548 | 0.0291 | 0.0154 |
| | | | | | 0.0485 | 0.0257 | 0.0137 |
| | | | | | | 0.0227 | 0.0121 |
| | | | | | | | 0.0107 |
| Sum | 1.0000 | 1.0000 | 1.0000 | 1.0000 | 1.0000 | 1.0000 | 1.0000 |

**Probabilities of arriving at each node**

| | Step 0 | Step 1 | Step 2 | Step 3 | Step 4 | Step 5 | Step 6 |
|---|---|---|---|---|---|---|---|
| | 1.0000 | 0.5308 | 0.2817 | 0.1495 | 0.0794 | 0.0421 | 0.0224 |
| | | 0.4692 | 0.4981 | 0.3966 | 0.2807 | 0.1862 | 0.1186 |
| | | | 0.2202 | 0.3506 | 0.3722 | 0.3292 | 0.2621 |
| | | | | 0.1033 | 0.2193 | 0.2910 | 0.3090 |
| | | | | | 0.0485 | 0.1286 | 0.2048 |
| | | | | | | 0.0227 | 0.0724 |
| | | | | | | | 0.0107 |
| Sum | 1.0000 | 1.0000 | 1.0000 | 1.0000 | 1.0000 | 1.0000 | 1.0000 |

(b)

| | | | | | | | |
|---|---|---|---|---|---|---|---|
| $E^P[S]$ | 100.000 | 100.837 | 101.681 | 102.532 | 103.390 | 104.255 | 105.127 |
| $S_0 exp(rndt)$, n= 0,1,2,...,6 | 100.000 | 100.837 | 101.681 | 102.532 | 103.390 | 104.255 | 105.127 |

By comparing the expected stock returns under EMM with $S_0 exp(rndt)$, n= 0,1,2,...,6, we can see that the stock (underlying asset) return is the same as risk-free rate of return!

**Figure E2.6**

| | | | | | | | 0.05 |
|---|---|---|---|---|---|---|---|
| | | | | | | 0.05 | 0.05 |
| | | | | | 0.05 | 0.05 | 0.05 |
| | | | | 0.05 | 0.05 | 0.05 | 0.05 |
| | | | 0.05 | 0.05 | 0.05 | 0.05 | 0.05 |
| Risk-neutral rate of return on stock | | 0.05 | 0.05 | 0.05 | 0.05 | 0.05 | 0.05 |

**Figure E2.7**

5. We know that there are five variables that determine a European call option on nondividend-paying stocks. These variables are a stock price, an exercise price, the time to maturity, stock volatility, and the risk-free rate of return. When the stock price rises with other variables being constant, we know that the call option price also rises. However, it is not clear what would happen to the call option value when the risk-free rate rises. Of course, in this case, the other variables except the risk-free rates remain unchanged. The reason for this is that we have two opposing factors to influence the call option value when the risk-free rate rises. When the risk-free rate rises, we have a higher discounting rate to discount the future cash flow, which leads to a lower call option price. This is a negative factor on the call option price. On the other hand, we have a lower present value of the exercise price, which is good to the call option holders, because the option holder can deposit less money for the possible use on the maturity date. This is a positive factor. Therefore, the overall effect depends on which factor is more dominant. If the positive factor is stronger than the negative factor, we can see that the higher risk-free rate might lead to a high call option value. To see this point, we can construct a binomial lattice to calculate a call option and change the risk-free rate to see how the call option value changes. We can do the same thing for the other variables. This type of work is called comparative statics analysis.

*Answer:* Calculate the rho ($\rho$) in the binomial tree and see the performance profile of the $\rho$. Since the $\rho$ is a sensitivity of the call option with respect to the risk-free interest rate, we disturb the risk-free interest rate ($\Delta r$) to calculate $\rho$ and then calculate the call price at time 0, with a small upward shift of the yield curve ($C_{\Delta r+}$) and a downward shift of the yield curve ($C_{\Delta r-}$) . The difference between $C_{\Delta r+}$ and $C_{\Delta r-}$ divided by $2\Delta r$ is the sensitivity of the call option with respect to the risk-free rate of return. Algebraically, rho can be expressed as follows.

$$\rho = \frac{C_{\Delta r+} - C_{\Delta r-}}{2\Delta r}$$

The graph in figure E2.8 shows how $\rho$ depends on the stock prices. Intuitively, the European call option is the expected stock price at expiration conditional on the stock price exceeding the exercise price net of the exercise price and then multiplied by the probability of expiring in the money at expiration. When the stock price is very high or low, the probability that the option will expire in the money or out of the money would be nearly constant. On top of that, the marginal increase in the expected stock price will be canceled out by the increase in the interest rate. Therefore, when the stock price is very high, $\rho$ exhibits an almost constant pattern.

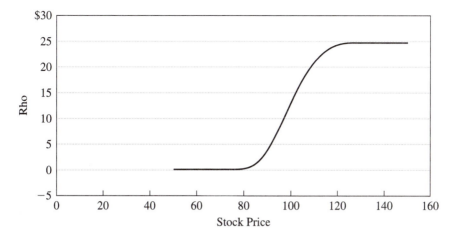

**Figure E2.8**

## Further Exercises

1. Construct a Cox-Ross-Rubinstein tree when we assume time-dependent stock volatility.

   *Answer:* If the stock volatility is time-varying, we cannot guarantee that the stock lattice is recombining. To make the stock lattice recombining, we have to adjust the length of one period depending on the time. So far, we have assumed a fixed time period. The length of the first period is 0.20729, the second period is 0.18802, and so on; see figure E2.9. The sum of the six periods is the time to maturity of one year. We should adjust the other parameters such as the upward movement size and the risk-neutral probability accordingly.

2. On January 14, 2004, we have the following data from the *Wall Street Journal*.

   Treasury Bill
   Maturity March 18, 2004
   Days to maturity 64
   Bid 0.84
   Asked 0.83

   Call Option
   Underlying stock Oracle (NASDAQ)
   Maturity March
   Exercise price 12.5
   Stock price (January 13, 2004) 14.36
   Stock price (January 12, 2004) 14.66
   Option premium (January 13, 2004) 2.05
   Option premium (January 12, 2004) 2.3

   We assume that the call option expires on March 18, the risk-free rate applicable for the option life is the Treasury bill rate, and the underlying stock does not pay dividends until the option matures on March 18, 2004.

| Inputs | | | | | | | | | |
|---|---|---|---|---|---|---|---|---|---|
| Stock price ($) | S | 100 | | | | | | | |
| Strike price ($) | K | 100 | | | | | | | |
| Time to expiration (year) | T | 1 | | | | | | | |
| Upward movement | u | 1.09533 | | | | | | | |
| Downward movement | d | 0.91296 | | | | | | | |

Changing cell for solver

| Time period | 0 | 1 | 2 | 3 | 4 | 5 | | Sum |
|---|---|---|---|---|---|---|---|---|
| Flat yield curve | $r_i$ | 0.05 | 0.05 | 0.05 | 0.05 | 0.05 | 0.05 | |
| Volatility | $\sigma_i$ | 0.2 | 0.21 | 0.22 | 0.23 | 0.24 | 0.25 | |
| $\Delta t_i$ | 0.20729 | 0.18802 | 0.17132 | 0.15674 | 0.14395 | 0.13267 | 0 | 1 Target cell for solver |
| $p_i$ | 0.53438 | 0.52904 | 0.52442 | 0.52039 | 0.51686 | 0.51375 | | |

| Outputs | | | | | | |
|---|---|---|---|---|---|---|
| | | | | | | 72.6946 |
| | | | | | 58.3251 | 43.9415 |
| | | | | 45.3151 | 32.0745 | 19.9756 |
| | | | 33.5569 | 21.3492 | 10.1945 | 0 |
| | | 23.8194 | 13.5127 | 5.23136 | 0 | 0 |
| | 16.3557 | 8.29954 | 2.70112 | 0 | 0 | 0 |
| European call option lattice | 10.9564 | 5.00497 | 1.40444 | 0 | 0 | 0 | 0 |

Figure E2.9

**m = 1/Δ**

| | | | | | |
|---|---|---|---|---|---|
| 1.16955883 | 1.048125 | 1 | 1 | 1 | 1 |
| | 1.33515237 | 1.10505491 | 1 | 1 | 1 |
| | | 1.71812605 | 1.2450777 | 1 | 1 |
| | | | 2.89597602 | 1.68790963 | 1 |
| | | | | 12.3851886 | 6.40344539 |
| | | | | | N/A |

**The number of stocks to buy (a)**

| | | | | | |
|---|---|---|---|---|---|
| 1 | 0.9722531 | 0.95833308 | 0.95833308 | 0.95833308 | 0.95833308 |
| | 1.01872347 | 0.98113005 | 0.95833308 | 0.95833308 | 0.95833308 |
| | | 1.04364703 | 0.99473953 | 0.95833308 | 0.95833308 |
| | | | 1.07646828 | 1.01541891 | 0.95833308 |
| | | | | 1.12801902 | 1.06215676 |
| | | | | | N/A |

**(S − mC)a**

| | | | | | | |
|---|---|---|---|---|---|---|
| 11.9624044 | 11.965196 | 11.9679882 | 11.970781 | 11.9735745 | 11.9763687 | 11.9791635 |
| | 11.965196 | 11.9679882 | 11.970781 | 11.9735745 | 11.9763687 | 11.9791635 |
| | | 11.9679882 | 11.970781 | 11.9735745 | 11.9763687 | 11.9791635 |
| | | | 11.970781 | 11.9735745 | 11.9763687 | 11.9791635 |
| | | | | 11.9735745 | 11.9763687 | 11.9791635 |
| | | | | | N/A | N/A |
| | | | | | | N/A |

Figure E2.10

**Levered portfolio (ΔS + B = C)**

| | | | | | | |
|---|---|---|---|---|---|---|
| 2.050000 | 2.811999 | 3.715306 | 4.721164 | 5.769823 | 6.925193 | 8.131428 |
| | 1.328026 | 1.956313 | 2.762741 | 3.709477 | 4.715334 | 5.783991 |
| | | 0.732575 | 1.192146 | 1.865832 | 2.756911 | 3.703645 |
| | | | 0.296915 | 0.553564 | 1.021317 | 1.860000 |
| | | | | 0.053569 | 0.110060 | 0.226124 |
| | | | | | 0.000000 | 0.000000 |
| | | | | | | 0.000000 |

Figure E2.11

(a) We can think of other rates such as a two-month CD rate or a commercial paper rate as a risk-free rate. Can you explain why the Treasury bill rate is the most appropriate rate to price the call option?
*Answer:* The Treasury bill rate has no default risk while the two-month CD or commercial paper rates have default risk.

(b) To see whether the option price is reasonable by the Black-Scholes model, we need five variables for the model input. They are the stock price, the exercise price, the risk-free rate, the time to maturity, and the stock volatility. However, we cannot observe the stock volatility on the market. How can we estimate the stock volatility given the data?
*Answer:* We have two ways to estimate the stock future volatility, because we cannot observe the stock volatility during the option life. One way is based on historical volatility and the other way is based on implied volatility. As long as the option prices reflect future market expectation, the implied volatility reflects the market expectation. If we estimate the implied volatility using the stock price data on January 13, 2004, and the option premium on January 13, 2004, the implied volatility is 36.24%

(c) Can we create a risk-free asset over one day by combining the Oracle stock and the call option? See figure E2.10.

(d) Can we duplicate the option position using the underlying stock and the risk-free bond? See figure E2.11.

(e) If Oracle announces an unexpected dividend payment, which will be paid before the option matures, how does the call option price respond to the announcement?
*Answer:* If Oracle pays the unexpected dividend before the option expiration, the option price decreases, because the stock price at expiration will be lower due to the dividend payment during the option life.

## E2.2   THE PUT-CALL PARITY

### Definition

The description of the input parameters to the put-call parity can be found in the Cox-Ross-Rubinstein model.

### Description of the Model

The put-call parity is based on the perfect capital market arbitrage-free assumption. The model provides a relationship between the put and call options that have the same expiration date and strike price, and the underlying stock does not pay dividends.

Specifically, the model says that the put option is the same as holding the call option, shorting the stock, and holding a zero-coupon bond with the maturity equaling the time to expiration and the face value, which is the same as the strike price.

Alternatively, a call option is the same as holding the put option and the stock, while shorting the zero-coupon bond as described above.

### Numerical Example

We assume that the stock price is 100, the strike price is 100, and time to expiration is 6 years. Assume further that the stock volatility is 20% and the continuously compounding

| Inputs | | | | | |
|---|---|---|---|---|---|
| Stock price ($) | S | 100 | | | |
| Strike price ($) | K | 100 | | | |
| Volatility | σ | 0.2 | | | |
| Time to expiration (year) | T | 6 | $0 < T \leq 6$ | | |
| Dividend yield | d | N/A | | | |
| The number of periods | n | 6 | $dt = T/n$ | | |
| | | | | | |
| Upward movement | u | 1.2214 | $= \exp(\sigma\sqrt{dt})$ | | |
| Downward movement | d | 0.8187 | $= 1/u$ | | |
| | | | | | |
| Time period (year) | | 0 | 1 | 2 | 3 |
| Yield curve | | 0.05 | 0.05 | 0.05 | 0.05 |
| | | | | | |
| Outputs | | | | | |
| | | | | | |
| Put-call parity holds | | S + P | C + Ke⁻ʳᵀ | C - P | S - Ke⁻ʳᵀ |
| | | 106.091 | 106.091 | 25.918 | 25.918 |
| | | No arbitrage | | No arbitrage | |

Figure E2.12

risk-free rate is 5%. We use the Cox-Ross-Rubinstein model to price the call option and the put option. Note that we can also use the Black-Scholes model to price these options. See figure E2.12.

The result shows that the Cox-Ross-Rubinstein option pricing model is consistent with the put-call parity. $S + P$ and $C + Ke^{-rT}$ are equal to each other. If we move $P$ and $Ke^{-rT}$ to the other side of the equality sign, we have $C - P$ and $S - Ke^{-rT}$, which are also equal to each other. This way, we have many different forms of the put-call parity.

## Applications

1. Using the call option price, we can determine the put option price.
2. By monitoring arbitrage opportunities in the pricing of the stock, call, put, and the zero-coupon bonds, we can catch the arbitrage opportunities.

## Case: Proprietary Trading Desk

The Quanta Arbitrage Group is a private proprietary equity trading company. The partners trade with their own capital. They have computerized their trading and they can monitor market prices across a selected set of stocks and their options. They take positions when they recognize the markets will move in a certain way. They unwind their positions when they do not think their bet is profitable, after adjusting for the risks. The duration of holding a particular position can be as short as a few minutes. To avoid holding excessive risks, they would sell off their positions by the end of the day, avoiding any unexpected news after the market is closed.

One set of strategies they take is exploiting the put-call parity. The put-call parity is rather straightforward, but in practice, many of the assumptions made in the theory are not strictly correct. That means that the put-call parity is only an approximation in practice. The arbitrage opportunity predicted by the theory when the price relationship of the stock, call, and put options are violated is really a "risk arbitrage," an arbitrage trade with risks. This concept of "risk arbitrage" truly bothers one of the partners, Lili Zeus, and she raises this issue in their partners meeting.

"I think we are doing more and more risk arbitrage trades" is Lili's opening remark, "and I do not like it." "But we take risk from day one. What is new Lili?" "Previously, we consciously take risks. Now we kid ourselves saying: 'We look for the arb to come along' but we may in fact pack our positions with risks." "I don't know. It seems to me the put-call parity is transparent. How much risk can you pack in there?" Lili insists: "But the put-call parity has many assumptions, and all are unrealistic. The model risk is truly obvious." "So, what do you suggest that we do?"

The partner responsible for the systems suggests: "Well, I can build a simulator taking interest rate risks, stochastic dividends, and all the things that Lili can think of. We can then simulate our exposures and measure our risks." But Lili is not convinced: "No. The simulations can only be as good as what you assume." "That is amazing. You now want to measure risks that you do not know that you have assumed? Sounds a bit circular to me."

*"I need to understand the risks intuitively,"* murmured Lili. *"May be I should list all the risks in these trades and understand how the risks correlate with each other. There are operational risks too. What if some of the trades are not executed? What if the market becomes illiquid and the relationship breaks apart for a day or two? My partners just do not see my point—so frustrating."*

## Exercises and Answers

1. The traders have to make a judgement by doing more research to properly exploit the put-call parity to generate profitable trades. For example, they ask: Does the put-call parity hold with American options, instead of the European options? Can we use the numerical example to support the answer?

   *Answer:* The put-call parity is saying that the portfolio that consists of shorting a call and longing a put is equivalent to the portfolio of shorting a stock and a riskless lending. To see this point, recall that the put-call parity is $C - P = S - PV(K)$. Here we can interpret that the $+$ sign and $-$ sign represent cash inflow and cash outflow, respectively. Therefore $+C$ means shorting the call, because shorting brings cash inflow. With these in mind, we can manipulate the put-call parity equation to duplicate one security with other securities. For example, if we move $-P$ to the other side of the equality sign, we have $C = P + S - PV(K)$. Therefore, shorting a call can be duplicated by a portfolio of shorting a put, shorting a stock, and lending at the risk-free rate. See figure E2.13.

   The put-call parity holds only for the European options, because the early exercise features in the American options produce uncertain interim cash flow. Since the put-call parity does not allow the interim cash flow, the put-call parity does not hold for the European options with unknown dividend payments before the option maturity. In the Excel example, we can see that $S + P$ is not equal to $C + PV(K)$. $C + PV(K)$ in the American case is the same as in the corresponding European case, because the American call option on a nondividend-paying stock is equal to the corresponding European call. However, an American put has been early-exercised in the example, $S + P$ is different from the corresponding European case. Since the American put

| Inputs | | | | | | | | |
|---|---|---|---|---|---|---|---|---|
| Stock price ($) | S | 100 | | | | | | |
| Strike price ($) | K | 100 | | | | | | |
| Volatility | $\sigma$ | 0.2 | | | | | | |
| Time to expiration (year) | T | 6 | $0 < T \leq 6$ | | | | | |
| Dividend yield | d | N/A | | | | | | |
| The number of periods | n | 6 | dt = T/n | | | | | |
| | | | | | | | | |
| Upward movement | u | 1.2214 | $= \exp(\sigma\sqrt{dt})$ | | | | | |
| Downward movement | d | 0.8187 | = 1/u | | | | | |
| | | | | | | | | |
| Time period (year) | 0 | 1 | 2 | 3 | 4 | 5 | 6 |
| Yield curve | 0.05 | 0.05 | 0.05 | 0.05 | 0.05 | 0.05 | 0.05 |

| Outputs | | | | | | |
|---|---|---|---|---|---|---|
| Put-call parity does not hold | S + P | $C + Ke^{-rT}$ | | C - P | $S - Ke^{-rT}$ | |
| with American options. | 109.607 | 106.091 | | 22.402 | 25.918 | |

**Figure E2.13**

**Table E2.1**

| | January 6, 2005 | February 6, 2005 |
|---|---|---|
| Bid | 97 13/32 | 96 20/32 |
| Ask | 97 14/32 | 96 21/32 |
| Ask Yield | 1.29 | 1.63 |

value is higher than the corresponding European put, the put-call parity does not hold for the American options.

As another numerical example, we have the following data from the *Wall Street Journal* on January 13, 2004. Consider U.S. Treasury STRIPS maturing January 6, 2005, and February 6, 2005. See table E2.1.

Consider the option on Microsoft stock, expiring January 2005, with exercise price 27.50. Stock price is 27.43 and the call and put option premiums are 2.65 and 2.70 respectively.

We assume that Microsoft pays a quarterly dividend of 0.16 per share. We find that the model does not hold exactly. Several factors may lead to this result. For example, since Microsoft pays the quarterly dividends, the American call option is different from the corresponding European call option because of the early exercise possibility. STRIPS rate may not be the appropriate risk-free rate in the hedging. The put option is American.

2. Quanta Arbitrage Group also considers the use of the "risk-free" rate more carefully. They ask: Have we assumed that the yield curve is flat? What if the yield curve is not flat or there is a significant interest rate risk?

*Answer:* If the interest rate is zero, the put-call parity reduces to $C - P = S - K$. However, for positive interest rates, the value of an at-the-money call always exceeds the value of an at-the-money put. Since the put-call parity assumes no interim

| Inputs | | | | | |
|---|---|---|---|---|---|
| Stock price ($) | S | 100 | | | |
| Strike price ($) | K | 100 | | | |
| Volatility | σ | 0.2 | | | |
| Time to expiration (year) | T | 6 | 0 < T ≤ 6 | | |
| Dividend yield | d | N/A | | | |
| The number of periods | n | 6 | dt = T/n | | |
| | | | | | |
| Upward movement | u | 1.2214 | = exp(σ√dt) | | |
| Downward movement | d | 0.8187 | = 1/u | | |
| | | | | | |
| Time period (year) | 0 | 1 | 2 | 3 | 4 |
| Yield curve | 0.05 | 0.053 | 0.056 | 0.059 | 0.062 |
| | | | | | |
| **Outputs** | | | | | |
| | | | | | |
| Put-call parity holds when yield | S + P | C + Ke$^{-rT}$ | | C - P | S - Ke$^{-rT}$ |
| curve is not flat. | 103.672 | 103.672 | | 33.502 | 33.502 |
| | No arbitrage | | | No arbitrage | |

**Figure E2.14**

cash flows, only the interest rate, which is applicable from time zero up to the expiration date, matters. The interest rate up to the maturity date is known at time zero regardless of the term structure shape. Therefore the put-call parity still holds under the upward-sloping yield curve or the downward-sloping yield curve. What if there exists uncertainty about the interest rate? Put-call parity still holds when there is interest rate risk. See figure E2.14.

3. Finally, the Quanta Arbitrage Group evaluates the impact of dividends on the put-call relationship. What is the impact on the put-call parity if the stock pays dividends? *Answer:* If we manipulate the put-call parity, we can express $S$ as a combination of $C$, $PV(K)$, and $-P$. If the stock pays dividends, the equation would not hold, because we do not expect the interim cash flow from the call, the put, and riskless borrowing in the put-call parity. See figure E2.15.

When the stock pays a known dividend yield, the put-call parity condition is slightly changed as follows.

$$S - PV(Div.) + P = C + K \cdot e^{-rT}$$

Since the expected stock price at $T$ when dividends are paid during the option life is the current stock price adjusted by the present value of the dividend payment, we can change the put-call parity to hold by reflecting this feature.

4. Quanta Arbitrage Group wants to evaluate a particular trade using the S&P index, given that on December 23, 2003, the put and call option prices are as in table E2.2. Are the option prices consistent with the put-call parity, even though the assumptions of the put-call parity do not hold exactly? *Answer:* Since some of the stocks contained in the S&P 500 index will pay dividends before the option expiration, we can expect that the put-call parity does not hold. However, if the dividend yield is low, the put-call parity still holds approximately.

| Inputs | | | | | | |
|---|---|---|---|---|---|---|
| Stock price ($) | S | 100 | | | | |
| Strike price ($) | K | 100 | | | | |
| Volatility | $\sigma$ | 0.2 | | | | |
| Time to expiration (year) | T | 6 | $0 < T \leq 6$ | | | |
| Known dividend yield | $\delta$ | 0.02 | | | | |
| The number of periods | n | 6 | dt = T/n | | | |
| | | | | | | |
| Upward movement | u | 1.2214 | $= \exp(\sigma\sqrt{dt})$ | | | |
| Downward movement | d | 0.8187 | = 1/u | | | |
| | | | | | | |
| Time period (year) | | 0 | 1 | 2 | 3 | 4 |
| Yield curve | | 0.05 | 0.05 | 0.05 | 0.05 | 0.05 |

| Outputs | | | | | |
|---|---|---|---|---|---|
| Put-call parity relationship is | S - PV(Div.) + P | C + Ke$^{-rT}$ | | C - P | S - PV(Div.) - Ke$^{-rt}$ |
| slightly changed when stock | 98.228 | 98.228 | | 14.502 | 14.502 |
| pays known dividend yield. | No arbitrage | | | No arbitrage | |

**Figure E2.15**

Table E2.2  S&P 1076.48

| Strike | Expiration | Call | Put |
|---|---|---|---|
| 1070 | March | 34.50 | 31 |
| 1075 | March | 32 | 31.50 |

## Further Exercises

1. If we assume European options on stocks that pay unknown dividends, the put-call parity becomes an inequality. To derive this inequality, we assume that there is only one dividend payment. Furthermore, the largest dividend possible and the smallest dividend possible on the dividend payment date are denoted by $\bar{D}$ and $\underline{D}$, respectively.

   *Answer:* $S - \underline{D}(1 + r)^{-t} - K(1 + r)^{-T} \geq C - P \geq S - \bar{D}(1 + r)^{-t} - K(1 + r)^{-T}$

2. Describe a portfolio of stocks, call, and put options that would generate behavior like a zero-coupon bond with maturity $T$.

   *Answer:* $S - C + P = K \cdot e^{-rT}$. See figure E2.16.

3. If the stock price makes an instantaneous small rise, the call option price would make a small rise and the put option price would make a small fall. Use the put-call parity to derive the relationship of these small changes of prices. Use the Excel models to verify that this relationship is correct by computing these changes using a numerical example and show that the derived relationship holds.

   *Answer:* If the stock price increases by 1($\Delta S = 98 - 97$), the call option goes up by 0.6888 ($= 30.6315 - 29.9427$) and the put option goes down by 0.3112 ($= 7.0245 - 6.7133$). Therefore, $\Delta C - \Delta P$ is 1, which is the same amount of the stock price increase. The put-call parity still holds for the small changes. See figure E2.17.

| | | | | | | | | 100.000 |
|---|---|---|---|---|---|---|---|---|
| | | | | | | | 95.123 | 100.000 |
| | | | | | | 90.484 | 95.123 | 100.000 |
| | | | | | 86.071 | 90.484 | 95.123 | 100.000 |
| | | | | 81.873 | 86.071 | 90.484 | 95.123 | 100.000 |
| | | | 77.880 | 81.873 | 86.071 | 90.484 | 95.123 | 100.000 |
| S - C + P | | 74.082 | 77.880 | 81.873 | 86.071 | 90.484 | 95.123 | 100.000 |
| | | | | | | | | |
| | | | | | | | | 100.000 |
| | | | | | | | 95.123 | 100.000 |
| | | | | | | 90.484 | 95.123 | 100.000 |
| | | | | | 86.071 | 90.484 | 95.123 | 100.000 |
| | | | | 81.873 | 86.071 | 90.484 | 95.123 | 100.000 |
| | | | 77.880 | 81.873 | 86.071 | 90.484 | 95.123 | 100.000 |
| Ke$^{-rT}$ | | 74.082 | 77.880 | 81.873 | 86.071 | 90.484 | 95.123 | 100.000 |

Figure E2.16

| Stock price | 97 | 98 | $\Delta S =$ | 1 |
|---|---|---|---|---|
| Call option price | 29.9427 | 30.6315 | $\Delta C =$ | 0.6888 |
| Put option price | 7.0245 | 6.7133 | $\Delta P =$ | -0.3112 |

Figure E2.17

## E2.3  THE BLACK-SCHOLES OPTION PRICING MODEL

### Definitions

The stock price is a current price of an underlying stock. The strike price is an agreed-upon price between a buyer and a seller of the option. When exercised, the call option buyer pays the exercise price to the seller to exercise his right. The time to expiration is the remaining time to the option expiration date in terms of years. The risk-free rate is a continuously compounding rate. The dividend yield is zero, because the Black-Scholes model assumes that there are no dividend payments before the option expiration date.

### Description of the Model

Under the perfect capital market assumptions and the arbitrage-free condition in a continuous-time world, the model provides the European option price, given the underlying stock volatility. The European call option gives the holder the right, but not the obligation, to buy the underlying stock at the strike price at the expiration date. The European put option gives the holder the right, but not the obligation, to sell the underlying stock at the strike price at the expiration date.

### Numerical Example

Suppose that the options are at the money where the current stock price equals the strike price at 100. Let the options have the expiration date of one year. Assume a stock

| Inputs | | |
|---|---|---|
| Stock price (S) | 100 | |
| Strike price (K) | 100 | |
| Time to expiration (T) | 1 | |
| Stock volatility (σ) | 0.2 | |
| Risk-free rate (r) | 0.04 | |
| Dividend yield | N/A | |
| | | |
| Outputs | | |
| | | |
| | Call | Put |
| Price | 9.9250 | 6.0040 |

Figure E2.18

volatility of 20% and a one-year risk-free rate of 4%. Then the European call option price is 9.925 and the European put option price is 6.0040. See figure E2.18.

## Applications

1. The model provides pricing of the European call and put option on a stock.
2. Using an observed option price, we can determine the implied volatility of the stock, the volatility of the underlying stock that determines the observed option price.

## Case: Use of Put Options in Hedging

Henry Smith was an analyst working at the structured product department of a securities firm. An account executive, Mary Lee, who was working with her client, a hedge fund, called him. The hedge fund would like to protect the downside potential loss of this equity portfolio. Her client thought the S&P index may fall over 20% over the next month, and the hedge fund would like to buy a put option on S&P index from his department, but the problem was pricing. The hedge fund complained about the hedging cost. Specifically, the hedge fund was uncomfortable with the assumptions used in the Black-Scholes model that Henry was using.

Mary went to Henry's office and said: "Look, my client is a really sophisticated quant. He said that he would not use the Black-Scholes model. He would use a blah blah blah model. Can you talk to him about it?" "Models are just tools. The question is: What does he want? We can only give him the right tool when he tells us his problem that needs to be solved." "Well, he needs a put option to hedge his downside risks, and he thinks the Black-Scholes model gives an unreasonably high price." "But the market determines that option price and not the model. We can only buy the option for him from the market. It has nothing to do with which model we are using." "Henry, do me a favor and talk to the guy." Mary rushed out for another meeting.

*Henry sat by himself shaking his head. "Account execs are all alike. Now what am I supposed to do? I do not know the guy and do not know what he wants. May be I should not focus on giving him an answer. Maybe I should make out a list of questions for him first. What are the questions? Does he need liquidity? Does he want structured product?"*

## Exercises and Answers

1. One of the assumptions for the Black-Scholes option pricing model is that the stock's return is lognormally distributed. "Why use a lognormal distribution? Why don't you use a normal distribution?" Henry had to compare the lognormal distribution and the normal distribution. How should he justify the use of the lognormal distribution and not the normal distribution? Note that a random variable $x$ is lognormally distributed if the logarithm of $x$ is normally distributed.

   *Answer:* If the random variable $x$ is normally distributed, the lowest possible value is minus infinity: however, if $x$ is lognormally distributed, the lowest possible value is zero. Since the worst possible case for stock investment is to lose the initial investment amount to buy the stock, the lognormal assumption is more valid than the normal assumption. In other words, the lowest possible price of the stock is zero, such that the rate of return is −100%. While the normal distribution is symmetric, the lognormal distribution exhibits positive skewness, which means that the distribution is skewed towards higher returns.

   For example, let $\mu$ be a continuously compounding rate of return. Then the stock price at time $T$ is $Se^{\mu T}$, where $\mu$ follows a normal distribution as we assumed. Then if we take a logarithm, $Se^{\mu T}$ will become $\log S + \mu T$, which follows also a normal distribution. Therefore, we can say that the stock price follows a lognormal distribution.

   If we simulate the stock prices (figure E2.19), calculate the returns (figure E2.20), and determine the return distribution (figure E2.21), we can see that the return distribution looks like a normal distribution.

   As we can see in figure E2.21, the normal distribution is symmetric, however, the lognormal distribution is asymmetric. In addition to that, lognormal distribution always has positive value, but normal distribution has negative as well as positive value. We have drawn a normal distribution and a lognormal distribution. The means and the standard deviations of the two distributions are (0,1) and (0,1) respectively.

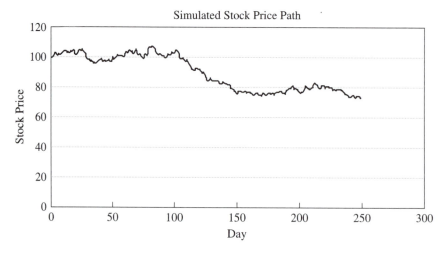

**Figure E2.19**

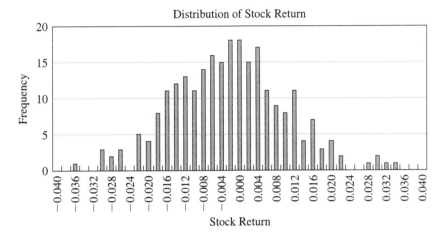

Figure E2.20

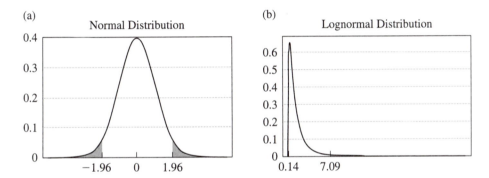

Figure E2.21

If $\ln X$ is normally distributed such as $\ln X \sim N(\mu, \sigma^2)$, then $X$ is lognormally distributed such as $X \sim \ln(\exp(\mu + \frac{1}{2}\sigma^2), e^{2\mu+\sigma^2}(e^{\sigma^2} - 1))$. The probability that a normally distributed variable falls beyond 1.96 or less than −1.96 is 2.5% each. The probability that a lognormally distributed variable has a value more than 7.09 or less than 0.14 is 2.5% each. Since the normal distribution is symmetric, the left shaded area is the same shape as compared to the right shaded area. However, this is not the case for the lognormal distribution.

2. Mary Lee called back the next day and said that her client was now concerned with the dividends of the S&P index. The hedge fund argued that the S&P index pays dividends but the Black-Scholes model assumes the stock pays no dividend. How did Henry take dividends into account in the pricing? Since the Black-Scholes model is to calculate a European call option on nondividend-paying stocks, we cannot apply the Black-Scholes model to price a European call option on known dividend-paying stocks. However, we can change the Black-Scholes model to do that. The intuition behind the Black-Scholes model is that once we can calculate the terminal call option value, we can discount the terminal value at the risk-free rate to get the option value

| Inputs | | |
| --- | :---: | --- |
| Stock price (S) | 100 | |
| Strike price (K) | 100 | |
| Time to expiration (T) | 1 | |
| Stock volatility ($\sigma$) | 0.2 | |
| Risk-free rate (r) | 0.04 | |
| Dividend yield ($\delta$) | 0.01 | |
| | | |
| **Outputs** | | |
| | | |
| | Call | Put |
| Price | 9.3197 | 6.3937 |

Figure E2.22

at time 0. We need the lognormal assumption of stock prices at the maturity date to calculate the terminal call option value, which is $Max[S_T - X, 0]$. To take care of dividend payments during the option life, we subtract the present value of the dividend payments from the current stock price to get an adjusted stock price. We plug the adjusted stock price into the Black-Scholes formula. Can you defend this method to calculate the European call option on dividend-paying stocks?

*Answer:* If the stock pays dividends during the option life, we can assume that the terminal stock price will be lowered by the dividend payments, because dividend payments lower the firm value, with other things being constant. To adjust for this effect, we subtract the present value of the dividend payment from the current stock price. See figure E2.22.

Since the continuous dividend yield is 0.01, the stock continuously pays 1% of the stock price as a dividend. Therefore, the adjusted stock price at the present time is $100 \times e^{-0.01 \times 1year}$, which will be plugged to the Black-Scholes model. We can see that the call option value is less than the option premiums in the numerical example, because of the dividend payments.

3. On January 13, 2004, we have the following data from the *Wall Street Journal*. The U.S. Treasury STRIPS reaches maturity on January 6, 2005, with the bid price of 97:13 and the ask price of 97:14. Another U.S. Treasury STRIPS reaches maturity on February 6, 2005, with the bid price of 96:20 and the ask price of 96:21. (Note: By market convention, 0:1 means 1/32.)

Consider the following option. The underlying stock is Microsoft. The time to expiration is January 2005, with the exercise price of 27.50. The stock price is $27.43. We assume that the stock volatility is 20% for simplicity. We further assume that Microsoft pays a quarterly dividend of 0.16 per share.

(a) Since Microsoft pays dividends before the option expires, we cannot directly use the Black-Scholes model to price the call option on Microsoft. One way would be to calculate the present value of the dividend payments and subtract it from the current stock price to determine the dividend-adjusted stock price. Calculate the option price using the Black-Scholes model with or without the stock price adjustments and see how different the two values are. See figure E2.23.

(a)

| Inputs | | | | | |
|---|---|---|---|---|---|
| Stock price (S) | 27.43 | | | | |
| Strike price (K) | 27.5 | | | | |
| Time to expiration (T) | 1 | | | | |
| Stock volatility (σ) | 0.2 | | | | |
| Bid price: PV(100) | 97.40625 | | | | |
| Risk-free rate (r) | 0.0263 | | | | |
| Dividend schedule (T) | Quarterly | 0.25 | 0.5 | 0.75 | 1 |
| Dividend amount | 0.16 | 0.16 | 0.16 | 0.16 | 0.16 |
| PV (Div.) | 0.62959092 | 0.15895225 | 0.15791137 | 0.1568773 | 0.15585 |
| Div.-adjusted stock price (S*) | 26.8004091 | | | | |

(b)

| Outputs | | | |
|---|---|---|---|
| | 0 | 2.49610 | 1.85282 |
| | 0.16 | 2.14111 | 2.12742 |
| | Dividend | Call | Put |

Figure E2.23

(b) If we assume that the dividend payment is large, like $20 per share, what would you like to do as an option holder just before the ex-dividend date? From this, we can see that the dividend amount has something to do with an early exercise decision. *Answer:* The option holder will exercise the option and receive the dividend. Otherwise, he has to experience a decline of the option price.

4. An investor has a pessimistic view about the stock market. To capitalize his view, he could short a stock or he could buy a put option. After he makes several calls to the brokers, he realizes that shorting a stock has many institutional constraints such as the up-tick rule (shorting a stock is allowed only when the stock transaction occurs at a higher price than the previous one). Therefore, he wants to buy a put option. However, he is uncertain about the reasonableness of the put option prices quoted in the market. What would be his best way to check whether the put prices are overpriced? Assume that he is considering buying a European option.
*Answer:* If we use the put-call parity and the Black-Scholes model, we can calculate the European put.

5. One of the five variables to use the Black-Scholes model is stock volatility, which we cannot observe in the market. We have two different ways to estimate the stock volatility. One is historical volatility, and the other is implied volatility. Can you tell why the two volatilities are different from each other?
*Answer:* The historical volatility is backward-looking and the implied volatility is forward-looking. Therefore the two volatilities are not the same.
*Example:* On Tuesday, February 3, 2004, the premium of the stock option on Microsoft is 0.15 with the strike price of 30 and the expiration date of March 19, 2004. The closing price of the underlying asset is 27.29. We use the 4-week Treasury

bill rate as the risk-free rate, 0.85% per annum. (Data: http://finance.yahoo.com/, http://www.federalreserve.gov/)

We assume that the stock does not pay dividends before the option expiration. We use the Black-Scholes option pricing model to estimate the implied volatility, which is consistent with the observed option market price under the Black-Scholes assumptions. See figure E2.24.

The implied volatility is 22.31%. Next we calculate the historical volatility of the underlying asset for the last thirty-four days. We sample thirty-four stock prices from December 15, 2003, to February 3, 2004. See figure E2.25. (Data: http://finance.yahoo.com/)

6. As a stock analyst responsible for equity research at Simon Research, John Matthew has discovered that the corporate activities had increased significantly recently at Fast Call Communications. He spotted corporate jets coming to the small local airstrip and noted the heavy traveling schedules of the senior management at Fast Call. John suspected that there might be a possible merger negotiation between Fast Call and a cable company. Or, Fast Call may be an acquisition target of White Mountains International, a global communication company. John was not certain about what

| Inputs | | |
|---|---|---|
| Stock price (S) | 27.29 | |
| Strike price (K) | 30 | |
| Time to expiration (T) | 0.1360 | |
| Stock volatility (σ) | 0.2231 | Changing cell for solver |
| Risk-free rate (r) | 0.0085 | |
| Dividend schedule (T) | Quarterly | |
| Dividend amount | 0 | |
| PV (Div.) | 0 | |
| Div.-adjusted stock price (S*) | 27.29 | |
| Option premium (market value) | 0.15 | |
| **Outputs** | | |
| | Call | Put |
| European option price | 0.15 | 2.83 |
| (Market value - BSOPM)$^2$ | 5.1268E-22 | Target cell for solver |

**Figure E2.24**

| Historical Volatility for the Last 34 Days | |
|---|---|
| Daily average | -0.000617 |
| Daily standard deviation | 0.01014637 |
| Annual average | -0.1542406 |
| Annual standard deviation | 0.16042824 |

**Figure E2.25**

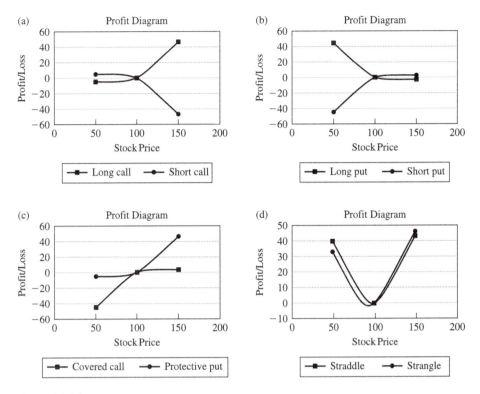

**Figure E2.26**

actually was happening, but he thought that the company stock would rise at least 10% when either event was made public. He drew eight profit diagrams: longing a call, shorting a call, a covered call, longing a put, shorting a put, a protective put, a straddle, and a strangle (see figure E2.26). Which strategy is the best for him to exploit his research?

*Answer:* We can see from the profit diagrams in figure E2.26 that the protective put is as good as the long call in terms of the payoffs at expiration, but the rate of return of longing a call is much better than the protective put, because we have to spend more money to long the protective put than to long the call. See figure E2.27.

## Further Exercises

1. Consider two call options, identical except that the underlying stock of one option pays dividends while the other does not pay dividends. Which option should have a higher price?

   *Answer:* The call option on a nondividend-paying stock has a higher price.

2. How do you determine the hedge ratio of a call option? Use the Excel model to show the effectiveness of the hedge by holding the hedge position and simulate the change in the value of the hedged position with a small change in the stock price.

   *Answer:* Option deltas are often called hedge ratios. The delta, $\Delta$, of a call option is $\Delta = \partial C / \partial S = N(d_1)$. Delta describes the change in the option, given a small change

(a)

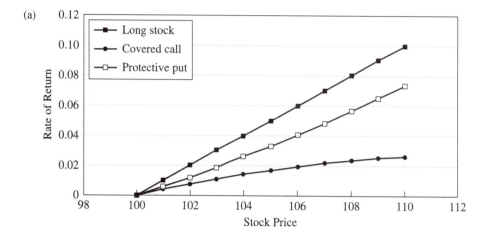

(b)

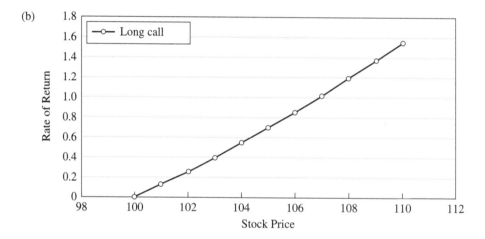

**Figure E2.27**

in the underlying security. For example, if the stock price ($S$) is 100, the strike price ($K$) is 100, the time to expiration ($T$) is one year, the stock volatility ($\sigma$) is 20%, the risk-free rate ($r$) is 4%, and the stock does not pay dividends, the delta of the call option is 0.6179. This means that the option value changes by $0.6179 when the underlying stock changes by $1.

3. A warrant is a long-dated option, an option with a long time to expiration. Consider an at-the-money warrant on a stock with a time to expiration of ten years. The warrant is a call option. Suppose that the yield curve is 4% flat. Use the Excel model to simulate the impact of a rise of interest rate by 1% on the call option. Is the impact higher or lower than an otherwise similar option with a three-month expiration?

*Answer:* The warrant on a stock with a time to expiration of ten years has a higher impact than the otherwise similar option with three-month expiration.

4. On January 14, 2004, we have the following data from the *Wall Street Journal*.

Treasury Bill
Maturity March 18, 2004
Days to maturity 64
Bid 0.84
Asked 0.83

Call Option
Underlying stock Oracle (NASDAQ)
Maturity March
Exercise price 12.5
Stock price (January 13, 2004) 14.36
Stock price (January 12, 2004) 14.66
Option premium (January 13, 2004) 2.05
Option premium (January 12, 2004) 2.3

We assume that the call option expires on March 18, the risk-free rate applicable for the option life is the Treasury bill rate, and the underlying stock does not pay dividends until the option matures on March 18, 2004.

(a) Since Oracle will not pay dividends until the option expiration, it is known that the option will be never exercised. To see this point, first calculate the intrinsic value and compare it with the option premium. If the intrinsic value is greater than the option premium, what can we do to make money using this opportunity? From this, we can see that the option premium should be below the intrinsic value.
*Answer:* On January 13, 2004, the intrinsic value is 1.86 (= $Max[0, 14.36 - 12.5]$), and the option premium is 2.05. The option premium is greater than the intrinsic value. If the intrinsic value is greater than the option premium, we buy options, exercise, and sell the stock.

(b) Actually, we can show that the American call option on nondividend-paying stocks should be greater than $Max[S - Ke^{-ri}, 0]$. If this does not hold, what can we do to use this "possible" arbitrage opportunity?
*Answer:* We buy the call option, sell the stock, and lend today. Then we have $S - CKE^{-ri} > 0$ today. At expiration, when $S_T > K$, the cash flow from the initial portfolio is zero, because $Max[S_T - K, 0] - S_T + K$ is zero. When $S_T < K$ at expiration, the cash flow is $-S_T + K > 0$, because the call option expires without value. Regardless of which state occurs at expiration, we can see that the arbitrage has a zero or positive cash flow at expiration.

(c) We can easily check that $Max[S - Ke^{-ri}, 0]$ is greater than $Max[S - K, 0]$, which is an intrinsic value. From this reasoning, what can we conclude about the early exercise of the American option?
*Answer:* $Max[S - K, 0]$ is the value of the option when it is exercised, and the call option must be worth at least $Max[S - Ke^{-ri}, 0]$. Therefore, it is not optimal to exercise the American option before the expiration. For the American call option on nondividend-paying stocks, it is always optimal not to exercise before the expiration.

## E2.4    THE RELATIONSHIP OF RISK-NEUTRAL AND MARKET BINOMIAL LATTICES

### Definitions

The risk-neutral binomial lattice is a lattice where a risk-neutral probability and a risk-free rate of return are used. The one-period rate of return for a stock is $r$. The market binomial lattice is a lattice where a market (actual) probability and risk-adjusted rate of return are used. The local drift of a stock return ($\mu$) is the expected return on a stock in the actual world. The expected stock price at period 1 on the binomial lattice is $qSu + (1 - q)Sd$ and the expected stock price in the actual world is $Se^{\mu dt}$. By matching the expected stock price on the binomial lattice with the actual stock price, we can have that $q = \frac{e^{\mu dt} - d}{u - d}$, which we can observe in the risk-averse world.

### Description of the Model

The risk-neutral and the market binomial lattice have the same node values. In the market binomial lattice, we can see that the option rates of return depend on the nodes, which means that the option risk is varying over periods and states. However, in the risk-neutral lattice, the option rates of return are constant across periods and states, yielding the risk-free rates of return.

### Numerical Example

Suppose that the options are at the money where the stock price is 100. The underlying volatility of the stock is assumed to be 20%, and the market risk-free rate over one year is 4%. Show that the rates of return on the call option in the risk-neutral world is constant at the risk-free rate. See figure E2.28.

### Application

The model values the dynamic hedging strategy of the options.

### Case: Asset Allocation and the Expected Returns of an Option

The equity market in the last two quarters had fallen significantly, with the S&P index losing 15% of the value. The portfolio strategy group of an asset management company that focused on investment funds for high net worth individuals was meeting to discuss the asset allocation strategy for their clients. The group consisted of a general partner of the firm, an equity manager, a fixed-income manager, and the account executive who was responsible for servicing some of the clients. In the meeting, the equity portfolio manager said that he was convinced that the equity market had reached the lowest point, "has bottomed." More precisely, he said that the equity index, S&P specifically, would outperform the risk-free rate by 3% next quarter. At this point, the general partner said. "Maybe we should even consider buying some European call options." The account executive nodded her head, suggesting that the clients could accept the risks of holding derivatives in their portfolios and that the investment guidelines did allow for a maximum of 10% in derivatives.

| Inputs | | | |
|---|---|---|---|
| Stock price ($) | S | 100 | |
| Strike price ($) | K | 100 | |
| Volatility | σ | 0.2 | |
| Time to expiration (year) | T | 1 | |
| Risk-free rate | r | 0.04 | |
| Local drift of stock return | μ | 0.05 | |
| Known dividend yield | δ | 0 | |
| The number of periods | n | 6 | |
| Time increment | dt | 0.16666667 | = T/n |
| Upward movement | u | 1.0851 | = exp(σ√dt) |
| Downward movement | d | 0.9216 | = 1/u |
| Risk-neutral probability | p | 0.5205 | =(exp(rdt)-d)/(u-d) |
| Actual probability | q | 0.5308 | =(exp(μdt)-d)/(u-d) |

| Outputs | | | | | |
|---|---|---|---|---|---|
| | | | | | 0.04 |
| | | | | 0.04 | 0.04 |
| | | | 0.04 | 0.04 | 0.04 |
| | | 0.04 | 0.04 | 0.04 | 0.04 |
| | 0.04 | 0.04 | 0.04 | 0.04 | 0 |
| Risk-neutral rate of return (r)   0.04 | 0.04 | 0.04 | 0.04 | 0 | 0 |

Figure E2.28

The fixed-income portfolio manager said that he thought options were usually associated with the Black-Scholes model and that they would be related to dynamic hedging, and that he would have no idea of the expected rate of return they would be delivering to the clients by using options. "Not so," said the equity portfolio manager. "If we are willing to assume that the equity market outperforms the risk-free rate by 3%, then we should be able to calculate the expected return of an at-the-money European call option with a three-month expiration." The general partner was silent, waiting for an answer. The equity portfolio manager then said: "Let me ask my analyst to give me an answer on this." He put his assistant, Logan Ghana, on the speaker phone.

"Logan, I am at an asset allocation meeting here." "Yes, what can I do for you, boss." "We want to know how you use that Black-Scholes model to determine the expected return of a call option. Kimmy thinks that he is god and he knows that the market will move three points next quarter. We want to know the expected returns of a call option, given Kimmy has control over the market." Kim, the general partner, chuckled and added: "I am a dangerous guy here."

"Boss. I don't know. I know you guys are all in the Parthenon among the gods. But you are asking the wrong questions. The Black-Scholes model gives you the fair value of an option, but that does not mean that you need to use it to calculate the expected returns of the option. Given a simulation of the stock returns over a three-month horizon, you can determine the option payoff in three months. You then calculate the expected returns of the option. Are you with me?"

"Logan, do we need to use the Black-Scholes model if we want to hold six-month options?" "Yes. Now you need to know the option value three months from now and

Time-state dependent rate of return ($R_{adj}$)

| | | | | | |
|---|---|---|---|---|---|
| 0.10359202 | 0.09772589 | 0.0907973 | 0.08284613 | 0.07462919 | 0.06939851 |
| | 0.12427295 | 0.11907462 | 0.11193061 | 0.10149705 | 0.08482226 |
| | | 0.15724848 | 0.15724848 | 0.15724848 | 0.15724848 |
| | | | 0.15724848 | 0.15724848 | 0.15724848 |
| | | | | 0 | 0 |
| | | | | | 0 |

**Figure E2.29**

Time-state dependent rate of return ($R_{adj}$)

| | | | | | |
|---|---|---|---|---|---|
| 0.13041585 | 0.12707208 | 0.12277631 | 0.11705446 | 0.1090551 | 0.09708053 |
| | 0.15724848 | 0.15724848 | 0.15724848 | 0.15724848 | 0.15724848 |
| | | 0 | 0 | 0 | 0 |
| | | | 0 | 0 | 0 |
| | | | | 0 | 0 |
| | | | | | 0 |

**Figure E2.30**

Time-state dependent rate of return ($R_{adj}$)

| | | | | | |
|---|---|---|---|---|---|
| 0.08230236 | 0.07716921 | 0.07211123 | 0.06768846 | 0.06455123 | 0.06221591 |
| | 0.09384252 | 0.0874954 | 0.08034892 | 0.07309341 | 0.06836184 |
| | | 0.11182773 | 0.10526633 | 0.09605758 | 0.08206238 |
| | | | 0.14029704 | 0.13902108 | 0.13753741 |
| | | | | 0.15724848 | 0.15724848 |
| | | | | | 0 |

**Figure E2.31**

therefore you can apply the Black-Scholes model in the simulation." "Thanks Logan—that's all we need to know."

*Kim was thinking aloud: "Which option should we then be buying? We need to have a way to narrow down our choices. Like Logan said, asking the right question is the first step."*

## Exercise and Answer

1. We have shown that the rates of return on the call option on the risk-neutral binomial lattice are constant over time and state. Show that the rate of return on the option is time-varying depending on the stock price on the market binomial lattice.

   *Answer:* We can see that the rate of return of each node on the risk-neutral lattice is always a risk-free rate of return. However, the rate of return on the market binomial lattice is not constant, reflecting that the risk of the call option is changing. We can observe that when the call option is out of the money (the stock price is less than the exercise price), the call option is riskier as compared to the in-the-money option. When the call option is getting more in the money, the call option rate of return approaches the risk-free rate of return. For example, at time 4 and state 4, the rate of return is 7.46%. However, at time 5 and state 5, the option rate of return is 6.94%, which is closer to the risk-free rate of return (4%). When the call option becomes out of the money, the rate of return goes up to 15.72%. Because of this change in the risk of the call option, we cannot apply the risk-adjusted rate of return approach to evaluate the risky cash flow. See figure E2.29.

## Further Exercises

1. Suppose that the option is out of the money where the stock price is 80 and the strike 100. The underlying volatility of the stock is assumed to be 20%, and the market risk-free rate over one year is 4%. Show that the option rates of return across the nodes are changing.

   *Answer:* See figure E2.30.

2. Suppose that the option is in the money where the stock price is 120. The other input data is the same as in question 1. Repeat the same question here. Show that the option risk is rapidly changing depending on whether the option is in the money or out of the money.

   *Answer:* The more out-of-the-money an option becomes, the more rapidly the option's risk changes. See figure E2.31.

## Notes

1. Visit www.amex.com/ for further information.
2. Visit www.cbot.com/ for detailed information.
3. "True lattice" is used interchangeably with "risk-averse lattice."

## Bibliography

Black, F., and M. Scholes. 1973. The pricing of options and corporate liabilities. *Journal of Political Economy*, 81, 637–654.

Brennan, M. J. 1979. The pricing of contingent claims in discrete time model. *Journal of Finance*, 34, 53–68.

Britten-Jones, M., and A. Neuberger. 2000. Option prices, implied price processes, and stochastic volatility. *Journal of Finance*, 55(2), 839–866.

Chung, S. L., and M. Shackleton. 2000. The binomial Black-Scholes model and the Greeks. Working paper, Lancaster University Management School.

Cox, J. C., S. Ross, and M. Rubinstein. 1979. Option pricing: A simplified approach. *Journal of Financial Economics*, 7, 229–264.

Jarrow, R. A., and A. Rudd. 1983. *Option Pricing*. Homewood, IL: Richard D. Irwin.

Levy, H. 1985. Upper and lower bounds of put and call option value: Stochastic dominance approach. *Journal of Finance*, 40(4), 1197–1218.

MacBeth, J. D., and L. J. Merville. 1980. Tests of the Black-Scholes and Cox call option valuation models. *Journal of Finance*, 35(2), 285–300.

Merton, R. C. 1973. Theory of rational option pricing. *Bell Journal of Economics and Management Science*, 4, 141–183.

Rendleman, R. J., and B. R. Bartter. 1979. Two state option pricing. *Journal of Finance*, 34(5), 1092–1110.

Stoll, Hans R. 1969. The relationship between put and call option prices. *Journal of Finance,* 31, 319–332.

# 3

# Exotic Options

In practice, options are not simply European put and call options. Nor do options often have one underlying risk source (e.g., the stock price risk). There is a broad range of options. Finance is a social science, not a natural one. Options are made and designed every day, and they are not found in nature. Making an exhaustive list of possible options found in the market may be a futile exercise.

What is useful is to describe the types of options in terms of their economics. What are the designs in the options that make them valuable? What options can we use as building blocks for other options? Which options are similar in terms of their economics even though they have different names? These are the questions that this chapter will seek to answer.

*Exotic options* are options that are not standard—in our case, any options that are not European. Elsewhere, many option types are considered standard, and exotic options are options not commonly used. The purpose of this chapter is to provide an overview of different important features of options.

## 3.1 OPTIONS WITH ALTERNATIVE PAYOFFS AT EXPIRATION

European stock options or bond options have a relatively simple specification of the payoff at the terminal date; the payment is $Max [S_T - X, 0]$ for a call option. But the payoff can take alternative specifications. One example is a digital option (or binary option).

The *binary option* pays $\$Q$ if the underlying asset has a value above the strike price on the expiration date. There is no payment if the underlying asset has a value below the strike price. There are two main differences between a digital option and a European call option. First, the payoff function is discontinuous at the strike price for the digital option. That means that near the expiration, implementing a delta hedge will be difficult.

Second, the payoff of the digital option is truncated on the upside. The maximum payment is $Q$. For a deep-in-the-money option, the expected payoff in all likelihood will be a fixed payment of $Q$ at expiration. Therefore, the option will behave like a bond.

Consider an option that is out of the money. As the stock value rises, the option value increases at an accelerated pace because the likelihood of being paid $Q$ increases. We then have a positive gamma. In this region, we will also have a time decay effect.

As the stock price continues to rise, the positive gamma turns into a negative gamma. This is because a digital option has the payoff capped at $Q$. In this region, there is a significant downside risk that the option will pay nothing when the stock price falls, but there is a limited upside, capped at $Q$. As the stock price increases, the option value reaches its maximum of the present value of $Q$. As time passes, and if the stock price remains unchanged, the option will appreciate in value as the likelihood of receiving payment $Q$ increases. (See figure 3.1.)

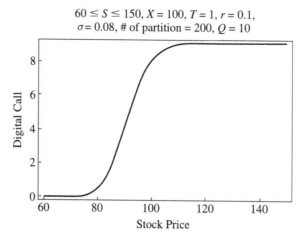

**Figure 3.1** Performance profile of a digital option. The digital call option pays $10 (Q) if the stock price exceeds $100 (X) at time period 1; otherwise there is no payment. The standard call option pays $Max[S - X, 0]$ at time period 1. The stock price varies from 60 to 150 for simultion purposes. The continuously compounding risk-free rate is 10%. The stock volatility is 0.08. We partition one period into 200 subperiods to enhance the accuracy.

The valuation method is the same as the European option. We will roll back the value from the terminal date. We assume that the stock price is 100, the exercise price is 100, the stock volatility is 10%, the time to maturity is one year, the continuously compounding risk-free rate is 10%, and the number of partitions is six. (See figure 3.2.)

If we think that the underlying asset price will be above the strike price at expiration, we might buy either a European call or a digital call. The European call has upside potential, growing with the underlying asset price beyond the strike price, whereas the digital option can never pay off more than Q. If we expect the underlying asset to rise significantly, then we should buy the European call; otherwise, we should consider the digital call, which may cost less because it does not give the potentially high returns that are offered by the European call.

Digital options can be used as building blocks for European options. For example, suppose the European option has a strike price of $10. Then let us hold a portfolio of digital options, one option for each strike price: $10, $11, $12, ..., with $Q = \$1$. We can see that this portfolio of digital options has a payoff at the expiration similar to that of the European option. Therefore, in general, a portfolio of digital options with different strike prices with payoff Q can approximate a European option because its payoff schedule approximates that of the European option.

If we long a digital option and short another with a higher strike, it leads to a security that has a payoff for a range of stock prices. Using this combination of digital options, we can construct a broad range of payoffs for a portfolio of options. We can also create more gamma by increasing the number of digital options with increasing strike price. The payoff can be a power function like $S^n$ at the expiration of the option, where S is the stock price and n is some number. Therefore, this payment is no longer one-to-one with the stock price but a power of the stock price. Creating a high gamma leads to an

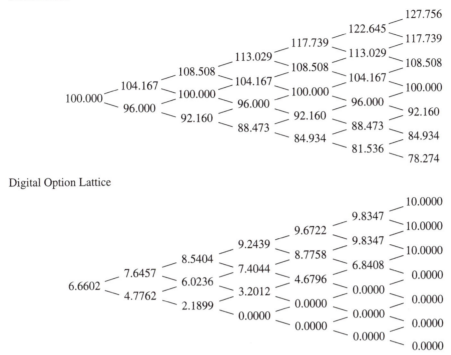

**Figure 3.2** The binomial lattice of a digital option. The binomial lattice of the stock prices is shown in the upper panel. We assume that the initial stock price is 100, the stock volatility is 10%, the time to maturity is 1 year, and the continuously compounding risk-free rate is 10%. Since the number of partitions is 6, we adjust the upward parameter, $u$, the downward parameter, $d$, and the risk-free rate over one subperiod to 1.04167, 0.959997, and 0.01681, respectively. The risk-neutral probability is 0.695573. The parameters are $u = \exp\left\{\sigma\sqrt{1/m}\right\} = 1.04167, d = 1/u = 0.959997, S = 100, \sigma = 0.1, r = 0.1, T = 1$, and $p = (\exp\left[\frac{r}{m}\right] - d)/(u - d) = 0.695573, 1 - p = 0.304427, m = 6$. The binomial lattice of the digital option is represented in the lower panel. At maturity, the digital option prices are Q if the stock prices exceed the exercise price. At one subperiod before the maturity, the digital option prices are determined by backward substitition. For example, we get 9.8347 by discounting the expected value with the risk-free rate over one subperiod. That is $(10 \times 0.695573 + 10 \times 0.304427)/1.01681$.

accelerated positive payoff when the stock price rises. The holder can benefit more from the stock price increase.

## 3.2    OPTIONS WITH BOUNDARY CONDITIONS

Options may have conditions, called *boundary conditions*, imposed on the payoff from the initial date to the expiration date. An important example of this type of option is the barrier option. There are two kinds of barrier options. The *knockout* option is a European put or call option that ceases to exist when the underlying stock reaches the barrier (a prespecified stock level), which may be above or below the current stock price, any time before the expiration. The *knock-in* option is a European option (put or call) that comes into existence whenever the underlying stock reaches the barrier any time before expiration.

The economic reason for the design of the barrier option is to allow the investor to buy or sell options at any stock price level, which is not subject to the current stock price. In other words, we can activate or deactivate an option depending on the prevailing stock price over a horizon period.

The barrier option is the same as the European option except for one important feature: it depends on the path of the stock price. If a stock falls below the barrier and rises back to the initial value, the knockout option will have no value, because as soon as the stock reaches the barrier, the option expires. However, a European option value stays alive until the expiration date. Thus we can say that the barrier option is *path-dependent*. Similarly, for the knock-in option, if the stock falls below the barrier and rises back, the

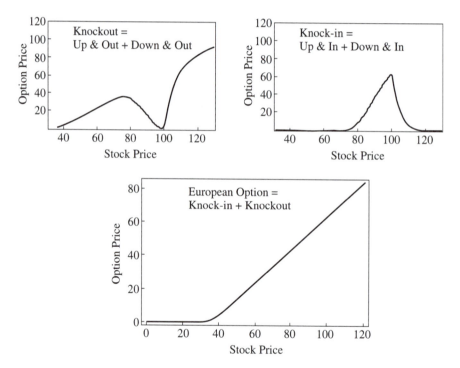

**Figure 3.3** Performance profile of knock-in and knockout options. The European knockout call option becomes a standard European call option whenever the underlying stock price does not touch the barrier before expiration. If it touches, the European knockout call option is worthless even though the stock price is above the strike price at the maturity. The stock price varies from 30 to 130 for simulation purposes. The continuously compounding risk-free rate is 10%. The variance of the stock returns is 0.1. The time to maturity is 1 year. The knockout barrier is 100 and the strike price is 40. We partition one year into 100 subperiods to enhance the accuracy. The upper-left diagram shows two knockout options. One is up and out and the other is down and out. The up and out knockout option has value when the stock prices are below 100, which is the knockout barrier. The down and out knockout option has value when above 100, which is the knockout barrier. Similar interpretation can be given to the knock-in options in the upper-right diagram. If we combine the two options, we get the European option profile shown in the lower diagram.

option will have value. However, if the stock price stays constant, the knock-in option has no value. Therefore, the knock-in option also is path-dependent.

Consider the following example. Let $C$ be a European call option with strike price $X$ and time to maturity $T$. Suppose that we have a knockout barrier at $X$ (the strike price). Then the option pays nothing if the stock price falls below $X$ at any time before expiration. Such a barrier option should be worth less than the equivalent European option. The barrier may be referred to as the absorption barrier, since the option expires when the stock price hits the barrier and the option is "absorbed."

We can use the rolling-back method on a binomial lattice to value such a barrier option. We assume that the option survives and is not absorbed until the expiration. We know the payoff, and we roll back to one step before expiration. For all the nodes (state and time) that the stock price falls below the strike, we let the option price be 0. Then we proceed to use backward substitution until we reach the initial time, and that is the price of the option. (See figures 3.3 and 3.4.)

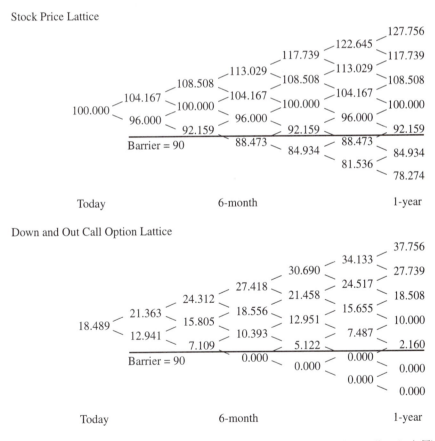

Figure 3.4 The binomial lattice for barrier option pricing (European knockout call option). The European knockout call option becomes a standard European call option whenever the underlying stock prices do not touch the barrier before expiration. The initial stock price is 100 and the barrier is 90. Therefore, if the stock price touches 90, the option will expire. The strike price is 90. As we can see in the second panel, the knockout option is nil below the stock price of 90, which is the barrier.

The European knockout call option becomes a standard European call option whenever the underlying stock prices do not touch the barrier before expiration. The European knock-in call option becomes a standard European call option whenever the underlying stock prices reach the barrier before expiration. Since the probability that stock prices will or will not touch the barrier is 1, a portfolio of a European knockout call option and a European knock-in call option is a standard European call option.

$$\text{Knockout} + \text{Knock-in} = \text{European Call Option}$$

If we want to have a call option when the stock price reaches a certain level, we can buy a knock-in option today. Thus, we have bought such a strategy at a fixed price. By contrast, if we buy the call option when the stock meets the price level, the option cost will be uncertain because the option price depends on when the stock price hits the barrier.

## 3.3  OPTIONS WITH THE EARLY EXERCISE FEATURE (AMERICAN) AND THE BELLMAN OPTIMIZATION

*Early exercise* is a feature that allows the holder to exercise the option at any time before, and right up to, the expiration date, not just at the expiration date (as in the case of a European option). This type of option, called the *American option*, can apply to a call or put option.

An American option has an added feature that can only be valuable for the holder. The holder can always treat an American option as a European option without bothering to exercise early, and therefore an American option should be valued higher than or equal to the European option. The possibility of the early exercise feature having no value (which means the European option is priced identically to the American option) exists because it is possible that for some options it is never profitable to exercise them early. For example, we will show that an American call option on a nondividend-paying stock should be priced like a European call option because there is no rational reason to exercise the option early.

One common variation of an American option is called the *Bermuda* option. A Bermuda option allows the holder to exercise the option at certain times, for example, at the end of each month or each week. Therefore, it is similar to an American option in that it can be exercised early—but only at specific dates, instead of at any time.

An American option is similar to a barrier option in terms of being path-dependent; the stock price may reach a level that makes early exercise desirable. It is different from a barrier option because the early exercise decision may not be a simple rule that is specified in the term sheet of the option. The exercise rule depends on the investor. Indeed, the American option introduces an important aspect to option decisions in finance. The questions the American option poses are as follows: Is there an optimal early exercise rule that a rational investor should follow? If such a rule exists, what is it?

Understanding this optimal early exercise rule is central to pricing an American option. More important, the concept is applicable to many financial theories that can be used to model an individual's behavior in the capital market. For this reason, we will first discuss a mathematical concept introduced by Bellman. The decision rule is dynamic in the sense that it depends on the current state of the world: the stock price, time to expiration, and all the other market variables. Therefore the decision has to be revised continually—and hence is dynamic.

The pricing of American options requires an extra argument. The initial price of an American option must depend on its optimal exercise at any future time prior to the expiration date. We must consider all the stock price paths and the optimal exercise point, and discount the payoff at the risk-free rate to determine the present value. The option price is the highest of all the possible exercise rules. A rule such as "exercise when the stock price reaches a certain level at time $t$ without any dip in the price history" may be included. The optimal exercise rule is to search for such a rule that maximizes the value of an option. This would be an enormous search. For example, we can search through the binomial tree and explore all the possible early exercise rules. Given that any exercise rule can determine an option price, we can in principle search for a solution. However, this search to determine the optimal value seems mathematically intractable.

The *Bellman optimization* procedure provides a very elegant solution to this problem. Bellman's argument proposes that if the option price is given by the optimal exercise strategy, then that strategy has to be optimal over any period. This means that at any time before expiration, the optimal exercise rule must assume that it will be used in the subsequent time steps.

Following Bellman's argument, we must therefore solve the problem backward. At time $(n-1)$, we need to decide whether we would exercise the option. The optimal rule, therefore, states that we should exercise the option if the payoff is higher than the option price. Therefore, the option price at each node is the maximum of the option payoff if exercised early at that node and the rolled-back option value. We repeat this procedure iteratively backward from step $n-2$ to step 0.

The results show that the Bellman optimal decision depends on the current option price, which is determined by the stock price and other parameters of the option model. The optimal rule takes the value of waiting into account. Since the option can be exercised only once, we need to consider the probability of future stock price movements. Bellman's solution takes all the future contingencies into consideration and decides what action is optimal at present, and it does not look only at the immediate future.

In an American call option on a stock that does not pay dividends, there should be no optimal early exercise. The option holder should never exercise the option early, because he is always better off selling the option than exercising it. This assertion can be derived as follows. First, note that the option price should always be above the stock price net of the present value of the strike price.

$$C > S - PV(X) > S - X \qquad (3.1)$$

If not (i.e., $C \leq S - PV(X)$), we should buy the call option, short the stock, and invest the present value of the strike price at the risk-free rate. The net investment is the arbitrage profit, because the payoff at the expiration of this arbitrage position is always positive. At the expiration, the cash flow of the arbitrage position is $Max[S - X, 0] - S + X$, which is always positive or 0 regardless of $S$ relative to $X$. It follows that the call option value at any time must exceed the stock price net the exercise price. Thus, at any node point on the binomial lattice, the call option price is never below the value of earlier exercise $(S - X)$, and hence there should be no early exercise.

However, this is not the case with put options. By the same argument made above, put options should always trade above the present value of the exercise price net of the stock price.

$$P > PV(X) - S \tag{3.2}$$

But in this case, it is possible for the put option to have a value less than the strike price (not the present value of the strike price) net of the stock price (i.e., $X - S > P > PV(X) - S$). In these instances, early exercise of the put option is optimal, because the put option holder will get $X - S$ by exercising the option. However, the put option holder will get $P$ by selling it. Therefore, it is to his benefit to exercise early rather than sell it. (See figures 3.5–3.7.)

The value of the early exercise option of an American put option can be analyzed. Figure 3.8 plots the American put option and the European put option.

Both the American put option and the dividend-paying American call option have values for early exercise. As we have shown, the put-call parity does not allow any possibility of early exercise, and therefore the parity condition does not hold for American options. Unfortunately, most options on the exchanges are American, and any put-call parity trading strategies have to take early optimal exercise into consideration.

An American option offering holders early exercise is valuable in many ways. In practice, there are times when there may be liquidity problems in the option market. Selling an option at an inappropriate time may be expensive. An American option offers flexibility to the holder.

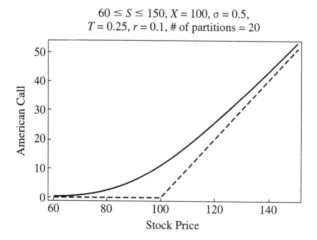

$60 \le S \le 150, X = 100, \sigma = 0.5,$
$T = 0.25, r = 0.1, \text{\# of partitions} = 20$

**Figure 3.5** Performance profile of an American call option. The American call option has an early exercise feature that the holder can exercise before the expiration date, which is the only difference from the European counterpart. To properly price the American options, we should determine the early exercise boundary, which is not a simple job. However, since the American call option on nondividend-paying stocks will never exercise early, we price the American call option as if it were the European call option. The stock price varies from 60 to 150 for simulation purposes. The continuously compounding risk-free rate is 10%. The variance of the stock returns is 0.5. The time to maturity is 0.25 year. We partition a period of 0.25 year into 20 subperiods to enhance the accuracy.

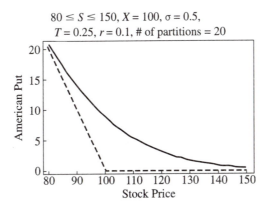

$80 \leq S \leq 150, X = 100, \sigma = 0.5,$
$T = 0.25, r = 0.1, \#\ \text{of partitions} = 20$

**Figure 3.6** Performance profile of an American put option. The American put option has an early exercise feature that the holders can exercise before the expiration date, which is the only difference from European counterparts. To properly price American options, we should determine the early exercise boundary, which is not a simple job. For this reason, we do not have a closed-form solution for American put options. The stock price varies from 80 to 150 for simulation purposes. The continuously compounding risk-free rate is 10%. The variance of the stock returns is 0.5. The time to maturity is 0.25 year. We partition a period of 0.25 year into 20 subperiods to enhance the accuracy.

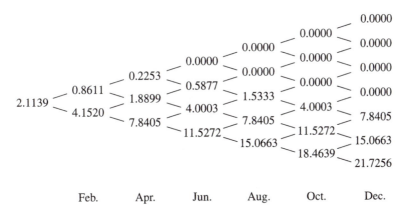

Feb.    Apr.    Jun.    Aug.    Oct.    Dec.

**Figure 3.7** The binomial lattice of an American put option. The underlying stock prices are the same as before. The exercise price of the American put option is 100. At maturity, prices are determined by $Max[X - S_T, 0]$. The prices at the months before maturity are determined by comparing the intrinsic values of $Max[100 - S_T, 0]$ with the values of the backward substitution. For example, 11.5272 in June is determined by comparing 11.527 ($= Max[100 - 88.473, 0]$) with 10.5321 ($= (7.8405 \times 0.61285 + 15.0663 \times 0.38715)/1.01005$). The continuously compounding risk-free rate is 6%.

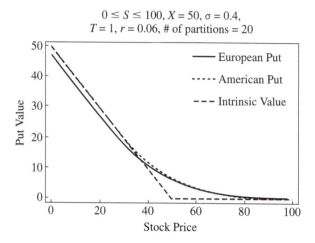

$0 \leq S \leq 100, X = 50, \sigma = 0.4,$
$T = 1, r = 0.06,$ # of partitions $= 20$

**Figure 3.8** American put vs. European put option. The only difference between the American put option and the European put option is whether the option holders have the right to exercise early. Therefore, the price differential between them will reflect the early exercise premium. The early exercise premium is higher when the option are in-the-money rather than out-of-the money. The stock price varies from 0 to 100 for simulation purposes. The continuously compounding risk-free rate is 6% per period. The volatility of the stock return is 0.4. The time to maturity is 1 year. We partition one period into 20 subperiods to enhance the accuracy.

## An Intuitive Explanation of the Bellman Optimization Solution

Determining an optimal dynamic rule is very valuable for financial decisions. For this reason, an extended discussion of the intuition behind this optimization method is in order. The intuition can be related by using an anecdote.

A physicist sitting in his backyard saw an apple on the grass. An ant was crawling from the bottom of the apple to the top. The physicist picked up the apple and traced the path of the ant on the apple. Next he took a rubber band and anchored its ends at the beginning of the path and the end of the path. He found that the rubber band lay on top of the ant's path, demonstrating that the ant took the shortest distance between two points.

This was somewhat surprising to the physicist. How could an ant possibly know that it was taking the shortest path between two points far apart, when it could feel and see only a rather short distance? How should the ant make the decision for each step forward?

Consider the ant that is standing on the apple, pondering the next step. Bellman's optimization solution says that the ant should take the next step that has the shortest distance between the point where it took the last step and the point where it will be in the next step. The ant has to make optimal local decisions. For a path that is optimal globally, from one point of the apple to another point far away, we must require the path to be optimal locally, ensuring that it is the shortest from the last step to the next step.

In pricing an option with an early optimal exercise feature, the thought process suggests that we need to make an optimal decision at each point to attain the optimal solution at large. Like the ant, we always seek the optimal decision at each local point. On the binomial lattice, we always choose the optimal decision among all the alternatives at each node point, as we have described.

## 3.4  COMPOUND OPTIONS

A *compound option* is an option on another option, and not on a stock. Stock risk is the only risk source for the compound option. The compound option of a stock can behave differently from other options. It tends to be more sensitive to the underlying stock price. Compound options can be a series of options, each option (choice) being an option on another option. These options can be put or call options.

One common compound option is the *retention option*. It has a series of strike prices. Instead of having an option to buy an asset (for example, stock) at a strike price $X$, a retention option offers the holder the opportunity to buy the asset in installments. However, if any installment payment is skipped, the holder loses the right to buy the

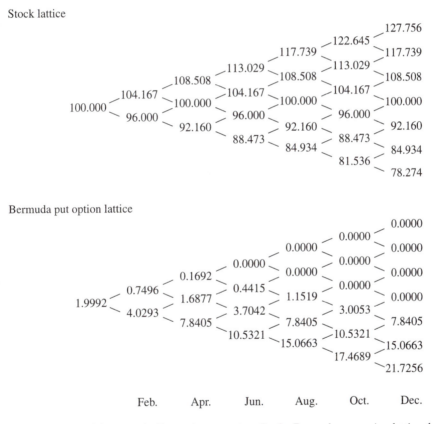

Figure 3.9 Binomial lattices of a Bermuda put option. In the Bermuda put option lattice the underlying stock prices are the same as those of the digital call option. The exercise months of the Bermuda put options are April, August, and December. At maturity, the Bermuda put options' prices are the intrinsic values of $Max[X - S_T, 0]$. The prices at the exercise months except maturity are determined by comparing the intrinsic values at the nodes with the values determined by backward substitution. For example, in August we get 15.0663 by comparing the intrinsic value of $Max[100 - 84.934, 0]$ with the backward substitution value of 13.0862 (= $(10.5321 \times 0.61285 + 17.4689 \times 0.38715)/1.01005$). The continuously compounding risk-free rate is 6%. The prices except in exercise months are determined only by backward substitution, because early exercise is not allowed.

asset. In other words, if we are offered an option to buy an asset, and we can pay for the asset in installments, and we can let the option expire, then this flexibility has value, and the value is the retention option price.

The retention option is a compound option; the decision to exercise the first option to pay the first installment has to depend on the optimal decisions that one will be making for all the subsequent periods. For example, if the asset value is significantly higher than the first payment, we should pay the first installment. The retention option spreads out the buy decision into a series of options. Of course, we have to take the cost of all the installments into account.

The valuation of a compound option using a rollback method is the same as that of an American option or a Bermuda option. The valuation begins from the expiration date, assuming that all the installments have been paid to retain the option. Then backward substitution determines the option price on the expiration date of the last option. The terminal condition of the next option is *Max* [option prices − strike prices, 0]. In rolling back the value of the options, we can determine the value of the option at the next expiration date. Then we will continue the backward substitution procedure until we reach the initial position. (See figures 3.9 and 3.10.)

There are many compound options. For example, the stock of a firm with coupon bonds outstanding is a compound option. Since the shareholders have to pay the coupons every six months and the principal at the bond maturity date in order to retain ownership of the firm, the stock could be treated as a compound option.

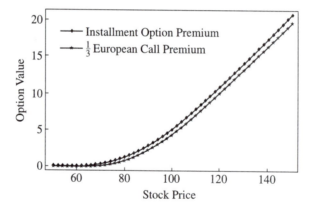

**Figure 3.10** An installment option is a European option in which the premium is paid in a series of installments rather than being paid up-front. If all installments are paid, the holder has the corresponding European option, but the holder has the right to terminate payments on any payment date, in which case the option lapses with no further payments. In other words, the holder has a series of opportunities to decide whether he continues holding the option or terminates the option. The corresponding European option holder does not have this flexibility. Stock price varies between 50 and 150. The volatility of the underlying stock is 0.2. The time-to-maturities of both options are 1. The continuously compounding risk-free interest rate is 0.1. We assume 3 equal installment payments, i.e., one up-front payment and two interim payments of the same amount. We partition 1 year into 6 periods for convenience purposes. For example, when the initial stock price is 100, the equal installment premium is 5.06037, which is greater than one third of the corresponding European call price, 4.31009 (= 1/3 × 12.9303), the difference between them being the value of a put option on the call.

# EXCEL MODEL EXERCISES

## E3.1    AMERICAN STOCK OPTION

### Definition

The parameters in specifying the binomial stock option movement are given in the Cox-Ross-Rubinstein model.

### Description of the Model

An American call option gives the holder the right and not the obligation to buy the underlying stock at the strike price anytime before the expiration of the option. An American option has an added feature that can only be valuable for the holder. The holder can always treat an American option as a European option without bothering to exercise early, and therefore an American option should be valued higher than or equal to the European option. The model is a binomial model framework of Cox-Ross-Rubinstein, assuming a perfect capital market with no arbitrage opportunity at any node point.

### Numerical Example

We divide the time to expiration by the number of subperiods to enhance accuracy. Therefore, the number of subperiods in a year is two in the numerical example, because the time to expiration is three years and the number of subperiods is six. If we change the time to expiration up to six years in the numerical example, the length of one period adjusts accordingly. For example, if we set the time to expiration to be four, the length of one period is eight months. The yield curve is flat at 6% for simplicity. See figure E3.1.

Let an American option have a strike price of 100 on an underlying stock priced at 100. The stock volatility is assumed to be 20% and the interest rate is flat at 6%. The option expires in three years. We divide one year into two subperiods. The American call option price is 21.933.

### Applications

1. The model prices an American put and call option.
2. The model determines the optimal exercise boundary of an American option.
3. Given the option price, the model determines the implied volatility of the stock.

### Case: Valuing Employee Stock Options

Pooja Patel is a vice president of a corporation in the human resource department. The CFO recently has decided to include the fair value of the employees' options on the company in their quarterly financial reporting. For accounting purposes, he has been asked to use a standard option pricing model to determine the fair value of the options, even though these options are not publicly traded, or cannot be traded at all. One of the standard models is called a "binomial lattice" model.

Pooja began with understanding the firm's employee option. There is only one type of option offered to the employees, irrespective of the seniority of the option holder.

| Inputs | | | | | | | | |
|---|---|---|---|---|---|---|---|---|
| Stock price ($) | S | 100 | | | | | | |
| Strike price ($) | K | 100 | | | | | | |
| Volatility | σ | 0.2 | | | | | | |
| Time to expiration (year) | T | 3 | 0 < T ≤ 6 | | | | | |
| Known dividend yield | δ | 0 | | | | | | |
| The number of periods | n | 6 | dt = T/n = 0.5 | | | | | |
| | | | | | | | | |
| Upward movement | u | 1.1519 | = exp(σ√dt) | | | | | |
| Downward movement | d | 0.8681 | = 1/u | | | | | |
| | | | | | | | | |
| Time period (year) | 0 | 1 | 2 | 3 | 4 | 5 | 6 | |
| Yield curve | 0.06 | 0.06 | 0.06 | 0.06 | 0.06 | 0.06 | 0.06 | |

| Outputs | | | | | | | |
|---|---|---|---|---|---|---|---|
| | | | | | | | 133.621 |
| | | | | | | 105.767 | 76.065 |
| | | | | | 81.889 | 55.802 | 32.690 |
| | | | | 61.453 | 38.513 | 18.146 | 0.000 |
| | | | 44.731 | 25.563 | 10.073 | 0.000 | 0.000 |
| | | 31.689 | 16.513 | 5.592 | 0.000 | 0.000 | 0.000 |
| American call option lattice | 21.933 | 10.456 | 3.104 | 0.000 | 0.000 | 0.000 | 0.000 |

Figure E3.1

A typical option has a time to expiration of five years. The strike price is determined to be the prevailing stock price. Therefore, on the grant date, the option is always at-the-money. There is a two-year vested period, where, during this period, the option holder cannot exercise the option, and if the option holder leaves the firm during this period, the option is worthless. After the vested period, the person can exercise the option anytime till the expiration date. And if the option holder leaves the company, voluntarily or otherwise, the option holder can exercise the option.

Since the company pays high dividends, Pooja believes that the option holders may early-exercise these options and therefore the American aspect of the option is valuable. He then investigated the historical database of the employees' behavior. He calculated that the attrition rate, the rate at which the employees leave the company voluntarily or not, was 10%. That is, if the year started with options granted to ten employees, one employee would leave the company the first year and 0.9 persons would leave the second year and so on. In valuing the options, Pooja first stated all the assumptions that he would make in a memo to the CFO. These assumptions would be discussed and he would have to justify them with the internal auditing department and the external auditors before they are finally approved by the CFO. For these reasons, he was careful in valuing the options objectively and simply, without sacrificing the accuracy of the model. These are his assumptions:

1. The "risk-free rates" are based on the U.S. STRIPS curve.
2. The stock volatility was calculated based on the historical daily return data of the past three years.

3. Given the same option with expiration of six years, one-tenth of the option holders know at the grant date that he/she would leave in one year. The same portion would leave each year for the next five years, and they would exercise the options optimally accordingly.

He proceeded to assume that there were five groups of people, with the $n$th group being the people leaving the company in the $n$th year. He then would calculate the value of the American option that does not allow any early exercise in the first two years. The total employee option cost would be the sum of the options of these five groups of people.

*He started to anticipate some of the questions that the auditors may ask him about the model. Is the model conservative in giving a higher option cost than it should? Is the use of historical data to estimate the future volatility appropriate? What else will the auditor ask?*

## Exercises and Answers

1. He was satisfied with all the assumptions, but he needed to know more about the "binomial lattice" model. He decided to investigate the pricing model further. Evaluate the stock option value, given the above assumptions.
   *Answer:*

   - Generate the stock price lattice assuming a high dividend yield of 10%.
   - The STRIPS curve is flat at 6%, and the stock volatility is 0.2.
   - The company has ten employees who joined the company at the same time.
   - The first option can be exercised from the first year, the second option can be exercised from the second year, and the rest of the options can be exercised from the third year.

   The employee stock option value is 73.068. See figure E3.2.
2. What is the put option value given the same assumptions of the numerical example?
   *Answer:* Given the same parameters on the binomial lattice, the American put option value is 7.665. See figure E3.3.
3. Does the put-call parity apply to the American options?
   *Answer:* No. The put-call parity does not apply to American options. The put-call parity assumes no interim payments other than the payments on the expiration date. However, possible early exercise would result in payments before the expiration.
   Considering the numerical example, the stock, the call, and the put option value are 100, 21.933, and 7.665 respectively. The present value of the strike is 83.53. According to the put-call parity, the call option price is the stock price net of the present value of the strike plus the put option, which is 24.138, which exceeds the value of the call option.
4. Determine the optimal exercise boundary of the American put and call options.
   *Answer:* It is essential to determine the optimal exercise boundary for pricing the American options, because we have an intrinsic value on the optimal exercise boundary.
   Note that for the American call option on the nondividend-paying stock, there is no early exercise of the American option even though the American option holder has the right to exercise early. The American option holder does not exercise early because the call option value is always greater than the intrinsic value. Such is not the case

**Outputs**

American option 1

| Time period (year) | 0 | 1 | 2 | 3 | 4 | 5 | 6 |
|---|---|---|---|---|---|---|---|
| | 7.5468112 | 12.5605301 | 20.8378005 | 32.8324605 | 46.0177403 | 60.5118237 | 76.4446258 |
| | | 1.08585896 | 1.90979704 | 3.35893046 | 5.90765072 | 10.3903125 | 18.2743697 |
| | | | 0 | 0 | 0 | 0 | 0 |
| | | | | 0 | 0 | 0 | 0 |
| | | | | | 0 | 0 | 0 |
| | | | | | | 0 | 0 |
| | | | | | | | 0 |

American option 2

| Time period (year) | 0 | 1 | 2 | 3 | 4 | 5 | 6 |
|---|---|---|---|---|---|---|---|
| | 7.5468112 | 12.5605301 | 20.8378005 | 32.8324605 | 46.0177403 | 60.5118237 | 76.4446258 |
| | | 1.08585896 | 1.90979704 | 3.35893046 | 5.90765072 | 10.3903125 | 18.2743697 |
| | | | 0 | 0 | 0 | 0 | 0 |
| | | | | 0 | 0 | 0 | 0 |
| | | | | | 0 | 0 | 0 |
| | | | | | | 0 | 0 |
| | | | | | | | 0 |

American option 3

| Time period (year) | 0 | 1 | 2 | 3 | 4 | 5 | 6 |
|---|---|---|---|---|---|---|---|
| | 7.25048852 | 12.039361 | 19.9211738 | 32.8324605 | 46.0177403 | 60.5118237 | 76.445 |
| | | 1.08585896 | 1.90979704 | 3.35893046 | 5.90765072 | 10.3903125 | 18.274 |
| | | | 0 | 0 | 0 | 0 | 0.000 |
| | | | | 0 | 0 | 0 | 0.000 |
| | | | | | 0 | 0 | 0.000 |
| | | | | | | 0 | 0.000 |
| | | | | | | | 0.000 |

| Employee stock option value | 73.0678983 | = option1+0.9*option2+8.1*option3 |
|---|---|---|

Figure E3.2

| | | | | | | | 0.000 |
|---|---|---|---|---|---|---|---|
| | | | | | | 0.000 | 0.000 |
| | | | | | 0.000 | 0.000 | 0.000 |
| | | | | 0.000 | 0.000 | 0.000 | 0.000 |
| | | | 0.945 | 2.275 | 5.477 | 13.188 | 24.636 |
| | | 3.339 | 6.775 | 13.273 | 24.636 | 34.575 | 43.203 |
| American put option lattice | 7.665 | 13.993 | 24.636 | 34.575 | 43.203 | 50.693 | 57.196 |

Figure E3.3

(a)

| | | | | | | | Payoff |
|---|---|---|---|---|---|---|---|
| | | | | | | Backward | Payoff |
| | | | | | Backward | Backward | Payoff |
| | | | | Backward | Backward | Backward | 0 |
| | | | Backward | Backward | Backward | Backward | 0 |
| | | Backward | Backward | Backward | Backward | Backward | 0 |
| Call option exercise boundary | Backward | Backward | Backward | Backward | Backward | Backward | 0 |

(b)

| | | | | | | | 0 |
|---|---|---|---|---|---|---|---|
| | | | | | | Backward | 0 |
| | | | | | Backward | Backward | 0 |
| | | | | Backward | Backward | Backward | Payoff |
| | | | Backward | Backward | Backward | Exercise | Payoff |
| | | Backward | Backward | Backward | Exercise | N/A | Payoff |
| Put option exercise boundary | Backward | Backward | Exercise | Exercise | N/A | N/A | Payoff |

Figure E3.4

for the put option. In figure E3.4, the analysis shows that the backward-substituted American put option value can be less than the intrinsic value on the early exercise boundary, and at those nodes on the early exercise boundary, the option holder will optimally early-exercise the put option. In figure E3.4, "Backward" represents that a backward substitution takes place on the node, and "Exercise" means that a backward-substituted value is replaced by the intrinsic value because of the early exercise.

5. Given the same parameters in the numerical example, calculate the European call option value and compare with the American counterpart to see which option is more valuable. Confirm that the American put option is more valuable than the European put option on the early exercise boundary. Finally, calculate the early exercise premium of the American put option.

*Answer:* The American call option is the same as the European call option, because there is no early exercise for the American call option. However, this is not the case for the American put option. For example, at period 5 and state 2, the backward-substituted value from period 6 is 10.232 and the intrinsic value at that node is 13.188. Therefore, the backward-substituted value is replaced by the intrinsic value for the American put option value at that node. See figure E3.5.

| | | | | | | | 133.621 |
|---|---|---|---|---|---|---|---|
| | | | | | | 105.767 | 76.065 |
| | | | | | 81.889 | 55.802 | 32.690 |
| | | | | 61.453 | 38.513 | 18.146 | 0.000 |
| | | | 44.731 | 25.563 | 10.073 | 0.000 | 0.000 |
| | | 31.689 | 16.513 | 5.592 | 0.000 | 0.000 | 0.000 |
| American call option lattice | 21.933 | 10.456 | 3.104 | 0.000 | 0.000 | 0.000 | 0.000 |
| | | | | | | | 133.621 |
| | | | | | | 105.767 | 76.065 |
| | | | | | 81.889 | 55.802 | 32.690 |
| | | | | 61.453 | 38.513 | 18.146 | 0.000 |
| | | | 44.731 | 25.563 | 10.073 | 0.000 | 0.000 |
| | | 31.689 | 16.513 | 5.592 | 0.000 | 0.000 | 0.000 |
| European call option lattice | 21.933 | 10.456 | 3.104 | 0.000 | 0.000 | 0.000 | 0.000 |
| | | | | | | | 0.000 |
| | | | | | | 0.000 | 0.000 |
| | | | | | 0.000 | 0.000 | 0.000 |
| | | | | 0.000 | 0.000 | 0.000 | 0.000 |
| | | | 0.945 | 2.275 | 5.477 | 13.188 | 24.636 |
| | | 3.339 | 6.775 | 13.273 | 24.636 | 34.575 | 43.203 |
| American put option lattice | 7.665 | 13.993 | 24.636 | 34.575 | 43.203 | 50.693 | 57.196 |
| | | | | | | | 0.000 |
| | | | | | | 0.000 | 0.000 |
| | | | | | 0.000 | 0.000 | 0.000 |
| | | | | 0.000 | 0.000 | 0.000 | 0.000 |
| | | | 0.733 | 1.765 | 4.250 | 10.232 | 24.636 |
| | | 2.569 | 5.205 | 10.173 | 18.813 | 31.619 | 43.203 |
| European put option lattice | 5.461 | 9.714 | 16.432 | 25.968 | 37.379 | 47.738 | 57.196 |
| The early exercise premium of the American put option | | 2.205 | | | | | |

Figure E3.5

6. We consider a European call option and an American call option on the nondividend-paying stock. Using the backward substitution method, calculate the two option prices. Since the American call option has an early exercise feature as compared to the European call option, the value of the American call option is at least equal to or greater than the European call option. Explain why the two options have the same value regardless of the early exercise feature of the American call option.

*Answer:* If the intrinsic value is larger than the option market value, the American option holder will exercise the American option. Otherwise, it is more profitable to sell the American call option rather than exercise. Since the American call option on the nondividend-paying stock is always larger than its intrinsic value, the American call option holder would not exercise it. Therefore, the American call option will never be early-exercised, which leads to the same value as the European counterpart.

7. Consider the put option in question 2; the present value of 100 is 83.53. Suppose that the stock is now trading below 16.47 (= 100 − 83.53). Explain why you would early-exercise at this stock price level?

*Answer:* The put option holder receives positive payment when the stock price is below the exercise price, and the payment from the exercise is highest when the stock price reaches the lowest possible value of zero. Therefore, in this example, the highest payoff from exercising the put option at expiration is 100. If the stock trades below 16.47, the put option holder should exercise the option and receive a payment greater than 83.53, the strike net the stock price. When investing the proceedings of 83.53 to buy a zero-coupon bond that matures on the expiration date, the investor will receive the principal on the expiration date. The principal of the bond, 100, is equal to the highest possible payoff of the put option at expiration. Hence the option holder should exercise the option in this case.

## Further Exercises

1. An American option has a strike price of 100 on an underlying stock priced at 100. The stock volatility is assumed to be 30% and the interest rate is flat at 6%. The option expires in three years. Calculate the American call option price and compare with the numerical example. The only difference between this exercise and the numerical example is the volatility. The number of subperiods per year is 2.
   *Answer:* The American call option price is 27.335, whereas the American call option price in the numerical example is 21.933. Since the volatility is higher in this exercise than that in the numerical example, we can expect that the American call in this exercise should be higher. See figure E3.6.
2. Repeat the numerical example, but with the risk-free rate of return at 7%.
   *Answer:* The American call option price is 23.536, whereas the American call option price in the numerical example is 21.933. Since the risk-free rate is higher in this exercise than that in the numerical example, we can expect that the American call in this exercise should be higher. From these exercises, we can see that the higher the risk-free rate is, the higher the option premium is. See figure E3.7.
3. Determine the optimal exercise boundary of the American put option when the risk-free rate is 7%, and compare it with the optimal exercise boundary in question 4.
   *Answer:* See figure E3.8.

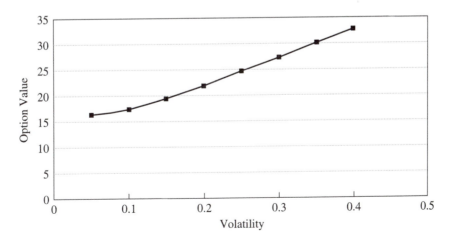

**Figure E3.6**

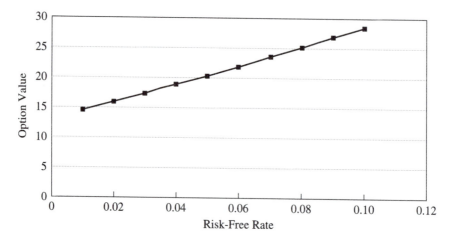

**Figure E3.7**

| Put option exercise boundary | | | | | | | 0 |
|---|---|---|---|---|---|---|---|
| | | | | | | Backward | 0 |
| | | | | | Backward | Backward | 0 |
| | | | | Backward | Backward | Backward | Payoff |
| | | | Backward | Backward | Backward | Exercise | Payoff |
| | | Backward | Backward | Exercise | Exercise | N/A | Payoff |
| | Backward | Backward | Exercise | N/A | N/A | N/A | Payoff |

**Figure E3.8**

# E3.2   COMPOUND OPTION

## Definition

A compound option is an option on an option. The underlying option can be a compound option itself.

## Description of the Model

The Geske model of the compound option is an extension of the Black-Scholes model that values the compound option in a continuous time framework, providing a closed-form solution. The model presented here is an extension of the Cox-Ross-Rubinstein binomial lattice model. Therefore, the model assumes a perfect capital market with no arbitrage opportunity at each node point.

## Numerical Example

In the market, the stock price is observed to be 100 with volatility of 10%, and the risk-free rate is 6%. The option expires in one year. The holder of the option can buy the underlying option at the end of the fourth month at 20, and the underlying option

| Inputs | | | | | | | | |
|---|---|---|---|---|---|---|---|---|
| Stock price ($) | S | 100 | | | | | | |
| | K(6) | 50 | | | | | | |
| Strike price at period n ($) | K(4) | 30 | | | | | | |
| | K(2) | 20 | | | | | | |
| | sum | 100 | | | | | | |
| Volatility | σ | 0.1 | | | | | | |
| Time to expiration (year) | T | 1 | | | | | | |
| Risk-free rate | r | 0.06 | | | | | | |
| The number of periods | n | 6 | dt = T/n = 0.1667 | | | | | |
| | | | | | | | | |
| Upward movement | u | 1.0417 | = exp(σ√dt) | | | | | |
| Downward movement | d | 0.9600 | = 1/u | | | | | |
| Risk-neutral probability | p | 0.6128 | = (exp(rdt)-d)/(u-d) | | | | | |

| Outputs | | | | | | | | |
|---|---|---|---|---|---|---|---|---|
| | | | | | | | | 77.7556 |
| | | | | | | | 73.1425 | 67.7389 |
| | | | | | | 38.7290 | 63.5265 | 58.5076 |
| | | | | | 34.8053 | 29.4976 | 54.6645 | 50.0000 |
| | | | | 11.0621 | 25.9432 | 20.9901 | 46.4972 | 42.1595 |
| | | | 7.6911 | 2.5546 | 17.7760 | 13.1495 | 38.9704 | 34.9337 |
| Compound option lattice | | 5.2607 | 1.5500 | 0.0000 | 10.2491 | 5.9238 | 32.0336 | 28.2744 |
| Time period | | 0 | 1 | 2 | 3 | 4 | 5 | 6 |

Figure E3.9

provides the holder the right to buy an option at the end of the eighth month at 30, where the underlying option offers the holder the right to buy the stock at 50 at the end of the year. We divide one year into six subperiods. Therefore, each subperiod represents two months. The value of the compound option is 5.2607. See figure E3.9.

## Applications

1. The compound option premium offers the option holder the right to retain the possibility of buying the stock as the stock prices evolve over time.
2. The compound option can be used to value coupon bonds that have default risks.
3. The compound option is equivalent to a retention option in corporate finance.

## Case: Project Financing and the Compound Option

Global Mining is a precious-metal mining company based in Australia. The company has found a large deposit base of gold in the basin. However, a significant infrastructure has to be built before the mining can start. The infrastructure will take six years to build. Given the market price of gold and other factors, if Global Mining ignores the infrastructure cost, the find should be worth around $10 billion today. But of course, the value of the find changes over time depending on the gold price and other factors. The management believes that the volatility of this estimate is around 10% annually.

Bob Stanley is the president of the project financing company, a subsidiary of Global Mining. The financing company is responsible for seeking financing for projects including this infrastructure cost. He goes to Tokyo to meet a potential investor. The investor is a development fund that specializes in long-term direct investment on development projects. The fund typically holds an equity position of the projects, and the fund managers are familiar with the mining business. Naoki Takahashi is the managing director of the fund. The fund has studied the proposal ahead of the meeting in detail, and Takahashi-san began the meeting with his concerns about investing in the project. "We have carefully evaluated your project. But we have some concerns. We tend to agree with your estimate of $10 billion valuation. But the infrastructure project has five tranches in the investment payments. We have to invest according to this schedule. Year 6 is $4.5 billion, and then years 4, 2, and 0 are $3, $2, and $0.5 billion, respectively. The value of the deposit can barely cover the present value of the costs. What do you think?" Bob is quick to respond. "At each installment of the payment, we, the equity holders, can abandon the project if the gold price has come down and the cost of continuing the building of the infrastructure would not justify the project." Bob then proceeds to show details of Global Mining's calculations.

The methodology Global Mining used is based on a compound option. This means that at the beginning of each phase of the installment, the firm together with the investors has the option of not proceeding with the project by not exercising the option, paying the installment costs. He has calculated the value of the project to be $2.7273 billion. With a net of $0.5 billion, the net present value of the project is $2.2273 billion. Bob then comes to his bottom line in a matter-of-fact way: "We will give you 18.33% (= 0.5/2.7273) interest in the project for $500 million, which we will use to pay for the initial installment. "Global thinks that this is a fair deal. What do you think?"

*Takahashi-san suggested that their team would evaluate the project further and would like to discuss the financing further. He reasons that there are many assumptions made in this capital budgeting problem. "What should I tell my team to look into? How should we go about making a decision on this proposal? I should make an outline for my team." Takahashi-san wondered.*

## Exercises and Answers

1.  What if the volatility is not 10%? What if it is higher, like 40%? What would be the compound option value? See figure E3.10.
    *Answer:* The compound option value is $2.2273 billion when the volatility is 10%. The 10% volatility is assumed in the above case study. The compound option value is $3.3965 billion when the volatility is 40%. See figures E3.11 and E3.12.

2.  Given question 1 above (with 40% volatility), if the risk-free rate is 0%, what is the compound option value? See figure E3.13.
    *Answer:* If we assume a zero interest rate, the compound option value is $2.3131 billion, which is less than $3.3965 billion. If the risk-free rate goes down, we should put aside more money for the exercise price, which makes the option less attractive. On top of that, if the risk-free rate goes down, the discount rate also goes down, which makes the option more valuable. Since in this case the former effect is dominating the latter effect, the option price goes down when the risk-free interest rate goes down. See figure E3.14.

3.  Given the compound option in question 2, the present value of all the strike prices is 10. Calculate the standard European call option expiring in one year on the underlying stock with a strike price of 10. Does the standard call option or the compound option have a higher premium?

## Inputs

| | | | |
|---|---|---|---|
| Stock price ($) | S | 10 | |
| Strike price at period n ($) | K(6) | 4.5 | |
| | K(4) | 3 | |
| | K(2) | 2 | |
| | K(0) | 0.5 | |
| | sum | 10 | |
| Volatility | σ | 0.1 | |
| Time to expiration (year) | T | 6 | |
| Risk-free rate | r | 0.06 | |
| The number of periods | n | 6 | dt = T/n = 1 |
| Upward movement | u | 1.1052 | = exp(σ√dt) |
| Downward movement | d | 0.9048 | = 1/u |
| Risk-neutral probability | p | 0.7837 | = (exp(rdt)-d)/(u-d) |

## Outputs

| | 0 | 1 | 2 | 3 | 4 | 5 | 6 |
|---|---|---|---|---|---|---|---|
| | | | | | | | 13.7212 |
| | | | | | | 12.2493 | 10.4182 |
| | | | | | 7.9271 | 9.2606 | 7.7140 |
| | | | | 6.9146 | 5.2229 | 6.8138 | 5.5000 |
| | | | 4.0134 | 4.4677 | 3.0089 | 4.8104 | 3.6873 |
| | | 3.3287 | 1.7994 | 2.4644 | 1.1962 | 3.1702 | 2.2032 |
| Compound option lattice | 2.2273 | 1.3281 | 0.0000 | 0.8828 | 0.0000 | 1.8274 | 0.9881 |
| Time period | 0 | 1 | 2 | 3 | 4 | 5 | 6 |

Figure E3.10

## Outputs

| | 0 | 1 | 2 | 3 | 4 | 5 | 6 |
|---|---|---|---|---|---|---|---|
| | | | | | | | 105.7318 |
| | | | | | | 69.6526 | 45.0303 |
| | | | | | 42.5392 | 28.9632 | 17.7554 |
| | | | | 26.6172 | 15.2643 | 10.6803 | 5.5000 |
| | | | 14.0552 | 8.3350 | 3.0105 | 2.4686 | 0.0000 |
| | | 7.4949 | 2.4071 | 1.3512 | 0.0000 | 0.0000 | 0.0000 |
| Compound option lattice | 3.3965 | 1.0804 | 0.0000 | 0.0000 | 0.0000 | 0.0000 | 0.0000 |
| Time period | 0 | 1 | 2 | 3 | 4 | 5 | 6 |

Figure E3.11

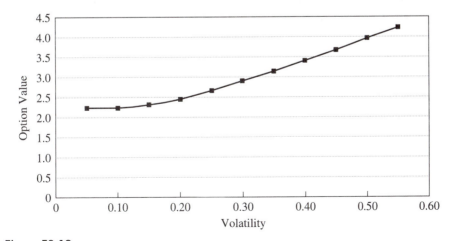

Figure E3.12

| Outputs | | | | | | | |
|---|---|---|---|---|---|---|---|
| | | | | | | | 105.7318 |
| | | | | | | 69.3906 | 45.0303 |
| | | | | | 42.0303 | 28.7012 | 17.7554 |
| | | | | 25.7012 | 14.7554 | 10.4182 | 5.5000 |
| | | | 12.7563 | 7.4197 | 2.5024 | 2.2072 | 0.0000 |
| | | 6.0645 | 1.5788 | 1.0042 | 0.0000 | 0.0000 | 0.0000 |
| Compound option lattice | 2.3131 | 0.6336 | 0.0000 | 0.0000 | 0.0000 | 0.0000 | 0.0000 |
| Time period | 0 | 1 | 2 | 3 | 4 | 5 | 6 |

**Figure E3.13**

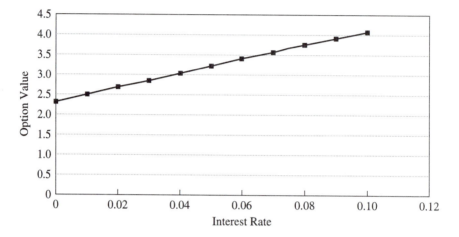

**Figure E3.14**

| | | | | | | | 100.2318 |
|---|---|---|---|---|---|---|---|
| | | | | | | 63.8906 | 39.5303 |
| | | | | | 39.5303 | 23.2012 | 12.2554 |
| | | | | 23.2012 | 12.2554 | 4.9182 | 0.0000 |
| | | | 12.9629 | 6.0999 | 1.9738 | 0.0000 | 0.0000 |
| | | 6.9516 | 2.9222 | 0.7921 | 0.0000 | 0.0000 | 0.0000 |
| European call option | 3.6058 | 1.3630 | 0.3179 | 0.0000 | 0.0000 | 0.0000 | 0.0000 |

**Figure E3.15**

*Answer:* The European call option is more valuable than the compound call option. See figure E3.15.

4. Suppose a car dealer offers to sell a new car model, which has not been released to the showroom yet. The car will be delivered in one year. The car is expected to be priced at $105,748.8. The dealer offers the prospective buyer the right to buy the car at this price when the car is delivered if he pays $16,082.20 to the dealer now as a non-recoverable down payment. Alternatively the prospective buyer can pay $16,082.20 in installments such that the buyer pays $16,082.20/3 at periods 0, 2, and 4 to retain the right to buy the car at 105,748.8 at period 6. If the buyer is willing to choose one

| | | | |
|---|---|---|---|
| Stock price ($) | S | 105748.8 | |
| Strike price ($) | K | 105748.8 | |
| Volatility | σ | 0.4 | |
| Time to expiration (year) | T | 1 | |
| Continuous compounding rate | r | 0 | |
| The number of periods | n | 6 | dt = T/n = 0.1667 |
| Equal installments | ep | 6850.6456 | This is a control variable for solver. |
| Installment periods | | 0, 2, 4 | The initial value is set to be the European call option value divided by the number of installments. |
| Upward movement | u | 1.1774 | exp(σ√dt) |
| Downward movement | d | 0.8493 | 1/u |
| Risk-neutral probability | p | 0.4593 | (exp(rdt)-d)/(u-d) |

**Outputs**

| | 0 | 1 | 2 | 3 | 4 | 5 | 6 |
|---|---|---|---|---|---|---|---|
| | | | | | | 133514.1249 | 175956.7475 |
| | | | | | 90615.3925 | 66849.0667 | 97466.0381 |
| | | | | 59998.4211 | 33994.2967 | 18758.6790 | 40844.9423 |
| | | | 29662.6856 | 16566.5771 | 1764.5713 | 0.0000 | 0.0000 |
| | | 14269.7867 | 1196.0291 | 810.4070 | 0.0000 | 0.0000 | 0.0000 |
| Installment option lattice | 6850.6456 | 549.2951 | 0.0000 | 0.0000 | 0.0000 | 0.0000 | 0.0000 |

| Time period | 0 | 1 | 2 | 3 | 4 | 5 | 6 |
|---|---|---|---|---|---|---|---|

Finding the no-arbitrage value of the equal premium, ep, where V = the fair value of installment option

| ep = V(S, ep) | 0.0000 |
|---|---|

This is a target cell for solver.

We have to minimize the difference between the equal premium and the installment option value to find the no-arbitrage value of the installment premium.

Installment option value > (European option value)/3, where 3 is the number of installments.

| Installment option value | 6850.6456 |
|---|---|
| (European call option)/3 | 5360.7328 |

Figure E3.16

from the two options, which one should the buyer take? If the second option is more valuable, how much more added to the installment is the buyer willing to pay for the second option?

*Answer:* The buyer should take the second option because the second option is more valuable than the first. We can compare the installment option value with the European option value divided by the number of installments. The European option value divided by three is 5,360.7328 and the installment option value is 6,850.6456. The installment option is more valuable because it is more flexible as compared to the European option. See figure E3.16.

## Further Exercises

1. In the market, the stock price is observed to be 100 with volatility of 10%, and the risk-free rate is 6%. The option expires in one year. The holder of the option can buy the underlying option at the end of the second period at 10, at the end of the fourth period at 20, and at the end of the fifth period at 30, where the underlying option offers the holder the right to buy the stock at 40 at the end of the year. Calculate the compound option value.

   *Answer:* The compound option value is 5.5078.

2. Increase the risk-free rate and the volatility to 7% and 12%, respectively. Recalculate the compound option value and compare the answers with those in question 1.

   *Answer:* The compound option value is 6.4523, which is larger than the compound option in question 1.

## E3.3   DIGITAL OPTION

### Definitions

The digital option pays a binary payoff when the underlying stock prices are larger than the strike price. Even though the binary payoff is usually $1, it can be any amount depending on the digital option contracts.

### Description of the Model

The digital option pays a binary payoff amount whenever the underlying stock price exceeds the strike price at expiration. The model is an extension of the Cox-Ross-Rubinstein model for a specific payoff of the option at the expiration date. Therefore, the model assumes a perfect capital market in a discrete time framework, with no arbitrage opportunity at each node point.

### Numerical Example

The market-observed risk-free rate is 6%, with the stock price at 100 with volatility of 20%. The digital option expires in one year, with a digital payment of $1 and strike of 100. Then the digital option value is 0.3989. See figure E3.17.

| Inputs | | | | | | | |
|---|---|---|---|---|---|---|---|
| Stock price ($) | S | 100 | | | | | |
| Strike price ($) | K | 100 | | | | | |
| Volatility | σ | 0.2 | | | | | |
| Time to expiration (year) | T | 1 | | | | | |
| Risk-free rate | r | 0.06 | | | | | |
| The number of periods | n | 6 | dt = T/n = 0.1667 | | | | |
| Binary payoff ($) | Q | 1 | | | | | |
| | | | | | | | |
| Upward movement | u | 1.0851 | $= \exp(\sigma\sqrt{dt})$ | | | | |
| Downward movement | d | 0.9216 | = 1/u | | | | |
| Risk-neutral probability | p | 0.5411 | = (exp(rdt)-d)/(u-d) | | | | |

| Outputs | | | | | | | |
|---|---|---|---|---|---|---|---|
| | | | | | | | 1.0000 |
| | | | | | | 0.9900 | 1.0000 |
| | | | | | 0.9802 | 0.9900 | 1.0000 |
| | | | | 0.8766 | 0.7738 | 0.5357 | 0.0000 |
| | | | 0.7172 | 0.5449 | 0.2870 | 0.0000 | 0.0000 |
| | | 0.5485 | 0.3617 | 0.1537 | 0.0000 | 0.0000 | 0.0000 |
| Digital option lattice | 0.3989 | 0.2312 | 0.0823 | 0.0000 | 0.0000 | 0.0000 | 0.0000 |
| Time period | 0 | 1 | 2 | 3 | 4 | 5 | 6 |

| Interim Calculations | | | | | | | |
|---|---|---|---|---|---|---|---|
| | | | | | | | 163.2150 |
| | | | | | | 150.4181 | 138.6245 |
| | | | | | 138.6245 | 127.7556 | 117.7389 |
| | | | | 127.7556 | 117.7389 | 108.5076 | 100.0000 |
| | | | 117.7389 | 108.5076 | 100.0000 | 92.1595 | 84.9337 |
| | | 108.5076 | 100.0000 | 92.1595 | 84.9337 | 78.2744 | 72.1373 |
| Stock lattice | 100.0000 | 92.1595 | 84.9337 | 78.2744 | 72.1373 | 66.4814 | 61.2689 |

Figure E3.17

## Applications

1. Using a portfolio of digital options, we can construct a synthetic option with a certain payoff function.
2. In writing the option, the seller can limit the potential loss.

## Case: IPO Incentive Option and Executive Option Design

Diwan Technologies is a software company providing application software to financial companies. In recent years, the company has seen significant growth in its sales and is contemplating bringing the company to the public in one year. To implement such a corporate strategy, the firm is recruiting a chief financial officer to prepare the firm for listing, with the goal that the firm valuation at the initial public offering (IPO) can reach a certain target value. Therefore, the firm offers the incoming CFO an incentive employee option. If the stock closing price on the day of the IPO is at or above $30, the CFO would receive $1 million. The option expires on the expected IPO day, one year from the commencement of the employment. While the board of directors is contemplating such an offer, a number of questions arise.

The chairman favored a standard employee option, one-year vested period, expiring in five years. He argued that the standard employee option was simple to implement and the option would provide the appropriate incentive for the CFO. He suggested that the director of human resources should prepare a memo providing the pros and cons of these two alternatives of the option plan.

*"Can you describe to us with no mathematics why we would use a digital option and not a standard employee option for our CFO?"* the chairman gave his order.

## Exercises and Answers

1. Suppose the volatility of the underlying stock has increased to 40%. What is the option value, where the option is described in the numerical example?

   *Answer:* It is known that the higher volatility leads to the higher option prices, because the option holders can take only the upside return and the higher volatility brings more upside returns.

   However, the binary option value decreases as the volatility increases, because the probability that the stock price will exceed the exercise price decreases as the volatility goes up, and the binary option payoffs are constant regardless of the stock prices. The reason for having a lower probability is that when the volatility increases, the asset becomes riskier and the asset's distribution should shift to the left to have a risk-free rate of return in the risk-neutral world. To understand this statement, recall that every risky asset has the risk-free rate of return in the risk-neutral world. For an asset with higher volatility to have the risk-free rate in the risk-neutral world, its distribution should be lowered. When its distribution shifts to the left as the volatility increases, the probability that the stock price exceeds the exercise price will decrease. For example, what would happen to a digital option when its stock volatility increases to infinity? The answer is that the digital option price will converge to zero. See figure E3.18.

2. Using the numerical example (where 20% volatility is used), what is the value of the digital option if the digital payment is $2 million instead of $1 million?

   *Answer:* Since the payoff at each state has doubled, we can see that the digital option value will also double, as the calculation confirms. See figure E3.19.

3. One board member suggests a hedging strategy on the employee option. He argues that if Diwan were traded in the market, its stock would be similar to that of its competitor, McAlister, Inc., a publicly traded company. Therefore, he thinks that Diwan should use McAlister stock to hedge this employee option. Describe how Diwan would use the digital options to replicate a European stock option with expiration of one year, strike at 100. Verify the goodness of the replication with the digital model.

   *Answer:* The only difference between a European option and a digital option is the cash flow when exercised. The European option generates the difference between the stock price and the exercise price, while the digital option gives the option holder only $1 regardless of the stock price. Therefore, we can duplicate the payoff of the European call option with the digital options.

   The European call option value is 10.6623. To duplicate the European call option, we need three digital options whose exercise prices are 100, 117.7389, and 138.6245. The digital option prices and the number of the corresponding digital options are

| Outputs | | | | | | | |
|---|---|---|---|---|---|---|---|
| | | | | | | | 1.0000 |
| | | | | | | 0.9900 | 1.0000 |
| | | | | | 0.9802 | 0.9900 | 1.0000 |
| | | | | 0.8416 | 0.7252 | 0.4850 | 0.0000 |
| | | | 0.6458 | 0.4705 | 0.2353 | 0.0000 | 0.0000 |
| | | 0.4576 | 0.2858 | 0.1141 | 0.0000 | 0.0000 | 0.0000 |
| Digital option lattice | 0.3061 | 0.1666 | 0.0553 | 0.0000 | 0.0000 | 0.0000 | 0.0000 |
| Time period | 0 | 1 | 2 | 3 | 4 | 5 | 6 |

| Interim Calculations | | | | | | | |
|---|---|---|---|---|---|---|---|
| | | | | | | | 266.3912 |
| | | | | | | 226.2559 | 192.1675 |
| | | | | | 192.1675 | 163.2150 | 138.6245 |
| | | | | 163.2150 | 138.6245 | 117.7389 | 100.0000 |
| | | | 138.6245 | 117.7389 | 100.0000 | 84.9337 | 72.1373 |
| | | 117.7389 | 100.0000 | 84.9337 | 72.1373 | 61.2689 | 52.0379 |
| Stock lattice | 100.0000 | 84.9337 | 72.1373 | 61.2689 | 52.0379 | 44.1977 | 37.5388 |

Figure E3.18

| Outputs | | | | | | | |
|---|---|---|---|---|---|---|---|
| | | | | | | | 2.0000 |
| | | | | | | 1.9801 | 2.0000 |
| | | | | | 1.9604 | 1.9801 | 2.0000 |
| | | | | 1.7533 | 1.5475 | 1.0714 | 0.0000 |
| | | | 1.4344 | 1.0898 | 0.5739 | 0.0000 | 0.0000 |
| | | 1.0971 | 0.7235 | 0.3074 | 0.0000 | 0.0000 | 0.0000 |
| Digital option lattice | 0.7978 | 0.4624 | 0.1647 | 0.0000 | 0.0000 | 0.0000 | 0.0000 |
| Time period | 0 | 1 | 2 | 3 | 4 | 5 | 6 |

Figure E3.19

given in the second and the third column, respectively. The fourth column gives the total amount by multiplying the second column with the third column. The sum of the total amount for the three digital options is equal to the European call option. See figure E3.20.

4. Diwan's board of directors further considers other performance-based options for the incoming CFO. The payments to provide incentives to the CFO have to balance with the cost to the company. Describe how Diwan would use the digital options to synthetically create an option that has a payoff $Max[(S - 100)^2, 0]$, where $S$ is the stock price on the expiration date, and the option expires in one year. What is the value of the portfolio? What is the price of the synthetic option?

*Answer:* As we have explained in question 3, we can duplicate the payoff of the European option with a portfolio of digital options. Even though the payoff of the European option is not linear to the stock price, we can duplicate the European option with the same degree of accuracy as the linear case.

| ① | ② | ③ | ②x③ |
|---|---|---|---|
| Strike | Digital Price | Required # | Total Amount |
|  | 0.3989 |  |  |
| 138.6245 | 0.0236 | 24.5905 | 0.5811 |
| 117.7389 | 0.1439 | 20.8856 | 3.0053 |
| 100.0000 | 0.3989 | 17.7389 | 7.0760 |
| 84.9337 | 0.6873 | 0.0000 | 0.0000 |
| 72.1373 | 0.8707 | 0.0000 | 0.0000 |
| 61.2689 | 0.9330 | 0.0000 | 0.0000 |
| 0.0000 | 0.9418 | 0.0000 | 0.0000 |
| European option value || | 10.6623 |

Figure E3.20

| ① | ② | ③ | ②x③ |
|---|---|---|---|
| Strike | Digital Price | Required # | Total Amount |
|  | 0.3989 |  |  |
| 138.6245 | 0.0236 | 2504.2800 | 59.1794 |
| 117.7389 | 0.1439 | 1177.1830 | 169.3869 |
| 100.0000 | 0.3989 | 314.6687 | 125.5200 |
| 84.9337 | 0.6873 | -226.9936 | -156.0079 |
| 72.1373 | 0.8707 | -549.3352 | -478.3214 |
| 61.2689 | 0.9330 | -723.7699 | -675.2530 |
| 0.0000 | 0.9418 | 1500.0988 | 1412.7398 |
| European option value || | 457.2437 |

Figure E3.21

Since the payoff is nonlinear with respect to the stock price, we need seven digital options to duplicate the option with the final payoff of $Max[(S - 100)^2, 0]$. We can see that the option is duplicated with seven digital options. See figure E3.21.

## Further Exercises

1. Consider the above numerical example. Suppose the option pays $1 when the stock price is above 100 but less than or equal to 120 and $2 when the stock price exceeds 120. What is the price of the option, using the Excel model in the numerical example?
   *Answer:* The digital option price is 0.5428.
2. Consider the above numerical example. Suppose that the time to expiration increases to ten years. Can we calculate the digital option price?
   *Answer:* The digital option price is 0.3409.
3. Does the digital option price increase or decrease with a rise in interest rates for question 2?
   *Answer:* We have to consider two effects on the digital option value when we increase the risk-free rate. The positive effect of the interest rate increase on the digital option value comes from the smaller present value of the exercise price. The negative effect comes from the smaller present value of the final payoff on expiration. When interest rate is less than 7%, the positive effect is dominating the negative effect. However, the negative effect is dominating beyond 7%. See figure E3.22.

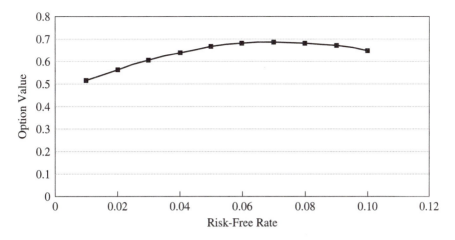

**Figure E3.22**

4. Suppose that the above option is an American call option. What would be the price of the option?
   *Answer:* The American call option price is 1.4540, which is larger than the corresponding European option.
5. A European put digital option is defined as an option that offers the holder the right and not the obligation to receive a fixed amount, say $1, if the stock price is below the exercise price at expiration. What is the price of the option in the numerical example if the option is a put option and not a call option?
   *Answer:* The European put digital option price is 0.2545.

## E3.4   GREEKS (DELTA, GAMMA, THETA, VEGA, RHO, OMEGA): A BINOMIAL LATTICE VERSUS A CLOSED-FORM SOLUTION

### Definitions

Delta ($\Delta$) is the price sensitivity of the option to the stock price. Gamma ($\Gamma$) is the sensitivity of the delta to the changes of the stock price. Vega ($\nu$) is the price sensitivity of the option to the changes of the stock volatility. Theta ($\Theta$) is the price decay of the option over time. Rho ($\rho$) is the price sensitivity of the option to the changes of the risk-free rate. Omega ($\Omega$) is the elasticity of the option to the underlying asset. Sensitivity to dividend yield is the price sensitivity of the option to the change of the dividend yield.

### Description of the Model

The Greeks describe the behavior of the options given small changes of the market parameters or the terms and conditions of the contracts. We can calculate the Greeks by a closed form that is derived from the Black-Scholes model or by a simulation based on a binomial lattice. Since the Black-Scholes model is only valid for a European option,

| Inputs | | |
|---|---|---|
| Stock price (S) | 100 | |
| Strike price (K) | 100 | |
| Time to expiration (T) | 1 | |
| Stock volatility (σ) | 0.2 | |
| Risk-free rate (r) | 0.04 | |
| Dividend yield (δ) | 0 | |
| **Outputs** | | |
| | Call | Put |
| Price | 9.92504 | 6.00399 |
| Δ (Delta) | 0.61791 | -0.38209 |
| Γ (Gamma) | 0.01907 | 0.01907 |
| ν (Vega) | 38.13878 | 38.13878 |
| Θ (Theta) | -5.88852 | -2.04536 |
| ρ (Rho) | 51.86609 | -44.21285 |
| Ω (Omega) | 6.22578 | -6.36392 |
| Sensitivity to dividend yield (∂f/∂δ) | -61.79114 | 38.20886 |

Figure E3.23

the Greeks from the closed-form solution are only applicable for the European option. For this reason, the simulation method by the binomial lattice is widely used in practice.

## Numerical Example

Suppose that the options are at the money where the stock price is 100. The underlying volatility of the stock is assumed to be 20%, and the market risk-free rate over one year is 4%. Let the options expire in one year. Then the Greeks for the put and call options are given in figure E3.23.

## Applications

1. We formulate the dynamic hedging strategy of the options using Greeks.
2. We replicate put options in portfolio insurance using Greeks.

## Case: Valuing an Equity-Structured Product from a Term Sheet

Pedro Santos is the quantitative analyst at the derivative group of the medium-size securities firm Gem Stone Company. The firm has a large corporate parent that guarantees its high credit rating in the swap market. Pedro has in his hand a "term sheet" that has been sent to him. His group is considering a trade as expressed in this term sheet, and he is evaluating the proposed trade. The term sheet reads as follows:

S&P Index Option Swap
Commencement date: January 31, 2004
Termination date: January 31, 2005
Party: Gem Stone Company

Counter party: Smith Company

Pay: floating one-month LIBOR

Receive: fixed annual interests 1%

Notional amount: $10 million

Additional amount to receive: Let $S(0)$ be the S&P index at the commencement date. Let $S(T)$ be the S&P index on the terminal date. The amount to be received on the terminal date is

$$\text{Notional amount} \times Max[(S(T)/S(0)) - 1, 0]$$

The risk-free rate is 4% and the S&P index is 100 at the commencement date. The volatility of the S&P index is 25%. The continuous-time known dividend yield of the S&P index is 1%. Pedro has to decide whether Gem Stone should enter into this swap and if so, how should he hedge the position? He proceeds to analyze the term sheet systematically. He first breaks down the problem into its separate components. In essence, there are three components in this swap agreement: sell a floating-rate note, buy a fixed-rate bond, and buy an at-the-money call option on the bond. Using the LIBOR swap curve as the time value of money, the value of the swap to Gem Stone is therefore

$$V = B + C - F$$

where

$$B = \text{the value of the fixed-rate bond}$$

$$C = \text{the value of the call option}$$

$$F = \text{the value of the floating-rate bond}$$

*Before he started doing the valuation, he wondered which option pricing model he should use. He wanted to pick two alternatives and consider their pros and cons.*

## Exercises and Answers

1. The following questions are related to the case above. Using the market data given in the numerical example, he can proceed to determine $B$. He shows that it is $\$10.1e^{-0.04}$. Since the floating-rate note is paying interests based on the market rate, the value is the par, which is $10 million. He just needs to price the call option and determine the hedge position.

   *Answer:* Let us denote the notional amount by $N$. Since the additional amount to receive is $N \times Max[S(T)/S(0) - 1, 0]$, we can manipulate it to $N \times 1/S(0) \times Max[S(T) - S(0), 0]$. $Max[S(T) - S(0), 0]$ is the call option payoff at expiration, where $S(0)$ is the exercise price. By using the Black-Scholes model, we can calculate the call option price, which is 11.2356. The additional amount to receive at option maturity is $N \times 1/S(0) \times Max[S(T) - S(0), 0]$. Therefore, the present value of the additional amount to receive is $10 million $\times 1/S(0) \times$ 11.2356.

   To duplicate the call option, we sell short 0.59083 shares of stock and invest 47.8478 in the one-year bond. The hedge portfolio value is 11.82107, and the call option value is 11.81690, which shows that the hedge portfolio is effective to duplicate the call option. See figure E3.24.

| Hedge Portfolio | Time 0 | After 1 Day | |
|---|---|---|---|
| Stock price | 100 | 101 | |
| Sell short ΔS | 59.08338 | 59.67421 | |
| Invest | -47.84782 | -47.85314 | |
| Sum | 11.23555 | 11.82107 | |

| Call Option | | Maturity | |
|---|---|---|---|
| | 11.23555 | 1 | 0.99722 |
| Stock price | 100 | 11.23555 | 11.21856 |
| | 101 | 11.83399 | 11.81690 |

Figure E3.24

2. We have bought an at-the-money call option based on the terms and conditions of the contract, given the market conditions, except that we assume the dividend yield to be zero. How much of the stock do we need to short and how much should we invest in the one-year bond to hedge the option position?
   *Answer:* Sell short 0.61218 shares of stock and invest 49.38075 in the one-year bond.
3. We would like to replicate the put option as described above using the dynamic hedging strategy based on the underlying stock and the zero-coupon bond maturing in one year. Describe the short and long position at the initial time.
   *Answer:* Long 0.38782 shares and borrow 46.6982 for one year.

## Further Exercises

1. To see how the sensitivities vary as stock prices change, we should calculate the sensitivities at each stock price. We assume that the exercise price is 100 and the stock prices vary from 0 to 200. Mr. A is concerned with how the option price changes for a given small change of the stock price. He thinks that when the stock price moves from $50 to $51, the call option value does not move much, because the call option is still out-of-the-money. However, when the stock price moves from $149 to $150, the call option price change by $1, because the call option is deep-in-the-money. Which diagram can we use to confirm his reasoning? Furthermore, Mr. A thought that since gamma is a measure of delta change, the gamma is a small number when the call option is in-the-money or out-of-the-money, because the delta would not change when the call option is deep-in-the-money or deep-out-of-the-money. Which diagram can we use to confirm his thought?
   *Answer:* When the European call option is in the deep-out-of-the-money, the delta is nearly zero, because the slope of the call option price is parallel to the x-axis where the y-axis and the x-axis represent the call option premium and the stock price, respectively. When the European call option is deep-in-the-money, the delta is nearly one, because the slope is parallel to the 45° line. Therefore, the gamma of the deep in-the-money or out-of-the-money call option is close to zero. See figures E3.25 and E3.26.
2. Suppose that the call option is out of the money where the stock price is 80. The underlying volatility of the stock is assumed to be 20%, and the market risk-free rate over one year is 4%. Let the options expire in one year. Calculate the Greeks for the call option. Repeat the same question for the put options when the stock price is 120.
   *Answer:* See figure E3.27.

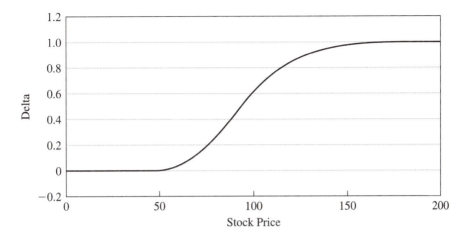

Figure E3.25

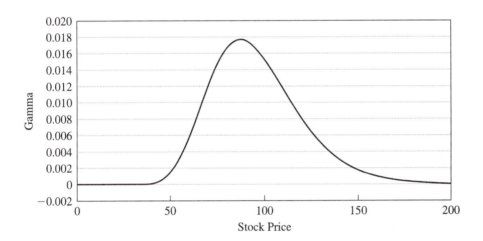

Figure E3.26

| Outputs | | |
|---|---|---|
| | Call(S=80) | Put(S=120) |
| Price | 1.7056 | 1.4354 |
| $\Delta$ (Delta) | 0.2073 | -0.1128 |
| $\Gamma$ (Gamma) | 0.0179 | 0.0080 |
| $\nu$ (Vega) | 22.8829 | 22.9784 |
| $\Theta$ (Theta) | -2.8835 | -1.6988 |
| $\rho$ (Rho) | 14.8809 | -14.9751 |
| $\Omega$ (Omega) | 9.7249 | -9.4329 |
| Sensitivity to dividend yield ($\partial f/\partial \delta$) | -16.5865 | 13.5398 |

Figure E3.27

3. Even though we can use the Black-Scholes model to calculate sensitivities, we can also use the binomial lattice. If the option is an American option, we can use only the binomial lattice to calculate the sensitivities, because we do not have a closed-form solution for American options.

*Answer:* See figures E3.28 and E3.29.

$$\Delta = \frac{C_{0,1} - C_{0,-1}}{S_{0,1} - S_{0,-1}}$$

$$\Gamma = 2 \times \left[ \frac{C_{0,1} - C_{0,0}}{S_{0,1} - S_{0,0}} - \frac{C_{0,0} - C_{0,-1}}{S_{0,0} - S_{0,-1}} \right] / (S_{0,1} - S_{0,-1})$$

$$\Theta = \frac{1}{2} \times \left[ \frac{(C_{2,1} - C_{0,0}) + (C_{0,0} - C_{-2,-1})}{2\Delta t} \right]$$

$$\nu = \frac{C_{\Delta\sigma^+} - C_{\Delta\sigma^-}}{2\Delta\sigma}$$

where $C_{0,1}(S_{0,1})$ and $C_{0,-1}(S_{0,-1})$ are the call option (stock) price at time 0 and state 1 and the call option (stock) price at time 0 and state $-1$, respectively. $C_{\Delta\sigma^+}$ and $C_{\Delta\sigma^-}$ are the call price when the volatility increases and decreases, respectively.

To numerically calculate the sensitivities, we use a binomial lattice, because we have already constructed the binomial lattice to price options. We can easily calculate the sensitivities as a by-product of pricing options, because we have to calculate the option value at every node to price the option at time 0.

| Inputs | | | | | | |
|---|---|---|---|---|---|---|
| Stock price ($) | S | 100 | | | | |
| Strike price ($) | X | 100 | | | | |
| Stock volatility | σ | 0.2 | | | | |
| Time to expiration (year) | T | 0.25 | | | | |
| Risk-free rate | r | 0.05 | | | | |
| The number of periods | n | 6 | dt = T/n | | | |
| The increment of σ | Δσ | 0.01 | | | | |
| | | | | | | |
| Upward movement | u | 1.0417 | exp(σ√dt) | | | |
| Downward movement | d | 0.9600 | 1/u | | | |
| Risk-neutral probability of u | p | 0.5153 | (exp(rdt)-d)/(u-d) | | | |
| | | | | | | |
| **Outputs** | | | | | | |
| | | | | | | |
| | | Delta | Gamma | Theta | Vega | |
| Call option Greeks | | 0.5730 | 0.1387 | -10.91502 | 9.4257518 | |

**Figure E3.28**

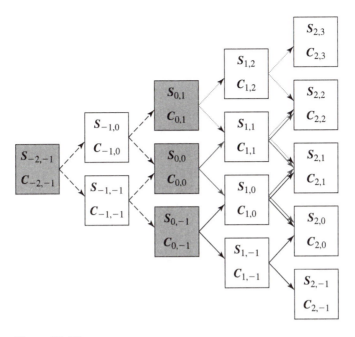

**Figure E3.29**

## Bibliography

Babbs, S. 2000. Binomial valuation of lookback options. *Journal of Economic Dynamics & Control*, 24, 1499–1525.

Babsiri, M. E., and G. Noel. 1998. Simulating path-dependent options: A new approach. *Journal of Derivatives*, 6 (2), 65–83.

Barone-Adesi, G., and R. E. Whaley. 1987. Efficient analytic approximation of American option values. *Journal of Finance*, 42 (2), 301–320.

Boyle, P. P. 1998. A lattice framework for options pricing with two state variables. *Journal of Financial and Quantitative Analysis*, 23 (1), 1–12.

Boyle, P. P., J. Evinde, and S. Gibbs. 1989. Numerical evaluation of multivariate contingent claims. *Review of Financial Studies*, 2 (2), 241–250.

Boyle, P. P., and J. S. H. Lau. 1994. Bumping up against the barrier with the binomial method. *Journal of Derivatives*, 1 (4), 6–14.

Brennan, M. J., and E. S. Schwartz. 1977. The valuation of American put options. *Journal of Finance*, 32 (2), 449–462.

Brodie, M., P. Glasserman, and G. Jain. 1997. Enhanced Monte Carlo estimates for American option prices. *Journal of Derivatives*, 5 (1), 25–44.

Carriere, J. F. 1996. Valuation of the early-exercise price for options using simulation and non-parametric regression. *Insurance: Mathematical and Economics*, 19, 19–30.

Chriss, N. A. 1997. *Black-Scholes and Beyond Option Pricing Models*. New York: McGraw-Hill.

Conze, A., and R. Viswanathan. 1991. Path dependent options: The case of lookback options. *Journal of Finance*, 46, 1893–1907.

Gao, B., Jz. Huang, and M. Subrahmanyam. 2000. The valuation of American barrier options using the decomposition technique. *Journal of Economic Dynamics & Control*, 24 (11), 1783–1827.

Geske, R. 1979. The valuation of compound options. *Journal of Economics*, 7, 63–81.

Geske, R., and H. E. Johnson. 1984. The American put option valued analytically. *Journal of Finance*, 39 (5), 1511–1524.

Goldman, M. B., H. B. Sosin, and M. A. Gatto. 1979. Path dependent options: Buy at the low, sell at the high. *Journal of Finance*, 34 (5), 1111–1127.

Thompson, A. C. 1995. Valuation of path-dependent contingent claims with multiple exercise decision over time: The case of take-or-pay. *Journal of Financial and Quantitative Analysis*, 30 (2), 271–293.

Turnbull, S. M., and L. M. Wakeman. 1991. A quick algorithm for pricing European average options. *Journal of Financial and Quantitative Analysis*, 26 (3), 377–389.

# 4

# Bond Mathematics, Treasury Securities, and Swaps

---

Bonds are important in our capital markets. Some are traded in the financial markets, and some are agreements made between parties. To a large extent, the bond values are more dependent on the time value of money than stocks. Therefore, bond pricing demands a different analytical framework, something that we will discuss in this chapter.

## 4.1 BOND MATHEMATICS

A bond is a financial contract to receive specified payments over time. These payments are usually called principal and interest (or coupons).

### Principal and Coupons

A bond is often specified by the *coupons* and the *principal*. The coupons usually represent regular, periodic payments to the holder. Principal (often called the face value) is the sum that is promised to be repaid by the borrower to the lender. The coupon amount or interest is calculated as a percent of the principal. That percentage is referred to as the coupon rate. For an investor, the key determination in buying a bond is the return on the investment, which is the combination of the coupons and principal. Together, we call these cash flows. One relevant distinction between coupons and principal is tax. The coupons are subject to income tax. The appreciation of the price is subject to the capital gains tax.

The time until the final payment of a bond is called the *maturity*. The price of the bond is the price the bond transacted in the market, as in the case of a stock. The price quoted is often considered a percent of the principal amount, and therefore a bond price is quoted with the face value based on 100. In general, the terms and conditions of a bond that specify the future payments can be varied, and there are only broad guidelines. Since these payments are often specified as fixed-amount promised payments over time, bonds are more appropriately called *fixed-income securities*. Fixed-income securities that have no maturity (or infinite time to maturity) are called *perpetual bonds*.

### Accrued Interest

*Accrued interest* is an accounting entity that amortizes the coupon payment over the period between two coupon dates. The accrued interest at any time $t$ is calculated to be the portion of the next coupon payment such that the proportion of the accrued interest to the next coupon payment is the time lapse from the last coupon date to the time interval between the last and the next coupon dates. The *quoted price* (also called the clean price) is the price at which the bond will be bought or sold, and the amount transacted is the quoted price plus the accrued interest. This amount is called the *invoice price* (or the dirty price). The invoice price is the true economic value of the bond. For example, consider the value of a bond one day before the maturity date. The annual coupon rate is 10% and the principal is 100. The total payment at the maturity date is therefore 110. Since the accrued interest is 10, the quoted price, which is the present value of the bond net of the accrued interest, is 100 (= 110 − 10).

The quoted price is a market convention and not the economic value of the bond. Why do we not quote a bond price incorporating the accrued interest? Suppose the yield curve is flat. When the bond is sold, the coupon rate will be the same as the market interest rate and the price is par (100). Suppose the interest rate has not changed for the entire year. The invoice price will rise to the coupon payment and then drop immediately to reflect the coupon payment, whereas the quoted price will remain constant, appropriately reflecting the constant interest rate. When we quote a bond price at par (or 100), we can infer the market interest rate from the coupon rate. However, if we use the invoice price, we have to take the accrued interest into account before we can make such an inference.

## Yield

Yield measures the rate of return of a bond. There are several yield measures. The most commonly used measure is called *yield to maturity*. It is the internal rate of return of a bond. More specifically, the yield to maturity is given by

$$Invoice\ Price = \frac{coupon}{(1+YTM)} + \frac{coupon}{(1+YTM)^2} + \cdots + \frac{coupon+principal}{(1+YTM)^T} \quad (4.1)$$

where YTM is the yield to maturity.

The above equation refers to the coupon being paid annually. But in the United States many bonds have coupons paid semiannually. In that case, the formula is

$$Invoice\ Price = \frac{coupon/2}{(1+YTM/2)} + \frac{coupon/2}{(1+YTM/2)^2} + \cdots + \frac{coupon/2+principal}{(1+YTM/2)^{2T}}$$

This yield to maturity is semiannual compounding and is called the bond yield.

The coupon payment period does not have to be semiannual. It can be daily, monthly, or some other regular period. The yield to maturity can be defined as daily compounding or monthly compounding. When a bond has a continuously compounding yield, then the continuously compounding yield $r$ over a term $T$ for a $1.00 payment at time $T$ is given by

$$Price = \exp(-rT)$$

It is important to specify the compounding period of the yield that is quoted. For example, a bond that has a 10% monthly compounding rate has a higher return than a bond quoted 10% at an annual compounding rate.

When the yield to maturity equals the coupon rate, the bond price is the same as the principal (the face) value. In this case, we say that the bond is trading at par. If the yield to maturity is higher than the coupon rate, the bond price is below par. In this case, we say the bond is trading at discount. Finally, when the bond yield to maturity is below the coupon rate, the bond price will exceed the par price and we say that the bond is trading at premium.

An increase in the yield will result in a lower bond price, and a fall in the yield will lead to an increase in the bond price. The bond price is negatively related to the yield. These relationships are direct results from the yield to maturity in equation (4.1).

For the perpetual bond (also called the consol bond), which has no maturity, the bond price is related to the coupon rate and the yield to maturity, the time value of money, in a simple way. The perpetual bond price is given by

$$Price = \frac{annual\ coupon}{YTM} \tag{4.2}$$

The yield to maturity of a perpetual bond can be considered the yield of a bond with the longest maturity that one can observe in the market.

## 4.2  BONDS AND BOND MARKETS

### Money Markets

*Money markets* are investments with a short time value of money, ranging from daily to annual rates. There are quite a few markets providing different rates, depending on the borrowers and lenders. The following are some examples of money market instruments. The *London Interbank Offered Rate* (LIBOR) is the British Bankers Association average of interbank offered rates for dollar deposits in the London market, based on quotations at major banks. This market is very active, and the LIBORs are often considered the benchmarks for the time value of money. The *prime rate* is the base rate on corporate loans. These rates should be higher than the LIBORs with the same term to maturity because they represent the lending rates of the banks. The *discount rate* is the charge on loans to depository institutions by the Federal Reserve banks. This rate represents an administered rate, a rate not fully representing the market supply of and demand for funds. *Federal funds* are reserves traded among commercial banks for overnight use. Commercial banks use federal funds to manage their short-term liquidity needs. *Commercial paper* consists of short-term unsecured promissory notes issued by corporations. They are sold in the open market, typically with maturity less than a year. *Bankers' acceptances* are negotiable, bank-backed business credit instruments that typically finance an import order. The *overnight repurchase rate* (repo rate) is the dealer financing rate for overnight sale and repurchase of Treasury securities. Each rate indicates the required returns for the risk and time value of money for each market segment. For example, consider the money market rates on February 7, 2002, in table 4.1. The LIBORs (annualized) show that the interest rates increase with the term. The discount rate, federal funds, and repo rates are annualized daily rates.

### Treasury Securities

Treasury securities are fixed-income securities and have three submarkets: bills, notes, and bonds. *Bills* are discount instruments (which have no coupon payments) with a maturity of less than one year at issuance. They are important to the money markets for their size in the market and their creditworthiness. *Treasury notes* are fixed-income

**Table 4.1** Money Market Rates on
February 7, 2002

| Money Market Rates | Rate (%) |
| --- | --- |
| LIBOR (month) | |
| 1 | 1.84 |
| 3 | 1.90 |
| 6 | 2.02 |
| 12 | 2.42 |
| Discount rate | 1.24 |
| Federal funds | 1.50 |
| Repo | 1.68 |
| Banker's acceptance | 1.86 |
| Prime rate | 4.75 |

Money markets refer to investments with a short
time value of money, ranging from daily to annual
rates. The LIBOR rates are increasing with the
term. The discount rate, federal funds, and repo
rates are annualized daily rates. Each rate indicates the required returns for the risk and time
value of money for each market segment.

securities with coupons paid semiannually and a maturity of less than ten years at
issuance. *Bonds* are similar to notes and have a maturity of thirty years at issuance. Some
Treasury bonds have call features such that the Treasury can call (buy back) the bonds at
par over the five years before maturity. The call feature gives the Treasury some control
over the scheduling of the bonds' principal payments coming due. Some recent bond
issues (since 1997) have the principal linked to the inflation rate. These bonds are called
*Treasury inflation protection securities*, or TIPS. The principal of the bond is adjusted by
the semiannual inflation rate. Therefore the principal of the bond at time $T$ is the initial
principal amount compounded at the published inflation rate at semiannual intervals.
The coupon payments are based on the fixed coupon rate on the adjusted principal
amount. When the inflation rate is high, the bond pays higher coupons and higher
adjusted principal at maturity. Therefore these bonds offer a hedge against inflation for
the investors.

There is an active secondary market. There are over 300 Treasury securities outstanding in the market that participants can buy or sell. As of 2001, the Treasury markets have
had a value of over $3 trillion. The market is very liquid, particularly for some of the re-
cent issues. These issues are called *on-the-run issues*. For such issues, a $10 million trade
would not have much (if any) impact on the market because many market participants
stand ready to trade these securities. However, an investor can buy as little as $10,000
of the bonds without incurring significant transaction costs. Since Treasury notes and
bonds are sold at a coupon rate such that the market price is 100% of the principal (that
is, the bonds are sold at 100 or par), these bonds' yields are benchmarks for the market to
infer the time value of money. These yields are called the *par rates*. The plot of these par
rates against their maturities is called the *par yield curve*. The par yield curve therefore
defines the yields of par bonds for different times to maturity.

Some of these coupon issues (notes and bonds) are held by the U.S. Treasury, and are
then "stripped" into coupons and principal payments. Each payment becomes a zero-
coupon bond. The zero-coupon bonds have no coupon payments, just one payment at
maturity. These bonds appeal to investors who need to have a particular payment at a

specific time. This market is called the STRIPS market. In February 1985, the Treasury began its *Separate Trading of Registered Interest and Principal of Securities* (STRIPS) program, which facilitated the stripping of designated Treasury securities.

In general, the Treasury markets (including the STRIPS market) are assumed to have no default risks. Considering that most bonds are liquid, they become the standard for measuring the time value of money.

When a bond is quoted as traded at par, it means that the bond price is 100. When the price is above 100, the bond is called premium, and when the price is below 100, the bond is discount. Treasury bills do not pay any interest, and they are always traded at discount. The same observation applies to the STRIPS bonds (zero-coupon bonds).

The yield curve observed from the STRIPS market is the *market-observed spot curve*, and the prices of the STRIPS bonds form the *discount function*. By convention, the discount function is quoted on the basis of a face value of 1 (not 100, as in the case of the STRIPS bond prices). The STRIPS prices can be used to price Treasury bonds because a Treasury coupon bond can be viewed as a portfolio of STRIPS bonds. Each coupon payment and its principal is a zero-coupon bond. Each zero-coupon bond can be valued by using the observed STRIPS bond prices (the discount function). The portfolio value can be calculated by summing the values of all the STRIPS bonds. This portfolio value should be close to the observed coupon bond price.

There is a reason for this observed closeness of the prices. The market allows for arbitrage between the Treasury markets and the STRIPS markets. When the Treasury bond (note) is priced below the fair price, dealers can buy these (*cheap*) bonds and strip them to sell the coupons and principals at the observed higher price. The stripping will continue until the fair price and the quoted price are aligned again. Conversely, if the bond price is traded above the fair price, the dealers can "reconstitute" the bond by buying the STRIPS bonds. The portfolio of STRIPS bonds replicates the actual bond. Then the portfolio can be sold as a bond.

### Other Bonds

The issuers can be quite varied. Corporations are often borrowers, promising the investors coupons and principals. Such bonds are called corporate bonds. Typically, bondholders do not have claims on any real assets or corporate entities. They are not subject to any charter of a corporation, nor are they directly rewarded by the returns of the real sector and real processes, as stockholders are.

Municipalities' borrowings are called *municipal bonds*. Bonds that use real estate properties as collateral are called *mortgages*. Some bonds' coupons and principals are derived from a portfolio of other bonds. These bonds are called *pass-through certificates*, suggesting that the cash flows are just passed from one type of bond to other bonds, changing the bond characteristics in the process. Most bonds are traded in the OTC markets. (Some corporate bonds are traded on the New York Stock Exchange, but the market is less liquid.)

## 4.3   SWAP MARKETS

A *swap* is an over-the-counter instrument that is not issued by any corporation or government agency. It is an exchange of payments between two parties. These payments are interest payments that may be based on a floating rate or a fixed rate, on the same amount of principal and maturity. *Floating rates* are short-term interest rates that may be daily (for example, 2 percent above the federal fund rate), accruing over time and paid monthly or semiannually. A *fixed rate* is a coupon rate fixed to the end of the contract. As a result, only the interests (floating and fixed) are exchanged, since the principals are the same on both sides of the swap. The maturity (or the term of the agreement) is called the *tenor*. The principal is called the *notional amount*, since it will never result in a payment.

*Vanilla swap* refers to a swap where one party pays a standard floating rate (for example, daily LIBOR) and receives a fixed rate, as described above, without any embedded options or contingencies, or any nonstandard fixed or floating payments. A vanilla swap has two components: (1) borrowing at the short-term rate, "short term funding," and (2) buying a fixed-rate bond. Therefore, entering into a vanilla swap is equivalent to securing short-term funding and investing in a bond. For this reason, the fixed rate for a given tenor of the swap (time to the termination of a swap) reflects the term structure of interest rates in the capital market. When the parties are highly rated (have minimal default risk), the *swap rates* can be used as a benchmark for the time value of money. Since the swap rate is the coupon rate determined for the fixed payments, it refers to the rate on the notional amount such that if we view the fixed payments as a bond, the market value of the bond is par. Swap rates are equivalent to the par rates of the bond market, and the swap curve is the par curve in the swap market.

Not all swaps are vanilla. Since swaps are agreements between two parties in the over-the-counter market, there is no standardization of designs. The fixed payment can be a *bullet payment* (a bond that accrues all the interest to be paid at the termination date), or an amortization schedule, or coupon-paying but with nonstandardized payment dates.

Unlike bonds, a swap has no multiple borrowers or lenders, only parties who exchange the cash flows. Such arrangements offer significant flexibility in the design. The terms and conditions of each swap are summarized in a confirm sheet, which includes the names of the parties, the notional amount, specifications of the exchange of payments, and the termination date.

Swap markets are very liquid in the United States. Swaps can be arranged in large notional amounts (in billions of dollars) continually. In countries where there is no long-term national debt, swap rates are often used as benchmarks for the time value of money. Indeed, the swap rates for bullet payments build the spot curve for the market. The spot curve provides the discount rate for a bullet payment.

## 4.4    ECONOMICS OF THE YIELD CURVE

### Yield Curves

A *spot curve* is defined as the relationship between the required rate of return of $1.00 invested over a time horizon $T$. It is represented by $r(T)$, and it measures the time value of money required by the market. There are several ways to construct the yield curve.[1] We will describe three ways to construct the theoretical yield curves for Treasuries, depending on which bonds we include in the construction. The candidates are Treasury STRIPS, on-the-run Treasury issues, and all Treasury coupon securities and bills.

The STRIPS market is one practical measure of the spot curve. U.S. Treasury securities are bonds that best approximate the theoretical construct of "default-free" bonds.

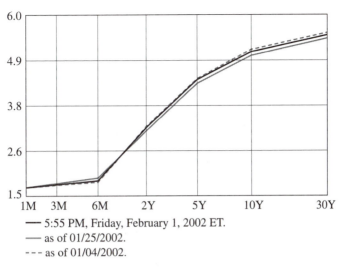

— 5:55 PM, Friday, February 1, 2002 ET.
— as of 01/25/2002.
- - - as of 01/04/2002.

**Figure 4.1** Treasure market spot curve. Since the Treasury market is a liquid market with no default risks, its spot curve is often used as a benchmark for the time value of money. Here, yield curves at different points in time show how yield curves fluctuate over time.
Source: http://www.bondmarkets.com

The probability that the U.S. government will default on its debt is perceived as negligible at present. As long as the U.S. Treasury can print more money, the government's debt obligations can be repaid. The Treasury spot curves are important to the fixed-income markets in pricing other bonds because of Treasury bonds' liquidity and creditworthiness. (See figure 4.1.)

The plot of the yields to maturity of the Treasury securities outstanding in the marketplace against their maturities is called the *nominal yield curve*. Since each bond has both the coupons and the principal payments, the nominal yield curve is only an approximation of the time value of money, since it does not precisely specify the present value of $1.00 at time $T$.

Another commonly used yield curve is the *par curve*. The par curve is used for the most closely watched bonds, the on-the-run issues. These are the most recently issued Treasury bills, notes, and bonds. These bonds are the most actively traded, and their movements represent the market's view of the equilibrium values of the bonds. Since these Treasury securities are the most recently issued and they are issued at par (except for the bills), their yields are close to their coupon rates. If we construct a yield curve by linearly interpolating the yields to maturity of these par bonds, the yield curve will represent the time value of money best represented at any one time by these most actively traded bonds. This yield curve is called the par curve.

The market has established the convention of quoting the price as a spread off the Treasury rate. For example, a bond may be quoted as 100 basis points off the ten-year Treasury, meaning that the bond yield to maturity is the yield to maturity of the ten-year on-the-run Treasury bond, plus 100 basis points. For this reason, the par curve is important on trading floors.

The bonds are continually traded and the prices are continually updated. Therefore, the yield curve fluctuates in an uncertain fashion over time. But two bonds with similar maturities cannot have price movements independent of each other. The yield of a $T$-year bond should be similar to that of a bond with maturity $T$ year plus one month. After all, the time value of money represents the market participants' preferences for returns over a time horizon, and therefore, the time value of money should be a smooth function related to the time to maturity.

If the yield $r(T)$ is constant and not dependent on the time to maturity $T$, we say that the spot yield curve is flat. If $r(T)$ rises (falls) with time $T$, we say the curve is an upward (downward)-sloping curve. The shape of the curve depicts the market supply and demand for funds over time.

In recent years, as a result of the U.S. government's effort to retire the national debt, the Treasury securities market has become smaller and, in some of the maturity spectrum, less liquid. At times the spot yield may fail to reflect the market supply of and demand for funds over time for lack of liquidity in part of the yield curve. An alternative benchmark to measure the time value of money is the swap market.

The swap market is a highly liquid market. Further, many countries do not have a liquid government bond market with longer maturities; their debts have maturities extending only one year. The swap curve becomes a necessary market benchmark for these countries. However, since swaps are contracts arranged between two parties, and the market swap rates are gathered by the market from the global financial institutions, there is a possibility that credit risks may affect these swap rates. The choice of the benchmark bonds to determine the yield curve and the choice of yield curve (spot curve or par curve) depend on the applications of the yield curve.

## Real Rate and Nominal Rate

The interest rates of the yield curves that we have discussed so far are called *nominal rates*. These are the yields of the bonds or the interest that we receive on our investments. Our study focuses on the nominal interest rate, which has two components: inflation and the real rate. The *real rate* reflects the real sector, where there is no impact of money on the purchase of goods. If the economy has higher productivity, investment increases and consumption falls. In addition to the real rate, the inflation rate affects the nominal interest rate. When we expect a higher inflation rate, the nominal interest rate will increase. This is summarized by the Fisher equation, stated as

$$nominal\ interest\ rate = real\ rate + expected\ inflation\ rate \tag{4.3}$$

The Fisher equation is particularly relevant for the long-term rate. The short-term rate is often affected by government monetary policy. For example, when the market expects persistent recession (hence low inflation and real rate), the long-term rate will fall. At this point the government may seek to lower the interest rate by using short-term instruments, which directly affects the cost of funds to the banks. For example, the monetary authority uses the *discount window* (central banks provide short-term liquidity needs of banks) and *open market operations* (central banks buy and sell government securities in the secondary markets) to lend or to buy short-term bonds, and such trading may affect the market short-term rates. In this case, the yield curve will fall, but the short-term rate will fall faster. Such was the case in the United States during the period 1990–1992.

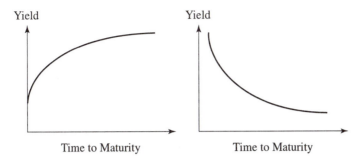

**Figure 4.2** Yield curve shapes. Yield curves are upward- or downward-sloping, depending on factors such as the market supply of and demand for funds. Various interpretations have been put forward to explain why the yield curves are upward- or downward-sloping. For example, if the yield curve is downward-sloping, we expect that the spot rates in the future will decrease, according to the expectation hypothesis. However, this is not always the case for the liquidity premium hypothesis.

Conversely, the market may experience a high inflation rate, resulting in a high long-term rate. The government may combat the inflation via lowering the money supply. It may then raise the short-term rate higher. In this case, the yield curve will move up, but the short-term rate will move up faster. This movement will result in an inverted (downward-sloping) yield curve. Such was the case in the United States during the period of 1975–1978. (See figure 4.2.)

## Expectation Hypothesis

The movement of the yield curve should be dependent on market expectations. When market participants anticipate that the interest rate will rise, the long-term yield of bonds should rise. Suppose we predict that the one-year rate will rise in one year; then the two-year bond yield should rise to reflect the market expectation. The new two-year rate should rise by an amount such that the investor rolling over the one-year bond has the same expected return as one locking in the two-year returns.

Establishing notations is in order at this point. We denote the $t$ year interest rate prevailing at time 0 as $r_{0,t}$. Extending this notation to future periods, we denote the $T^* - t$ year interest rate prevailing at time $t$ as $r_{t,T^*}$. In other words, $r_{t,T^*}$ is the interest rate that will be applied during the period from $t$ to $T^*$, where $t$ and $T^*$ denote the times. Then the expectation hypothesis asserts that

$$(1 + r_{0,1})(1 + E(\tilde{r}_{1,2})) = (1 + r_{0,2})^2 \tag{4.4}$$

The left-hand side of the equation represents the investment of \$1.00 at the one-year interest rate in the first year and reinvested in the second year at the prevailing one-year rate. One expects that the total return should equal the return of investing in a two-year bond compounded at the two-year rate over two years. For example, let the one-year and two-year interest rates be 6% and 7%, respectively. Then the implied expected one-year rate, one year from now, $E(\tilde{r}_{1,2})$, is solved from the following equation:

$$1.06 \times (1 + E(\tilde{r}_{1,2})) = 1.07^2 \text{ or } E(\tilde{r}_{1,2}) = 8.01\%$$

## Liquidity Premium Hypothesis

The U.S. Treasury bond market has bonds that mature in thirty years. One may argue that most investors have an investment horizon much shorter than thirty years. For investors to hold these bonds, they will demand a higher return for taking the price risks, in case the yield curve changes and they sell the bond at the prevailing (uncertain) price. Therefore, they should be compensated with an additional return, called the *liquidity premium*. In such a case, the yield curve should generally be upward-sloping, reflecting the liquidity premium that increases with maturity.

## Preferred Habitat Hypothesis

*Preferred habitat* refers to the segment of the yield curve that each investor occupies. Typically, banks tend to hold short-term securities because their deposit accounts and other fundings are short-term. Life insurance companies hold long-term bonds because their liabilities are life policies, which often require insurers to make payments in a fairly distant future, such as forty years. To ensure that the investments can support these obligations, life insurers often seek to buy long-term bonds. The change in supply and demand of a type of bond within each segment will prompt the yield curve to change its shape if there is a preferred habitat effect.

## 4.5   THE BOND MODEL

The market becomes efficient because market participants trade in a way that assures that the prices fully reflect the underlying value. The arbitrage mechanism is particularly important in this trading process to assure market efficiency.

Short selling is part of the arbitrage mechanism. When a security is underpriced, investors will buy the security. The buy orders will continue until the price rises to the level at which the security is no longer underpriced. When a security is underpriced, we say that it is cheap; if it is overpriced, it is rich. When a security is rich, investors will sell the security. But the investor who is aware that the security is rich may not own the security to sell. Short selling allows such an investor to make use of his private information. The security can first be borrowed, with the investor being obligated to return it over a time horizon. After borrowing the security, the investor sells it in the market and reinvests the proceeds. If the investor is correct about the security's price movement, and the price falls within this time horizon, then he can buy back the security at a lower price. The security is returned, and the profit is the difference between the sold price and the buy price.

*Arbitrage opportunity* occurs in a situation where two or more identical securities are priced differently. Then the investor will buy the cheap security and sell short the rich security as much as possible. The trade does not require capital, since the investment in the cheap security is always equal to the proceeds from the short selling net of the arbitrage profits. Arbitrage trade therefore ensures that two identical securities have the same price. The arbitrage profit is risk-free. Furthermore, the arbitrage depends only on the relative values of two securities, and not on their value relative to the true investment value. A consequence of the availability of the arbitrage mechanism is the law of one price.

**Figure 4.3** The relationship between no arbitrage and law of one price. No arbitrage opportunity is represented by the phrase "no free lunch." The law of one price means that the same price will be assigned to the same securities. The law of one price does not imply no arbitrage opportunity. For example, assume that the price of two identical stocks is −$10. Since we assigned the same price to two identical securities, the law of one price clearly holds. However, since the price is negative, we have an arbitrage opportunity. In this case, we would hold the stock (since we are paid to hold it) and wait to profit from the captial gains on it since there is limited liability on the firm (and hence the stock).

The *law of one price* states that if two securities have the same cash flows, they should have the same price. More to the point, if the law of one price does not hold, there will be an arbitrage opportunity, which cannot exist in an efficient capital market. The law of one price should hold in an efficient capital market. (See figure 4.3.)

## Model Assumptions

We assume that the bond market is *complete* by asserting that it has default-free discount bonds traded at all maturities. A discount bond with maturity $T$ is a bond that pays $1.00 at time $T$. The bond market is complete because under this assumption any default-free, fixed-income security is a portfolio of discount bonds that are traded in the market.

Let $P(T)$ be the price of a discount bond with maturity $T$ years with $1.00 principal. $P(T)$ as a function of maturity $T$ is called a discount function. For example, the prices of the STRIPS bonds divided by 100 in the Treasury bond market form a discount function. The prices of the bullet payment (single payment without coupons) swaps can be used as a discount function for the same reason that the STRIPS prices are used for the spot curve. The bullet payments enable an investor to identify the time value of money.

We define the yield $r_{0,T}$ to be

$$P(T) = \frac{1}{(1 + r_{0,T})^T} \tag{4.5}$$

where $r_{0,T}$ is a function of $T$ and is called the spot (yield) curve based on annual compounding.

Let us assume that the law of one price holds. If we can estimate the discount function at any moment, then given any cash flow, we can determine its present value by viewing the cash flow as a portfolio of payments. The present value of each payment can be calculated because we know the present value of $1.00, which is the discount factor. Now, according to the law of one price, the present value of the cash flow is simply the sum of the present values of all the payments. As a result, we can replicate a portfolio of zero-coupon bonds such that the bond portfolio has the same cash flow as the bond. The bond price must therefore be equal to the value of the portfolio. (See figure 4.4.)

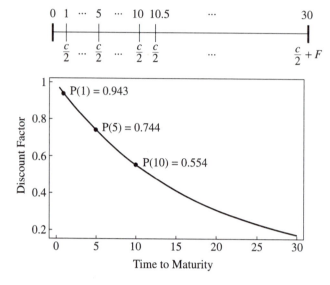

**Figure 4.4** Bond pricing. Since the bond price is the present value of future cash flow, we need a discount function and future cash flow of the bond to calculate the price. The numbers above and below the time line in the upper diagram represent the time and the corresponding cash flow, respectively. The discount function indicates the time value of money. The bond price is the sum of cash flows discounted by the corresponding discount function.

$$Price = \frac{coupon}{2} \times P(0.5) + \frac{coupon}{2} \times P(1) + \cdots + (\frac{coupon}{2} + principal) \times P(T) \quad (4.6)$$

where $P(i)$ is the discount function and $i$ denotes the time to the payment.

The above discussion can be summarized by the bond model shown below. Suppose a bond has coupon and principal payments $CF(i)$ every year $i$ until maturity year $T$. Then the value of the bond is

Bond Model

$$B = \sum_{i=1}^{T} P(i) \times CF(i) \quad (4.7)$$

The discount function is the set of present-value discount factors inferred from the capital market by observing the traded prices of the discount bonds. These factors measure the time value of money in the capital market and can be used as benchmark values for other fixed-income securities. The time value of money can be represented by the discount function or by the spot yield curve.

Let us take a numerical example. Consider the following zero-coupon bonds.

| Price | Maturity (years) | Yield to Maturity | Discount Factor |
|-------|------------------|-------------------|-----------------|
| 90 | 1 | 0.1111 | 0.9 |
| 80 | 2 | 0.118 | 0.8 |
| 70 | 3 | 0.1262 | 0.7 |

Suppose we have a bond maturing in three years with coupon rate of 10 percent. Can we calculate the price?

The cash flow for each year is shown below.

| Term | 1 | 2 | 3 |
|---|---|---|---|
| Coupon | 10 | 10 | 10 |
| Principal | | | 100 |
| Cash flow | 10 | 10 | 110 |

The price, by the law of one price, is

$$Price\ (P) = 10 \times 0.9 + 10 \times 0.8 + 110 \times 0.7 = 94 \qquad (4.8)$$

If a bond is trading below the fair value, we can buy and then resell it as three separate zero-coupon bonds. If the bond is trading above the fair price, we can buy the zero-coupon bonds, repackage them, and sell them on the coupon bond market. This method assumes that the law of one price holds.

The law of one price used in equation (4.8) can be explained quite intuitively. Suppose that we walk into a grocery store and note that apples are 50 cents each, oranges are 40 cents each, and mangoes are a dollar each. Later, we see a fruit basket with five apples, six oranges, and seven mangoes. What would be a guess for the price of the fruit basket? An educated guess would be $11.90 ($= 0.5 \times 5 + 0.4 \times 6 + 1.0 \times 7$). Every day the STRIPS market determines the price of $1.00 for each maturity date. Therefore, if we have a stream of future promised payments, we can use the market prices from the STRIPS market to determine the value of the payments, just as we used the prices of the fruit in the grocery store. Of course, thus far we are assuming that the payments have the creditworthiness of the U.S. government.

## 4.6  FORWARD PRICES AND FORWARD RATES

Bond markets are often called cash markets because investors buy the bonds at the time of the transaction. By way of contrast, a forward or futures bond market determines the bond price at a future delivery.

### Futures and Forward Contracts

Interest rate *futures* and *forward contracts* are financial contracts similar to those for equity indices. Interest rate futures are traded on the exchange that ensures the marking to market mechanism. Interest rate forwards are traded in the over-the-counter markets without any marking to market. The interest rate futures' and forwards' underlying assets are interest rate sensitive. Examples of exchange-traded interest rate futures are Treasury bond futures, Treasury note futures (five-year and two-year Treasury note futures), and Eurodollar futures.

Unlike the index futures, bond futures have deliverable assets: the corresponding bonds. Since the market needs to assure that there is liquidity in the market, the seller of a futures contract can deliver any bond in the deliverable basket of bonds. The basket is determined by the futures exchange, through defining the bonds to be included in the basket.

Futures and forward contracts are not priced in the same way because of the daily marking to market in a futures contract. When there is money exchanged at the end of each day, the cash has to be reinvested, and this reinvestment is subject to uncertain interest rate levels. However, a forward contract does not necessarily have any money change hands during the life of the contract. For this reason, it is valued differently, but typically the differences in prices are quite small relative to the price risks.

A forward contract of a bond is the agreement to deliver a bond with time to maturity $T$ at a future date $T^*$ (the termination date) at a price stated in the agreement. Note that when we "buy" a forward contract, there is no exchange of money at the time of the agreement. Only at the termination date there is an exchange where the buyer pays the agreed-upon price (the forward price) and receives the $T$ time to maturity bond. This exchange will not take place even when there is a significant change in market interest rate during this period before the termination date.

Given the forward price, we can calculate the yield of the bond. Suppose we buy a $1.00 $T^*$-year bond. At maturity $T^*$, we will receive the principal and interest. If we also have a forward contract that requires us to buy the $T$-year bond for which the maturity date of the contract is $T^*$, then at year $T^* + T$, we will receive the total of the interest and principal reinvested at the forward rate. The main point is that by holding a $T^*$-year bond and a $T$-year forward contract with a delivery date at year $T^*$, we can assure a fixed return, which has to be the return of the $T^* + T$ year bond. (See table 4.2.)

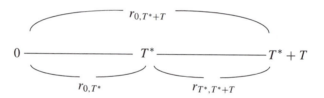

In other words, the law of one price suggests that if we know the yields of $T^* + T$ year and $T^*$-year bonds, we can determine the yield of the forward contract (the *forward rate*). Therefore, given the spot curve, we can determine the forward rate, the interest rate that we will receive on the forward contract. Now if we assume that there is only one possible way for the yield curve to move in the future (that there is no uncertainty), then the yield curve must move according to the forward curve. In that sense, the forward

**Table 4.2** Forward Contract Pricing Model

| *Time* | 0 | $T^*$ | $T^* + T$ |
|---|---|---|---|
| Holding a $T^*$-year bond | $-P(T^*)$ | *coupon + principal =* $P(T^*)(1 + r_{0,T^*})^{T^*}$ | |
| Holding a $T$-year forward contract with a delivery date at year $T^*$ | | $-(coupon + principal)$ | $(coupon + principal)$ $\cdot (1 + r_{T^*,T^*+T})^T$ |
| Cash flow | $-P(T^*)$ | 0 | $P(T^*)(1 + r_{0,T^*})^{T^*}$ $\cdot (1 + r_{T^*,T^*+T})^T$ |

The cash flow at time $T^* + T$ is $P(T^*)(1 + r_{0,T^*})^{T^*}(1 + r_{T^*,T^*+T})^T = P(T^*)(1 + r_{0,T^*+T})^{T^*+T}$ by no arbitrage condition.

rate is the "expected rate" from the market. The relationship between the forward rate and the spot rate is often called the expectation hypothesis.

The above discussion is summarized by the forward contract pricing model.

$$P(T^* + T) = P(T^*)F(T^*, T) \tag{4.9}$$

$F(T^*, T)$ is the forward price, with a delivery date at time $T^*$, delivering a bond with face value 1 and time to maturity $T$. Equation (4.9) is important because it shows that the discount function (or the spot yield curve) can determine the forward price.

The above equation can be expressed in terms of rates:

$$\frac{1}{(1 + r_{0,T^*+T})^{T^*+T}} = \frac{1}{(1 + r_{0,T^*})^{T^*}} \times \frac{1}{(1 + r_{T^*,T^*+T})^{T}} \tag{4.10}$$

where $r_{T^*,T^*+T}$ is the forward rate with a delivery date at time $T^*$.

A specific forward rate with special importance is the one-period forward rate, $r_{T^*,T^*+1}$. This is the one-period forward rate $T^*$ periods from the present. Given these relationships, we have the following results that are useful in fixed-income analytics.

$$\frac{1}{(1 + r_{0,T^*+1})^{T^*+1}} = \frac{1}{(1 + r_{0,T^*})^{T^*}} \times \frac{1}{(1 + r_{T^*,T^*+1})} \tag{4.11}$$

$$1 + r_{T^*,T^*+1} = \frac{(1 + r_{0,T^*+1})^{T^*+1}}{(1 + r_{0,T^*})^{T^*}} = \left(\frac{1 + r_{0,T^*+1}}{1 + r_{0,T^*}}\right)^{T^*}(1 + r_{0,T^*+1})$$

$$r_{0,T^*+1} > r_{0,T^*} \Leftrightarrow r_{T^*,T^*+1} > r_{0,T^*+1}$$

$$r_{0,T^*+1} < r_{0,T^*} \Leftrightarrow r_{T^*,T^*+1} < r_{0,T^*+1}$$

That is, if the spot curve is upward-sloping, then the one-period forward rate exceeds the yield of the bond with maturity $T^* + 1$. Conversely, if the spot curve is downward-sloping, then the one-period forward rate is lower than the yield of the bond with maturity $T^* + 1$.

Forward rates and spot rates are related. For a flat spot curve, the one-period forward rate is constant and is the same as the spot rate. The forward rate rises for an upward-sloping spot curve and the forward rate falls for a downward-sloping spot curve. (See figure 4.5.)

Note that the one-period forward rate with a delivery date at time 1 is in fact

$$r_{1,2} = \frac{(1 + r_{0,2})^2}{(1 + r_{0,1})} - 1 \tag{4.12}$$

Here, $r_{1,2}$ is the one-period forward rate with a delivery date at time 1; $r_{0,2}$ is the two-year rate (or yield of the two-period bond); and $r_{0,1}$ is the one-year rate.

Thus, if equation (4.4) holds, then the forward rate (which is simply calculated from the observed yield curve) equals the expected future spot rate. When the expected future one-period spot rate equals the forward rate, we say that the *local expectation hypothesis* holds. Unfortunately, this hypothesis defies simple testing. There is no easy way to ask the market participants what they think the future spot rates will be and compare their expected numbers with the forward rates. But the hypothesis does provide us with some guidelines to why the yield curve moves.

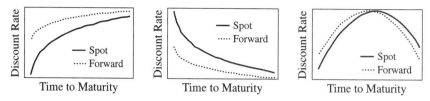

**Figure 4.5** Forward and spot rates. The relationship between the spot and the forward curves is that if the spot curve is upward-sloping, the forward curve is above the spot curve, whereas if the spot curve is downward-sloping, the forward curve is below the spot curve. Therefore, the forward curve crosses from above the highest point of the spot curve according to the rightmost panel. By analogy, the spot rate could be treated as if it were an average batting average and the forward rate as if it were a marginal batting average. (The marginal batting average is a batting average in the current game.) If the marginal batting average is larger than the average batting average, the average batting average including the current game will be rising, and vice versa.

If the expectation hypothesis is true, then an upward-sloping yield curve can be interpreted as predicting rising interest rates and the future yield curve can be specified exactly by the forward curve. Similarly, the downward-sloping curve would predict falling interest rates. To the extent that the forward curve does predict the future yield curve, the expected return of a bond over a time horizon must be the same as the return of the risk-free bond over that period. The movement of this short-term rate is therefore dependent on the shape of the yield curve.

We assume the following upward-sloping yield curve for illustration purposes. We can determine the forward yield curve according to equation (4.12).

| Maturity (T) | 1 | 2 | 3 |
|---|---|---|---|
| Spot rate (%) | $r_{0,1} = 8\%$ | $r_{0,2} = 9\%$ | $r_{0,3} = 10\%$ |
| Forward rate | $r_{1,2} = 10.01\%$ | $r_{1,3} = 11.01\%$ | N/A |
| Forward rate | $r_{2,3} = 12.03\%$ | N/A | N/A |

$$r_{1,2} = \frac{(1 + r_{0,2})^2}{(1 + r_{0,1})} - 1 = \frac{(1.09)^2}{1.08} - 1 \approx 10.01\%$$

$$r_{1,3} = \sqrt{\frac{(1 + r_{0,3})^3}{(1 + r_{0,1})}} - 1 = \sqrt{\frac{(1.1)^3}{(1.08)}} - 1 \approx 11.01\%$$

$$r_{2,3} = \frac{(1 + r_{0,3})^3}{(1 + r_{0,2})^2} - 1 = \frac{(1.1)^3}{(1.09)^2} - 1 \approx 12.03\%$$

Specifically, under the expectation hypothesis, the yield curve at time 1 will be the forward yield curve implied by the current yield curve. The return on each bond for the one-year holding period is 8%. The implied forward one-year rate (i.e., $r_{1,2} = 10.01\%$) is the one-year spot rate at year 1.

The return of the one-year zero-coupon bond over one year is

$$\left(100 \Big/ \frac{100}{1 + r_{0,1}}\right) - 1 = \left(100 \Big/ \frac{100}{1 + 0.08}\right) - 1 = 8\%$$

The return of the two-year zero-coupon bond over one year is

$$\left(\frac{100}{1+r_{1,2}}\Big/\frac{100}{(1+r_{0,2})^2}\right)-1=\left(\frac{100}{1+0.1001}\Big/\frac{100}{(1+0.09)^2}\right)-1=8\%$$

The return of the three-year zero-coupon bond over one year is

$$\left(\frac{100}{(1+r_{1,3})^2}\Big/\frac{100}{(1+r_{0,3})^3}\right)-1=\left(\frac{100}{(1+0.1101)^2}\Big/\frac{100}{(1+0.1)^3}\right)-1=8\%$$

This numerical example shows that the return of a bond on the yield curve over one year is always the one-year rate (the risk-free rate over the year) if the forward curve prevails at the end of the first period.

However, if the spot rate curve at year 1 is different from the forward curve, the return on each bond for the one-year holding period is not 8%. To show that the return over the one-year holding period is not 8%, we assume that the spot rate curve at year 1 is a horizontal yield curve at 9.5%. Then the return of a one-year zero-coupon bond over one year is

$$\left(100\Big/\frac{100}{1+0.08}\right)-1=8\%$$

The return of a two-year zero-coupon bond over one year is

$$\left(\frac{100}{1+0.095}\Big/\frac{100}{(1+0.09)^2}\right)-1\approx 8.5\%$$

The return of a three-year zero-coupon bond over one year is

$$\left(\frac{100}{(1+0.095)^2}\Big/\frac{100}{(1+0.1)^3}\right)-1\approx 11.01\%$$

The returns of the two-year and the three-year zero-coupon bonds are different from the one-period risk-free interest rate of 8%.

## Forward Rate Movement

Let us consider a money market forward contract expiring at time $T^*$. A one-month Eurodollar forward contract is an example when it agrees on the price of a one-month discount Eurodollar payment for a forward delivery. Suppose, at time 0, we have a particular shape of a yield curve. We all agree on this for the next month. There is no uncertainty. When the yield curve moves according to the market anticipation, this forward rate should not move at all. If today we all believe that the one-month borrowing rate will be 10% for the year 2005 and one year later, if there is no new information (no uncertainty), then there is no reason for the forward rate to change. It will still be 10%.

More formally, let us denote the discount curve as $P(T)$. Let the forward contract price that delivers a $T$-year maturity bond at time $T^*$ be denoted by $F(T^*, T)$.[2]

$$F(T^*, T) = \frac{P(T^* + T)}{P(T^*)} \tag{4.13}$$

Now suppose that after time $t$ ($t < T^*$), the new discount function is the same as the forward discount function implied by today's discount function.

$$P^*(T) = \frac{P(t + T)}{P(t)} \qquad (4.13a)$$

Further suppose that after time $t$, the time to expiration of the contract is now ($T^* - t$), and therefore the forward contract price at time $t$ is $F^*(t, T^*, T)$. By equation (4.13), we can rewrite the equation as

$$F^*(t, T^*, T) = \frac{P^*(T^* + T - t)}{P^*(T^* - t)}$$

By using equation (4.13a) to relate $P^*$ to $P$, we can derive

$$F^*(t, T^*, T) = \frac{P^*(T^* + T - t)}{P^*(T^* - t)}$$
$$= \frac{P(t + T^* + T - t)}{P(t)} \bigg/ \frac{P(t + T^* - t)}{P(t)} = \frac{P(T^* + T)}{P(T^*)}$$

But by the definition of the forward price, we have

$$\frac{P(T^* + T)}{P(T^*)} = F(T^*, T)$$

Therefore, we have $F^* = F$. That means the forward contract price remains unchanged as long as the prevailing yield curve is the forward curve. Therefore, a change of the forward price is not the result of a change in the spot curve, but rather the deviation of the spot curve from the forward curve.

The following numerical example is offered as illustration. Consider a flat yield curve where the interest rate is 6%. The discount factors for the one-year, two-year, and three-year terms are 0.9433, 0.8899, and 0.8396, respectively. Therefore the forward contract price that delivers the one-year maturity bond at year 2 is 0.9433 (= 0.8396/0.8899) by equation (4.13). Here $T^*$ is 2 and $T$ is 1. Suppose the future discount function at year 1 is the same as the forward discount function implied by today's discount function (equation (4.13a)). The time elapsed, $t$, is 1. The forward discount function at year 1, which is implied by today's discount function, is given by the one-year discount factor, 0.9433 (= 0.8899/0.9433), and the two-year discount factor, 0.8899 (= 0.8396/0.9433). Given this forward discount function, the one-year forward contract is 0.9433 (= 0.8899/0.9433), and therefore the one-year forward contract price has not changed over the first period, as long as the prevailing discount function is the forward discount function.

## 4.7   DURATION AND CONVEXITY

### Durations

Perhaps the most commonly used analytical measure for bonds is the duration. The terminology "duration" is somewhat misleading and is a source of confusion in many instances. Duration, sometimes called effective duration, is defined as the price sensitivity of a bond to a parallel shift of the spot curve, where the spot yield is typically assumed to be semiannual compounding. The (*effective*) duration is defined as

$$\frac{\Delta P}{P} = -effective\ duration \times \Delta\ spot\ yield \tag{4.14}$$

For a default-free zero-coupon bond, the duration is approximately the same as the maturity of the zero-coupon bond. For example, for a zero-coupon bond with maturity $T$, the price $P$ is given by

$$P = \frac{1}{(1 + r_{0.5}/2)^{2T}}$$

where $r_{0.5}$ is a semiannually compounding rate.

When we apply equation (4.14) by letting the $\Delta$ spot yield be a small change in the interest rate $r_{0.5}$, we can derive the duration by differentiating $P$ with respect to $r_{0.5}$ and have

$$Duration = \frac{T}{(1 + r_{0.5}/2)} \tag{4.15}$$

where $r_{0.5}$ can be called the yield of the bond. The term $1 + r_{0.5}/2$ is a modifier that is required to calculate the duration. Duration is the price sensitivity of a bond to the spot yield change. But the spot yield can be specified as an annual compounding yield, a semiannually compounding yield, a monthly, or even a daily compounding yield. Surely, a 1% change of a daily compounding yield has a larger impact on the bond price than a 1% change in the annual compounding yield. $(1 + r_{0.5}/2)$ is used to adjust for a semiannual compounding. In general, the modifier is $1 + r_{1/n}/n$ where $n$ is the number of periods used in one year.

For example, suppose a zero-coupon bond has a maturity of ten years and the semi-annual compounding yield is 6%. The duration is 9.708 ($= 10/(1.03)$). The price of the bond is $100/(1 + r_{0.5}/2)^{20}$. For a special case, cash has zero duration, and by convention the price of the cash is 100.

|                                       | Zero-Coupon Bond | Cash |
|---------------------------------------|:----------------:|:----:|
| Maturity (years)                      | 10               | 0    |
| Spot yield (semiannual compounding)   | 6%               | —    |
| Price                                 | 55.36            | 100  |
| Duration                              | 9.708            | 0    |

That means that when the spot yield curve falls 1% (or equivalently stated, by convention, drops 100 basis points) in a parallel fashion, the bond price will rise 9.708%. The change of the interest rate level does not affect the cash. That is, the cash has zero duration.

The duration measure has a very convenient property. The duration of a portfolio is the weighted average durations of each bond, where the weights are defined as the proportion of the bond market value to the portfolio market value. That is,

$$Duration_P = \sum_i \left(\frac{B_i}{P}\right) Duration_i \tag{4.16}$$

where $Duration_P$ and $Duration_i$ are the durations of the portfolio and bond $i$, respectively. $B_i$ is the market value of the bond position and $P$ is the portfolio value, such that the sum of $B_i$ is the portfolio value $P$.

Continuing the above numerical example, if the portfolio has $10 million in bonds and $20 million in cash, then the portfolio value is $30 million and the duration is 3.236 years (9.708/3).

We can think of any bond with specified cash flows as a portfolio of zero-coupon bonds. Following the above argument, the duration of the bond is very close to the weighted average life of the bond. The weighted average life of a bond is called the *Macauley duration*. This duration measure is very helpful in providing insight into bond behavior. For example, for a ten-year coupon bond with an average life of six years, a 1 percentage point shift upward in the interest rate will lead to an approximately 6% drop in value. However, we must recognize the limitation of this link between the life of a bond and its duration. The link is true for bonds without embedded options.

What does the duration mean for a bond with no embedded options? Suppose we have a bond with two payments: $100 in one year and $100 in five years. And suppose that the duration of the bond is 2.8 years. Suppose the interest rates fall instantaneously in a parallel fashion by 1 percentage point and remain constant for the subsequent years. The first $100 will have to be reinvested at a lower market rate (lowered by 1%), while the second $100 will have a higher present value because of the lower interest rate. The duration is like a fulcrum balancing the capital gains from the five-year payment and loss of reinvestment of the one-year payment. The duration is the break-even point in the sense that after 2.8 years, when we liquidate the bond position, the unrealized capital gains from the five-year payment exactly offset the loss of the reinvestment interest payment of the one-year payment. Duration is calculated to find this point in time. If the investment horizon of the investor is 2.8 years, then this shift of interest rates does not affect his portfolio value when he liquidates the position.

Duration is a useful measure for managing the interest rate risks of an investment portfolio. For swaps and bond trading, where the positions can have positive or negative value, a measure of proportional change in the portfolio value or a swap value has little meaning. For those purposes, dollar duration is used. Dollar duration is defined to measure the dollar change in value with a parallel shift of the spot yield curve. In this case, one can measure the dollar duration of any trading position. The position is hedged when the dollar duration is 0 and the value is unchanged with a small change in interest rates. Dollar duration is related to duration in a simple manner for a bond or an option.

$$\$\ Duration = Duration \times Value \tag{4.17}$$

*Dollar duration* is measured in dollars and is the value sensitivity of the bond portfolio to the yield curve. By market convention, a similar measure of risk is also used, called the *price value of a basis point* or PV 01. The "01" refers to a 1 basis point shift of the yield curve, and PV 01 is the change in the bond price or portfolio value by 1 basis point shift of the yield curve. Thus dollar duration and PV 01 are related by

$$Price\ Value\ 01 = \$\ Duration \times 0.0001 \tag{4.18}$$

Continuing the above numerical example:

|  | *$ Duration* |
| --- | --- |
| Cash | 0 |
| Bond position | $97.08 million |
| Portfolio | $97.08 million |
| PV 01 | $9,708 |

Note that the bond position and the portfolio have the same dollar durations. This is because the cash does not contribute any price risk to changes in the interest rates.

## Modified Duration

Another duration measure is the *modified duration*. As we have discussed, the price and the yield to maturity of a bond are mathematically related. Yield to maturity is the internal rate of return of a bond's cash flows. The price has the same informational content as the yield. They are just two ways of expressing the value of a bond. The price is the present value of the bond's cash flows. The yield is the return of the bond over its life. Modified duration is the price sensitivity to the changes in the yield to maturity.

$$\frac{\Delta P}{P} = -modified\ duration\ \times \Delta\ yield\ to\ maturity \qquad (4.19)$$

Often we want to know a small change of price in relation to a small change of yield. Maybe the investor is interested in knowing how the price quote may be affected by a small change in the yield. Modified duration relates the small change of the yield to maturity to the change in the bond price. For example, a bond has a modified duration of five years. We are told that the yield to maturity of the bond is 7%. If the yield to maturity increases to 8%, then the bond price will fall by 5%.

The mathematical relationship can be derived from the price yield formula. For a bond without any embedded options, the formula is similar to that of the weighted average life of the bond where the weights are the present value of the payments discounted at the yield.

## Key Rate Duration

The yield curve does not always make parallel shifts, whereby each interest rate moves by $x$ basis points along the entire yield curve. This is the underlying assumption of the use of the effective duration to measure the risk of a bond. In reality, the yield curve makes many types of movements. A measure of the price sensitivity to the yield curve risk, which is the impact of the uncertain yield curve movement on the price of the bond, is called the key rate duration. The key rate duration is the proportional change in the bond price in response to a small change in the key rate. The dollar key rate duration is defined as the dollar change in value with a small shift of the key rate.

A spot yield curve is a continuous function of the maturity. We need to represent the movement of this yield curve by a finite set of points. One approach is to use the terms of the on-the-run issues of the Treasury markets. As explained before, the

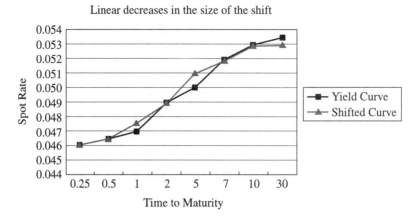

**Figure 4.6** Yield curve and shifted curve. This illustrates the upward shifts of key rates at year 1 and year 5. In addition to the upward shifts at year 1 and year 5, the figure also shows a downward shift at the 30-year term. However, in this illustration there are no shifts on the 0.25-, 0.5-, 2-, 7-, and 10-year terms. If an upward or a downward shift occurs at a certain term, we draw a straight line connecting the upward or downward shift point to the adjacent terms to denote how the adjacent rates will be changed due to the shift.

on-the-run bond or note issues are the most watched securities in representing the spot yield curve movements. They are three-month, six-month, twelve-month, two-year, three-year, five-year, seven-year, and ten-year. The Treasury recently stopped issuing thirty-year bonds. To measure the yield curve sensitivity, we should add twenty- and thirty-year rates. If we can identify bond price sensitivities to these key rate movements, we in principle can capture the price risk of the bonds.

Using this observation, we can now define an $i$th key rate shift to be a rise of 10 basis points at the $i$th key rate. Now we need to describe the changes of the other interest rates, given the change of one key rate. We assume that the size of the shift decreases linearly on both sides of the $i$th key rate, reaching 0 at the $(i - 1)$th and $(i + 1)$th key terms. (See figure 4.6.)

Figure 4.6 illustrates the upward shift of key rates at one-year and five-year terms and a downward shift at the thirty-year term; there is no shift in the rest of the terms.

Then the $i$th *key rate duration*, $KRD(i)$ is defined as

$$\frac{\Delta P}{P} = -KRD(i) \cdot \Delta r(i) \tag{4.20}$$

where the $i$th key rate shift is represented by $\Delta r(i)$.

One useful property of the key rate duration is that the sum of key rate durations is the duration. We can therefore think of key rate durations as a decomposition of a duration number. More generally, we can add any subset of the key rate durations as a measure of interest rate risk to a particular segment of the yield curve. For example, we can use the sum of the first three key rate durations to measure a bond's sensitivity to the short-term segment of the yield curve. Another useful property of key rate duration is that the key rate duration of a portfolio of bonds and options is the weighted average

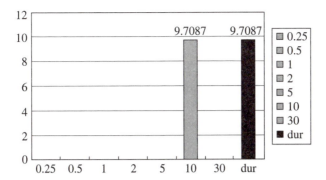

**Figure 4.7** Duration and key rate duration of a zero-coupon bond. This shows that the sum of the key rate durations is equal to the duration. The duration of a zero-coupon bond is 9.7087. Its key rate duration is 9.7087 at the ten-year term because there is no cash flow except the ten-year term.

of the key rate durations of all the securities in the portfolio weighted by the proportion of the value of the bond or option position in the portfolio.

Consider a zero-coupon bond with $T$-year maturity. The bond price is not affected by any change in the key rates except those that lead to a change in the spot curve at the $T$-year term. This is somewhat nonintuitive at first glance. Suppose an investor is holding a long-term zero-coupon bond, and the short-term interest rates have just shifted. The bond price should not be affected, since the bond pricing model shows that the bond price is determined by discounting the bond's cash flows at the long-term interest rates rather than the short-term interest rate. For clarity, assume that the $T$-year term is a key rate. Then the key rate durations are all 0 except for the $T$th year key rate. The key rate duration of this key rate is the duration of the bond $T/(1 + r_{0,T})$, where $r_{0,T}$ is the $T$th year spot rate. The key rate duration is the same as the duration in this case because the sum of key rate durations must equal the duration number.

For a leveraged position, where the position involves shorting or borrowing of securities, such as in swaps, the value of the position may not be positive and can at times have a zero or negative value. In such a case the measure of exposure is the *dollar key rate duration* $\$KRD(i)$, as defined by

$$\Delta P = -\$KRD(i) \cdot \Delta r(i)$$

Price value 01 is defined analogously, as the dollar change in value for 1 basis point change in each key rate.

*Key rate duration profile* refers to the relationship of the key rate durations and the key rates. For example, consider the key rate duration profile of the bond discussed in figure 4.7.

## Convexity

Bond prices do not change proportionally to the shift in the interest rate as specified by the effective duration. As the spot curve falls, a bond value may increase at an accelerated or decelerated rate. Convexity provides a measure of such an acceleration or deceleration to better describe the behavior of the bond price in relation to the changing yield curve. *Convexity* is defined as

$$Convexity = \frac{1}{2}\left(\frac{d^2P}{dr^2}\right)/P \tag{4.21}$$

where $P$ is the bond price and $r$ is the interest rate. For example, consider a zero-coupon bond with maturity $T$ and a semiannually compounding market yield of $r_{0.5}$. Then

$$P = \frac{1}{(1 + r_{0.5}/2)^{2T}} \tag{4.22}$$

A straightforward calculation shows that the convexity of such a bond is

$$Convexity = \frac{1}{4} \times \frac{T(2T + 1)}{(1 + r_{0.5}/2)^2} \tag{4.23}$$

In general, when a bond has embedded options or the yield curve is not flat, both effective duration and convexity do not have simple mathematical expressions like the ones shown above. In practice, both effective duration and convexity are numerically simulated, using a valuation model of a bond.

The estimated convexity value can be given by

$$Convexity = \frac{1}{2}\frac{[P(\Delta) - 2P + P(-\Delta)]}{\Delta^2}\frac{1}{P}$$

where $P(\Delta)$ and $P(-\Delta)$ are the bond prices with the spot curve shifted by $\Delta$ up and down, respectively.

Given the definition of convexity, it can be shown that the changes of a bond value can be approximated by the duration and convexity as follows:

$$\Delta P = -Duration \cdot P \cdot \Delta r_{0.5} + Convexity \cdot P \cdot (\Delta r_{0.5})^2 \tag{4.24}$$

The above equation holds even for bonds with embedded options, not just for bonds with fixed cash flows. This relationship of the change in price to the change in interest rates, using duration and convexity, is derived by using a Taylor expansion of $P$ as a function of interest rate $r$. Using the above numerical example, we have cash with a convexity of 0, a bond position with a convexity of 49.486, and a portfolio with a convexity of 16.49 ($= 49.486 \times 10/30$).

The change in bond price as a function of a parallel shift of interest rates is

$$\Delta P = -9.708 \times 55.36\Delta r_{0.5} + 49.486 \times 55.36\Delta r_{0.5}^2$$

For example, if the yield curve shifts 2% or 200 basis points upward, then $\Delta r_{0.5}$ is 0.02, and the change of the bond price is

$$\Delta P = -9.708 \times 55.36 \times 0.02 + 49.486 \times 55.36 \times (0.02)^2 \approx -9.65$$

That means that if the yield curve rises 200 basis points, the bond would drop in price from $55.36 to $45.71, as approximated by using duration and convexity.

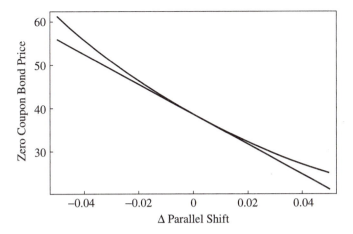

**Figure 4.8** Performance profiles of a bond. We plot the prices of a zero-coupon bond against parallel shifts of interest rates from −5% to 5% with an interval of 1 basis point. The face value is $100 and the maturity is ten years hence. The current yield curve is 10% flat. The curve is a zero-coupon bond profile and the straight line is a tangent line at the no shift point, where the yield is 10%. Since the curve is above the straight line, the bond profile is convex rather than concave. In other words, the appreciating amount of the bond when the rate goes down is larger than the depreciating amount when the rate goes up. In this sense, the more convex a bond is, the more valuable it is, other things being equal.

## Performance Profile

*Performance profile* depicts the value of a bond over a range of instantaneous parallel movements of the interest rate level. The performance profile can clearly depict how the behavior of the bond price changes with the level of interest rates. For a bond with a positive duration, the price will fall as the interest rate increases, and therefore the performance profile of the bond will have a negatively sloped curve. The curvature of the performance profile is related to the convexity of the bond. The higher the convexity of the bond, the higher is the curvature of the performance profile, with an accelerated increase in the price as the interest rate falls.

The performance profile is particularly useful for understanding the interest rate exposure of a bond portfolio position. If the bond portfolio is not sensitive to the interest rate parallel movement, then the performance profile will be horizontal. (See figure 4.8.)

## 4.8   APPLICATIONS OF THE BOND ANALYTICS

In this section, we present two applications using the bond analytics described. One refers to a commonly used bond trading strategy called "barbell trade," and the other is the use of key rate duration to manage an enhanced indexed Treasury portfolio.

### A Barbell Trade

A *barbell position* refers to buying bond positions with short-term bonds and long-term bonds while selling medium-term bonds such that the net portfolio position is 0. The dollar duration of the barbell position is also 0. The combination of the use of short-term bonds and long-term bonds (hence the name "barbell") leads to a higher convexity in the buy position than in the sell position. The reason that the barbell has a higher convexity will be explained below. As a result, the barbell position leads to positive returns when the yield curve rises or falls in a parallel way.

Assume that the market has a flat yield curve at 6%. Consider an example of a barbell trade: holding a bond position of $100 in a one-year zero-coupon bond and $100 in a five-year zero-coupon bond and shorting $200 in a 2.999-year zero-coupon bond.

|  | Bond Position Value | Maturity | Duration | Convexity |
|---|---|---|---|---|
| A | $100 | 1 | 0.9708 | 0.7069 |
| B | $100 | 5 | 4.8543 | 12.9606 |
| Total | $200 | 3 | 2.9125 | 6.8337 |
| Short-selling | $200 | 2.999 | 2.9125 | 4.9486 |

The holding portfolio value as a function of parallel shifts of the yield curve is given by

$$\Delta V(holding) = -2.9125 \times 200 \times \Delta r_{0.5} + 6.8337 \times 200 \times \Delta r_{0.5}^2$$

Similarly, the short-selling position value is given by

$$\Delta V(short\ selling) = -2.9125 \times 200 \times \Delta r_{0.5} + 4.9486 \times 200 \times \Delta r_{0.5}^2$$

The net position is given by

$$\Delta V = \Delta V(holding) - \Delta V(short\ selling)$$
$$= 377.02 \Delta r_{0.5}^2$$

For example, if the spot yield curve shifts 100 basis point up or down, then $\Delta r_{0.5} = 0.01$, and the profit is $\Delta V = \$0.0377$.

This description of the barbell trade, according to the above equation, seems to suggest that the bond position can realize profits as long as the yield curve moves up or down. Of course it is not always possible to attain a position where only profitable situations occur. If the medium-term rate falls more relative to the short-term and long-term rates, then the barbell trade will realize a loss.

If we analyze the barbell position, we should find positive dollar key rate durations at the one- and five-year terms and a negative dollar key rate at the 2.999-year term. The dollar key rate durations for the terms are given below.

| Year | Dollar Key Rate Duration × 0.0001 = PV 01 |
|---|---|
| 1 | 0.9708 × 100 × 0.0001 = 0.009708 |
| 2.999 | −2.9125 × 200 × 0.0001 = −0.05825 |
| 5 | 4.8543 × 100 × 0.0001 = 0.04854 |
| Total | 0 |

Since the net dollar key rate duration is 0, the price of the barbell position is insensitive to the parallel shifts of the spot yield curve. However, for example, a fall of 1 basis point at the 2.999-year rate, while the other rates remain unchanged, would lead to a loss of $0.05825. Indeed, there are many possible yield curve movements that may lead to losses in holding the barbell position. This trade is designed to bet on parallel yield curve movements.

### Replicating a Treasury Index—Passive Portfolio Management

In bond portfolio management, asset managers may offer a portfolio managed against a Treasury bond index. A *Treasury bond index* is defined as a portfolio constructed from all the Treasury notes and bonds outstanding, subject to some liquidity constraints on each bond issue. Asset managers offer to manage a client investment that will mimic the Treasury index monthly total returns. Such management style is called *passive* because the asset management is not actively seeking to provide high returns for the clients but passively reacting to the performance of the bond index.

Suppose the investment is $100 million. The size of the investment would prohibit the portfolio manager from buying all the Treasury bonds and notes outstanding in proportion to each bond's outstanding amount relative to the total Treasury securities market. Also, given the size of the investment, the transaction costs would be prohibitive.

A commonly used approach to this problem is to choose various characteristics of the index and then determine the value of the Treasury bond position as a proportion of the outstanding amount that has those characteristics. Such characteristics may be the coupon rate range, maturity range, and yield range. The portfolio can then be constructed to replicate the Treasury index by matching the portfolio values to each of the cells. For example, according to the Treasury index, the proportion of bonds that have yields 5%–5.5%, coupon rates 6.0%–6.5%, and maturities of three to five years is 10%. Then the replicating portfolio can be constructed by assigning 10% of the investment to bonds that satisfy the above criteria.

Much of the risk of the Treasury index return is driven by the changing shape and level of the yield curve. Another approach is to use key rate duration. McCoy (1993) uses a portfolio of 12 bonds that match the key rate durations of the Treasury index at the beginning of the month, and continually revises the portfolio at the end of the month. He empirically tests the strategy using historical data from January 1990 to December 1990. The test shows that the average absolute difference in returns was only 2 basis points. He then tests various strategies for enhancing the portfolio returns, including choosing cheap bonds. The return generated by various strategies ranges from 22 basis points to 238 basis points. Of course, we have to note that the test was conducted with observed bond prices; transaction costs have not been properly accounted for. In any case, the test does show that controlling the risk of yield curve movements is important in managing a bond, particularly a Treasury bond, portfolio.

# EXCEL MODEL EXERCISES

## E4.1   EFFECTIVE DURATION

### Definitions

The spot yield curve is based on a specified compounding rate. The shift of the spot yield curve is assumed to be parallel for the duration measure. The bond price is the value of the bond derived from the bond model, using the spot yield curve. The key rates are the principal rates, which mainly determine the yield curve movements. Since the yield curve makes many types of movements in reality, we need the key rates to describe nonparallel shifts. $P(r + \Delta)$ is a bond price when the interest rises by $+\Delta$ from the current level of r. $P(r - \Delta)$ can be defined similarly. $P(r)$ is a current bond price when the interest rate is r. $(P(r + \Delta) - P(r - \Delta))/2$ is the average price change and $(P(r+\Delta)-P(r-\Delta))/(2 \cdot P(r))$ is the more accurate percentage or relative price change than $(P(r + \Delta) - P(r))/P(r)$ or $(P(r) - P(r - \Delta))/P(r)$.

## Description of the Model

Effective duration measures the sensitivity of the bond value to a small parallel shift of the yield curve. The measure is an approximation, applicable to a small parallel shift of the spot yield curve. Specifically, effective duration is the proportional change in the bond value to the change in spot yield curve.

## Numerical Example

Consider a zero-coupon bond with maturity of ten years. Suppose that the spot yield curve is flat at 6%. The duration of the bond is 9.7087. That is, if the spot yield curve falls one basis point to a level of 5.99%, then the bond price would rise 0.097087%

| Inputs | | | | |
|---|---|---|---|---|
| Compounding frequency (m) | 2 | | | |
| Bond maturity (years) | 10 | $0 < T \le 10$ with 0.5 step size | | |
| Principal | 100 | | | |
| Coupon rate (annual compounding) | 0 | | | |
| $\Delta$ Spot yield (shift amount) | 0 | | | |
| Key rate | 0 | Key rate "0" means parallel shift. | | |

| Year | 0 | 0.5 | 1 | 1.5 |
|---|---|---|---|---|
| Spot curve (semiannual compounding) | 0.06 | | 0.06 | |
| Shifted curve | 0.06 | 0.06 | 0.06 | 0.06 |
| | | | | |
| Cash flow | | 0 | 0 | 0 |
| PV(CF) | | 0 | 0 | 0 |
| Bond price | 55.3675754 | | | |

| Outputs | | | | |
|---|---|---|---|---|
| $\Delta$ Spot yield (shift amount) | | -0.0001 | 0.0000 | 0.0001 |
| Bond price | | 55.4214 | 55.3676 | 55.3138 |
| | | | | |
| Effective duration (numerical value) | 9.7087 | $=-(P(r+\Delta)-P(r-\Delta))/(2\Delta P(r))$ | | |
| | | | | |
| Effective duration of zero-coupon bond | 9.7087 | $=T/(1+r_{0.5}(T)/2)$ | | |
| (closed form) | | | | |

Figure E4.1

$(= 9.7087 \times 0.0001 \times 100)$, because the effective duration is defined as $(-\Delta P/P)/\Delta r$. It is interesting to note that the effective duration of a zero-coupon bond is similar to the maturity of the bond. In general, the effective duration of a bond with no embedded option is approximately the same as the weighted average life of the cash flows of a bond. See figure E4.1.

## Applications

1. Duration is used to measure the interest rate exposure of a bond or a bond portfolio.
2. The duration measure can be used in the delta-normal method to determine the VaR (value at risk) of a bond or a bond portfolio.
3. By matching the durations of the assets and the liabilities, we can immunize the asset and liability portfolio to interest rate risks.

## Case: Interest Rate Bet Using Effective Duration

Directional Asset Management is a fixed-income asset management company. Its clients are endowment funds of universities, some retirement funds, and other institutional investments. Directional Asset Management invests in relatively liquid bonds such as government securities and investment grade corporate bonds with large amounts outstanding in the market. The expertise of the company is the forecast of interest rate movements. The portfolio management's strengths are based on its bet on the cycles when the interest rates fall or rise. The investment policy has a given guideline arranged with its clients in terms of the risk exposure to the interest rate risks. The guideline is that the portfolio duration should be between two years and seven years. Duration is defined as the price sensitivity to the yield curve shifts. In comparing with the industry standards, this duration constraint does allow the asset management to take significant interest rate directional bets.

In a meeting with one potential client, which is considering allocating a small portion of their endowment fund to Directional Asset Management, this issue of the duration constraint is being reviewed.

*The client wants to understand the implication of the constraint better. "How much risk are we talking about?" the client asks. "When you take the maximum risks under this constraint, would you be taking the risks equivalent to holding an S&P index? Maybe you can give me a comparison relative to some benchmarks. I know you have to make some assumptions. That is OK as long as you state them clearly to me."*

## Exercises and Answers

1. What is the effective duration of the bond in the numerical example if the principal amount is 1,000? How is the duration of a bond dependent on the principal value in general? See figure E4.2.

   *Answer:* In the numerical example, we assume $100 principal; however here we assume $1,000 principal. Even though we have different principal, the effective duration is the same, because the effective duration measures the bond price sensitivity with respect to a small change of interest rate. To calculate the effective duration, we can use either a formula or a numerical method. The basic procedure of the numerical method is that first we disturb the interest rate by a small amount to

| Inputs | | | | |
|---|---|---|---|---|
| Compounding frequency (m) | 2 | | | |
| Bond maturity (years) | 10 | 0 < T ≤ 10 with 0.5 step size | | |
| Principal | 1000 | | | |
| Coupon rate (annual compounding) | 0 | | | |
| Δ Spot yield (shift amount) | 0 | | | |
| Key rate | 0 | Key rate "0" means parallel shift. | | |
| | | | | |
| Year | 0 | 0.5 | 1 | 1.5 |
| Spot curve (semiannual compounding) | 0.06 | | 0.06 | |
| Shifted curve | 0.06 | 0.06 | 0.06 | 0.06 |
| | | | | |
| Cash flow | | 0 | 0 | 0 |
| PV(CF) | | 0 | 0 | 0 |
| Bond price | 553.675754 | | | |

| Outputs | | | | |
|---|---|---|---|---|
| Δ Spot yield (shift amount) | | -0.0001 | 0.0000 | 0.0001 |
| Bond price | | 554.2136 | 553.6758 | 553.1385 |
| | | | | |
| Effective duration (numerical value) | 9.7087 | =-(P(r+Δ)-P(r-Δ))/(2ΔP(r)) | | |
| | | | | |
| Effective duration of zero-coupon bond (closed form) | 9.7087 | =T/(1+$r_{0.5}$(T)/2) | | |

Figure E4.2

| Inputs | | | | |
|---|---|---|---|---|
| Compounding frequency (m) | 2 | | | |
| Bond maturity (years) | 10 | 0 < T ≤ 10 with 0.5 step size | | |
| Principal | 1000 | | | |
| Coupon rate (annual compounding) | 0.1 | | | |
| Δ Spot yield (shift amount) | 0 | | | |
| Key rate | 0 | Key rate "0" means parallel shift. | | |
| | | | | |
| Year | 0 | 0.5 | 1 | 1.5 |
| Spot curve (semiannual compounding) | 0.06 | | 0.06 | |
| Shifted curve | 0.06 | 0.06 | 0.06 | 0.06 |
| | | | | |
| Cash flow | | 50 | 50 | 50 |
| PV(CF) | | 48.5436893 | 47.1297955 | 45.757083 |
| Bond price | 1297.5495 | | | |

| Outputs | | | | |
|---|---|---|---|---|
| Δ Spot yield (shift amount) | | -0.0001 | 0.0000 | 0.0001 |
| Bond price | | 1298.4313 | 1297.5495 | 1296.6685 |
| | | | | |
| Effective duration (numerical value) | 6.7930 | =-(P(r+Δ)-P(r-Δ))/(2ΔP(r)) | | |

Figure E4.3

measure how much the bond price changes. Since the bond price change is different depending on whether we increase or decrease the interest rate by a small amount, we calculate both of them and average them to measure the effective duration. The empirical results show that two methods generate the same effective duration. For a straight bond, we have a closed form; however we do not have a closed form for an option-embedded bond. In this case, we have to resort to the numerical method. The closed form of the effective duration for a zero-coupon straight bond is a $T/(1 + r_{0.5}(T)/2)$ where $r_{0.5}(T)$ is a semiannually compounded $T$-year interest rate.

2. What is the effective duration of a bond with a 10% coupon rate, keeping all the other assumptions in the numerical example above? See figure E4.3.

*Answer:* If the coupon rate increases from a zero rate to a positive rate, the effective duration decreases. The effective duration of the coupon bond decreases from 9.7087 to 6.7930. 9.7087 is the effective duration of the zero-coupon bond as we have seen in question 1. The reason for this is that whenever the coupon rate increases, we will receive more cash inflow before the maturity. To understand this point, we can think of the duration as the weighted average of the coupon payment dates and the maturity. The weight is the proportion of the present value of the cash flow to the bond price. Since the sum of the present value of the cash flow is the price, the sum of the weights should be 1. For example, we have a five-year bond with the coupon rate of 10%. We assume an annual coupon payment for simplicity. The coupon payment dates are 1, 2, 3, 4, and 5 years and the maturity date is year 5. For each year we have $10 as a coupon payment and $100 only at year 5 as a principal. Therefore we have $10 for the period of year 1 to year 4 and $110 at year 5. The weight average life can be calculated as $(PV(10) \times 1 + PV(10) \times 2 + \ldots + PV(110) \times 5)/\text{Price}$.

From the calculation, we can see that the weighted average life for a coupon bond is shorter than that for a zero-coupon bond. For example, compare two bonds. One is a zero-coupon bond and the other is a 10% coupon bond. For simplicity, we assume annual coupon payments, and the two bonds have the same ten-year time to maturity. The cash flow of the zero-coupon bond is 100 at year 10. The cash flow of the coupon bond before the maturity is 90 (= $10 \times 9$ years) and 110 at the maturity. For this reason, the effective duration of the coupon bond is smaller than the corresponding zero-coupon bond.

3. What is the duration of the portfolio of $100 million (market value) in the ten-year zero-coupon bond and $100 million (market value) in the coupon bond described in question 2?

*Answer:* The duration of the portfolio is the weighted sum of the individual bond durations, where the weight is the proportion of the market value.

$$Duration_p = \sum_i \left(\frac{B_i}{P}\right) Duration_i$$

$$= \tfrac{1}{2} \times 9.7087 + \tfrac{1}{2} \times 6.7930$$

$$= 8.2509$$

4. Suppose the yield curve is 12%. What is the impact on the duration of the zero-coupon bond? See figures E4.4 and E4.5.

*Answer:* The modifier decreases in value with the increase of the risk-free rate.

| Inputs | | | | |
|---|---|---|---|---|
| Compounding frequency (m) | 2 | | | |
| Bond maturity (years) | 10 | 0 < T ≤ 10 with 0.5 step size | | |
| Principal | 1000 | | | |
| Coupon rate (annual compounding) | 0 | | | |
| Δ Spot yield (shift amount) | 0 | | | |
| Key rate | 0 | Key rate "0" means parallel shift. | | |
| | | | | |
| Year | 0 | 0.5 | 1 | 1.5 |
| Spot curve (semiannual compounding) | 0.12 | | 0.12 | |
| Shifted curve | 0.12 | 0.12 | 0.12 | 0.12 |
| | | | | |
| Cash flow | | 0 | 0 | 0 |
| PV(CF) | | 0 | 0 | 0 |
| Bond price | 311.804727 | | | |
| | | | | |
| Outputs | | | | |
| | | | | |
| Δ Spot yield (shift amount) | | -0.0001 | 0.0000 | 0.0001 |
| Bond price | | 312.0990 | 311.8047 | 311.5107 |
| | | | | |
| Effective duration (numerical value) | 9.4340 | =-(P(r+Δ)-P(r-Δ))/(2ΔP(r)) | | |
| | | | | |
| Effective duration of zero-coupon bond (closed form) | 9.4340 | =T/(1+r_{0.5}(T)/2) | | |

Figure E4.4

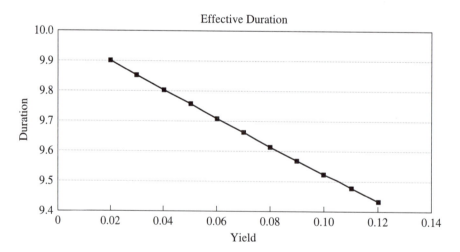

Figure E4.5

## Further Exercises

1. Consider a coupon bond with a coupon rate of 10% and a five-year maturity. We assume a semiannual coupon payment. The yield curve is flat at 10%. Since we have ten cash flows from the bond, we can calculate the present value of the ten cash flows. We know that the sum of ten present values is the bond price. Calculate the weighted sum of the periods when we have cash flows. Since we know ten cash flow periods, which are $0.5, 1, 1.5, \ldots, 5$, we should determine the weights, which are the present value of the corresponding cash flow at each period divided by the price. After we calculate the weighted sum, we divide the weighted sum by 1.05, which is equal to the effective duration.

   *Answer:* The effective duration is 3.8609.

2. Use the effective duration in question 1 and calculate the bond price when the yield curve shifts to 11%.

   *Answer:* Using the effective duration, we can approximate the bond price change when the yield curve shifts to 11%. We can also calculate the new bond price when the yield curve is flat at 11%. The approximated price using the effective duration is 961.391. The exact bond price using the shifted yield curve is 962.312. The difference between the two values comes from the fact that we use only the first derivative to determine the effective duration. The formula to approximate the bond price change is $\Delta P = -D_{effective} \times \Delta r \times P$.

## E4.2    PAR YIELD CURVE, SPOT YIELD CURVE, DISCOUNT FUNCTION, AND FORWARD PRICES

### Definitions

The par yield curve is the yield curve based on the yields of the par bonds, where their market prices equal the par value. The spot yield curve is the yield curve based on the yields of the zero-coupon bonds.

The yields can be determined using different compounding rates. For example, they can be annually, semiannually, monthly, daily, and continuously compounded. The frequency $m$ is the number of subperiods per year. For example, $m = 12$ means compounded monthly.

Discount function is the market value of $1 to be paid at a future specified date. The forward price is the $T$-year zero-coupon bond price to be delivered at a future date, determined by the forward contract pricing model.

The forward discount function is the function of forward prices of zero-coupon bonds $1 par over a range of maturities to be delivered at time $t$.

### Description of the Model

The discount function, spot yield curve, and the par yield curve are all mathematically related by definition.

Given the discount function, spot yield curve, or the par yield curve from the market place, we can determine the forward price of a $T$-year zero-coupon bond to be delivered in time $t$ based on the arbitrage-free assumption in a perfect capital market.

| Inputs | | | | | | | |
|---|---|---|---|---|---|---|---|
| Year | 0 | 1 | 2 | 3 | 4 | 5 | 6 |
| Spot rate (continuous compounding) | Changing cells | 0.0617 | 0.0617 | 0.0617 | 0.0617 | 0.0617 | 0.0617 |
| Target spot curve w/ frequency m | 12 | 0.0618 | 0.0618 | 0.0618 | 0.0618 | 0.0618 | 0.0618 |
| Solver target cell | 0.0000 | | | | | | |
| Target par curve | | 0.0127 | 0.0155 | 0.0198 | 0.0243 | 0.0287 | 0.0314 |
| Solver target cell | 0.0126 | | | | | | |

| Outputs | | | | | | | |
|---|---|---|---|---|---|---|---|
| Year | 0 | 1 | 2 | 3 | 4 | 5 | 6 |
| Discount function | 0 | 0.9402 | 0.8839 | 0.8311 | 0.7814 | 0.7346 | 0.6907 |
| Forward prices | 1 | | 0.9402 | 0.8839 | 0.8311 | 0.7814 | 0.7346 |
| F(t,T) | 2 | | | 0.9402 | 0.8839 | 0.8311 | 0.7814 |
| =P(T)/P(t) | 3 | | | | 0.9402 | 0.8839 | 0.8311 |
| =F(t-1,T)/F(t-1,t) | 4 | | | | | 0.9402 | 0.8839 |
| | 5 | | | | | | 0.9402 |
| | 6 | | | | | | |
| | 7 | | | | | | |
| | 8 | | | | | | |
| | 9 | | | | | | |
| | Future date | | | | | | |

**Figure E4.6**

## Numerical Example

Suppose that the monthly compounding spot yield curve is flat, at a rate of 6.18%. Then we can determine the continuously compounding spot yield curve to be 6.17%. Given this market condition, the forward price for a two-year zero-coupon bond, to be delivered in three years, is 88.39 for a 100 par. See figure E4.6.

## Applications

1. The forward discount function can then be used to derive the forward spot yield curve at a future date.
2. The model can be used to price a forward contract of any bond, including coupon-paying bonds, using the bond model.

## Case: The Law of One Price and Marking a Bond Position

The room was silent. John Lawson felt the tension, sitting next to his boss, Alan Modigliani, the risk manager of a fund management company. John was staring at his notes, but not reading, and Alan was looking straight at the white wall. Also in the room were four assistants of the portfolio manager of the corporate bond portfolios.

The silence was broken as the door swung open and closed noisily. "Alan, good to see you," Pierre Cartier announced his entrance and took the seat at the head of the table, the only vacant seat left for him. "You know, your idea of marking to market with the law of one price is exactly right, and this is precisely the right way for us to deal with these illiquid bond positions that we are taking," he continued. "Last month, the rates fell and our putable bonds booked the profits according to the models you developed. Your models are exactly right and your approach is exactly what we need here." "Pierre, glad you like what we have done. This is exactly why I called this meeting." "Alan, you got more ideas! When do you sleep?"

"No, Pierre. I want to review your position in Yeong Leung Industries. We are holding over 50% of their long bond issues, and we noticed that last week their stocks came down 20% after their poor earnings announcement." "Alan, I know the stock has fallen. But we are holding the bonds. Am I missing something?" "You know as well as I do. Stocks and bonds are related." "This is like saying I am related to my wife." "OK. We also know that a similar Yeong Leung issue was traded five points down last week." "Right. Ha. That was a $1 million trade, probably sold by some kid who needed to fix his home. That trade said nothing for us in marking our position. Look, what do you want us to do." "You need to adjust the price on that bond in marking your portfolio. Use the law of one price model. We notice that you are still using the same price as the one two weeks ago."

"Alan, you are kidding, right? That bond has not traded for a month. Where do I find a price for the bond, and why should I mark it down anyway," Pierre protested, as he raised his voice. "Your model does not apply to that bond issue." "Pierre, how do you then decide which bond should be priced by the risk department model and which should not?" "Simple. We are in the market every minute and we know the market. Period." Pierre slammed the table in anger. He jumped up to the side table where there was phone. He picked up the white phone and stared intently at Alan. "If you want, you can call Dave up and ask him which number he wants to mark our bond position!" (Dave is the president of the company.) "Dave is not there to give you numbers every week," Alan retorted. "Go and call him." Pierre pushed the phone to Alan, becoming physically aggressive. Alan picked up his papers and got up, leaving the room. " We will talk about this in our credit committee next week," he said, as he walked out. John Lawson quickly followed.

Out on the street, John felt that his jaw muscles were all tensed and noticed that he had not uttered one word in the meeting, nor had four other assistants. "Alan, I thought the law of one price is a principle in finance. Pierre even agreed to that at the beginning of the meeting." "John, that is right. But there is one overriding principle in finance." "What is that?" "Self-interest."

*John was emotionally drained by the confrontation, but he could not resist attempting to untangle the apparent contradiction between the two principles in finance. What will Dave say in the credit committee meeting next week? How would Dave resolve this confrontation?*

## Exercises and Answers

1. Suppose that the annual compounding spot yield curve is flat at a rate of 6.17%. What is the forward price of a bond to be delivered in three years with an annual coupon rate of 6.17%, with maturity of two years?

   *Answer:* From the current yield curve, we can calculate the implied forward curves, which are the expected future term structure of interest rates. From these forward curves, we can calculate the forward price. At year 3, the term structure of the forward rates are 0.941886 and 0.887149 for year 1 and year 2, respectively. Therefore, the forward price is 100 (= 106.17 × 0.887149 + 6.17 × 0.941886). Intuitively, since

| Inputs | | | | | | |
|---|---|---|---|---|---|---|
| Year | 0 | 1 | 2 | 3 | 4 | 5 |
| Spot rate (continuous compounding) | Changing cells | 0.059871 | 0.059871 | 0.059871 | 0.059871 | 0.059871 |
| Target spot curve w/ frequency m | 1 | 0.0617 | 0.0617 | 0.0617 | 0.0617 | 0.0617 |
| Solver target cell | 0.0000 | | | | | |
| Target par curve | | 0.0127 | 0.0155 | 0.0198 | 0.02425 | 0.0287 |
| Solver target cell | 0.0114 | | | | | |
| **Outputs** | | | | | | |
| Year | 0 | 1 | 2 | 3 | 4 | 5 |
| Discount function | 0 | 0.941886 | 0.887149 | 0.835593 | 0.787033 | 0.741295 |
| Forward prices | 1 | | 0.941886 | 0.887149 | 0.835593 | 0.787033 |
| F(t,T) | 2 | | | 0.941886 | 0.887149 | 0.835593 |
| =P(T)/P(t) | 3 | | | | 0.941886 | 0.887149 |
| =F(t-1,T)/F(t-1,t) | 4 | | | | | 0.941886 |
| | 5 | | | | | |
| | 6 | | | | | |
| | 7 | | | | | |
| | 8 | | | | | |
| | 9 | | | | | |
| | Future date | | | | | |
| | | | | B(3,5) | c | c+F |
| | | | | 100 | 6.17 | 106.17 |
| | | | | P.V. | 5.811434 | 94.18857 |

**Figure E4.7**

the initial spot curve is flat at 6.17%, we know that the forward curve is also flat at 6.17. Therefore, the coupon bond price is par if the coupon rate is the same as the interest rate. See figure E4.7.

2. Using the market assumption from question 1, what is the price of the bond with 6.17% annual coupon, with maturity of two years?

*Answer:* As we have indicated in question 1, the bond price is par as long as the coupon rate is equal to the current interest rate. See figure E4.8.

3. Would the answers to the above questions change if the yield curve has not changed, even though the market expects much higher market volatilities in the future, and more uncertainty about the future, as reflected by anticipated changes in the interest rates?

*Answer:* Since the current yield curve reflects all the market expectations about the future interest rate, we do not have to worry about how the market expectations would change the future yield curves in order to calculate the current bond prices when the bonds have no embedded options.

4. Using the U.S. STRIPS market, we observe that the spot yield (annual compounding) curve is given in table E4.1. What is the forward price of a two-year zero-coupon bond with a one-year delivery date?

*Answer:* We calculate the term structure of forward rates at year 1. The one-year forward price at year 1 is 0.976559 and the two-year forward price at year 1 is 0.933445. From this forward price, we can calculate the two-year zero-coupon bond at year 1, which is 0.933445. See figure E4.9.

| Inputs | | | | | | |
|---|---|---|---|---|---|---|
| Year | 0 | 1 | 2 | 3 | 4 | 5 |
| Spot rate (continuous compounding) | Changing cells | 0.059871 | 0.059871 | 0.059871 | 0.059871 | 0.059871 |
| Target spot curve w/ frequency m | 1 | 0.0617 | 0.0617 | 0.0617 | 0.0617 | 0.0617 |
| Solver target cell | 0.0000 | | | | | |
| Target par curve | | 0.0127 | 0.0155 | 0.0198 | 0.02425 | 0.0287 |
| Solver target cell | 0.0114 | | | | | |
| | | | | | | |
| Outputs | | | | | | |
| Year | 0 | 1 | 2 | 3 | 4 | 5 |
| Discount function | 0 | 0.941886 | 0.887149 | 0.835593 | 0.787033 | 0.741295 |
| Forward prices | 1 | | 0.941886 | 0.887149 | 0.835593 | 0.787033 |
| F(t,T) | 2 | | | 0.941886 | 0.887149 | 0.835593 |
| =P(T)/P(t) | 3 | | | | 0.941886 | 0.887149 |
| =F(t-1,T)/F(t-1,t) | 4 | | | | | 0.941886 |
| | 5 | | | | | |
| | 6 | | | | | |
| | 7 | | | | | |
| | 8 | | | | | |
| | 9 | | | | | |
| | Future date | | | | | |
| | | | | | | |
| | B(0,2) | c | c+F | | | |
| | 100 | 6.17 | 106.17 | | | |
| | P.V. | 5.811434 | 94.18857 | | | |

Figure E4.8

Table E4.1

| Year | Yields (%) |
|---|---|
| 1 | 2 |
| 2 | 2.2 |
| 3 | 3.0 |
| 4 | 3.8 |
| 5 | 4 |

| Inputs | | | | | | |
|---|---|---|---|---|---|---|
| Year | 0 | 1 | 2 | 3 | 4 | 5 |
| Spot rate (continuous compounding) | Changing cells | 0.019803 | 0.021761 | 0.029559 | 0.037296 | 0.039221 |
| Target spot curve w/ frequency m | 1 | 0.02 | 0.022 | 0.03 | 0.038 | 0.04 |
| Solver target cell | 0.0000 | | | | | |
| Target par curve | | 0.0127 | 0.0155 | 0.0198 | 0.02425 | 0.0287 |
| Solver target cell | 0.0004 | | | | | |
| | | | | | | |
| Outputs | | | | | | |
| Year | 0 | 1 | 2 | 3 | 4 | 5 |
| Discount function | 0 | 0.980392 | 0.957411 | 0.915142 | 0.861412 | 0.821927 |
| Forward prices | 1 | | 0.976559 | 0.933445 | 0.87864 | 0.838366 |
| F(t,T) | 2 | | | 0.955851 | 0.899731 | 0.85849 |
| =P(T)/P(t) | 3 | | | | 0.941288 | 0.898142 |
| =F(t-1,T)/F(t-1,t) | 4 | | | | | 0.954163 |
| | Future date | | | | | |

Figure E4.9

| Year | 0 | 1 | 2 | 3 | 4 | 5 |
|---|---|---|---|---|---|---|
| Spot curve (continuous compounding) | 0 | 0.019803 | 0.021761 | 0.029559 | 0.037296 | 0.039221 |
| Forward curves (continuous compounding) | 1 | | 0.02372 | 0.034437 | 0.043127 | 0.044075 |
| f(t,T) | 2 | | | 0.045153 | 0.05283 | 0.05086 |
| =-ln(P(T)/P(t))/(T-t) | 3 | | | | 0.060507 | 0.053714 |
| =-lnF(t,T)/(T-t) | 4 | | | | | 0.04692 |
| | Future date | | | | | |

**Figure E4.10**

| Year | 0 | 1 | 2 | 3 | 4 | 5 | 6 | 7 | 8 | 9 | 10 |
|---|---|---|---|---|---|---|---|---|---|---|---|
| Interpolations | | 0.0127 | 0.0155 | 0.0198 | 0.0243 | 0.0287 | 0.0314 | 0.0341 | 0.0358 | 0.0375 | 0.0392 |

**Figure E4.11**

5. What is the forward yield curve, given the above spot yield curve over a one-year period?
   *Answer:* The forward yield curve is the expected spot yield curve at year 1. See figure E4.10.
6. For an upward-sloping spot yield curve, should the forward curve be higher than the spot yield curve? Hint: compare the discount function with the forward discount function.
   *Answer:* The forward curve is above the spot yield curve if the spot yield curve is upward-sloping.

## Further Exercises

1. Assume an upward-sloping yield curve. The quarterly compounding (m = 4) yield starts at 4% at year 0 and increases by 1% annually until year 10. Calculate the forward curve at year 1 and year 2. Given the target par curve observed in the market, calculate the par rate at year 1 and year 2 if the expected future spot curve is the forward curve. Finally, calculate the discount function.
   The target par curve observed in the market is given in figure E4.11.
   *Answer:* See figures E4.12 and E4.13.
2. Assume the same upward-sloping curve in question 1. Calculate a 10% coupon bond with eight-year maturity. If the future spot curve at year 1 is the forward curve, calculate the same bond price at year 1 and the rate of return of the bond over the first year.
   *Answer:* See figure E4.14.

## E4.3   DOLLAR DURATION

### Definitions

Compounding frequency is the number of compoundings in a year for the yield calculation. For semiannual compounding, the compounding frequency is 2.

| Outputs | | | | | | | | | | | |
|---|---|---|---|---|---|---|---|---|---|---|---|
| Year | 0 | 1 | 2 | 3 | 4 | 5 | 6 | 7 | 8 | 9 | 10 |
| Discount function | 0 | 0.961 | 0.9054 | 0.8364 | 0.7576 | 0.673 | 0.5862 | 0.5009 | 0.4197 | 0.345 | 0.2782 |
| Forward prices | 1 | | 0.9422 | 0.8703 | 0.7884 | 0.7003 | 0.6101 | 0.5212 | 0.4368 | 0.359 | 0.2895 |
| F(t,T) | 2 | | | 0.9238 | 0.8368 | 0.7433 | 0.6475 | 0.5532 | 0.4636 | 0.3811 | 0.3073 |
| =P(T)/P(t) | 3 | | | | 0.9058 | 0.8046 | 0.7009 | 0.5989 | 0.5018 | 0.4125 | 0.3327 |
| =F(t-1,T)/F(t-1,t) | 4 | | | | | 0.8883 | 0.7738 | 0.6611 | 0.554 | 0.4554 | 0.3672 |
| | 5 | | | | | | 0.8711 | 0.7443 | 0.6237 | 0.5127 | 0.4134 |
| | 6 | | | | | | | 0.8544 | 0.716 | 0.5885 | 0.4746 |
| | 7 | | | | | | | | 0.838 | 0.6889 | 0.5555 |
| | 8 | | | | | | | | | 0.822 | 0.6629 |
| | 9 | | | | | | | | | | 0.8064 |
| | Future date | | | | | | | | | | |
| Year | 0 | 1 | 2 | 3 | 4 | 5 | 6 | 7 | 8 | 9 | 10 |
| Spot curve (continuous compounding) | 0 | 0.0398 | 0.0497 | 0.0596 | 0.0694 | 0.0792 | 0.089 | 0.0988 | 0.1085 | 0.1182 | 0.1279 |
| Forward curves (continuous compounding) | 1 | | 0.0596 | 0.0694 | 0.0793 | 0.0891 | 0.0988 | 0.1086 | 0.1183 | 0.128 | 0.1377 |
| f(t,T) | 2 | | | 0.0793 | 0.0891 | 0.0989 | 0.1087 | 0.1184 | 0.1281 | 0.1378 | 0.1475 |
| =-ln(P(T)/P(t))/(T-t) | 3 | | | | 0.0989 | 0.1087 | 0.1185 | 0.1282 | 0.1379 | 0.1476 | 0.1572 |
| =-lnF(t,T)/(T-t) | 4 | | | | | 0.1185 | 0.1282 | 0.1379 | 0.1476 | 0.1573 | 0.167 |
| | 5 | | | | | | 0.138 | 0.1477 | 0.1574 | 0.167 | 0.1767 |
| | 6 | | | | | | | 0.1574 | 0.1671 | 0.1767 | 0.1863 |
| | 7 | | | | | | | | 0.1767 | 0.1864 | 0.196 |
| | 8 | | | | | | | | | 0.196 | 0.2056 |
| | 9 | | | | | | | | | | 0.2152 |
| | Future date | | | | | | | | | | |

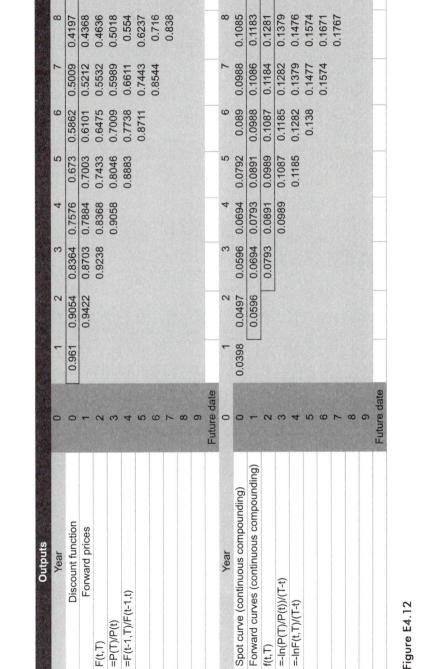

Figure E4.12

| Year | 0 | 1 | 2 | 3 | 4 | 5 | 6 | 7 | 8 | 9 | 10 |
|---|---|---|---|---|---|---|---|---|---|---|---|
| Spot curve (continuous compounding) | 0 | 0.0127 | 0.0155 | 0.0198 | 0.0244 | 0.029 | 0.0319 | 0.0348 | 0.0366 | 0.0385 | 0.0405 |
| Forward curves (continuous compounding) | 1 | | 0.0183 | 0.0234 | 0.0283 | 0.0331 | 0.0357 | 0.0385 | 0.04 | 0.0417 | 0.0435 |
| f(t,T) | 2 | | | 0.0285 | 0.0333 | 0.0381 | 0.0401 | 0.0425 | 0.0437 | 0.0451 | 0.0467 |
| =-ln(P(T)/P(t))/(T-t) | 3 | | | | 0.0381 | 0.0429 | 0.0439 | 0.046 | 0.0467 | 0.0479 | 0.0493 |
| =-lnF(t, T)/T-t | 4 | | | | | 0.0476 | 0.0469 | 0.0487 | 0.0489 | 0.0498 | 0.0512 |
| | 5 | | | | | | 0.0461 | 0.0492 | 0.0493 | 0.0504 | 0.0519 |
| | 6 | | | | | | | 0.0523 | 0.0509 | 0.0518 | 0.0533 |
| | 7 | | | | | | | | 0.0495 | 0.0515 | 0.0537 |
| | 8 | | | | | | | | | 0.0536 | 0.0558 |
| Future date | 9 | | | | | | | | | | 0.058 |

Figure E4.13

## Outputs

| Year | 0 | 1 | 2 | 3 | 4 | 5 | 6 | 7 | 8 |
|---|---|---|---|---|---|---|---|---|---|
| Discount function | 0 | 0.961 | 0.9054 | 0.8364 | 0.7576 | 0.673 | 0.5862 | 0.5009 | 0.4197 |
| Forward prices (1) | 1 | | 0.9422 | 0.8703 | 0.7884 | 0.7003 | 0.6101 | 0.5212 | 0.4368 |
| F(t,T) (2) | 2 | | | 0.9238 | 0.8368 | 0.7433 | 0.6475 | 0.5532 | 0.4636 |
| =P(T)/P(t) (3) | 3 | | | | 0.9058 | 0.8046 | 0.7009 | 0.5989 | 0.5018 |
| =F(t-1,T)/F(t-1,t) (4) | 4 | | | | | 0.8883 | 0.7738 | 0.6611 | 0.554 |
| (5) | 5 | | | | | | 0.8711 | 0.7443 | 0.6237 |
| (6) | 6 | | | | | | | 0.8544 | 0.716 |
| (7) | 7 | | | | | | | | 0.838 |
| (8) | 8 | | | | | | | | |
| (9) | 9 | | | | | | | | |

| | Future date | 0 | 1 | 2 | 3 | 4 | 5 | 6 | 7 | 8 |
|---|---|---|---|---|---|---|---|---|---|---|
| Face value | | 100 | | | | | | | | |
| Coupon rate | | 0.1 | | | | | | | | |
| CF | | | 10 | 10 | 10 | 10 | 10 | 10 | 10 | 110 |
| Bond price at time 0 | | 98.37629 | 9.6098 | 9.054 | 8.3639 | 7.5762 | 6.7297 | 5.8625 | 5.0088 | 46.172 |
| Bond price at time 1 | | 102.3708 | | 9.4216 | 8.7035 | 7.8838 | 7.003 | 6.1005 | 5.2122 | 48.046 |
| Rate of return (quarterly compounding) | | 0.04 | | | | | | | | |
| Rate of return (continuous compounding) | | 0.0398 | | | | | | | | |

Figure E4.14

## Description of the Model

Dollar duration measures the increase in the bond portfolio with one unit parallel drop in interest rates. In particular, PV 01 is the increase of the portfolio value for a one–basis point drop in rates. The model can be used to calculate the dollar duration of the bond portfolio.

## Numerical Example

Consider a bond portfolio with $30 million in a ten-year zero-coupon bond and borrowing cash of $20 million. Suppose the yield curve is flat at 6%. A one–basis point fall in interest rates would lead to a $29,126 rise in the bond portfolio. The dollar duration is $291.2621 million. See figure E4.15.

| Inputs | | | |
|---|---|---|---|
| Compounding frequency (m) | 2 | | |
| Bond maturity (years) | 10 | 0 < T ≤ 10 with 0.5 step size | |
| Principal | 100 | | |
| Coupon rate (annual compounding) | 0 | | |
| Δ Spot yield (shift amount) | 0 | | |
| Key rate | 0 | | |
| | Key rate "0" means parallel shift. | | |
| Investment in bond ($mil.) | 30 | | |
| Investment in cash ($mil.) | -20 | | |
| Portfolio value ($mil.) | 10 | | |
| | | | |
| Year | 0 | 0.5 | 1 |
| Spot curve (semiannual compounding) | 0.06 | | 0.06 |
| Shifted curve | 0.06 | 0.06 | 0.06 |
| | | | |
| Cash flow | | 0 | 0 |
| PV(CF) | | 0 | 0 |
| Bond price | 55.3676 | | |

| Outputs | | | |
|---|---|---|---|
| $ Duration of bond position (million) | 291.2621 | | |

$$\$Duration = Duration \times Value$$
$$= -\frac{\Delta P/P}{\Delta r} \times P = -\frac{\Delta P}{\Delta r}$$

| | | | |
|---|---|---|---|
| $ Duration of portfolio (million) | 291.2621 | | |

$$\$D_P = D_P \times Value_P$$
$$= \left(\frac{B}{P}D_{Bond} + \frac{C}{P}D_{Cash}\right) \times Value_P$$

| | | | |
|---|---|---|---|
| PV 01 = $ Duration∗0.0001 | 29,126.2 | | |

$$PV01 = -\frac{1}{10000}\frac{\Delta P}{\Delta r}$$

Figure E4.15

## Applications

In measuring the bond portfolio sensitivity to one–basis point shifts in interest rates, dollar duration can be used for portfolio hedging. The portfolio can have both long and short positions, and the net portfolio value may be zero. The portfolio can also have interest rate derivatives, like options, forwards, and futures contracts.

Dollar durations or PV 01 can be used in managing the interest rate risks on the trading floor in aggregating all the interest rate risks from all the trading desks. The measure can be used to implement dynamic hedging of interest rate options.

## Case: Transfer Pricing and Hedging at a Treasury Desk

Jack Lau was the deputy treasurer at a bank, a medium-size bank in Singapore. He was in charge of the capital market activities doing the day-to-day activities in managing the bank's transfer pricing—taking a position or hedging as the bank made commitments to loans and received deposits. He had a bit of a challenge one day. At 10:00 a.m., he was told that the bank had sold a $10 million one-year certificate of deposit (CD), and the cash had been wired to the bank account. Almost at the same time, the bank made an unusually long-term loan to a major bank client, a five-year fixed rate, also $10 million. He checked the market swap rates at the time. The loan rate was 2% above the five-year swap rate and the CD was 0.25% below the one-year swap rate. "That's good. The spread is positive, even after adjusting for default risks," he said to himself. If the swap curve rose 1%, then the cost of funding using the CD would go up. Then this positive spread would not leave much of a profit margin. He knew that he could calculate the PV 01 to determine the interest rate risks.

The problem he was facing that day was that he did not want to take two swap positions at the same time to hedge the risk. The two positions would be: buy a one-year swap to hedge the CD position and sell a five-year swap to hedge the loan position. He was convinced that the swap curve would only move in a parallel fashion in the short term, and one swap position should suffice. He sat down to calculate the PV 01 of a swap position. The market was particularly active at the three-year tenor. He just needed to determine the notional amount that he would need such that the PV 01 of the hedge position would offset the PV 01 of the CD and loan positions. "Duration calculation would not be appropriate for these long-short positions. PV 01 tells me the dollar profit and loss, and therefore that measure would be more appropriate." He then proceeded to investigate such possible hedging strategies.

*Jack knew that his position was hedged if the yield curve movement was parallel. He at the same time knew that the yield curve could shift in many ways. Which instantaneous yield curve movement would result in a significant loss to his "hedged position"? Would that yield curve movement be likely to occur? Since he had to book all unrealized gains and losses on the mark-to-market basis, he was concerned about any temporary yield curve movements.*

## Exercises and Answers

1. Consider a portfolio of $10 million in a par bond with ten-year maturity and $20 million in a par bond with two-year maturity. The $30 million bond position is funded by a $20 million five-year par bond and $10 million cash. Suppose that the yield curve is flat at 6%. What is the duration and dollar duration of the portfolio? See figure E.4.16.

| Outputs | | | | | | |
|---|---|---|---|---|---|---|
| | | Di | | | | |
| Duration of asset (use "data-table") | Maturity | | Amount (mil.) | Weight | Dp | $ Dp (mil.) |
| | 10 | 7.4387 | 10 | 0.33 | 2.4796 | 74.3874 |
| | 2 | 1.8585 | 20 | 0.67 | 1.2390 | 37.1710 |
| | Value ⇒ | Sum | 30 | 1 | 3.7186 | 111.5584 |
| | | | | | | |
| | | Di | | | | |
| Duration of liability (use "data-table") | Maturity | | Amount (mil.) | Weight | Dp | $ Dp (mil.) |
| | 5 | 4.2651 | 20 | 0.67 | 2.8434 | 85.3020 |
| | 0 | 0.0000 | 10 | 0.33 | 0.0000 | 0.0000 |
| | Value ⇒ | Sum | 30 | 1 | 2.8434 | 85.3020 |
| | | | | | | |
| Dollar duration of portfolio | | | 0 | | 0.8752 | 26.2563 |

**Figure E4.16**

| Outputs | | | | | |
|---|---|---|---|---|---|
| Bond price | | | | Principal (mil.) | |
| | | 99.2596 | 10 | 20 | 20 |
| | Maturity (year) | 10 | 9.9260 | 19.8519 | 19.8519 |
| | | 2 | 9.9814 | 19.9629 | 19.9629 |
| | | 5 | 9.9575 | 19.9149 | 19.9149 |
| Investment in cash ($mil.) | 10 | | | | |
| Δ Portfolio value | -26,086 | | | | |

**Figure E4.17**

*Answer:* The portfolio duration is 0.8752 and the dollar duration is 26.2563. The duration is the relative price change with respect to a small interest change, and the dollar duration is the absolute price change with respect to a small interest change. Therefore, the dollar duration is the duration multiplied by the value. For example, a ten-year bond's duration is 7.4387 and the dollar duration is 74.3874 million (= 7.4387 × $10 million).

2. Given a parallel ten–basis point upward shift of the yield curve, what is the change in value of the portfolio?

*Answer:* Figure E4.17 shows the price of a bond depending on the principal and the maturity. For example, if the maturity is ten years and the principal is $10 million, the price is 9.9260 when the flat yield curve shifts upward by ten basis points. We generate all the combinations for illustration purposes. The total change of the portfolio is −$26,086.

3. If the trader is to mark to market the portfolio to determine the profit and loss of the bond position, should the trader report a gain or loss? How much?

*Answer:* The ten–basis point rise in the interest rate decreases the portfolio value by $26,086.

4. If the trader also has to report the dollar duration of the portfolio after the shift of the interest rates, what would be reported?

*Answer:* The dollar duration of the portfolio is 25.9174 after the shift of the interest rates. See figure E4.18.

| Duration of asset (use "data-table") | Maturity | Di 7.4253 | Amount (mil.) | Weight | Dp | $ Dp (mil.) |
|---|---|---|---|---|---|---|
| | 10 | 7.4253 | 9.9260 | 0.3321 | 2.4659 | 73.7031 |
| | 2 | 1.8576 | 19.9629 | 0.6679 | 1.2407 | 37.0822 |
| | Value ⇒ | Sum | 29.8888 | 1.0000 | 3.7066 | 110.7853 |
| | | | | | | |
| Duration of liability (use "data-table") | Maturity | Di 7.4253 | Amount (mil.) | Weight | Dp | $ Dp (mil.) |
| | 5 | 4.2615 | 19.9149 | 0.6657 | 2.8370 | 84.8679 |
| | 0 | 0.0000 | 10.0000 | 0.3343 | 0.0000 | 0.0000 |
| | Value ⇒ | Sum | 29.9149 | 1.0000 | 2.8370 | 84.8679 |
| | | | | | | |
| Dollar duration of portfolio | | | -0.0261 | | 0.8696 | 25.9174 |

Figure E4.18

## Further Exercises

1. Consider a portfolio with $30 million in a ten-year par bond and borrowing cash of $20 million. Suppose the yield curve is flat at 6%. Calculate the change in the portfolio value when the yield curve shifts downward by one basis point. Furthermore, calculate the dollar duration and compare it with the change in the portfolio value for the one–basis point drop.

   *Answer:* The portfolio value increases by $22,327 when the yield curve shifts downward by one basis point. The dollar duration is $223.162 million and PV 01 is $22,316. The dollar duration measures the increase in the bond portfolio value with respect to one unit parallel drop in interest rates, and PV 01 is the increase of the portfolio value for a one–basis point drop in rates. The actual change in the portfolio value is not identical to the estimated change of the portfolio value based on the duration. The reason for this is that we take only a linear relation between the interest and the bond price into consideration to calculate the duration. Note that the relationship between the bond price and the interest rate is convex rather than linear.

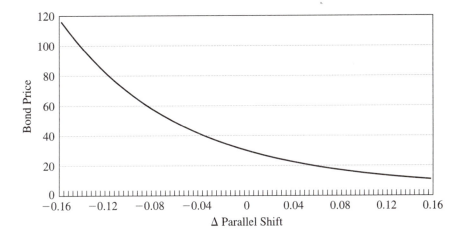

Figure E4.19

2. Calculate the change in the portfolio value when the yield curve shifts upward or downward by one basis point. Can you explain why the amounts of the change are different depending on the direction of the yield curve movements?

*Answer:* When the yield curve shifts upward by one basis point, the portfolio value decreases by $22,306, and when the yield curve shifts downward by one basis point, the portfolio value increases by $22,327. This shows that the relation between the bond price and the interest rate is not linear. Figure E4.19 clearly represents the convexity relation between the interest rates and the bond prices. The absolute amount of the price increase when the rate drops is larger than the absolute amount of the price decrease when the rate rises. This is called convexity.

## E4.4  SWAP MODEL

### Definitions

The notional amount is the principal used to calculate payments in an interest rate swap. The principal is "notional" because it is not actually exchanged between the parties.

### Description of the Model

A swap is an over-the-counter instrument that is issued by any corporation or government agency. It is an exchange of payments between two parties. These payments are interest payments that may be based on a floating rate or a fixed rate, on the same amount of principal and maturity. A vanilla swap (a fixed-rate receiver or a floating-rate payer) has two components: (1) borrowing at the short rate, "short financing," and (2) buying a fixed-rate bond. Therefore, entering into a vanilla swap is equivalent to securing short-term funding and investing in a bond or longing a fixed bond and shorting a floating bond.

### Numerical Example

Consider a three-year swap. The floating rate is the one-year LIBOR. Settlement payments are made annually. What is the fixed rate of the swap? The notional amount is $100 for simplicity. The setting of the fixed interest rate is called the pricing of interest rate swaps. See figure E4.20.

The floating rate that the floating-rate payer will pay at the next exchange period is determined one year before the next exchange period. For example, the current floating interest rate is 6%, and the floating rate one year hence is 8%. The fixed rate is 9% and the notional amount is $100. We assume that the exchange between the fixed rate and the floating rate is made annually. At the next exchange period, which is one year hence, the floating-rate payer should pay 6% rather than 8%. Therefore, the floating-rate payer will receive $3 from the fixed-rate payer.

### Applications

1. When the parties are highly rated (with minimal default risk), the swap rate can be used as a benchmark for the time value of money.

| Inputs | | | | |
|---|---|---|---|---|
| Year | 0 | 1 | 2 | 3 |
| Initial yield curve | 0.1 | 0.1 | 0.1 | 0.1 |
| Initial discount function p(n) | 1 | 0.904837 | 0.818731 | 0.740818 |
| 1-year forward curve | 0.1 | 0.1 | 0.1 | 0.1 |
| Lognormal spot volatility ($\sigma^s$) | 0 | 0.12 | 0.12 | 0.12 |
| Lognormal forward volatility ($\sigma^f$) | 0 | 0.12 | 0.12 | 0.12 |
| The number of partitions (m) | 1 | | | |
| | | | | |
| Forward price | 0.9048 | 0.9048 | 0.9048 | 0.9048 |
| Delta ($\delta$) | 1 | 0.976286 | 0.976286 | 0.976286 |
| | | | | |
| Notional amount | 100 | | | |

| Outputs | | | | |
|---|---|---|---|---|
| | | | 2.399539 | |
| | | 2.285383 | 0.028793 | |
| Swap lattice | 0.000000 | -2.285383 | -2.399539 | |
| Year | 0 | 1 | 2 | 3 |

Figure E4.20

2. The swap itself can be an underlying asset of an option contract, which is called a swaption.

## Case: A Hedging Program Designed by an Asset Liability Committee

The asset liability committee (ALCO) of the Pacific-Atlantic Bank met at 9:00 a.m. In this meeting the senior management team discussed both the strategic and tactical problems in relation to the assets and liabilities of the bank, with special interests directed to the interest rate risk management and to an extent the related issues in credit risks of the loan portfolio. The CEO often attended the meeting to listen to some of the issues. The meeting was chaired by the treasurer, Zena Christinson, who was also the head of the ALCO. The risk manager and the asset manager were also present. The meeting began with an overview of the risk exposure of the bank's assets, which were mostly loans together with a fairly liquid mortgage portfolio, and the liabilities, which were mostly deposit accounts.

After thirty minutes of presentation, showing the interest rate risk exposures and the recent trends in the deposit rates, the risk manager concluded that the asset and the loan portfolio had a longer duration than the liability portfolio.

Zena said "As you know, recently our marketing people have pushed our CDs (certificate of deposit accounts), and the volume has grown in that area. These are six-month CDs. Our marketing people said that these accounts are very qualified, and they would roll over, not the hot money type. How do you treat them with respect to their duration?" "Zena, we assume these papers to have a duration of six months. Even if they roll over, we will be paying them the prevailing market rates, which are tied to our transfer pricing rate. So this assumption is valid, we believe."

"I see. I never quite understand then why we do not assume our savings account to have a one-day duration." "Zena, I know we went through this before. Our savings account is different because our savings rate does not tie to our transfer pricing rate, which is the capital market rate. And therefore, we have to take into consideration when the customer takes the money from the account."

"OK. But are you suggesting that we should do something about our asset and liability mismatch?" "Zena, our asset portfolio is holding some real good mortgages. Selling them to shorten our duration would not make sense. I suggest maybe we slowly change our loan duration by switching our fixed-rate loan product to do more lending in floating rate," said the asset manager. But Zena replied: "But the market for fixed-rate loans is strong now."

The CEO said with authority, as it was often perceived, "But I am not sure we want to shorten the duration. Our yield curve is very steep now. We buy the long rate and lock in the interests and pay the short rate, making a good spread. I think this spread will go on for the rest of this year." Zena replied: "Sure, but what if the entire curve pops up next quarter?" "I am not sure why that would happen. It will take the short end of the curve rising up or the curve popping up a lot, before the funding cost hurts us. Neither scenario is likely."

Zena then said: "I tend to agree with you. But we really do not know what will happen when the interest rates move later in the year. I suggest that we should plan on putting a swap position to lower our duration. When we think the market is ready to go up, we can always put those swaps on." "Do we have a lot of swaps on our book now?" "No, not at all. We can put them on anytime. Let us first come up with a plan and see how the swaps would affect our net income, etc."

*Zena started making some notes about this swap position plan. What are the bullet points that she should take note of in preparation for putting on a swap position? She knew that it would not just be the valuation and calculation of the hedging. She had to think about the decision-making process, working out how the committee should be ready to make the decision with good timing. "The Swap Hedging Plan," she scribbled on the page.*

## Exercises and Answers

1. Explain why a six-month CD has duration of six months regardless of whether the CD would be rolled over or not.

   *Answer:* We know that duration is a measure of bond price sensitivity with respect to the interest. Since CD rates are determined at the then prevailing market rate, and the CD rates are fixed for six months, the CD duration is six months. Recall that a zero-coupon bond's duration is its maturity.

2. Bank A and bank B enter into a swap contract. The notional is $1,000,000. The trade date and the termination date are July 3, 2003, and July 3, 2005, respectively. Bank A is a fixed-rate payer, and bank B is a floating-rate payer. The LIBOR reset frequency is six months. One year is assumed to have 360 days. The floating rate is the LIBOR.

   (a) To determine the present value of the floating cash flows paid by bank B, what Zena has done is to first discount the notional at the two-year discount rate and then subtract the discounted value from the notional value. Explain the logic of this method.

   *Answer:* Since bank B pays the floating-rate cash flows during the swap tenor, and the present value of a floating coupon bond is par, the present value of the floating

| Swap rate calculation | | | | | | |
|---|---|---|---|---|---|---|
| Swap rate | 0.0512711 | Changing cell for solver | | | | |
| (semiannual compounding) | | | | | | |
| | 1.10517092 | = (1+swap rate)$^2$ | | | | |
| | 1.10517092 | = exp(0.1) | | | | |
| | | | | | | 105.12711 |
| | | | | | 102.582075 | 105.12711 |
| | | | | 101.830238 | 104.250054 | 105.12711 |
| | | | 102.704163 | 105.085327 | 105.946581 | 105.12711 |
| Par value | | 100 | 107.550057 | 108.451365 | 107.672144 | 105.12711 |
| Adjusted time period (year) | | 0 | 0.5 | 1 | 1.5 | 2 |
| | | | | | | |
| Squared error | | 0 | Target cell for solver | | | |
| | | | | | | |
| LIBOR rate calculation | | | | | | |
| (semiannual compounding) | | | | | | |
| exp{r(n,i,1)/2}-1 | | | | | | |
| | | | | | | 0.08819136 |
| | | | | | 0.07872502 | 0.06987996 |
| | | | | 0.06941798 | 0.06057291 | 0.05187669 |
| | | | 0.06026755 | 0.05142248 | 0.04272626 | 0.03417636 |
| LIBOR lattice | | 0.0512711 | 0.04242603 | 0.0337298 | 0.02517991 | 0.01677389 |

Figure E4.21

| Outputs | | | | | | |
|---|---|---|---|---|---|---|
| | | | | | 2.545035 | |
| | | | | 1.616947 | 0.877056 | |
| | | | 0.783985 | 0.027528 | -0.819471 | |
| Swap lattice | | 0.000000 | -0.783985 | -1.644331 | -2.545035 | |
| Adjusted time period (year) | | 0 | 0.5 | 1 | 1.5 | 2 |

Figure E4.22

cash flows is $1,000,000 minus the present value of the notional. The reason for this is that the difference between the floating coupon bond and the floating-rate cash flows in terms of the future cash flows is the notional at maturity. Therefore, we subtract the present value of the notional from $1,000,000, which is the price of the floating coupon bond when the par is 1,000,000.

(b) How do you determine the fixed rate paid by bank A?

*Answer:* Since bank B receives a fixed coupon, and the present value of the floating coupon bond is par, the fixed coupon bond price should be par. Therefore, we search for a coupon rate, which makes the fixed coupon bond price equal to par. See figures E4.21 and E4.22.

## Further Exercises

1. We assume that the swap tenor is five years rather than three years in the numerical example. Price the swap and check whether the present value of the fixed payer's cash flow is 100.

*Answer:* See figures E4.23 and E4.24.

2. What is the net present value of the floating interest receiver from a swap with a notional principal value of $100 and a period of five years remaining to maturity? Assume that the current term structure is flat at 10% and the swap rate at the origination is 8%. For simplicity, the swap settlement is made annually. Repeat the same question when the current yield curve is upward, starting from 10% at year 0 to 14% at year 5.

| Swap rate calculation | | | | | | |
|---|---|---|---|---|---|---|
| 5-year swap rate (annual compounding) | 0.105171 | Changing cell for solver | | | | |
| Year | 0 | 1 | 2 | 3 | 4 | 5 |
| | | | | | | 110.5171 |
| | | | | | 105.7208 | 110.5171 |
| | | | | 103.7435 | 108.0333 | 110.5171 |
| | | | 104.059 | 108.0993 | 110.402 | 110.5171 |
| | | 106.3627 | 110.3656 | 112.6637 | 112.8282 | 110.5171 |
| Par value | 100 | 114.6715 | 117.1214 | 117.4468 | 115.3134 | 110.5171 |
| | 2.02E-28 | Target cell for solver | | | | |

Figure E4.23

| Outputs | | | | | | |
|---|---|---|---|---|---|---|
| | | | | | 4.796317 | |
| | | | | 3.211120 | 2.483789 | |
| | | | 1.960112 | 1.173572 | 0.115090 | |
| | | 0.920075 | 0.071422 | -1.016297 | -2.311147 | |
| Swap lattice | 0.000000 | -0.920075 | -2.054779 | -3.367244 | -4.796317 | |
| Year | 0 | 1 | 2 | 3 | 4 | 5 |

Figure E4.24

| | | | | | 100 | |
|---|---|---|---|---|---|---|
| | | | | 100 | 100 | |
| | | | 100 | 100 | 100 | |
| | | 100 | 100 | 100 | 100 | |
| Floating-rate bond price | 100 | 100 | 100 | 100 | 100 | |
| Year | 0 | 1 | 2 | 3 | 4 | 5 |
| | | | | | | |
| 5-year swap rate (annual compounding) | 0.08 | | | | | |
| Year | 0 | 1 | 2 | 3 | 4 | 5 |
| | | | | | | 108 |
| | | | | | 101.0354 | 108 |
| | | | | 97.11647 | 103.2952 | 108 |
| | | | 95.62426 | 101.3248 | 105.61 | 108 |
| | | 96.18009 | 101.6511 | 105.7358 | 107.981 | 108 |
| Fixed-rate bond price | 90.58296 | 104.0392 | 108.1114 | 110.3593 | 110.4095 | 108 |
| | | | | | | |
| NPV of floating-rate receiver | 9.417037 | | | | | |

Figure E4.25

| | Year 0 | Year 1 | Year 2 | Year 3 | Year 4 | Year 5 |
|---|---|---|---|---|---|---|
| | | | | | 100 | |
| | | | | 100 | 100 | |
| | | | 100 | 100 | 100 | |
| | | 100 | 100 | 100 | 100 | |
| Floating-rate bond price | 100 | 100 | 100 | 100 | 100 | |
| Year | 0 | 1 | 2 | 3 | 4 | 5 |

| | Year 0 | Year 1 | Year 2 | Year 3 | Year 4 | Year 5 |
|---|---|---|---|---|---|---|
| Five-year swap rate (annual compounding) | 0.08 | | | | | |
| Year | 0 | 1 | 2 | 3 | 4 | 5 |
| | | | | | | 108 |
| | | | | | 91.33299 | 108 |
| | | | | 83.24165 | 94.59521 | 108 |
| | | | 80.54644 | 88.59671 | 97.98513 | 108 |
| | | 81.62317 | 87.48967 | 94.34259 | 101.5078 | 108 |
| Fixed-rate bond price | 77.62764 | 89.96045 | 95.13918 | 100.5082 | 105.1683 | 108 |
| | | | | | | |
| NPV of floating-rate receiver | 22.37236 | | | | | |

**Figure E4.26**

*Answer:* When the current yield curve is flat at 10%, the net present value of the floating receiver is 9.417. See figure E4.25. When the current yield curve is upward, starting from 10% at year 0 to 14% at year 5, the net present value of the floating receiver is 22.372. See figure E4.26.

## Notes

1. Generally speaking, the yield curve is defined as the relationship between the yields on bonds with or without coupons and their maturities. The spot yield curve is defined as the relationship between the yields on zero-coupon default-free bonds and their maturities. The spot yield curve correctly represents the time value of money.

2. Since $F(T^*, T)$ is the forward price at time 0, it can be denoted $F(0, T^*, T)$.

## Bibliography

Bierwag, G. O. 1977. Immunization, duration and the term structure of interest rates. *Journal of Financial and Quantitative Analysis*, 12, 725–742.

Bierwag, G. O., G. G. Kaufman, and C. Khang. 1978. Duration and bond portfolio analysis: An overview. *Journal of Financial and Quantitative Analysis*, 13, 671–681.

Carleton, W. T., and I. A. Cooper. 1976. Estimation and uses of the term structure of interest rates. *Journal of Finance*, 31, 1067–1083.

Cox, J. C., J. E. Ingersoll, and S. A. Ross. 1979. Duration and the measurement of basis risk. *Journal of Business*, 52, 51–61.

Cox, J. C., J. E. Ingersoll, and S. A. Ross. 1981. The relationship between forward prices and futures prices. *Journal of Financial Economics*, 9, 321–346.

Duffee, G. R. 1998. The relation between treasury yields and corporate bond yield spreads. *Journal of Finance*, 53(6), 2225–2241.

Fong, H. G., and O. Vasicek. 1983. The trade-off between return and risk in immunized portfolios. *Financial Analysts Journal*, 39(5), 73–78.

Ho, T. S. Y. 1992. Key rate duration: A measure of interest rate risks exposure. *Journal of Fixed Income*, 2(2), 29–44.

Jarrow, R. A., and G. S. Oldfield. 1981. Forward contracts and futures contracts. *Journal of Financial Economics*, 9, 373–382.

Longstaff, F. A. 2000. Arbitrage and the expectations hypothesis. *Journal of Finance*, 55, 989–994.

Macaulay, F. R. 1938. *Some Theoretical Problems Suggested by the Movements of Interest Rates, Bond Yields and Stock Prices in the United States since 1856*. Washington, DC: National Bureau of Economic Research.

McCoy, W. F. 1993. Enhancing the returns of a replicating portfolio. In Thomas S. Y. Ho, ed., *Fixed-Income Portfolio Management: Issues and Solutions*. Homewood, IL: Business One Irwin.

# 5

# Bond Options

---

Bond options can be traded in the exchanges or in the over-the-counter markets. Bond options can also be embedded in many interest rate securities or instruments on the firm's balance sheets. They may even be embedded in business contracts and agreements. The value of these options is dependent on the yield curve movements. Therefore, we need to model the yield curve movements and develop a framework to incorporate these movements to the bond option pricing model. This chapter will deal with this problem.

## 5.1  INTEREST RATE MOVEMENTS: HISTORICAL EXPERIENCES

Interest rate movements refer to the uncertain movements of the Treasury spot yield curve. Each STRIPS bond is considered a security. When the daily closing price is reported, the bond's yield to maturity can be calculated. The observed Treasury spot yield curve is the scattered plot of the yield to maturity against the maturity for all the STRIPS bonds. Since the spot yield curve is a representation of the time value of money, and the time value of money is related to the time to horizon in a continuous fashion, the scattered plots should be a continuous curve. Hence, we call the scattered plot a yield curve.

What are the dynamics of the spot yield curve? Let us consider the historical behavior of spot yield curve movements in relation to interest rate levels. The monthly spot yield curves from the beginning of 1994 until the end of 2001 are depicted in figure 5.1.

As figure 5.1 shows, the spot yield curves can take on a number of shapes. When the yields of the bonds increase with the bonds' maturities, the yield curve is said to be upward-sloping. Conversely, when the yield decreases with maturity, the spot curve is called downward-sloping. Although not shown in figure 5.1, the early 1980s displayed a yield curve that was downward-sloping. In 1998, the yield curve was level or flat. In the early part of 2001, the yield curve was humped, with yields reaching the peak at the one-year maturity. Historically, the spot yield curve has continually changed its shape as well as its level.

*The yield curve movement* is concerned with the change of the yield curve shape over a relatively short time interval, say one month. Describing yield curve movements is slightly more complicated than describing a stock movement. To describe the latter, we can decompose the stock movement into two parts: the expected drift or expected returns and the uncertain movement. The model is represented by

$$dS = \mu S dt + \sigma S dZ \tag{5.1}$$

where $dS$ is a small movement for a short interval $dt$. $\mu$ is the instantaneous returns of the stock, and $\sigma$ is the instantaneous standard deviation (or volatility) of the stock. $dZ$ represents a small, uncertain movement specified by a normal distribution. The mean and the standard deviation of the normal distribution are 0 and $\sqrt{dt}$, respectively. The

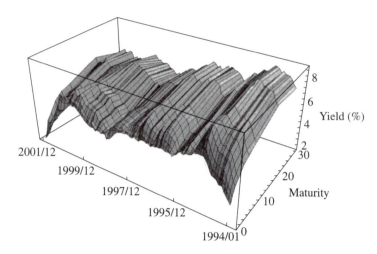

**Figure 5.1** A time series diagram of monthly spot yield curve movements (1994–2001). The Treasury spot yield curve continually exhibits random movements, changing its level as well as its shape over the period from January 1994 to December 2001. Interest rate movement models are supposed to specify such movements, for example, to price bonds with option provisions or bond options. Since the data are par yields at key rate maturities of 0.25, 0.5, 1, 2, 3, 5, 7, 10, 20, and 30 years, we convert them into spot yields, assuming that par yields are semiannually paid coupon rates. For example, if a par yield at year 7 is 10%, we convert the par yield into a spot yield by assuming that the semiannually paid coupon rate is 10% and the bond price is at par. Data from http//:www.economagic.com/.

first term, called the drift term, represents the expected movement of the stock price. If the first term is 0, then the future stock price is expected to be the same as the present observed price. Of course, the realized stock price in the future can deviate from the initial stock price because of the uncertain stock price movement specified by the second term. The random term $dZ$ can be viewed as a unit of risk, a normal distribution over an (infinitely) short interval.[1] The coefficient of $dZ$ represents the volatility of the process. If this coefficient is 0, then the process has no risk and the stock price movement has no uncertainty.

But specifying the movement of the yield curve in a way that is similar to equation (5.1), is more problematic. Since a yield curve is determined by all the U.S. STRIPS bonds, its movement should be represented by the movements of all the bond prices. But the movements of all the bond prices are not independent of each other. They have to be correlated. The following empirical evidence may suggest how the yield curve movements may best be specified.

## Lognormal Versus Normal Movements

The movements (often called the dynamics) of each interest rate of the spot yield curve can be specified as we have done for a stock. We can rewrite equation (5.1), replacing the stock price with a rate that is the yield to maturity of a zero-coupon bond of a specific maturity $T$. Thus we have

$$dr = \mu(r, t)rdt + r\sigma\, dZ \tag{5.2}$$

When a $T$-year rate is assumed to follow the process specified by equation (5.2), we say that the interest rate follows a *lognormal process*, and equation (5.2) is called a lognormal model. In comparing equation (5.2) with equation (5.1), note that the drift term of the interest rate model is any function of the short-term interest rate $r$ and time, while the lognormal model for stock tends to assume that the instantaneous stock return is a constant number. Therefore, the research literature of interest rate models has somewhat abused the language in calling equation (5.2) a lognormal model. The important point is that in a lognormal process, the volatility term is proportional to the interest rate level $r(t)$. When the interest rate level is high, we experience high interest rate volatility. When the interest rate level is low, we experience low interest rate volatility.

There is an alternative specification of the interest rate process, which the research literature calls the *normal process*. In the normal process, the volatility is independent of the interest rate level, and it is given below:

$$dr = \mu(r, t)dt + \sigma\,dZ \tag{5.3}$$

Equation (5.3) is called the *normal model*. Note that the distinction made between the lognormal model and the normal model depends only on the volatility term. For a normal model, the interest rate fluctuates with a volatility independent of the interest rate level over a short interval. For a lognormal model, the interest rate has a volatility related to

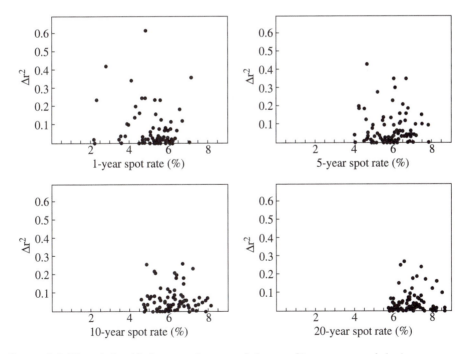

**Figure 5.2** The relationship between the squared change of interest rate and the interest rate level. The interest rate levels are plotted against the squared changes in the monthly interest rates over the following month during the period from 1994 to 2001. The results do not indicate any specific relationship between the interest rate level and its volatility, which can be interpreted to suggest that the volatility does not depend on the interest level. If that is the case, we cannot reject the normal interest rate models.

the interest rate level, in particular when the volatility becomes arbitrarily small when the interest rate level approaches 0. This way, the interest rates can never become negative. A lognormal process is written as

$$\frac{dr}{r} = \mu(r, t)dt + \sigma \, dZ \tag{5.3a}$$

Historical observations have shown the yield curve movements to be both normal and lognormal, depending on the interest rate levels. Which model is more appropriate to describe interest rate movements, the normal or the lognormal? We need to evaluate the model from an empirical perspective. Using U.S. historical interest rates, the squared change of the interest rate over one month is plotted against the interest rate level. Figure 5.2 presents the scattered plots for 1-, 5-, 10-, and 20-year rates.

As figure 5.2 indicates, over this time period the interest rate volatility has no relationship to the interest rate levels. If there were a positive relationship, we would see the higher volatility values related to higher interest rates. This result is consistent with Cheyette (1997), who shows that the positive correlation between the interest rate volatility and the interest rate level is weak when the interest rate level is below 10%. However, when the interest rate level was high in the late 1970s and early 1980s, the interest rate volatility was also high, showing positive correlations during that period.

## Interest Rate Correlations

We have discussed the dynamics of interest rates. Now let us consider the comovements of interest rates. Do interest rates move together in steps, such that they all rise or fall together?

While the yield curve in principle can take many shapes, historically, all the interest rates along the yield curve have been positively correlated. But the interest rates do not shift by the same amount. Their comovements can be investigated by evaluating the correlations of the interest rates, as presented in table 5.1.

The results show that all the correlations are positive, suggesting that all the interest rates tend to move in the same direction. The long rates, with terms over ten years, are

**Table 5.1** Correlation Matrix of the Interest Rates

|      | 0.25  | 0.5   | 1     | 2     | 3     | 5     | 7     | 10    | 20    | 30    |
|------|-------|-------|-------|-------|-------|-------|-------|-------|-------|-------|
| 0.25 | 1.000 | 0.936 | 0.837 | 0.701 | 0.630 | 0.533 | 0.443 | 0.377 | 0.087 | 0.083 |
| 0.5  | 0.936 | 1.000 | 0.938 | 0.832 | 0.770 | 0.675 | 0.587 | 0.509 | 0.224 | 0.154 |
| 1    | 0.837 | 0.938 | 1.000 | 0.940 | 0.895 | 0.816 | 0.731 | 0.654 | 0.379 | 0.291 |
| 2    | 0.701 | 0.832 | 0.940 | 1.000 | 0.989 | 0.950 | 0.898 | 0.832 | 0.573 | 0.426 |
| 3    | 0.630 | 0.770 | 0.895 | 0.989 | 1.000 | 0.980 | 0.945 | 0.887 | 0.649 | 0.493 |
| 5    | 0.533 | 0.675 | 0.816 | 0.950 | 0.980 | 1.000 | 0.982 | 0.946 | 0.736 | 0.595 |
| 7    | 0.443 | 0.587 | 0.731 | 0.898 | 0.945 | 0.982 | 1.000 | 0.976 | 0.821 | 0.670 |
| 10   | 0.377 | 0.509 | 0.654 | 0.832 | 0.887 | 0.946 | 0.976 | 1.000 | 0.863 | 0.750 |
| 20   | 0.087 | 0.224 | 0.379 | 0.573 | 0.649 | 0.736 | 0.821 | 0.863 | 1.000 | 0.867 |
| 30   | 0.083 | 0.154 | 0.291 | 0.426 | 0.493 | 0.595 | 0.670 | 0.750 | 0.867 | 1.000 |

The results show that all the correlations are positive so that all the interest rates tend to move in the same direction. The long rates (with terms over ten years) are highly correlated, which means that the rates in the ten- to thirty-year range tend to move up and down together. The interest rates that are closer together along the yield curves have higher correlations. However, the correlations of the short-term rates and the long-term rates are relatively low.

highly correlated, meaning that the segment of the yield curve in a range of ten to thirty years tends to move up and down together. The interest rates that are closer together along the yield curve have higher correlations.

## Term Structure of Volatilities

Interest rate volatility is not the same for all interest rates along the yield curve. By convention, based on the lognormal model, the uncertainty of an interest rate is measured by the annualized standard deviation of the proportional change in a bond yield over a time interval ($dt$). For example, if the time interval is one month, then $dt$ equals 1/12 year. This measure is called the interest rate volatility, and it is denoted by $\sigma(t, T)$, the volatility of the $T$th year rate at time $t$. More precisely, the volatility is the standard deviation of the proportional change in rate over a short interval, and it is given by

$$\sigma(t, T) = \sigma\left(\frac{\Delta r(t, T)}{r(t, T)}\right) \bigg/ \sqrt{\Delta t} \tag{5.4}$$

where $r(t, T)$ is the yield to maturity of the zero-coupon bond with time to maturity $T$ at time $t$ and $\sigma(\cdot)$ is a standard deviation over $dt$. We can relate equation (5.4) to (5.3a) by the following algebraic manipulations. For a small time step, equation (5.3a) can be written as

$$\frac{\Delta r(t, T)}{r(t, T)} \approx \mu \Delta t + \sigma(t, T) \Delta Z$$

For sufficiently small $\Delta t$, we have

$$\sigma\left(\frac{\Delta r(t, T)}{r(t, T)}\right) \approx \sigma(t, T)\sqrt{\Delta t}$$

Rearranging the terms, we can express $\sigma$ as equation (5.4) requires. Similarly, based on the normal model, the term structure of volatilities is given by

$$\sigma(t, T) = \sigma(\Delta r(t, T))/\sqrt{\Delta t} \tag{5.5}$$

The relationship of the volatilities to the maturity is called the *term structure of volatilities*. The interest rate volatilities can be estimated using historical monthly data ($\Delta t = 1/12$). The standard deviations of the rates for 0.25, 0.5, 1, 2, 3, 5, 7, 10, 20, and 30 years are presented in table 5.2.

**Table 5.2** Historical Term Structure of Volatilities: $\sigma(\Delta r(t)/r(t)) \cdot \sqrt{12}$

| Term | 0.25 | 0.5 | 1 | 2 | 3 | 5 | 7 | 10 | 20 | 30 |
|---|---|---|---|---|---|---|---|---|---|---|
| Volatilities | 0.1906 | 0.1908 | 0.1872 | 0.1891 | 0.1794 | 0.1632 | 0.1487 | 0.1402 | 0.1076 | 0.1137 |

The first row identifies the term of the yield, and the second row reports the volatilities. The relationship of the volatilities with respect to the maturity is called the term structure of volatilities. The interest rate volatilities can be estimated using historical data reported in figure 5.1. The historical term structure of volatilities shows that the short-term rates tend to have higher volatilities than the long-term rates, falling from 19.06% for the 0.25-year rate to 11.37% for the 30-year rate.

The historical term structure of volatilities shows that the short-term rates tend to have higher volatilities than the long-term rates, falling from 19.06% for the 0.25-year rate to 11.37% for the thirty-year rate. The empirical results suggest that we cannot think of interest rate volatility as one number. It depends on the term of the interest rate in question.

## Mean Reversion

Thus far the discussion has focused on the volatility term of the dynamics of the interest rates. Now we investigate the drift term. Research tends to argue that the yield curve cannot follow a random walk as a stock does, as in equation (5.1). The yields of Treasury bonds cannot rise and fall with the expected drift, yet be constant or a certain fixed proportion of the interest rate level. Since the nominal interest rate, which is what we are concerned with here, is decomposed into the real interest rate and the expected inflation rate, as stated in the Fisher equation, the movements of the nominal rates can be analyzed by considering the movements of the real rates and the inflation rate. One may argue that the real rate cannot follow a random walk because it is related to all the individuals' time value of money in real terms. We tend to think the real interest rate is quite stable and does not follow a random walk. To the extent that we believe the government seeks to control the inflation rate, the inflation rate cannot follow a random walk either. Therefore, we cannot assume that the (nominal) interest rate follows a random walk.

One may conclude that the interest rates tend to fall when they are high and, conversely, tend to rise when they are low. Research literature calls the dynamics that describe this behavior of interest rates a *mean reversion process*.

## 5.2   EQUILIBRIUM MODELS

The yield curve movement model described in the previous section is useful in specifying probable yield curve movements, but it cannot be used to value interest rate derivatives. What is needed in order to value interest rate derivatives? We will now examine the characteristics of an interest rate model.

First, consider pricing a *U.S. STRIPS bond option*. A bond option offers the holder the right to buy a specific U.S. STRIPS bond at the expiration date at a fixed price. Economists in the 1960s used the present-value method to price the bond option. They simulated interest rate scenarios based on an economic forecast to determine all the probabilities of interest rate levels at the expiration date. Then the expected payout of the bond option was calculated. Finally, the expected payment was discounted to determine the present value of the expected payment, the option price. However, the last step was the most difficult calculation. What was the appropriate discount rate? Would the discount rate be the observed rate from the yield curve? How would the forecast interest rate scenario be used to determine the discount rate? And should the risk premium be adjusted?

## Interest Rate Models

Interest rate models seek to specify the interest rate movements such that we can develop a pricing methodology for an interest rate option. We will describe two such models.

## The Cox-Ingersoll-Ross Model

The Cox-Ingersoll-Ross (CIR) interest rate model is based on the productive processes of an economy. According to the model, every individual has to make the decision between consuming and investing his limited capital. Investing in the productive process may lead to higher consumption in the following period, but it will sacrifice consumption today. The individual must determine the optimal trade-off.

Now assume that the individual can borrow capital from and lend capital to another individual. Each person has to make economic choices. The interest rates reach the market equilibrium rate when no one needs to borrow or lend. The model can explain the interest rate movements in terms of an individual's preferences for investment and consumption, as well as the risks and returns of the productive processes of the economy.

As a result of the analysis, the model can show how the short-term interest rate is related to the risks of the productive processes of the economy. Assuming that an individual requires a premium on the long-term rate (called term premium), the model continues to show how the short-term rate can determine the entire term structure of interest rates and the valuation of interest rate contingent claims.

CIR model

$$dr = a(b - r)dt + \sigma \sqrt{r}dZ \tag{5.6}$$

Cox, Ingersoll, and Ross (1985) made one of the early attempts at modeling interest rate movements. Their proposed equilibrium model extends from economic principles of interest rates. It assumes mean reversion of interest rates. As we discussed in section 5.1, mean reversion of interest rates means that when the short-term interest rate ($r$) is higher than the long-run interest rates ($b$), the short-term rate will fall, adjusting gradually to the long-run rate. Conversely, when the short-term interest rate is lower than the long-run, the short-term rate will rise gradually to the long-run rate. Note that the long-run interest rate is not the long-term rate. The long-term interest rate continuously moves stochastically, while the long-run rate is a theoretical construct which hypothesizes that the economy has a constant long-run interest rate to which interest rates converge over time. The constant ($a$) determines the speed of this adjustment. If ($a$) is high/low, the rate of adjustment to the long-term rate will be high/low. The CIR model is a lognormal model because the interest rate volatility is positively related to the interest rate level. The classification of lognormal and normal is based on the uncertain movement of the interest rate over a short period of time, as described above.

## The Vasicek Model

The second model was developed by O. Vasicek (1977). It is similar to the CIR model in that it assumes all interest rate contingent claims are based on short-term interest rates. The only difference is that the volatility is not assumed to be dependent on the interest rate level, and therefore it is a normal model.

Vasicek model

$$dr = a(b - r)dt + \sigma dZ, (a > 0) \tag{5.7}$$

This model assumes that there is only one source of risk and is referred to as a one-factor model. This assumption implies that all bond prices depend on the movements of the rate ($r$), and that all bond prices move in tandem because of their dependence on one factor. At first, this assumption seems to be unrealistic because, as we have discussed, the yield curve seems to have many degrees of freedom in its movements. Therefore, how can we confine our yield curve to exhibit a *one-factor movement*?

Dybvig (1989) shows that the one-factor model offers an appropriate first-order approximation for modeling the yield curve movement. Empirically, the dominant factor, the level movement, can explain much of the yield curve movements, and for the purpose of valuation, simplified models like the Cox-Ingersoll-Ross and the Vasicek may be justified. In other words, a one-factor model may be acceptable on an empirical basis.

## Market Price of Risk

From a theoretical perspective, neither the Cox-Ingersoll-Ross nor the Vasicek model for interest rates is a direct extension of the Black-Scholes model for stocks. In these models, the bond values are not determined by risk-neutral valuation (as in the Black-Scholes model), discounting the cash flows at the (stochastic) risk-free rate ($r$). These one-factor interest rate models cannot use the Black-Scholes relative valuation technique because the risk factor ($r$) is not a security that can be bought and sold to implement a dynamic hedging strategy. Therefore, the bonds cannot be valued relative to the observed interest rate level ($r$).

In a world where the yield curve has only one risk factor ($r$), the arbitrage-free condition in the bond market imposes a condition on the drift ($\mu$) and the risk ($\sigma$) for all the bonds. This condition is

$$\frac{\mu - r}{\sigma} = \lambda(r, t) \tag{5.8}$$

$\lambda(r, t)$ depends on the risk factor, $r$, and time, $t$. But more important, it is independent of the derivatives. Any derivatives depending on the risk factor must have the instantaneous drift $\mu$ and the risk $\sigma$ related by equation (5.8), for the same $\lambda$. Equation (5.8) suggests that the excess returns over a short period per unit risk, measured by the standard deviation, are the same for all the derivatives on the risk source. For this reason, Cox, Ingersoll, and Ross call $\lambda$ *market price of risk*, the excess return required for this risk factor per unit risk measure. The excess return ($\mu - r$) is the premium for bond returns, and is called the *term premium*.

Cox, Ingersoll, and Ross (1981) and Abken (1990) provide a discussion comparing the concept of term premium with the traditional hypothesis of liquidity premium of the term structure and the preferred habitat effect. The term premium or the market price of risk cannot be determined within the context of the model. Additional assumptions have to be made about the economy and the behavior of market participants to provide deeper insight into the value of the market price of risks. Cox, Ingersoll, and Ross propose that when there is no market price of risk, or equivalently no term premium, the market assumes the local expectation hypothesis to hold. In this case, all the bonds would have the expected return of the short-term rate ($r$) over one period.

# 5.3   ARBITRAGE-FREE MODELS

From the standard economic theory perspective, arbitrage-free modeling departs from the CIR approach. The main point of departure is sacrificing the economic theory by providing a model of the term structure of interest rates for a more accurate tool to value securities. Since the yield curve measures the agent's time value of money, the standard economic theory relates the interest rate movements to the dynamics of the economy. In contrast, arbitrage-free modeling assumes that the yield curve follows a random movement much like the model used to describe a stock price movement. Stock prices are assumed to be random, and such an assumption does not incorporate the modeling of the agent's behavior and the economy.

## The Ho-Lee Model

Ho and Lee (1986) take a different approach to modeling yield curve movements than do CIR and Vasicek. The *arbitrage-free interest rate model* uses the relative valuation of the Black-Scholes model. This concept becomes more complex in the interest rate theory. Arbitrage-free modeling argues, like the Black-Scholes model, that the valuation of interest rate contingent claims is based solely on the yield curve. Economic research focuses on understanding the inferences made from the yield curve shape and its movements. The arbitrage-free model omits all these fundamental issues, apparently ignoring part of the economic theory behind interest rate research. The model assumes that the yield curve moves in a way that is consistent with the arbitrage-free condition.

Let us assume that there is a perfect capital market in a discrete time world. But this time, the binomial model is applied to the yield curve movements. We assume the following:

1. Given the initial spot yield curve, the binomial lattice model requires that the yield curve can move only up and down.
2. The one-period interest rate volatility (the instantaneous volatility) is the same in all states of the world.
3. There is no arbitrage opportunity at any state of the world (at any node point on the binomial lattice).

Assumption (1) is a technical construct of the risk model. Assumption (2) is made simply for this example; it can be relaxed in the generalized models. Assumption (3), the arbitrage-free condition, is the most interesting and important. This condition imposes constraints on the yield curve movements.

Thus far, it seems that the extension is directly from the Black-Scholes model. But there is one problem: interest rate is not a security. We cannot buy and sell the one-period rate, though we can invest in the rate as the risk-free rate. Moreover, we cannot use the one-period rate to form an arbitrage argument, as the Black-Scholes model does with stock, since the one-period rate is the risk-free rate, which obviously cannot be the "underlying asset" as well. In an equity option, the stock is both the underlying instrument and the risk source or the risk driver.

## Arbitrage-Free Hedging

The conceptual extension of the interest rate arbitrage-free model from the Black-Scholes model is the introduction of the short-term interest rate as the risk source (or risk drive or state of the world). The Black-Scholes model's risk-neutral argument requires an underlying security and the risk-free rate. However, in the interest rate model, the risk-free rate is the risk source. One condition we want to impose on the interest rate movement is arbitrage-free, that is, the interest rate movements do not allow any possible arbitrage opportunity in holding a portfolio of bonds at any time. Research[2] shows that the interest rate movements are arbitrage-free if the following two conditions hold: (1) all the bonds at any time and state of the world have a risk-neutral expected return of the prevailing one-period rate, and (2) any bond on the initial yield curve has the risk-neutral expected return of the one-period interest rate of the initial yield curve. That is, for an interest rate movement to be arbitrage-free, there must be a probability assigned to each node of a tree such that all interest rate contingent claims have an expected risk-free return, which is the one-period rate. Note that this is the *risk-neutral probability*, whereas the market probability can be quite different.

## Recombining Condition

For tractability of the model, we require the discount function to recombine in a binomial lattice. This requirement is similar to the Black-Scholes model: the yield curve making an upward movement and then a downward movement must have the same value as the yield curve that makes a downward movement and then an upward movement. The difference between the yield curve movement and the stock movement is that we need the entire discount function (or the yield curve), and not just one bond price, to be identical when they recombine.

Under these restrictions, we can derive all the possible solutions. Let us consider the simplest solution in order to gain insight into these arbitrage-free models. Suppose the spot yield curve is flat. The spot curve can shift in a parallel fashion up and down. The binomial lattice represented is normal (or arithmetic) because the parallel shift of the curve is a fixed amount and not a proportion of the value at the node. The movements of the discount function can be represented by figure 5.3.

The purpose of the arbitrage-free model is not to determine the yield curve from any economic theory or to hypothesize that the yield curve should take particular shapes. The arbitrage-free model takes the yield curve (or the discount function) as given, and then hypothesizes the yield curve (or the discount function) movements in order to value other interest rate derivatives in relative terms. Using a dynamic hedging argument similar to the Black-Scholes model shows that we can assume the local expectation hypothesis to hold: the expected return of all the bonds over each time step is the risk-free rate, the one-period interest rate.

The Ho-Lee model is similar to the Vasicek model in that they are both normal models. The main difference, of course, is that the Ho-Lee model is specified to fit the yield curve, whereas the Vasicek model is developed to model the term structure of interest rates. For this reason, the Vasicek model has the unobservable parameter called term premium, and the yield curve derived from the Vasicek model is not the same as the observed yield curve in general. Unlike the Vasicek model, the arbitrage-free interest rate model does not require the term premium, which cannot be directly observed. Instead, the arbitrage-free interest model requires only the given observed yield curve to value bonds. Hence, the theoretical bond prices would be the same as those observed.

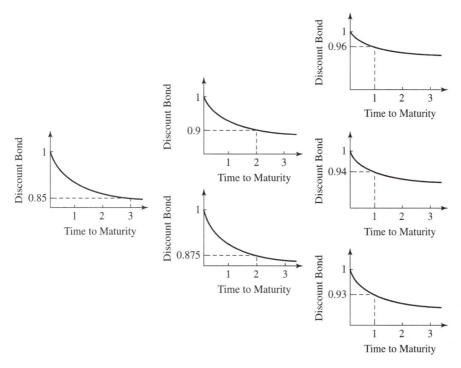

**Figure 5.3** Arbitrage-free movements of the discount function. The discount function is depicted in each state and time in a binomial lattice. The discount function always originates from value 1. It increases in value in an up state but drops in value in a down state. Consider the three-period bond. Initially, its value is $P(3)$. At time 1, it becomes a two-period bond, and its value can be either $P_1^1(2)$ or $P_0^1(2)$. At time 2, this bond becomes a one-period bond, and its value cannot deviate much from unity in any state of the world, and must converge to unity at maturity.

Specifically, let the initial discount function, the price of a zero-coupon bond with a face value of \$1 and with maturity $T$, be denoted by $P(T)$. $P(T)$ may be observed from the STRIPS market. The yield of the bond $P(T)$ is denoted by $r(T)$. Let $\sigma$ be the volatility of the interest rate. Interest rate volatility may be estimated from historical data. Then the price of a one-period bond $P_i^n(1)$ in time $n$ and state $i$ on the binomial lattice is given by

$$P_i^n(1) = 2\left(\frac{P(n+1)}{P(n)}\right) \cdot \frac{\delta^i}{(1+\delta^n)} \qquad (5.9)$$

where

$P_i^n(1) = $ a one-period bond price at time period $n$ and state $i$

$\delta = e^{-2 \cdot r(1) \cdot \sigma}$

$\sigma = $ standard deviation of $\left(\dfrac{\Delta r(1)}{r(1)}\right)$

Here, $-0.5 \ln \delta$ is the standard deviation of the change of the interest rate over each step size, and $\sigma$ is the standard deviation of the proportional change of the interest rate.

## A Numerical Illustration

For example, suppose the yield curve is 6% flat and the volatility is 15%.

$$P(n) = \frac{1}{1.06^n} \tag{5.10}$$

and

$$\delta = e^{-2 \times 0.06 \times 0.15} = 0.982161 \tag{5.11}$$

Then

$$P_i^n(1) = 2 \cdot \frac{1}{1.06} \frac{0.982161^i}{(1 + 0.982161^n)} \tag{5.12}$$

The Ho-Lee model captures many of the insights of arbitrage-free rate models. Because of its simplicity, it is useful for illustrating the salient features of arbitrage-free interest rate models. One shortcoming is that the interest rate movement does not exhibit any mean reversion process and the volatility of the one-period rate is constant at each node point. To be consistent with the historical behavior of the yield curve movements, the model should accept a term structure of volatilities as input. But this basic model can be extended to incorporate these features.

### Interest Rate Derivative Valuation and Verification of the Arbitrage-Free Property

We now consider using the interest rate model to value an interest rate contingent claim. Given an arbitrage-free interest rate model, the pricing of interest rate contingent claims is now relatively straightforward. The process is similar to that of pricing an equity option. We use the backward substitution procedure, starting from the terminal condition that specifies the value of the derivatives on the expiration date at each node point of the lattice. Then we determine the value of the derivative at each node point one period before that terminal date by discounting the risk-neutral expected value of the derivative (viewed from the node point where the derivative value is being calculated) at the prevailing one-period interest rate. The choice of the discount rate is the key in the development of the arbitrage-free rate model.

Unlike valuing an equity option in the binomial lattice, where the discount rate is the constant risk-free rate, in the case of uncertain interest rate movement, the one-period discount rate is determined by the interest rate model at the node point where the derivative value is being determined.

Once the derivative value is determined at all the node points one period before the terminal date, we can now determine the values of the derivatives at all the node points on the binomial lattice two periods before the terminal date, using the derivative values at the node point one period before the terminal date. We apply this procedure iteratively until we reach the initial date. This iterative procedure is identical to that of valuing the equity option. Therefore, the only difference between the equity option valuation and the interest rate derivative valuation is the use of a one-period discount rate in the backward substitution procedure. The equity option pricing uses a constant rate, while the interest rate derivative option pricing uses the prevailing one-period interest rate, as determined by the arbitrage-free interest rate model, at that node point.

The following binomial lattice of interest rates explains the backward substitution procedure for valuing a bond option. Suppose the bond option expires in two years. At the terminal date, the option holder has the right to buy a $T$-year zero-coupon bond at a strike price, $X$, given that the interest rate volatility is $\sigma$ and the market discount function is $P(T)$. Suppose we use the Ho-Lee model and determine the one-period discount factor $P_i^n(1)$ as described above. The following steps are then taken to determine the bond option price.

Step 1. Determine the two-year bond value on the terminal date at each node point on the binomial lattice using the backward substitution method. These bond prices are denoted by $P_i^n(T)$, where $T$ is the time to maturity (in this case, 2) of the bond at the terminal date, $n$ is the terminal date, and $i$ is the state of the world. Therefore, we can assign the price of the $T$-year bond at each node point, at the termination date. Denote $B(2, i, T) = P_i^2(T)$.

Step 2. Determine the terminal condition on the binomial lattice. The value of the bond option at the terminal date is given by $Max\,[B\,[2, i, T] - X, 0]$.

Step 3. Apply backward substitution at each node. If we denote the discount rate at each node $(n, i)$ by $r(n, i)$, then by definition of a discount factor, we have

$$P_i^n(1) = \frac{1}{1 + r(n, i)} \tag{5.13}$$

For the formulation of the Ho-Lee model presented, we assume that the risk-neutral probability $(p)$ is 0.5. Using this probability, we can calculate the expected derivative values one period ahead and discount the expected value using the prevailing interest rate, as shown in figure 5.4.

As a special case, we can use the same procedure to value a $T$-year zero-coupon bond. To value a zero-coupon bond price, the terminal date is the maturity of the bond $T$. The terminal condition at time $T$ is that the bond value is \$1 for all the nodes at the terminal

$IO[0, 0] = P(1)\{0.5 \times IO[1, 1] + 0.5 \times IO[1, 0]\}$

$IO[1, 1] = P_1^1(1)\{0.5 \times IO[2, 2] + 0.5 \times IO[2, 1]\}$

$IO[1, 0] = P_0^1(1)\{0.5 \times IO[2, 1] + 0.5 \times IO[2, 0]\}$

$IO[2, 2] = Max\,[B\,[2, 2, T] - X, 0]$

$IO[2, 1] = Max\,[B\,[2, 1, T] - X, 0]$

$IO[2, 0] = Max\,[B\,[2, 0, T] - X, 0]$

$IO[n, i]$ = Interest rate options value at time $n$ and state $i$

$B[n, i, T]$ = $T$-year bond value at time $n$ and state $i$

$X$ = Exercise price

**Figure 5.4** Pricing the interest rate option by recursive methods. For the formulation of the Ho-Lee model, we assume that the risk-neutral probability is 0.5. We can calculate the expected derivative values one period ahead with 0.5 risk-neutral probability and discount the expected value at the prevailing interest rate. $IO[n, i]$ is a interest rate option at time $n$ and state $i$. $B[n, i, T]$ is a $T$-year bond value at time $n$ and state $i$. $X$ is an exercise price.

One-period interest rate

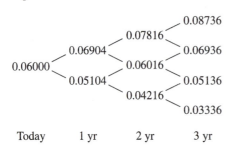

One-period discount factor movement

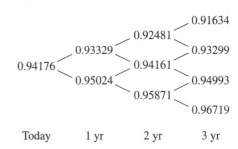

Zero-coupon bond price

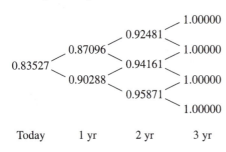

Pricing interest rate option

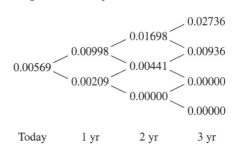

**Figure 5.5** The one-period interest rate, discount function movements, zero-coupon bond price and interest rate contingent claim (cap), using the assumptions as stated above, 6% yield curve. The zero-coupon bond price, which pays $1 for all nodes at the terminal date, is 0.83527, which is the same as $P(3)$ (= exp($-0.06 * 3$)). This is the essence of the arbitrate-free interest rate model. The terminal condition of the interest rate option is $Max[r(3, i) - 0.06, 0]$, $i = \{0, 1, 2, 3\}$, where $r(n, i)$ is the one-period interest rate for time $n$ and state $i$. The annual compounding rate is 6% and the volatility is 15%. The risk-neutral probability for upward movements is 0.5, the exercise price is 6%, and the notional amount is 1. The maturity of the option contract is three years. The one-period interest rates and corresponding one-period discount functions are shown in the figure. Based on them, the binomial lattice of interest rate options is represented in the subsequent diagram. At the highest state of year 3, the interst rate is 0.08736. If we subtract the exercise rate of 6% from the interest rate at that state and multiply the notional amount, we have the interest rate option value at the highest state of year 3.

date. When we conduct the backward substitution procedure, the initial value should exactly match the input discount bond prices $P(T)$. This is the essence of an arbitrage-free interest rate movement model, in the sense that the model takes the yield curve (of the discount function) as given, and the model prices any zero-coupon bond consistent with the input discount function. (See figure 5.5.)

There are two remarks that are important. First, note that given the one-period arbitrage-free discount rates specified at all the node points on the binomial lattice, we can always determine the zero-coupon bond price at any node point, using the method described above. Or we can value any derivatives at any node point. The important point is that specifying the one-period interest rate movement is sufficient to determine all interest rate derivatives. Second, this procedure of valuing an interest rate derivative relies only on the one-period arbitrage-free rate assigned to the binomial lattice. Therefore, this procedure is appropriate for any arbitrage-free rate models that can assign the one-period interest rate to all the nodes on the binomial lattice.

## 5.4   KEY RATE DURATION AND DYNAMIC HEDGING

### Duration

A valuation model of interest rate options or contingent claims enables us to develop the analytics of the securities, as we have done with stock options. The approach is very similar to stock options; they differ mainly in terminologies. Perhaps the most commonly used analytical measure for any interest rate contingent claim is the duration measure.

Duration is defined as the price sensitivity of an interest rate contingent claim to a parallel shift of the spot yield curve. Typically the spot yield curve is assumed to be semiannual compounding. Using an arbitrage-free interest rate model, we can simulate the duration of any interest rate contingent claim by shifting the spot yield curve (which is a model input) upward by a small amount, say five basis points.

As we have shown before, for a default-free zero-coupon bond, the duration turns out to be approximately the maturity. However, for a bond option, duration cannot be interpreted as maturity or time to expiration. For options, there is almost no relationship between the duration measure and the maturity or time to expiration. Indeed, for out-of-the-money call options, the duration can be very high—for example, 100 years. The duration for in-the-money call options approaches the duration of the underlying bond as the option becomes more in the money.

A similar analysis can be conducted for a put option. The bond put option has a negative duration. An out-of-the-money bond put option can have a duration of $-100$ years, and a deep-in-the-money put bond option's duration almost equals the negative of the duration of the underlying bond.

### Key Rate Duration

Since an arbitrage-free interest rate model takes the yield curve as given, we can input any shape of the yield curve to the interest rate model, and the valuation can still be assured to be consistent with arbitrage-free conditions. Specifically, we can use the shifts of the key rates as inputs to the interest rate model. The *key rate duration* of a bond option is the negative price change of the bond option with the key rate shift divided by the option price and the size of the shift. Since an arbitrage-free interest rate model can take any yield curve as given, we can appropriately define the key rate duration of an interest rate contingent claim using an arbitrage-free interest rate model.

The Black-Scholes model prescribes a methodology in replicating a stock option using the delta as the hedge ratio. We can implement the key rate durations of an interest rate contingent claim to determine the deltas (or hedge ratios) using zero-coupon bonds to dynamically hedge the interest rate contingent claim. Specifically, given an interest rate contingent claim, we can calculate its key rate durations ($KRD$) for key rates $1, 2, 3, \cdots, N$. Let the price of the contingent claim be $P$. Let the duration of each zero-coupon bond with maturity $T$ be $D(T) (= T/(1 + r(T)/2))$. Then the dollar amount we should hold to replicate the contingent claim for each zero-coupon bond is

$$X(i) = P \times \frac{KRD(i)}{D(i)} \text{ for } i = 1, 2, 3 \cdots, N$$

That is, given any small change in the $i$th key rate, the change in the zero-coupon bond value would equal the change in the price of the contingent claim attributed to the change in the key rate. The amount invested in cash is the price $P$ net of all the investments in all the zero-coupon bonds. Cash in this case represents all the short-term payments not captured by the first key rate. The cash portion of the bond has no interest rate sensitivity and therefore is not captured by the equation above. The sum of $KRD$ equals $D$. This portfolio replicates the interest rate contingent claims.

For example, we consider a call option on a ten-year zero-coupon bond. The option expiration date is five years and the initial yield curve is flat at 5%. The five-year key rate duration is −93.57 and the ten-year key rate duration is 196.67. Therefore the effective duration is 103.10. The call option price is \$1.58437. The durations of the five-year and ten-year zero-coupon bonds are 4.88 and 9.76, respectively. In this case, we sell \$−30.2952 (= 1.58 × (−93.57/4.878)) of five-year zero-coupon bonds and buy \$31.8507 (= 1.58 × 196.67/9.7561) of ten-year bonds. The amount invested in cash is \$0.02887 (= 1.58437 − (31.8507 − 30.2952)). The bond portfolio of the five-year bond and the ten-year bond replicates the call option over a short time interval. This bond portfolio will be revised, using the above procedure, at the end of this time interval.

## Key Rate Durations of Bonds and Options

Let us consider some examples: a zero-coupon bond, a call option, and a put option. The key rate durations of a $T$-year zero-coupon bond are all 0 except for the $T$th year. That key rate duration is $T/(1 + r/2)$ year at the $T$-year term.

Consider a floating-rate note. This bond has a principal of 100 maturing in $T$ years. A floating rate note pays interest as follows. The interest is accrued at the daily LIBOR. The accrued amount is paid out at the end of the year. Typically, interest is accrued with a margin (an additional spread) to a short-term interest rate and the interest payments are made quarterly or semiannually.

Although the floating-rate note described above is a bond with interest and principal, its behavior is more like a cash account. The bond is not different from a cash account that accrues interest and withdraws cash at regular intervals. Therefore, for such a floating-rate note, the key rate duration is 0.

Consider a European bond call option. At the expiration date, the call option can buy a zero-coupon bond at the strike price $X$. The relative pricing model shows that the call option is equivalent to buying the zero-coupon bond on margin. More specifically, we are shorting a zero-coupon bond maturing at the expiration date and buying the underlying zero-coupon bond. It is similar to the replication for a forward contract. However, the hedge ratios to replicate the option are different from that of the forward contract. The ratio of the two bonds is continually adjusted so that the hedging position can replicate the option value. Following this argument, we see that all the key rate durations are 0 except for the key rate duration at the expiration date and the maturity of the bond. The key rate duration is negative at the expiration date and is positive at the maturity. While we all know options have high duration values (are sensitive to interest rate shifts), the result shows that an option typically has an even larger exposure to the bends of the spot curve.

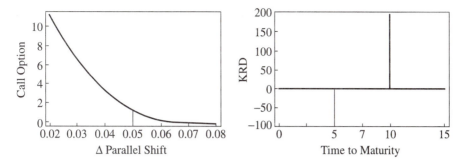

**Figure 5.6** The bond call option profile and key rate duration. This figure depicts the performance profile and the key rate durations of a call option on a bond. The maturity of the underlying bond is year 10 and the option expiration date is year 5. The initial term structure is flat at 5%. The exercise price is $78 and the face value is $100. The key rate duration of the bond call option at the expiration date is negative, and the key rate duration at the maturity of the underlying bond is positive.

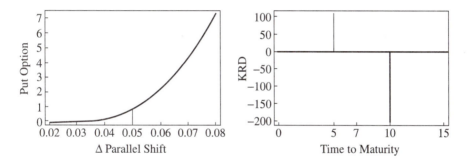

**Figure 5.7** The bond put option profile and key rate duration. This figure depicts the performance profile and the key rate duration of a put option on a bond. The maturity of the underlying bond is year 10 and the option expiration date is year 5. The initial term structure is flat at 5%. The exercise price is $78 and the face value is $100. The key rate duration of the bond put option at the expiration date is positive, and the key rate duration at the maturity of the underlying bond is negative.

A drop in the key rate at the option expiration date with a rise in the rate at the maturity date would simultaneously compound the effect of interest rate risks on the option.

In a similar fashion, we can analyze the key rate durations of a put option. Put options can be replicated by shorting the underlying zero-coupon bond and holding a position of a zero-coupon bond maturing on the expiration date. Again, the ratio of the two bond positions is continually adjusted, depending on the bond values. Therefore the key rate duration of a put option at the expiration date is positive and the key rate duration at the maturity of the underlying bond is negative. (See figures 5.6 and 5.7.)

## Dynamic Hedging

The importance of the equity option pricing model is based in large part on the specification of the delta. By specifying the replicating portfolio of an option, the market has a method to exploit any mispricing of an option. When an option is "mispriced," as judged by the Black-Scholes model, a trader can buy the option and sell the replicating portfolio, or vice versa, to realize an arbitrage profit. This can also be achieved in the bond option market. But for an interest rate option, in most cases we cannot use only one bond. We need to use the entire yield curve to hedge the interest rate option.

To extend the concept of hedging to interest rate options, we need to use more than one sensitivity number (delta); we need a vector of numbers. Key rate duration is based on the understanding that the yield curve movements are influenced by benchmark bonds in the market. Benchmark bonds are bonds with certain maturities that the market follows. Other bond yields tend to follow a blend of the yields for these bonds. For example, two-year and three-year Treasury bonds are benchmark bonds because the U.S. Treasury issues them, and the market accepts them as benchmark bonds. A bond with a maturity of 2.5 years is often quoted with a yield having a spread relative to the average of the two-year and three-year bond yields.

Therefore the movement of an entire yield curve is greatly affected by the key rate movements. Given an option with calculated key rate durations, we can construct a portfolio of bonds with no embedded options such that it has the same key rate durations and the same value as the option. This portfolio must dynamically replicate the option. If we want to hedge the option, then we should short this replicating portfolio. Holding the option and the short position of the replicating portfolio would lead to a dynamic hedging strategy instead of a dynamic replicating strategy.

If any option is priced above the arbitrage-free valuation, in theory we should sell the option and long the replicating portfolio of bonds (or swaps) based on fair value. The difference between the option price and the fair value (which is the same as the cost of the replicating portfolio) is the arbitrage profit. Similarly, if the option price is below the fair value of the arbitrage-free valuation, then the model suggests that we buy the option and sell the replicating portfolio.

## Convexity

Convexity, like the gamma of a stock option, measures the curvature of a price behavior. It is a historical accident that the converse of convexity is not concavity. There is no concavity. Therefore, we distinguish the option behavior as positive convexity or negative convexity. The measure is defined as

$$C = \frac{1}{2} \frac{\partial^2 P}{\partial r^2} \bigg/ P \qquad (5.14)$$

The definition comes from the expression of a Taylor expansion.

$$\Delta P = -D \cdot P \Delta r + C \cdot P (\Delta r)^2 \qquad (5.15)$$

A call option has positive duration because its value increases with the fall in interest rates. The option also has positive convexity. That means that when interest rates move up or down significantly, the option gains higher value than that predicted by the duration. The additional returns are attributed to the positive convexity.

A put option has negative duration because when interest rates fall, the option value falls along with them. However, since options always provide the holder with downside protection while offering upside returns, the put option also has positive convexity.

# EXCEL MODEL EXERCISES

## E5.1   COX-INGERSOLL-ROSS MODEL

### Definitions

The short-term rate is the shortest rate in the modeling, which may be the daily, weekly, or monthly rate. The long-run rate is the rate that the short-term rate converges to in the long run. The mean reverting speed is the rate at which the short-term rate is expected to converge to the long-run rate. The model assumes an instantaneous constant short-term rate volatility. The maturity is the bond maturity.

### Description of the Model

The model assumes a perfect capital market of bonds. The risk of the market is driven by the short-term rate. The model assumes a specific market price of risk for this short-term risk source that leads to an equilibrium bond pricing model.

### Numerical Example

Suppose that the observed short-term rate is 5% with volatility of 10%. Let the long-run rate be 6%, with the mean reversion speed of 15%; see figure E5.1. If we hypothesize that the market price of risk is zero, then the equilibrium term structure is shown in figure E5.2.

| Inputs | | | | | | | |
|---|---|---|---|---|---|---|---|
| The level of short rate (r(t)) | 0.05 | $dr = a(b - r)dt + \sigma\sqrt{r}dz$ | | | | | |
| The long-term mean (b) | 0.06 | | | | | | |
| The mean reverting speed (a) | 0.15 | | | | | | |
| The volatility of short rate (σ) | 0.1 | | | | | | |
| Maturity date (T) | 1 | | | | | | |
| Current date (t) | 0 | | | | | | |
| **Outputs** | | | | | | | |
| Time to maturity | | 0 | 1 | 2 | 3 | 4 | 5 |
| P(t,T) | 0.950622 | 1 | 0.950622 | 0.902866 | 0.857099 | 0.813492 | 0.772089 |
| r(t,T) | 0.050639 | 0.05 | 0.050639 | 0.051091 | 0.051401 | 0.051605 | 0.051731 |
| f(t,T) | | | | 0.050639 | 0.051543 | 0.052021 | 0.052217 | 0.052236 |

Figure E5.1

| Time to maturity | 0 | 1 | 2 | 3 | 4 | 5 |
|---|---|---|---|---|---|---|
| P(t,T) | 1 | 0.950622 | 0.902866 | 0.857099 | 0.813492 | 0.772089 |

Figure E5.2

## Applications

1. Given the specifications of the short-term rate movement, the model can derive the equilibrium yield curve.
2. Given the observed yield curve, the model can be used to specify a short-term interest rate process, which in turn can be used to value interest rate contingent claims.

## Case: Building a Model by Knowing Your Clients

Michelle India held a Ph.D. in experimental physics, and she had a strong educational background in empirical analysis. She recently got an assignment from the risk manager Elli Mohammed. As the risk manager put it: "We now need to bite the bullet by measuring our yen interest rate risk exposure by first developing our company's yen interest rate model." To begin, Michelle thought that she would assume that the interest rate would not be negative and that the interest rates should exhibit the mean reversion process. Given these assumptions, she thought that she would empirically estimate the Cox-Ingersoll-Ross model from the historical data.

Her first question was "What would be the appropriate 'short-term rate?'" The shortest rate she could find was the overnight swap rate. Another assumption was the long-term fixed rate. She then proceeded to assume that rate to be the observed twenty-year bond yield of 1.5%. Given these assumptions, she proceeded to estimate the overnight interest rate movements in yen using the fifteen-year historical data. She further assumed the market price of risk to be zero and proceeded to value the firm's securities in yen. When the work was completed, she discussed her results with the end users of the model in the firm.

"Michelle, I used your model to price the yen option. I think there is some mispricing. I am not sure if the market is mispricing the option or your model is inaccurate. How should I use your model?" asked the yen interest rate trader.

"Michelle, I deal with yen long-term contracts. These are private deals and have no markets. I do not see how your overnight rates are relevant to our ten-year contracts. Should you develop a long-rate model?" another question was raised.

"I have a simpler question. Our yen long rate is now 1.5%. But for the past fifteen years, yen rates have only been falling. In the early 1990s, no one would think the equilibrium long rate was 1.5%. How does model capture the changes of the expectations?"

The risk manager interjected saying: "I am sure there are many issues that we have not incorporated at this point. Maybe we will consider a more general model." "Elli, interest rates movements are very complex. I am not sure there is one model that would fit all our needs. May be we should first identify the users of your model, and then we can narrow our scope in the modeling development. What do you think?" asked one trader.

Michelle went back to her cubical somewhat dejected, looking absentmindedly at her physics books mixed with the finance books. Elli walked by. "Elli, I need to talk to you." "What's up?" "Look, I just walked into this job. I know my stuff. But I do not know 90% of the people here, and I do not know what they are shouting about all day." "You mean shouting for the clients' orders." "Whatever. But I am not a punching bag for these people. How can I go around to identify who uses the model, how they use the model, etc., when I do not even know what they do?" "Actually, most of them do not even know that they need models—that is the hard part." Elli concurred. "So, what should I do? Asking me to build such a model is unrealistic."

*"Michelle, no one is saying that you should come out with a holy grail model in one month. But people expect you to learn from the traders and find out what they need. One way to begin: Make up a list of the main users of the model and then think about their requirements of the model. And we will go from there."*

## Exercises and Answers

1. Suppose that the observed spot yield curve is 4% flat. What is the short-term rate model that can best fit the yield curve, if the short-term rate movement is assumed to follow the CIR model? Compare the results with the Vasicek model.
   *Answer:* Since we have a closed-form solution for the CIR model to calculate the yield curve, we can search for the parameters of the CIR model that best fit the given yield curve. See figure E5.3.
2. Using the results of question 1, suppose that a European call option on a zero-coupon bond with maturity at the end of the first year expires in 0.6 years. The strike price is 0.92. What is the price of the call option?
   *Answer:* We generate the yield curve given the estimated parameters up to year 1. Given the yield curve, we can calculate the zero-coupon bond price at year 0.6 and compare with the exercise price. If we have a positive cash flow at year 0.6, the discounted value is the call price at year 0. Note that the answer will change whenever we open the Excel sheet because of a new set of random numbers. See figure E5.4.
3. The only difference between the Vasicek and CIR model is the coefficient of the stochastic term. The CIR model has an additional term, which is $\sqrt{r}$, as compared to the Vasicek. What impact does this additional term have on the interest movements?
   *Answer:* If interest rate goes down to zero, the volatility of the short-term interest rates will decrease to zero. When the short-term interest is zero, the increase in

| Inputs | | |
|---|---|---|
| The level of short rate (r(t)) | 0.04 | $dr = a(b - r)dt + \sigma\sqrt{r}dz$ |
| The long-term mean (b) | 0.040001 | |
| The mean reverting speed (a) | 0.129001 | |
| The volatility of short rate (σ) | 0.000848 | Changing cells for solver |
| Maturity date (T) | 1 | |
| Current date (t) | 0 | |
| Option expiration (OT) | 0.6 | |
| Bond face value (F) | 1 | |
| Exercise price (K) | 0.92 | |

| Outputs | | | | | | | |
|---|---|---|---|---|---|---|---|
| Time to maturity | | 0 | 1 | 2 | 3 | 4 | 5 |
| P(t,T) | 0.960789 | 1 | 0.96078941 | 0.923116 | 0.8869203 | 0.852144 | 0.81873 |
| r(t,T) | 0.040000 | 0.04 | 0.04000003 | 0.04 | 0.0400001 | 0.04 | 0.04 |
| f(t,T) | | | 0.04000003 | 0.04 | 0.0400001 | 0.04 | 0.04 |
| | | | | | | | |
| | | | | | | | |
| Observed discount function: P*(t,T) | | | 0.96078944 | 0.923116 | 0.8869204 | 0.852144 | 0.818731 |
| Σ(P(t,T)-P*(t,T))² | 6.8E-12 | | 9.1184E-16 | 9.49E-15 | 3.108E-14 | 6.3E-14 | 9.76E-14 |
| | Target cells for solver | | | | | | |

Figure E5.3

| Outputs | | | |
|---|---|---|---|
| European bond option value | | 0.062615 | Simulation |

**Figure E5.4**

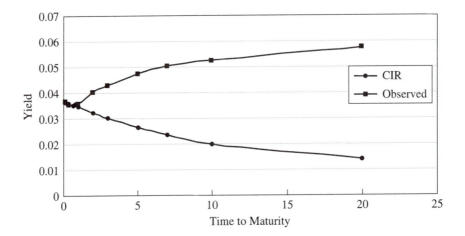

**Figure E5.5**

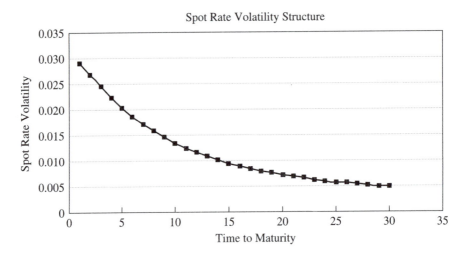

**Figure E5.6**

the interest rate is always positive, which guarantees that the interest rate is always positive. Therefore, it is impossible for the interest rate to go below zero. However, in the Vasicek model, it is possible to have negative interest rates.

4. Given the interest changes as input data, estimate the parameters of the CIR model. Based on the estimated parameters, draw the term structure of interest rates and the term structure of volatility. Compare the term structure of interest rate derived from the CIR with the actual term structure that we can observe in the market.

*Answer:* We collect the monthly Treasury yields from the Federal Reserve Board from July 2001 to April 2004. We use one-month interest rates as the short rates. The maximum likelihood method is used to estimate the parameters of the CIR model. The observed yield curve is different from the yield curve derived from the CIR model, which is a drawback of the CIR model. See figures E5.5 and E5.6.

## Further Exercises

1. Suppose that the observed short-term rate is 6% with volatility of 15%. Let the long-term rate be 8%, with the mean reversion speed of 20%. If we hypothesize that the market price of risk is zero, determine the equilibrium term structure.
   *Answer:* The equilibrium term structure by the CIR model is shown in figures E5.7 and E5.8.
2. Using the results of question 1, suppose that a European call option on a zero-coupon bond with maturity at the end of the first year expires in 0.6 years. The strike price is 0.9. What is the price of the call option?
   *Answer:* The price of the call option is 0.068734. See figure E5.9.

| Time to maturity | 0 | 1 | 2 | 3 | 4 | 5 | 6 |
|---|---|---|---|---|---|---|---|
| P(t,T) | 1 | 0.940187 | 0.881914 | 0.8262628 | 0.773702 | 0.724354 | 0.678156 |
| r(t,T) | 0.06 | 0.06167648 | 0.06283 | 0.0636141 | 0.064142 | 0.064495 | 0.06473 |

Figure E5.7

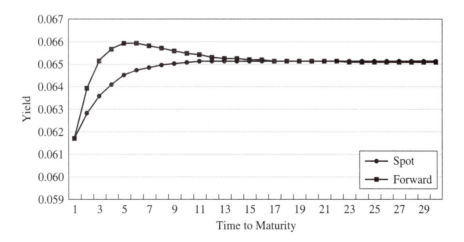

Figure E5.8

| Outputs | | |
|---|---|---|
| | | |
| European bond option value | | 0.068734 | Simulation |

Figure E5.9

## E5.2   VASICEK MODEL

### Definitions

The short-term rate is the shortest rate in the modeling, which may be the daily, weekly, or monthly rate. The long-term rate is the rate that the short-term rate converges to in the long term. The mean reverting speed is the rate at which the short-term rate is expected to converge to the long-term rate. The model assumes an instantaneous constant short-term rate volatility. The maturity is the bond maturity.

### Description of the Model

The model assumes a perfect capital market of bonds. The risk of the market is driven by the short-term rate. The model assumes a specific market price of risk for this short-term risk source that leads to an equilibrium bond pricing model.

### Numerical Example

Suppose that the observed short-term rate is 5% with volatility of 1%. Let the long-term rate be 6%, with the mean reversion speed of 15%; see figure E5.10. If we hypothesize that the market price of risk is zero, then the equilibrium term structure is shown in figure E5.11. The rate 0.050699 is a one-period rate that is applicable from time 0 to time 1. The other rate can be defined similarly.

| Inputs | | | | | | |
|---|---|---|---|---|---|---|
| The level of short rate (r(t)) | 0.05 | $dr = a(b - r)dt + \sigma dz$ | | | | |
| The long-term mean (b) | 0.06 | | | | | |
| The mean reverting speed (a) | 0.15 | | | | | |
| The volatility of short rate (σ) | 0.01 | | | | | |
| Maturity date (T) | 1 | | | | | |
| Current date (t) | 0 | | | | | |

| Outputs | | | | | | |
|---|---|---|---|---|---|---|
| Time to maturity | 0 | 1 | 2 | 3 | 4 | 5 |
| P(t,T) | 1 | 0.950565 | 0.902475 | 0.855973 | 0.811213 | 0.768287 |
| r(t,T) | 0.05 | 0.050699 | 0.051307 | 0.051839 | 0.052306 | 0.052718 |
| f(t,T) | | 0.050699 | 0.051915 | 0.052902 | 0.053708 | 0.054368 |

Figure E5.10

| Time to maturity | 0 | 1 | 2 | 3 | 4 | 5 |
|---|---|---|---|---|---|---|
| P(t,T) | 1 | 0.950565 | 0.902475 | 0.855973 | 0.811213 | 0.768287 |

Figure E5.11

## Applications

1. Given the specifications of the short-term rate movement, the model can derive the equilibrium yield curve.
2. Given the observed yield curve, the model can be used to specify a short-term interest rate process, which in turn can be used to value interest rate contingent claims.

## Case: Defined Benefits and Asset Management

George Paparigalo was a vice president in finance of a medium-size manufacturing company generating $100 million sales with 250 employees. He reported to the chief financial officer, and one of his responsibilities was managing the pensions of the employees. The company offered defined benefits to all full-time employees. For the participants of the pension plan, the retirees were entitled to a pension provided by the company for their retirement. The pension in essence was a liability cash flow to the company, a fixed annuity that commences on the retirement date. The pension actuaries retained by the company calculated the present value of these liabilities, and George had to make sure that the company had the assets assigned to support the total pension liabilities of the firm.

In addition, George had to manage the investment portfolio that supports the pension liability. Should he invest in equity or bonds? The performance of the portfolio would significantly affect the pension fund's ability to support the liabilities. Or, the fund performance could affect the profitability of the firm. If the fund underperforms, the firm may have to allocate more of the profits to support the pension liability, leading to a fall in the company's earnings.

He decided to begin understanding the risks of the pension liabilities. He would first begin by analyzing the pension liabilities under different interest rate scenarios. Using the Vasicek model was one way to begin building an interest rate model. The model could provide a set of interest rate scenarios, and from these scenarios he could then investigate the behavior of the combined pension asset and liability.

He picked up the phone and called the human resources department. "Mary, I am looking at our pension liability. This is a cash flow that goes on for fifty years or more." "Well, at least this is what our pension actuaries get us to believe. In fact, for our pension, we do take inflation into account, since our people's compensation is related to inflation." "How about people quitting the company?" "Yes, that too is taken into account. You got it. This cash flow that you have is only the expected cash flow." "It just seems to me that we need to look at our pension liability under a set of scenarios before we can formulate our investments." "I would think so. I would think interest rate risk is one risk driver. Interest rate risk is related to inflation risk, which in turn affects our pension liability."

*After hanging up the phone, George wondered about the appropriateness of using the Vasicek model. "Let me list all the assumptions of the model and evaluate them one by one. May be then I can see if the model is appropriate or not. If not, then I have to see if I can adjust the model accordingly."*

## Exercises and Answers

1. Supposing that the observed spot yield curve is 4% flat, what is the short-term rate model that can best fit the yield curve if the short-term rate movement is assumed to follow the Vasicek model?

*Answer:* We search for the parameters that minimize the differences between the estimated and the observed yield curves, such as the long-term mean, the mean reverting speed, and the volatility of the short rate. See figure E5.12.

2. Using the results of question 1, suppose that a European call option on a zero-coupon bond with maturity at the end of year 1 expires in 0.6 years. The strike price is 92. What is the price of the call option?

*Answer:* Once we know the parameters, we can generate the future interest rates so that we can price the European option on the zero-coupon bond. Note that the answer will change whenever we open the Excel sheet because of a new set of random numbers. See figure E5.13.

| Inputs | | | | | | |
|---|---|---|---|---|---|---|
| | | | | | | |
| The level of short rate (r(t)) | 0.04 | $dr = a(b - r)dt + \sigma dz$ | | | | |
| The long-term mean (b) | 0.040112 | | | | | |
| The mean reverting speed (a) | 0.113243 | | | | | |
| The volatility of short rate (σ) | 0.002038 | Changing cells for solver | | | | |
| Bond maturity (T) | 1 | | | | | |
| Current date (t) | 0 | | | | | |
| Option expiration (OT) | 0.6 | | | | | |
| Bond face value (F) | 100 | | | | | |
| Exercise price (K) | 92 | | | | | |
| | | | | | | |
| **Outputs** | | | | | | |
| | | | | | | |
| Time to maturity | | 0 | 1 | 2 | 3 | 4 |
| P(t,T) | 0.960784 | 1 | 0.960784 | 0.923099 | 0.886888 | 0.852097 |
| r(t,T) | 0.040005 | 0.04 | 0.040005 | 0.040009 | 0.040012 | 0.040014 |
| f(t,T) | | ◄ | 0.040005 | 0.040013 | 0.040018 | 0.040019 |
| | | | | | | |
| Observed discount function: P*(t,T) | | | 0.960789 | 0.923116 | 0.88692 | 0.852144 |
| Σ(P(t,T)-P*(t,T))² | 1.37E-07 | | 2.74E-11 | 3E-10 | 1.04E-09 | 2.23E-09 |
| | Target cells for solver | | | | | |

**Figure E5.12**

| Inputs | | | | |
|---|---|---|---|---|
| | | | | |
| The level of short rate (r(t)) | 0.04 | $dr = a(b - r)dt + \sigma dz$ | | |
| The long-term mean (b) | 0.040112 | | | |
| The mean reverting speed (a) | 0.113243 | | | |
| The volatility of short rate (σ) | 0.002038 | Changing cells for solver | | |
| Bond maturity (T) | 1 | | | |
| Current date (t) | 0 | | | |
| Option expiration (OT) | 0.6 | | | |
| Bond face value (F) | 100 | | | |
| Exercise price (K) | 92 | | | |
| **Outputs** | | | | |
| | | | | |
| European bond option value | | 6.252731 | | |
| | | Monte Carlo simulation | | |

**Figure E5.13**

3. Given the interest changes as input data, estimate the parameters of the Vasicek model. Based on the estimated parameters, draw the term structure of interest rates and the term structure of volatility. Compare the term structure of interest rate derived from the Vasicek model with the actual term structure that we can observe in the market.

*Answer:* We collect the monthly Treasury yields from the Federal Reserve Board from July 2001 to April 2004. We use the one-month interest rate as the short rate. To estimate the parameters, the maximum likelihood method is used. The observed yield curve is different from the yield curve derived from the Vasicek model. See figures E5.14 and E5.15.

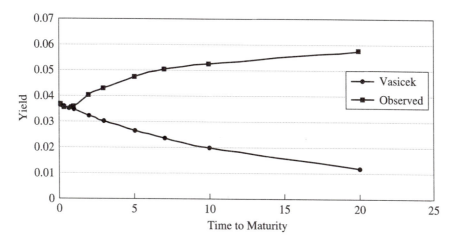

**Figure E5.14**

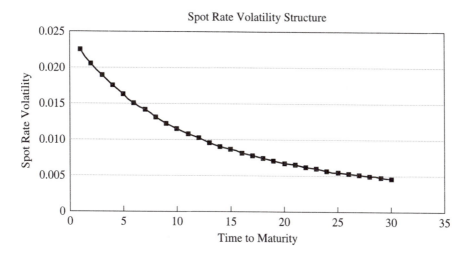

**Figure E5.15**

## Further Exercises

1. Suppose that the observed short-term rate is 6% with volatility of 2%. Let the long-term rate be 8%, with the mean reversion speed of 20%. If we hypothesize that the market price of risk is zero, determine the equilibrium term structure.
   *Answer:* See figures E5.16 and E5.17.
2. Using the results of question 1, suppose that a European call option on a zero-coupon bond with maturity at the end of the first year expires in 0.6 years. The strike price is 90. What is the price of the call option?
   *Answer:* The call option price is 7.467. See figure E5.18.

| Time to maturity | 0 | 1 | 2 | 3 | 4 | 5 | 6 |
|---|---|---|---|---|---|---|---|
| P(t,T) | 1 | 0.940056 | 0.881057 | 0.8239 | 0.769134 | 0.717067 | 0.667849 |
| r(t,T) | 0.06 | 0.061816 | 0.063316 | 0.064569 | 0.065623 | 0.066517 | 0.067282 |

Figure E5.16

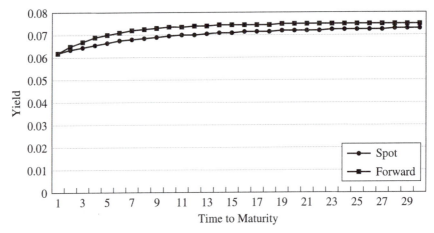

Figure E5.17

| Inputs | | |
|---|---|---|
| The level of short rate (r(t)) | 0.06 | $dr = a(b - r)dt + \sigma dz$ |
| The long-term mean (b) | 0.08 | |
| The mean reverting speed (a) | 0.2 | |
| The volatility of short rate ($\sigma$) | 0.02 | |
| Bond maturity (T) | 1 | |
| Current date (t) | 0 | |
| Option expiration (OT) | 0.6 | |
| Bond face value (F) | 100 | |
| Exercise price (K) | 90 | |
| | | |
| Outputs | | |
| | | |
| European bond option value | | 7.466881 |
| | | Monte Carlo simulation |

Figure E5.18

# E5.3   HO-LEE MODEL

## Definitions

The one-period forward rate is a one-period forward rate at each time period. The forward curve at time 1 is the term structure of forward rates that we can calculate at time 1. The lognormal spot volatility is a term structure of spot volatility. The lognormal forward volatility is the volatility of the one-period rate $n$ years from now. Delta, $\delta$, is a constant number to represent volatility, because $-0.5\ln\delta$ is the forward volatility of the interest rate model. $T$ is the time period of each step of the binomial lattice. The spot yield curve is assumed to be based on the continuously compounding rate.

## Description of the Model

The model is a binomial lattice interest rate model. The model is arbitrage-free, and it is consistent with the initial observed yield curve. The distribution of the interest rate is normal with a constant standard deviation.

## Numerical Example

The binomial lattice has a one-year step size. Suppose that the spot yield curve is increasing by 0.5%, starting at 6%. The binomial probability is 0.5. The forward volatility is constant at 0.0775. Even though the initial interest rate is 6%, the interest rates at year 5 vary from the lowest rate of 7.188% to the highest rate of 14.938%. The reason that we have higher interest rates at year 5 as compared to the initial one-period rate is that the term structure is upward-sloping. See figure E5.19.

## Applications

1. The model can determine the value of an interest rate option.
2. The implied volatility of the option can be determined when the value of the option is given.

## Case: Using an Arbitrage-Free Model to Determine Profit Release

General Financial Product Company (GFP) was a financial institution that sold interest rate financial products. The company was a subsidiary of a large conglomerate that had a very high credit rating. With a high credit rating backed by the parent company, GFP was engaged in selling interest rate options, many of them "exotic," not traded in the capital markets. Their sales force worked with manufacturing companies, hedged funds, asset management companies, and government agencies. GFP designed the interest rate contingent claims that fit the clients' needs and then sold the options, the financial products, to the willing buyer. A portion of the proceeds was then used to buy securities to hedge the option sold, and the remaining proceeds were released as profit to the firm. GFP recently hired a chief financial officer, who then set up an internal auditing team. The internal auditing team's first task was to review the hedging program, and they were concerned with the appropriateness in the measuring of the "profits." Their question

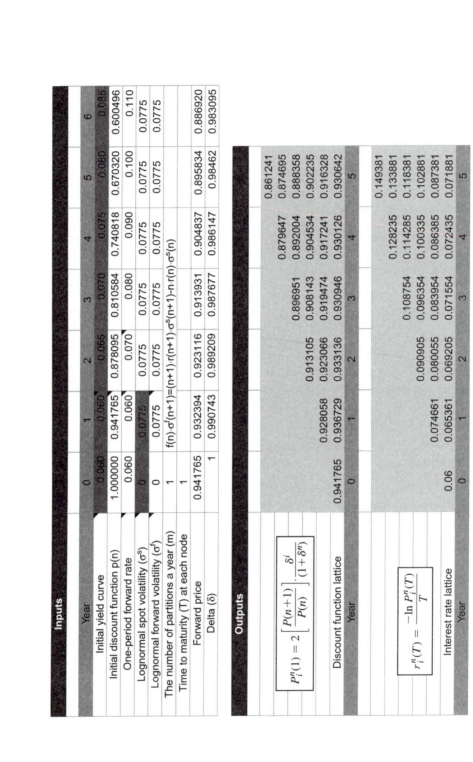

Figure E5.19

arose from the pricing of the interest rate contingent claim. "If these options are not traded in the market, and, therefore, there is no market price, how can we then determine the profits that we have made?" The CFO explained that the firm used the arbitrage-free interest rate model to determine the option values, and the model was then used to hedge the positions. Therefore the profit was properly measured. The internal auditing team was puzzled by the concept of "arbitrage-free" interest rate movement.

Angelika Parmagiano, the CFO, was taking a coffee break with Leslie Hawkins, the internal auditor. "Angie, so you do not see a touch of irony here. And you wouldn't consider a statement like 'booking profits using an arbitrage-free model' an oxymoron?" "Leslie, how do you like my coffee? What are you saying? I understand the part on 'booking profits.' But what is this about the arbitrage-free model?" "Your people told me that you assume the market is efficient and therefore there is no arbitrage opportunity out there and, therefore, your arbitrage-free model is appropriate. Then you turn around and use the model to book arbitrage profits. This is as oxymoronic as drinking caffeine-loaded coffee to stay awake over a break." "I see what you mean. Fuzzy logic begins with playing with words. Let's not get bogged down by the term 'arbitrage-free' for now. Our model in essence tells us the cost in replicating a structured product that we sell. If we sell the product above its cost, then we book the profit, just like any manufactured good."

"I am not sure I can entirely agree with you there. It costs me $1 to make this cup of coffee, and I sell it for $1.50, pocketing 50 cents. That is clean. In your case, in principle, it costs you $x millions to replicate the structured derivative. But you do not necessarily do that replication. Even if you replicate it, the derivative does not disappear like the cup of coffee. It sits on our book for many years to come. Anything can go wrong meanwhile. Who is to say your replication is perfect?" Leslie finished her cup of coffee to underscore that the transaction of coffee was simple and clean, but holding the derivatives on the book for many years was not. Angelika lowered her voice: "We probably cannot resolve this issue over a coffee break. Let's think about it."

*"I should write up a procedure in 'booking profits' for these derivatives," Leslie said to herself. "I am sure it will be a long process to finally get all parties to agree on an internal procedure since the procedure will affect the compensations of many people here."*

## Exercises and Answers

1. Verify that the interest rates in the Ho-Lee model are arbitrage-free by pricing a three-year zero-coupon bond using the backward substitution method.

   *Answer:* We can calculate a three-year zero-coupon bond by backward substitution on the binomial lattice. We can also calculate the three-year zero-coupon bond price using the initial term structure of interest rates. If the two values are the same, we can say that the interest rate lattice is arbitrage-free. To see this, we put $1 at every state of period 3. The zero-coupon bond price at state 2 and period 2 is 0.913105 (= $1.0 \times 0.913105$), where 0.913105 is the one-period discount function at state 2 and period 2. Similarly, we can calculate the zero-coupon bond price at state 1 and period 2. Rolling back by two more periods, we have the zero-coupon bond value at state 0 and period 0, which is 0.810584. To check whether this value is consistent with the zero-coupon bond value using the initial yield curve, we calculate the zero-coupon bond value by $\exp(-0.07 \times 3)$ (= 0.810584). Therefore, the Ho-Lee interest lattice is arbitrage-free. See figure E5.20.

2. What is the risk-neutral "expected" one-year rate over a three-year horizon according to the interest rate model in the numerical example? Is that the same as the one-year forward rate over a three-year horizon?

*Answer:* The interest rates at year 3 are 10.8754%, 9.6354%, 8.3954%, and 7.1554% from the highest states. The simple average of these interest rates is 9.0154%. Since the probability of arriving at each state $i$ at year 3 is $\binom{3}{i}\left(\frac{1}{2}\right)^3$, we multiply each interest at year 3 by this value and sum up to have 9.0154%. The one-year forward rate over a three-year horizon, $f(3, 4)$, is $r(4) \times 4 - r(3) \times 3$. See figure E5.21.

3. What is the two-year bond price at time 2 and state 2? (Note: State 0 has the lowest interest rate.)

*Answer:* If we assign $1 at all the states of year 4 and roll back to year 2, we can have the two-year zero-coupon bond price at year 2. In this way, we can construct a term structure of interest rate at each node of the lattice even though we have only the one-year interest rate lattice.

| | | | | | 1.000000 |
|---|---|---|---|---|---|
| | | | | 0.913105 | 1.000000 |
| | | | 0.852037 | 0.923066 | 1.000000 |
| Three-year zero-coupon bond | | 0.810584 | 0.869379 | 0.933136 | 1.000000 |
| Year | | 0 | 1 | 2 | 3 |
| Checking the arbitrage-free condition | | 0.810584 | | | |

Figure E5.20

| | | | 0.108754 |
|---|---|---|---|
| | | 0.102554 | 0.096354 |
| | 0.096354 | 0.090154 | 0.083954 |
| Expected one-year rate over a three-year horizon | 0.090154 | 0.083954 | 0.077754 | 0.071554 |
| Year | 0 | 1 | 2 | 3 |

Figure E5.21

| | | | | | 1.000000 |
|---|---|---|---|---|---|
| | | | | 0.896951 | 1.000000 |
| | | | 0.824120 | 0.908143 | 1.000000 |
| | | 0.773827 | 0.843505 | 0.919474 | 1.000000 |
| Four-year zero-coupon bond | 0.740818 | 0.799429 | 0.863346 | 0.930946 | 1.000000 |
| Year | 0 | 1 | 2 | 3 | 4 |

Figure E5.22

| | | | 0.096720 |
|---|---|---|---|
| | | 0.0909 | 0.085095 |
| Expected two-year bond yield at the end of period 2 | 0.0851 | 0.0793 | 0.073470 |
| Year | 0 | 1 | 2 |

Figure E5.23

At year 2, we have two-year zero-coupon bond prices, 0.824120, 0.843505, and 0.863346. If we continue rolling back to the initial period, we have a four-year zero-coupon bond price at the initial period, which is 0.740818. See figure E5.22.

4. What is the "expected" two-year bond yield at the end of period 2?

*Answer:* Since the two-year zero-coupon bond prices are 0.824120, 0.843505, and 0.8633461, we can calculate the bond yields, 9.672% (= −ln(0.82412)/2), 8.509%, and 7.347%. Once we have the two-year bond yield at each state of period 2, we can calculate the expected two-year return, which is 8.51%. See figure E5.23.

## Further Exercises

1. Since the Ho-Lee model is an arbitrage-free model, a binomial lattice of the Ho-Lee model should satisfy an initial term structure. To see this point, we calculate a zero-coupon bond price in two ways. The first way is to calculate the zero-coupon bond price using the initial term structure, and the second way is using the binomial lattice. Assume that the initial term structure is flat at 10% and the volatility is 15%. Generate the binomial lattice and calculate the five-year zero-coupon bond price by backward substitution. We can also calculate the zero-coupon bond price using the initial term structure. Compare the two prices to see whether they are identical. If they are different from each other, we can say that the law of one price does not hold, which means that there is an arbitrage opportunity. How does the conclusion change if we increase the volatility to 17%?

   *Answer:* The five-year zero-coupon bond price is the same regardless of the methods. Therefore, the bond price does not change even though we change the volatility of the interest rates. This property holds for the arbitrage-free interest models.

| Outputs | | | | | | | |
|---|---|---|---|---|---|---|---|
| $P_i^n(1) = 2\left[\dfrac{P(n+1)}{P(n)}\right]\cdot\dfrac{\delta^i}{(1+\delta^n)}$ | | | | | | 0.904837 | 0.904837 |
| | | | | | 0.904837 | 0.904837 | 0.904837 |
| | | | | 0.904837 | 0.904837 | 0.904837 | 0.904837 |
| | | | 0.904837 | 0.904837 | 0.904837 | 0.904837 | 0.904837 |
| | | 0.904837 | 0.904837 | 0.904837 | 0.904837 | 0.904837 | 0.904837 |
| Discount function lattice | 0.904837 | 0.904837 | 0.904837 | 0.904837 | 0.904837 | 0.904837 | 0.904837 |
| Year | 0 | 1 | 2 | 3 | 4 | 5 | |
| | | | | | | 0.1 | 0.1 |
| | | | | | 0.1 | 0.1 | 0.1 |
| $r_i^n(T) = \dfrac{-\ln P_i^n(T)}{T}$ | | | | 0.1 | 0.1 | 0.1 | 0.1 |
| | | | 0.1 | 0.1 | 0.1 | 0.1 | 0.1 |
| | | 0.1 | 0.1 | 0.1 | 0.1 | 0.1 | 0.1 |
| Interest rate lattice | 0.1 | 0.1 | 0.1 | 0.1 | 0.1 | 0.1 | |
| Year | 0 | 1 | 2 | 3 | 4 | 5 | |
| | | | | 0.1 | | | |
| | | | 0.1 | 0.1 | | | |
| | | 0.1 | 0.1 | 0.1 | | | |
| Expected one-year rate over a three-year horizon | 0.1 | 0.1 | 0.1 | 0.1 | | | |
| Year | 0 | 1 | 2 | 3 | 4 | 5 | |

Figure E5.24

2. We assume that the interest volatility is zero in question 1, which means that there is no interest rate risk. Generate the interest rate lattice and confirm that the interest rate at each period is the corresponding forward rate. From this, we expect that the forward rate is the expected future interest rate if there is no interest rate risk.
*Answer:* If the interest rate volatility is zero (i.e., $\delta = 1$), we have the same interest rate regardless of the states at each period. The expected future interest rate is 10%, which is the same as the forward rate, 10%. Since the yield curve is flat at 10%, the forward rate is also 10%. See figure E5.24.

## E5.4    THE BLACK MODEL OF THE BOND OPTION

### Definitions

The continuously compounding interest rate is the risk-free rate or the yield of the zero-coupon bond maturing at the time of the expiration of the option. The option price is the price that the holder of the call option should pay to have the right to buy the option or the price that the holder of the put option should pay to have the right to sell the option. The underlying bond is assumed to be a zero-coupon bond with as-specified maturity. Volatility refers to the bond return's volatility over the option life.

### Description of the Model

The Black model extends the Black-Scholes model for equity options to bond options. This model assumes that bond returns have a lognormal distribution like a stock in the Black-Scholes model.

### Numerical Example

Suppose that the two-year interest rate is 6% at a continuously compounding rate. The underlying bond is a zero-coupon bond with maturity of ten years, at par 100. The option has the time to expiration of two years and a strike price of 70. Assume that the bond return follows a process with a constant volatility of 10%. The European call and put option values are 0.8711 and 8.0744, respectively. The Black bond option model is as follows. $P(0, t)$ is the price at time 0 of the zero-coupon bond paying \$1 at time $t$. $F(0, t, T)$ is the forward price for a forward contract with maturity $t$. The underlying bond of the forward contract matures at time $T$. $X$ is the strike price of the bond option. $N(d)$ is the cumulative probability distribution function for a variable that is normally distributed with a mean of zero and a standard deviation of 1.0. $N(d)$ is the probability that a standard normally distributed variable is less than $d$. And $c$ and $p$ represent the Black bond call option and Black bond put option, respectively.

$$c = P(0, t)[F(0, t, T) \cdot N(d_1) - X \cdot N(d_2)]$$

$$p = P(0, t)[X \cdot N(-d_2) - F(0, t, T) \cdot N(-d_1)]$$

$$d_1 = \frac{\ln(F(0, t, T)/X) + \sigma^2 t/2}{\sigma \sqrt{t}}$$

$$d_2 = d_1 - \sigma \sqrt{t}$$

| Inputs | |
|---|---|
| Continuous compounding interest rate | 0.06 |
| Strike price | 70 |
| Volatility | 0.1 |
| Notional amount ($) | 100 |
| Maturity of bond (T) | 10 |
| Maturity of option (t) | 2 |
| | |
| **Outputs** | |
| | |
| Call option value | 0.8711 |
| Put option value | 8.0744 |

Figure E5.25

We can see that there are five variables: forward price, exercise price, discount function, time to maturity, and volatility of the forward price. In this numerical example, we can calculate the forward price of 61.8783, given the yield curve. See figure E5.25.

## Applications

1. The model gives a closed-form solution to European call and put options on bonds.
2. Given the agreed-upon inputs to the model, users of the model can obtain the option prices, and therefore the model is useful as a market convention in pricing bond options.
3. The model can be used to derive the implied volatility of the bond returns process precisely and therefore is used by the market participants to derive and quote the implied volatility of a bond's returns over a certain time horizon.

## Case: Proprietary Trading Desk

Gene Wahili is the head of the proprietary trading department of a securities firm. He and his team of ten occupy a corner area of the large fixed-income trading floor. They actively trade the over-the-counter interest rate derivative products. The team is in constant contact with the possible counter parties, soliciting their counter parties' bids and offers over a range of derivatives, including bond options. At the end of the day, they would liquidate or hedge their remaining positions. Then they would mark to market their positions, all long and short positions, with the market-available bid prices (for the long positions) and ask prices (for the short positions). The mark-to-market position can then determine the profit and loss of all the trading activities of the day. The profit and loss, together with the risk measures of their trading activities, are then reported to the internal audit department as well as the risk management department. At the end of each quarter, the proprietary trading department would share the profit, if any, with the firm, entitling it to a portion of the reported profits. The firm puts up the capital and the overhead costs in trading.

While Gene discloses his profit/loss and his risk measures to the internal audit and risk management on a confidential basis, his group does not reveal the trading strategies.

In fact, the group rarely interacts with anyone on the trading floors other than watching the market activities. One strategy the group employs is using the put-call parity on bond options. They seek the market prices of the spot (that is, the bond) prices and the call and put option prices continually in the market. When there is a discrepancy, violating the put-call parity, they would generate the trade accordingly. Gene recognizes that these trades are better described as "risk arbitrage" where not all risks are eliminated. These trades have to be tested in the market, and the risks have to be calculated. In using the Black model correctly, he has to understand all the assumptions made in the model. What are the assumptions behind the Black bond option model?

Gene talked to himself: "Since the Black model on the bond option is an extension of the Black-Scholes model on the stock option, the bond price in the Black model has a lognormal distribution, just like the stock price in the Black-Scholes model. Even though it is acceptable to assume a constant volatility in the stock option case, it is not appropriate to assume a constant volatility for bond options. But this may not affect my put-call parity trade. What other risks are there?"

## Exercises and Answers

1. Does the put-call parity apply to the bond options? Use the Black model to verify its applicability.

   *Answer:* Since a stochastic variable in the Black bond option model is the bond price at maturity, the put-call parity holds. The present value of the exercise price is 62.0844, and the sum of the present value of the forward price and the put value and the negative value of the call is equal to 62.0844. $P(0, t)F(0, t, T)$ is $100 \times P(0, T)$, because $F(0, t, T)$ is $100 \times \frac{P(0,T)}{P(0,t)}$. Therefore, the put-call parity for the bond option is $B(T) + p - c = XP(0, t)$, where $B(T)$ is the price of the underlying bond with maturity $T$. See figure E5.26.

2. A trader has accumulated a $3 million position of the call option as described above. He has decided to use the zero-coupon bonds to hedge his option position. What are the maturities of the bonds that he should use?

   *Answer:* The maturity of the underlying bond should be longer than the option time to expiration, because the option holder will decide whether he buys or sells the underlying bond at a prespecified price on the option expiration. Therefore, two bonds, which mature on the option expiration and on the underlying bond maturity, respectively will duplicate the bond option value.

3. Continue with question 2 and describe his initial dynamic hedging position.

   *Answer:* We can calculate the hedge ratio between two bonds to dynamically hedge one bond call option contract. See figure E5.27. If we change the interest rate to 7% from the current 6%, we can see that the changes of the Black bond option and the hedge position with two zero-coupon bond are the same, which confirms that

| Put-Call Parity Holds | |
|---|---|
| P(0,t)F(0,t,T) + P - C | 62.0844 |
| X P(0,t) | 62.0844 |

Figure E5.26

| Initial Hedging Position of Call Option | |
|---|---|
| Borrow $\alpha B(0,T)$, face = 100, $\alpha = N(d_1)$ | 11.6057 |
| Lend $\beta B(0,t)$, face = 70, $\beta = N(d_2)$ | -10.7347 |
| Sum | 0.8711 |

Figure E5.27

| Initial Hedging Position of Put Option | |
|---|---|
| Lend $\alpha B(0,T)$, face = 100, $\alpha = N(-d_1)$ | -43.2754 |
| Borrow $\beta B(0,t)$, face = 70, $\beta = N(-d_2)$ | 51.3498 |
| Sum | 8.0744 |

Figure E5.28

the hedge position duplicates the Black bond option. With a little algebra, using the Black bond call option and put option formula, we can express the Black bond call option as $P(0, t)F(0, t, T)(1 - N(-d_1)) - P(0, t)X(1 - N(-d_2))$, which is equal to $P(0, t)F(0, t, T)N(d_1) - P(0, t)XN(d_2)$. $(1 - N(-d_1))$ and $(1 - N(-d_2))$ are equal to $N(d_1)$ and $N(d_2)$, respectively, because the normal distribution is symmetric.

4. The trader now wants to explore the use of the two bonds to hedge his call option position. What is his appropriate hedging position now?

*Answer:* Since the call option, the put option, and the underlying bond have the same source of risk, it is possible to neutralize the risk involved in one security with other securities if we have the right combination among the securities. We can calculate the hedge ratio between two bonds to dynamically hedge one bond put option contract. See figure E5.28.

## Further Exercises

1. Suppose that the three-year interest rate is 8% at a continuously compounding rate. The underlying bond is a zero-coupon bond with maturity of eight years. The option has the time to expiration of three years, and a strike price of 80. Assume the bond price follows a returns process with a constant volatility of 10%. Calculate the European call and put option values.

   *Answer:* The European call option value is 0.7965. The European put option value is 10.9975.

2. In question 1, we assume that the call and bond price is given rather than the volatility. Calculate the implied volatility from the call and put price.

   *Answer:* The implied volatility is 0.1.

3. When we increase the volatility or the risk-free rate by one percentage point, describe what would happen to the call option prices and interpret the results.

   *Answer:* If we increase the risk-free rate by one percentage point, then the call option price decreases to 0.42. If we increase the volatility by one percentage point, then the call option price increases to 1.0434.

## E5.5   SWAPTION MODEL

### Definitions

The definitions in the swaption are the same as those in the swap or in the Ho-Lee model.

### Description of the Model

The holder of a swaption has the right at the expiration date to enter into a swap at a strike rate, such that the holder can pay the predetermined fixed rate (i.e., the strike rate) when the prevailing fixed rate exceeds the strike rate and pay the prevailing fixed rate if it is lower than the strike rate. The swaption is the same as the bond put option. At the expiration of a bond put option, if the market prevailing rate exceeds the bond coupon rate, then the bond price must fall below the face value. In this case, the holder of the bond put option exercises his right to sell the bond at the face value. Here, the bond coupon rate in the bond put option plays the same role as the predetermined fixed rate (i.e., the strike rate) in the swaption. Therefore, whenever the swaption is in the money, the bond put option is always in the money exactly in the same way.

### Numerical Example

The initial spot curve is flat at 10%. The volatility curve is also flat at 12%. Calculate the swaption. The swaption value is 0.0210. See figure E5.29.

| Inputs | | | | | | | | |
|---|---|---|---|---|---|---|---|---|
| Year | 0 | 1 | 2 | 3 | 4 | 5 | 6 | 7 |
| Initial yield curve | 0.1 | 0.1 | 0.1 | 0.1 | 0.1 | 0.1 | 0.1 | 0.1 |
| Initial discount function p(n) | 1 | 0.90484 | 0.81873 | 0.74082 | 0.67032 | 0.60653 | 0.54881 | 0.49659 |
| One-year forward curve | 0.1 | 0.1 | 0.1 | 0.1 | 0.1 | 0.1 | 0.1 | 0.1 |
| Lognormal spot volatility ($\sigma^s$) | 0 | 0.12 | 0.12 | 0.12 | 0.12 | 0.12 | 0.12 | 0.12 |
| Lognormal forward volatility ($\sigma^f$) | 0 | 0.12 | 0.12 | 0.12 | 0.12 | 0.12 | 0.12 | 0.12 |
| The number of partitions (m) | 1 | $f(n) \cdot \sigma^f(n+1) = (n+1) \cdot r(n+1) \cdot \sigma^s(n+1) - n \cdot r(n) \cdot \sigma^s(n)$ | | | | | | |
| | | | | | | | | |
| Forward price | 0.9048 | 0.9048 | 0.9048 | 0.9048 | 0.9048 | 0.9048 | 0.9048 | 0.9048 |
| Delta ($\delta$) | 1 | 0.97629 | 0.97629 | 0.97629 | 0.97629 | 0.97629 | 0.97629 | 0.97629 |

| Outputs | | | |
|---|---|---|---|
| | | | 0.0969 |
| | | 0.0448 | 0.0033 |
| Swaption lattice | 0.0210 | 0.0015 | 0.0000 |
| Year | 0 | 1 | 2 |

Figure E5.29

## Applications

1. When the parties are highly rated (i.e., minimal default risk), the swap rate can be used as a benchmark for the time value of money.
2. A swaption can be considered as a bond put option or bond call option.

## Case: Marking to Market an Illiquid Derivative Position

Nakiso, CFO of Sibanda Capital, called the meeting again on the valuation issue for the private wealth group's client portfolio. Nakiso began: "Look, we had a meeting last week and we have laid out the issues in valuing the clients' portfolios from the capital market, risk management, legal, and marketing perspective. One thing is clear. For many securities, the 'price' is not a number. For IBM stock, we have a price, a number. For a stock has no liquidity; when we sell it, the price can be much lower than what is quoted. For complex structured products, we can only give a distribution of the price, not a point estimate, as they say." Everyone in the room agrees. "So, a 'price' has to be defined depending on how that number get used." "Cannot agree more, Nakiso." "Also, I do not think that we need to think and discuss in pure abstraction. We can look at each security type and we can define the procedure, as long as we follow the principles that you pointed out last time." "What are they?" "They are (1) consistency, (2) transparency, (3) independence." "I hope you also add 'accuracy' to that list." Smiles went across all the faces.

"OK. It is clear what the use of the 'price' in this meeting is." "Right. Marking to market of our private wealth clients' portfolios." "OK, now let us go back to this spread option that we want to price. How should we price it?"

The risk manager proposes: "As our lawyer suggested, 'fair valuation' is a good start for the marking to market purpose, and that is what we do in risk management. The input to determine the spread option value is the volatility surface."

"Where do you get those numbers? Remember, we cannot say that we get those numbers from our traders, because that would not be independent." "In risk management, we want to be independent too. We back out those numbers from the market-observed swaption prices."

"Swaptions. Do we trade that many swaptions?" "No. But there is a liquid market out there. Every day, we can get quotes from the market for a broad range of swaptions, with tenor ranging from one month to thirty years." "And you have a systematic procedure to estimate the volatility surface from the swaption prices every day." "That is correct. And therefore, we can price the spread option with the estimated numbers."

"For our compliance work, I will have a hard time explaining your two-factor interest rate model and your swaptions and how that gives the price of the spread option," the lawyer said. "I will have the same problem with my investors," said the head of private wealth. "No, this process is really simple. All the procedure says is that given these swaption prices, we can replicate, or financial-engineer, the spread options at the 'fair price' that we determine."

*"Now, I just need to know what these swaptions are," joked the lawyer. The head of private wealth was more serious: "I had better prepare some charts and bullet points in explaining our approach to pricing these derivatives in our mark-to-market procedure. I cannot joke about it."*

## Exercises and Answers

1. To price a swaption on a binomial lattice, we consider two dates. The first date is the expiration date of the swaption when the swaption holder can exercise his right to enter a swap contract. The second date is the termination date of the swap contract. For example, if we have a two-by-five swaption, the swaption holder can exercise his right to enter a five-year swap in two years. We assume that the forward swap rate is the strike rate for the swaption. The forward swap rate is the forward par rate on the swaption expiration date. We calculate the swap rate at each node on the swaption expiration date. The swap rate at the swaption maturity date is the par rate, given the yield curve at each node. If the swap rate at the swaption expiration date is higher than the forward swap rate, the swaption holder will exercise his right to enter into the swap at the forward swap rate, because he can save the difference between the swap rate and the forward swap rate.

   (a) Calculate the forward swap rate and the swap rate.

   *Answer:* The yield curve is flat at 10% with continuous compounding. The reset rate is once a year. We can calculate the forward swap rate (annual compounding) from the initial yield curve by $\exp(0.1) - 1$, which is 0.105171. In other words, we calculate the yearly compounding interest rate that corresponds to the continuously compounding interest rate of 10%. We can calculate the forward swap rate at year 2 by searching for the fixed coupon rate that makes the fixed coupon bond a par bond given the implied forward yield curve at period 2. The implied forward yield curve can be derived from the initial flat yield curve of 10%. The fixed coupon bond matures at year 7, which is the end of the swap tenor.

   For the swap rate calculation at each state of year 2, we search for the par rate of the fixed coupon bond that matures at year 7, given the yield curve at each node of year 2. The swap rates of each node at year 2 are 0.13291, 0.10606, and 0.07985, from the highest state to the lowest state. See figure E5.30.

   (b) Calculate the interest amount saved over the swap tenor by exercising the option optimally.

| Forward swap rate calculation | | | | | | | | |
|---|---|---|---|---|---|---|---|---|
| Forward swap rate (annual compounding) | | | 0.10517 | Changing cell for solver | | | | |
| Year | 0 | 1 | 2 | 3 | 4 | 5 | 6 | 7 |
| CF | | | | 0.10517 | 0.10517 | 0.10517 | 0.10517 | 1.10517 |
| Forward discount function at time 2, F(2,t) | | | | 0.90484 | 0.81873 | 0.74082 | 0.67032 | 0.60653 |
| PV(CF) at the end of 2 year | | | 1 | 0.09516 | 0.08611 | 0.07791 | 0.0705 | 0.67032 |
| $(1-PV(CF))^2$ | | | 0 | Target cell for solver | | | | |
| | | | | | | | | |
| Swap rate calculation | | | | | | | | |
| (annual compounding) | | | | | | | | |
| SR(2,2) | | | 0.13291 | | | | | |
| SR(2,1) | | | 0.10606 | | | | | |
| SR(2,0) | | | 0.07985 | Changing cell for solver | | | | |
| Year | 0 | 1 | 2 | 3 | 4 | 5 | 6 | 7 |
| | | | | | | | | |
| Sum of squared errors | | | 1.9E-16 | Target cell for solver | | | | |

Figure E5.30

*Answer:* Since the forward swap rate is the strike rate, the payoff at option expiration is *Max*[swap rate − forward swap rate, 0] at each node of year 2. The difference between the swap rate and the forward swap rate is what the swaption holder can save per year over the swap tenor when the swap rate is larger than the forward swap rate. Therefore, we can calculate the present value of the total savings in the coupon rate over the tenor of the swap. They are 0.0969, 0.0033, and 0, from the highest state to the lowest state at year 2. See figure E5.31.

(c) Calculate the present value of the interest amount saved to get the swaption value.
*Answer:* Once we determine the cash flows at time 2, we apply backward substitution until the initial node to calculate the swaption value. See figure E5.32.

(d) Instead of going through questions (a) and (b), we calculate the fixed coupon bond prices on each node at the binomial lattice. The fixed coupon rate is determined by the forward swap rate. Once we calculate the fixed coupon bond price, we should compare it with the par to make an exercise decision at the option expiration date. If the fixed coupon bond price is less than the par, the

| Interest Amount Saved at Each Time During Swap Tenor | | | | | | | | |
|---|---|---|---|---|---|---|---|---|
| | | | 0.02774 | | | | | |
| | | | 0.00089 | | | | | |
| | | | 0 | | | | | |
| Year | 0 | 1 | 2 | 3 | 4 | 5 | 6 | 7 |
| | | | | | | | 0.0233 | |
| | | | | | | 0.04366 | 0.02386 | |
| | | | | | 0.06218 | 0.04522 | 0.02444 | |
| | | | | 0.0797 | 0.06509 | 0.04684 | 0.02504 | |
| PV (int. amt. saved) at time 2, state 2 | | | 0.09692 | 0.08432 | 0.06817 | 0.04852 | 0.02565 | |
| Year | 0 | 1 | 2 | 3 | 4 | 5 | 6 | 7 |
| | | | | | | | 0.00077 | |
| | | | | | | 0.00145 | 0.00078 | |
| | | | | | 0.00209 | 0.0015 | 0.0008 | |
| | | | | 0.00271 | 0.00219 | 0.00156 | 0.00082 | |
| PV (int. amt. saved) at time 2, state 1 | | | 0.00333 | 0.00287 | 0.00229 | 0.00161 | 0.00084 | |
| Year | 0 | 1 | 2 | 3 | 4 | 5 | 6 | 7 |
| | | | | | | | 0 | |
| | | | | | | 0 | 0 | |
| | | | | | 0 | 0 | 0 | |
| | | | | 0 | 0 | 0 | 0 | |
| PV (int. amt. saved) at time 2, state 0 | | | 0 | 0 | 0 | 0 | 0 | |
| Year | 0 | 1 | 2 | 3 | 4 | 5 | 6 | 7 |

Figure E5.31

| | 0 | 1 | 2 |
|---|---|---|---|
| | | | 0.0969 |
| | | 0.0448 | 0.0033 |
| Swaption lattice | 0.0210 | 0.0015 | 0.0000 |
| Year | 0 | 1 | 2 |

Figure E5.32

| Fixed Coupon Bond Price | | | | | | | | | |
|---|---|---|---|---|---|---|---|---|---|
| | | | 0.10517 | | | | | | |
| Forward swap rate (annual compounding) | | | 0.10517 | | | | | | |
| | | | 0.10517 | | | | | | |
| Year | | 0 | 1 | 2 | 3 | 4 | 5 | 6 | 7 |
| | | | | | | | | | 1.10517 |
| | | | | | | | | 1.0333 | 1.10517 |
| | | | | | | | 0.99369 | 1.05584 | 1.10517 |
| | | | | | | 0.97904 | 1.03516 | 1.07893 | 1.10517 |
| | | | | | 0.98476 | 1.03772 | 1.0786 | 1.10258 | 1.10517 |
| Bond price at time 2, state 2 | | | | 0.90308 | 1.06042 | 1.10058 | 1.12413 | 1.12681 | 1.10517 |
| Year | | 0 | 1 | 2 | 3 | 4 | 5 | 6 | 7 |
| | | | | | | | | | 1.10517 |
| | | | | | | | | 1.05584 | 1.10517 |
| | | | | | | | 1.03516 | 1.07893 | 1.10517 |
| | | | | | | 1.03772 | 1.0786 | 1.10258 | 1.10517 |
| | | | | | 1.06042 | 1.10058 | 1.12413 | 1.12681 | 1.10517 |
| Bond price at time 2, state 1 | | | | 0.99667 | 1.1432 | 1.16792 | 1.17184 | 1.15163 | 1.10517 |
| Year | | 0 | 1 | 2 | 3 | 4 | 5 | 6 | 7 |
| | | | | | | | | | 1.10517 |
| | | | | | | | | 1.07893 | 1.10517 |
| | | | | | | | 1.0786 | 1.10258 | 1.10517 |
| | | | | | | 1.10058 | 1.12413 | 1.12681 | 1.10517 |
| | | | | | 1.1432 | 1.16792 | 1.17184 | 1.15163 | 1.10517 |
| Bond price at time 2, state 0 | | | | 1.1012 | 1.23379 | 1.24006 | 1.22184 | 1.17705 | 1.10517 |
| Year | | 0 | 1 | 2 | 3 | 4 | 5 | 6 | 7 |

**Figure E5.33**

swaption holder will exercise the swaption and take the difference between the fixed coupon bond price and the par. Once we determine the cash flow at each node, we can determine the swaption price by backward substitution.

*Answer:* We can calculate the fixed coupon bond price at each node of year 2. The forward swap rate is the fixed coupon rate, and the time to maturity at year 2 is the swap tenor. Since we have a different yield curve at each node of year 2, the fixed coupon bond prices are 0.90308, 0.99667, and 1.1012 at the nodes in year 2. The swaption holder pays the fixed coupon rate and receives the floating rate. Therefore, if the fixed coupon bond price is less than the par, which is the floating-rate bond price, the cash flows at each node of year 2 are 0.09692, 0.00333, and 0.0, which are exactly same as question (c). See figure E5.33.

## Further Exercises

1. Assume an upward-sloping yield curve. The rate at year 0 is 10% and increases annually by 0.1% up to year 7. Generate the swaption lattice.
   *Answer:* See figure E5.34.
2. Assume a downward-sloping yield curve. The rate at year 0 is 10% and decreases annually by 0.1% up to year 7. Generate the swaption lattice. Interpret the results in question 1 and question 2.

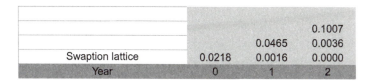

| Swaption lattice | 0.0218 | 0.0465 | 0.1007 |
| | | | 0.0036 |
| | | 0.0016 | 0.0000 |
| Year | 0 | 1 | 2 |

**Figure E5.34**

| Outputs | | | |
|---|---|---|---|
| | | | 0.0930 |
| | | 0.0430 | 0.0030 |
| Swaption lattice | 0.0201 | 0.0014 | 0.0000 |
| Year | 0 | 1 | 2 |

**Figure E5.35**

*Answer:* We can consider the swaption as a put option on a coupon bond where the exercise price is par. We know that the put option is increasing when the risk-free rate is going up. Therefore, the swaption value is going up in question 1 and down in question 2. See figure E5.35.

### Notes

1. Einstein first used the mathematical construct $dZ$ to study the random movements of particles.
2. Harrison and Kreps, 1979.

### Bibliography

Abken, P. A. 1990. Innovations in modeling the term structure of interest rates. *Economic Review*, 75(4). Federal Reserve Bank of Atlanta, July–August.

Baxter, M., and A. Rennie. 1996. *Financial Calculus*. Cambridge: Cambridge University Press.

Black, F. 1995. Interest rates as options. *Journal of Finance*, 50(5), 1371–1376.

Black, F., E. Derman, and W. Toy. 1990. A one-factor model of interest rates and its application to Treasury bond options. *Financial Analysts Journal*, 46, 33–39.

Black, F., and P. Karasinski. 1991. Bond and option pricing when short rates are lognormal. *Financial Analysts Journal*, 47, 52–59.

Brace, A., D. Gatarek, and M. Musiela. 1997. The market model of interest rate dynamics. *Mathematical Finance*, 7, 127–155.

Brennan, M. J., and E. S. Schwartz. 1979. A continuous time approach to the pricing of bonds. *Journal of Banking and Finance*, 3, 135–155.

Brennan, M. J., and E. S. Schwartz. 1982. An equilibrium model of bond pricing and a test of market efficiency. *Journal of Financial and Quantitative Analysis*, 17, 301–329.

Cheyette, Oren. 1997. Interest rate models. In Frank J. Fabozzi, ed., *Advances in Fixed Income Valuation, Modeling and Risk Management*. New Hope, PA: Frank J. Fabozzi Associates.

Cox, J. C., J. E. Ingersoll, Jr., and S. A. Ross. 1981. A reexamination of traditional hypothesis about the term structure of interest rates. *Journal of Finance*, 36, 769–799.

Cox, J. C., J. E. Ingersoll, Jr., and S. A. Ross. 1985. A theory of the term structure of interest rates. *Econometrica*, 53, 385–407.

Cox, J. C., S. A. Ross, and M. Rubinstein. 1979. Option pricing: A simplified approach. *Journal of Financial Economics*, 7, 229–263.

Dybvig, P. H. 1989. Bond and bond option pricing based on the current term structure. Working paper, Washington University, Saint Louis.

Flesaker, B. 1993. Testing the Heath-Jarrow-Morton/Ho-Lee model of interest rate contingent claims pricing. *Journal of Financial and Quantitative Analysis*, 28(4), 483–495.

Golub, B., and M. Tilman. 1997. Measuring yield curve risk using principal component analysis, value at risk, and key rate durations. *Journal of Portfolio Management*, 23(4), 72–84.

Grant, D., and G. Vora. 1999. Implementing no-arbitrage term structure of interest rate models in discrete time when interest rates are normally distributed. *Journal of Fixed Income*, 8, 85–98.

Harrison, J. M., and D. M. Kreps. 1979. Martingales and arbitrage in multi-period securities markets. *Journal of Economic Theory*, 20, 381–408.

Heath, D., R. Jarrow, and A. Morton. 1992. Bond pricing and the term structure of the interest rates: A new methodology. *Econometrica*, 60, 77–105.

Ho, T. S. Y. 1995. Evolution of interest rate models: A comparison. *Journal of Derivatives*, 2(4), 9–20.

Ho, T. S. Y., and S. Lee. 1986. Term structure movements and pricing of interest rate contingent claims. *Journal of Finance*, 41, 1011–1029.

Hull, J., and A. White. 1990. Pricing interest-rate-derivative securities. *Review of Financial Studies*, 3(4), 573–592.

Hull, J., and A. White. 1993. One-factor interest-rate models and the valuation of interest-rate derivative securities. *Journal of Financial and Quantitative Analysis*, 28(2), 235–254.

Jamshidian, F. 1989. An exact bond option formula. *Journal of Finance*, 44, 205–209.

Litterman, R., and J. A. Scheinkman. 1991. Common factors affecting bond returns. *Journal of Fixed Income*, 1(1), 54–61.

Longstaff, F., P. Santa-Clara, and E. Schwartz. 2000. The relative valuation of caps and swaptions: Theory and empirical evidence. Working paper, The Anderson School of UCLA, September.

Longstaff, F. A., and E. S. Schwartz. 1992. Interest rate volatility and the term structure: A two-factor general equilibrium model. *Journal of Finance*, 47, 1259–1282.

Richard, S. 1978. An arbitrage model of the term structure of interest rates. *Journal of Financial Economics*, 6, 33–57.

Ritchken, P., and L. Sankarasubramanian. 1995. Volatility structure of forward rates and the dynamics of the term structure. *Mathematical Finance*, 5, 55–72.

Rogers, L. C. G. 1995. Which model for term-structure of interest rates should one use? *Mathematical Finance*, 65, 93–115.

Tuckman, Bruce. 2002. *Fixed Income Securities*. New York: Wiley.

Vasicek, O. 1977. An equilibrium characterization of the term structure. *Journal of Financial Economics*, 5, 177–188.

# 6

# Corporate Bonds: Investment Grade

Corporations may raise funds by selling corporate bonds. The value of these bonds must therefore depend on all the provisions and conditions attached to the bonds. Moreover, these bonds also depend on the credit risk, as the corporation may default on its bonds. This chapter will discuss these issues surrounding the valuation of corporate bonds and their implications on the valuation of other related securities.

## 6.1 DESCRIBING A CORPORATE BOND

The corporate debt market is estimated to be $3.9 trillion,[1] approximately 21% of the entire U.S. debt market, which includes government securities, mortgages, municipal bonds, and consumer financing. Corporate debt is clearly a major sector in our fixed-income market. (See figure 6.1.)

Since the issuer of a corporate bond can be any type of firm, the bond does not have to adhere to any rigid format. There are some common bond types and designs, but there are also many varieties. The maturities can range from one day to 100 years. The coupons can be fixed or floating, changing according to a specified schedule. We will focus on the standard bond types in this chapter.

In order to have an overview of the salient features of a bond, we will review one example. Let us consider a typical description of a bond in the investment community. Wal-Mart Stores is the largest retailer in North America, operating discount department stores, wholesale clubs, and combination discount stores and supermarkets. The firm had a capitalization of $203 billion in 2000. The long-term debt level to the capitalization is 37%, showing that Wal-Mart has a significant debt outstanding, but the debt is supported by much of the shareholders' value, since it is less than 40% of the capitalization.

One of the bonds is described as follows:

Wal-Mart Stores WMT 8.57 01/02/10
Issuer: Wal-Mart Stores, retail discount
Bond type: Pass-through certificate
Coupon: 8.57    Fixed S/A    30/360
Issue size: USD 160,023,000;    Amount outstanding: USD 120,843,550
Call @ make whole
Pro rata sinking fund

An issuer's contractual terms reflect the market concerns at the time of issuance. These concerns range from existing interest rates and the probability of default on the bond to the supply of and demand for a particular bond type. After the issuance, the market may change (for example, the yield curve moves) but the agreement, as described above, will not. In the secondary market as well as in the primary market, participants

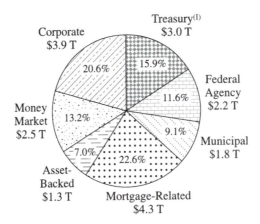

Total: $19.0 Trillion

**Figure 6.1** Outstanding bond market debt as of March 31, 2002*
[1]Includes marketable public debt.
*The Bond Market Association estimates
Sources: Federal Reserve System, U.S. Treasury, GNMA, FNMA, FHLMC.

need to evaluate the risks and rewards embedded in each corporate issue. We will proceed to discuss each item in the general description of the bond.

## Identification, Issuer, Sector: Wal-Mart Stores WMT 8.57 01/02/10, Retail Discount

WMT 8.57 means that the Wal-Mart (WMT) bond has a coupon rate of 8.57%. The last principal payment is paid on January 2, 2010.

Corporate bonds are often referred to by their issuer's symbol, followed by the coupon rate and the maturity date. The industry sector of the issuer is often relevant because the bond's credit risk is related to the business risk of the sector. Firms in the same sector tend to have similar debt structures and bond features. The sector can indicate whether the bond is sensitive to economic downturns or interest rate levels. For these reasons, portfolio managers tend to use the information to diversify their risk exposure across the sectors. In managing a corporate bond portfolio, investing a significant amount in one sector is called the *concentration risk*. A portfolio manager typically avoids concentration risk, since the risk exposure will not be properly diversified. To diversify the credit risk, a portfolio manager seeks to lower the concentration risk in terms of any one firm or firms legally related to any one entity, and also to any market segment or industry sector.

Corporate financial managers decide on the bond maturities, types of coupon rates (floating versus fixed), principal payment schedules, and other debt terms and conditions. These decisions depend on two things. The first is the debt structure of the firm, which describes the debts that the firm has already sold. The second is the market conditions on the demand for and supply of the bonds for different maturity spectra and credit risk levels. Firms may seek long-term debt financing when their assets have long economic lives. For example, utility firms often use long-term debt to finance their capital investments. The decisions on using debt to fund the firm's operation or on the type of the bonds to add to the existing debt structure are complex financial theory problems. For now, we will focus on the analysis of corporate bonds that have been issued.

## Bond Type: Pass-Through Certificate

The WMT bond is a pass-through certificate, a claim on a certain portion of the cash flows from the assets in a trust. For example, a firm may package its accounts receivable as assets. A trust, a legal entity representing a firm, is set up. The portfolio of accounts receivable becomes the assets of the trust's balance sheet. Pass-through certificates are issued as liabilities to raise funds in order to buy the accounts receivable. The cash flows from the accounts receivable are then passed to the investors in the pass-through certificates. Then the firm replaces its accounts receivable with cash. We say that the firm has securitized the accounts receivable. That is, in general, the interest and principal on these assets in the trust account will support the payments of the pass-through certificates. Wal-Mart Stores' operational cash flows are not used to support the bond. That means the principal and interest payments are passed from the financial securities— in this case, the lease incomes—of Wal-Mart to these pass-through certificates. This type of bond is an *asset-backed security*.

There are many other bond types. Mortgage bonds are secured by real estate; *equipment bonds* are secured by the firm's equipment. Unsecured bonds, called *debentures*, are perhaps the most common bond type. Bonds sold through agents without the full disclosure required by the Securities and Exchange Commission are called *medium-term notes*, a misleading term. "Medium-term note" does not mean that the bond maturities are not long-term or short-term. The distinction is made for a legal reason. Since these bonds are sold directly to a specific, targeted group of general investors, they are not subject to full disclosure. *Public bonds*, which are available to all general investors, are required to provide a full disclosure.

## Coupon Description: 8.57   Fixed S/A   30/360

The bond is a fixed-rate bond that pays coupons on a semiannual basis determined by the annual coupon rate of 8.57% (4.285% of the outstanding principal for each six-month period). In general, the interest payment can be floating. That means it can be based on a market rate like the three-month LIBOR or the one-year Treasury rate plus an interest margin (additional spread amount). Floating-rate bonds enable the firm to borrow at short-term rates that continually adjust to the market, even though the maturity of the bond may be long. These rates are continually reset over time at regular intervals. The dates for the resets are called *reset dates*. For example, a one-year Treasury rate can be reset every month, but the interest may not be paid out monthly. In such cases, the interest accrues and is paid out over a longer time period. For example, it can accrue monthly and be paid out semiannually.

In the United States, most corporate bonds have semiannual coupon payments. Their use is of a market convention. Other bonds, like mortgage-backed securities, pay interest monthly, and many bonds sold in Europe pay annual coupons. Therefore, the frequency of interest or coupon payment is based more on the market convention than on any fundamental economic reasons.

The accrual convention 30/360 is based on counting every month as thirty days, twelve months a year, for most corporate bonds in the United States. That means the amount of accrued interest is the proportion of the number of days from the last coupon date to the 180 days of the semiannual coupon payment. When the amount of accrued interest is added to the quoted price, the combined amount is the actual price that investors pay or receive.

## Issue Size: USD 160,023,000; Amount Outstanding: USD 120,843,550

The *issue size* is important to an investor because it indicates the liquidity in the market. However, the amount outstanding in the marketplace decreases with time to maturity because of the *sinking fund provision*, which we will discuss below in more detail. Briefly, a sinking fund provision requires the firm to retire a specified amount of debt over the life of a bond. For this reason, the amount outstanding is not the same as the issue size. Moreover, the investor needs to know the amount outstanding to evaluate the liquidity of a bond in the marketplace. The larger the amount outstanding, the higher the likelihood of a bond being more widely held; therefore, there is more trading activity, which means that more buyers and sellers of a bond are available. WMT bonds have over $120 million outstanding, which should indicate that the bond is quite liquid.

## Bond Call Provision: Call @ Make Whole

Firms have the option to call bonds. For a typical debenture, the *call provision* is represented by a call schedule that allows the corporation to buy back bonds at the call price at a specified date. When a bond is called, the firm pays the holders the call price and the accrued interest. Corporate bonds have precise *call schedules* stating the call prices at specific dates. Call schedules vary greatly. Typically, there is a first call date that stipulates the first date at which the bond is callable. A bond may be immediately callable, or it can be called at any time after the issuance. The first call price is often half the coupon rate in addition to the face value. For example, if the coupon rate of a bond is 10%, then the first call price is often 105. Then the call prices linearly decline to par (to 100, bond face value) some time before maturity or at maturity. If the call price reaches face value some time before maturity, its price will remain at par until maturity. For example, consider a ten-year bond with a 10% coupon rate. The first call price may be 105, effective immediately. The second year, the call price may be 104, then drop by 1 every year, reaching the call price of 100 in the fifth year. Then the call price will remain at 100 until maturity.

WMT's *call at make whole* is slightly more complicated. The make whole provision enables a firm to have control over the capital structure, but not the option of refinancing the bond when interest rates are favorable. This purpose is accomplished by requiring the firm to pay the investors a call price higher than they would otherwise receive independent of interest rate scenarios. This price is often set by discounting the bond cash flows at 5–15 basis points over the Treasury curve for investment grade, and 50 basis points for high-yield, bonds. Since such spreads are very low, judging by historical experience, in general calling bonds would be very expensive as measured by net present value. For example, consider an A-rated bond. Its value is based on discount rates that are the Treasury rates plus, say, 50 basis points. If the bond has a make whole provision and the firm seeks to use the call provision, then the firm can buy back the bond at a price determined by the present value of the coupons and principal, using the discount rates of the Treasury rates plus, for example, five basis points. This price would be higher than the price of a bond that is otherwise identical except for the call provision.

Bonds may be called for managerial reasons. The firm may wish to retire some debt in order to lower the debt ratio and consequently increase the corporate bond rating. Or it may wish to have a simpler balance sheet to ready itself for merger and acquisition activities. Perhaps, in a merger and acquisition, the bonds have to be retired as one of the conditions. In such cases, investors may not suffer financially from the call because the call price may be significantly higher than an equivalent bond without the make whole call provision.

## Bond Sinking Fund Provision: Pro Rata Sinking Fund

A sinking fund provision requires bonds to be retired over time according to a specified schedule. Sinking funds are designed so that the repayments are amortized over a period of time; these bonds are retired on a pro rata basis. That means investors will receive the coupons and a portion of the principal paid back over time, and this proportion is the same for all investors. For example, in this case, if the upcoming sinking fund is 10% of the outstanding amount, then each bondholder will receive 10% of the principal as an early payment. The proportion of the principal that remains outstanding to the amount issued is called the *factor*. For example, a bond's original issue amount is $100 million. After some years, a portion of the bonds has to be retired by the firm, and the outstanding amount in the market is $90 million. The bond factor is 0.9. The factor of the bond at issuance is 1, and it declines gradually until it reaches 0 at maturity. The factor of the WMT bond is 0.755161 ($= 120,843,500/160,023,000$).

In this case, the sinking fund is paid down semiannually in a slightly complicated way. This is because the schedule has to match the cash flows of the assets in the trust. (See table 6.1.)

The schedule continues until the maturity date. The last sinking fund payment can be quite small, since much of the debt will have been retired when we reach the last sinking fund payment. For this reason, the average weighted life of the bond can be significantly lower than is suggested by the maturity.

There are other sinking fund arrangements. For a debenture, typically there is no requirement for sinking funds for the first several years. After a deferment of a period, usually five years or more, a fixed amount of bonds must be retired at par to the trustee

**Table 6.1** Sinking Fund Amortization Schedule

| Date | Amount |
| --- | --- |
| 1/2/00 | 1,310,200 |
| 7/2/00 | 15,000 |
| 1/2/01 | 12,451,000 |
| 1/2/02 | 13,701,000 |
| 1/2/03 | 14,518,000 |
| 7/2/03 | 300,000 |
| 1/2/04 | 15,517,000 |
| 7/2/04 | 554,000 |
| 1/2/05 | 17,309,000 |
| 7/2/05 | 3,538,000 |

of the bond, who represents all the bondholders' interests. The trustee will ensure that the firm fulfills its sinking fund obligations. If such obligations are not fulfilled, then the trustee may decide to declare the firm in default. The sinking fund provision requires the firm to retire the bond gradually over the life of the bond. This can be accomplished by the firm's buying back some of the outstanding bonds over time and surrendering them to the trustee. There are two ways to retire the bond in this manner. First, the firm that has issued the bond can buy back portions of the bond in the open market. Second, the firm can make payments to the trustee, who will then call the bonds back at par through a lottery in which bond certificate numbers are drawn at random, and the firm can retire those selected bonds. The number of bonds selected will equal the number determined by the sinking fund requirement. If the firm cannot satisfy the sinking fund obligation (i.e., cannot get the required number of bonds to surrender to the trustee), the firm is considered in default of the debt.

## 6.2  VALUATION OF A BOND

### Price Quote in Terms of Yield

The price of WMT 8.57 10 is quoted at 114.4083 (6.25). The price quote is based on a percent of the principal. The yield (semiannually compounding) is 6.25%. The yield of a bond is calculated as the internal rate of return of the cash flow (coupon payments and sinking fund payments) given the price. It is important to note that the yield and price are mathematically related. For this reason, the yield of 6.25% and the price quote both indicate how the market values the bond.

There are alternative conventions in quoting a bond price. Another common convention is using the yield spread. Suppose the weighted average life of a bond is six years, and the yield of a Treasury seven-year on-the-run bond is 6%. Then the bond yield (or price quote) can be quoted as a spread in terms of basis points over the seven-year Treasury bond yield. For example, the spread may be quoted as 25 basis points, setting an arbitrary number. The 25 basis points is the yield spread to the nearest on-the-run Treasury bond. However, when the yield curve has a significant slope, a weighted average life of six years may no longer be comparable with the seven-year Treasury bond. In this case, we can have a blended rate as a benchmark comparison. The quote may be given as a spread from the linearly interpolated yields of two on-the-run Treasury bonds. Suppose another benchmark bond is the five-year Treasury bond with a yield of 5%. The blended yield for the six-year bond is 5.5%, which is the average of the seven-year on-the-run bond yield of 6% and the five-year Treasury bond yield of 5%. Using the yield spread of blended yields to determine the yield of the bond is often called *matrix pricing*. In matrix pricing, pricing or quoting a bond depends upon the market prices of actively traded bonds that reflect benchmark prices. Matrix pricing often does not depend on any financial modeling, but compares a bond against bonds similar in terms of their characteristics, such as maturity, coupon rate, sector, and rating.

For a callable bond with a call schedule, the yield to maturity does not represent the internal rate of return of holding a bond until maturity. This is because the maturity of the bond is no longer certain and the bond cash flow is not fixed. Rather, the yield to maturity depends on future interest rate scenarios. If the interest rate has fallen significantly and the bond is likely to be called, then the expected weighted average life of the bond will be shortened. As a result, the yield to maturity will entirely misstate the internal rate of return of the bond by still assuming that the bond will be held until maturity. For this reason, the bond price may be quoted as *yield to call*, which is the yield to the first call price. Alternatively, the bond price may be quoted as the *yield to worst*, which is the lowest yield number for all the possible call prices on the call schedule. The yield to worst is calculated by checking the yield for each call price along the call schedule to determine the lowest yield.

The central point in this discussion is that the price quote based on the yield spread is simply a market quote, a way to indicate the price. In contrast, the methodology that determines the appropriate present value of cash flows is called valuation. For the most part, the valuation of a bond (particularly an investment grade bond) is fundamentally different from valuing equity. A precise bond valuation model can explain much of the bond value. Unlike equity, bond values can be determined by comparing market prices of similar bonds. There are no empirically estimated parameters like beta or future estimates like earnings. For bonds, the cash flows are stated precisely and the discount rates can, by and large, be estimated. Developing an accurate bond valuation model is important because these models for investment grade bonds can provide a fairly accurate valuation of a bond in the market.

## Callability

The call provision affects the value of the bond. It has a dual purpose. First, it allows a firm to buy back bonds at a fixed price, enabling it to have control over its capital structure. For example, the firm may wish to reduce the debt outstanding because it wants to increase its creditworthiness. Or, for some sinking fund bonds, the remaining issues outstanding toward maturity may be only a small amount with little or no liquidity. The firm may "sweep" the remaining bonds away from the market and repackage the debt into a larger issue. When the firm needs to retire the debt, for whatever reason, it may prefer not to rely on the capital market to provide the liquidity necessary to purchase the bonds in the market. This is because the bonds may not be purchased at a fair price. For example, *accumulators* (investors who hold the bonds in anticipation of the firm's buying them back) may require a significant premium on the intrinsic value of the bonds to sell back to the issuer. A call provision can provide a cap on the price in these situations.

There is another motivation for the call provision: when interest rates fall, the firm can sell more bonds at current lower rates and buy back the bonds at the call price. The call provision provides the firm a way to re-fund the debt at a lower interest cost. This re-funding provision in essence offers the firm a call option to buy back the bonds at a fixed price, where the underlying risk is that of the interest rates.

$$\text{Callable Bond Price} = \text{Noncallable Bond Price} - \text{Call Option Value} \quad (6.1)$$

This equation shows that holding a callable bond is the same as holding a noncallable bond and shorting a call option. A fall in interest rates will lead to a higher price of the option-free bond, but part of that price increase is mitigated by the loss of the call option position.

We can also view the equation from an issuer's perspective. In issuing a callable bond, the firm has issued an option-free bond but simultaneously has bought some call options of the bond. In doing so, the firm has the right to retire the bond at a fixed price, but at the cost of the option premium. The proceeds to the firm of selling the bonds are the present value of the option-free bond net of the option cost. The proceeds are therefore less than those of selling an option-free bond.

The callable bond price is equal to the noncallable bond price minus the call option value, as suggested by equation (6.1). Therefore, the callable bond price should be lower than that of the corresponding noncallable bond because the call option value is subtracted from the noncallable bond price. Alternatively stated, the yield of a callable bond should be higher than that of a noncallable bond.

To maintain managerial control over the ability to retire bonds without paying a higher yield for the interest rate option, some bonds are issued with a "no refunding restriction" for a certain period. For the period when the bond is nonrefundable, the firm is not allowed to buy back the bond for the stated purpose of reselling a bond at a lower interest rate. But there are many ways to re-fund a nonrefundable bond. After all, firms sell bonds (or take out loans) and buy back bonds quite often. For example, a firm can take out a bank loan and use part of the proceeds to call a bond with nonrefunding restrictions. It is quite difficult to identify a particular purpose of a debt issuance or a bank loan, since the firm does not need to specify the purpose of a particular borrowing. For this reason, the re-funding restriction generally has little economic value.

## Sinking Fund

The sinking fund affects the bond value in two ways. In essence, a sinking fund specifies the timing of the principal repayments. Thus, the value of a sinking fund bond is affected by the shape of the yield curve. For example, consider two bonds with the same maturity $T$ but one has a sinking fund schedule and the other does not. Now suppose the $T$-year interest rate rises, while other rates remain the same; then the price for the bond without the sinking fund would fall more than that of the bond with the sinking fund. This is because the bond with the sinking fund has more obligated payments in earlier years, and therefore its value is more sensitive to changes in the shorter-term interest rates than to changes in the $T$-year rate. Beyond the cash flow timing issue, there is the option aspect. The sinking fund option provision offers the issuer the ability to retire the sinking fund obligation by an open market purchase or by a lottery, essentially calling the sinking fund bond at par. This option affects the bond price because of the call at the par price; or the firm can buy back the sinking fund bond at par value. The annual or semiannual sinking fund operation is similar to a call schedule such that it offers the firm the ability to buy back the bonds at a fixed price. The differences are, first, that the call price of the sinking fund option is par, whereas the call price of the call provision is often above par. Second, and more important, the sinking fund option applies to only a portion of the bond at each sinking fund operation date; a call option applies to the entire issue. Thus, the sinking fund option is a series of call options on the bond issue. At each sinking fund date, the issuer has the choice to call back the sinking fund amount at par or buy back the bonds at the market price.

Some sinking funds have an additional feature called the *double-up option*. At each sinking fund date, the firm can retire the stated sinking fund amount or double that amount. Using the double-up option, bonds can be retired faster.

Consider this example. For simplicity, we will assume that the bond has no call provision. It is a coupon bond with a three-year maturity, and the principal value is $100. The bond has a double-up sinking fund provision of a $10 principal at the end of each year.

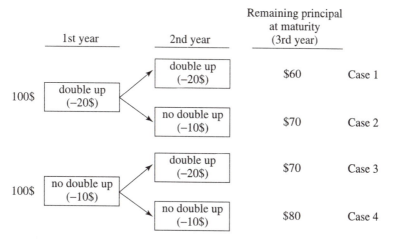

**Figure 6.2** The double-up option. The double-up option decision has the structure of a tree. At the end of each year, the firm can decide whether or not to double-up. When the double-up decision is made, the principal of the bond falls by $20. When no double-up decision is made, the principal amount falls by only $10, the sinking fund requirement.

The double-up option decision has the structure of a tree. At the end of each year, the firm can decide whether or not to double up. When the double-up decision is made, the principal of the bond falls by $20. When no double-up decision is made, the principal amount falls by only $10, the sinking fund requirement. The decision tree is illustrated in figure 6.2.

We now construct an arbitrage-free interest rate binomial lattice model over three years, using a monthly (or annual) step size. At the terminal date of the third year, each node has a bundle of information consisting of four values that keep track of the historical events: the bond is doubled up or not doubled up in the first year, and the same two possibilities apply in the second year. The remaining principals at maturity are $60, $70, $70, and $80, as depicted in figure 6.2. In other words, at each maturity node we have four remaining principals for the bond with the double-up sinking fund provision, whereas we have only one principal for a straight bond. We calculate the bond price based on a par value of 100 for simplicity.

Since there are four cases, we will construct the backward substitution to derive the market value of the bond prices for each case, depending on the history of the doubling up of the sinking funds. Refer to the four cases in figure 6.2. First, let us consider case 1. For each node at the end of second year, the firm exercises the double-up. Let the market value of the bond with $1 face value at the end of the second year at state $i$ have the value $B^*(i)$. This value is determined by rolling back the bond from the maturity date to the end of the second year. We will provide a numerical example of this valuation approach later in this chapter.

## Credit Risk Ratings

Credit risk is one major determinant of bond value. A number of corporations, called rating agencies, provide ratings of the creditworthiness of issuers and issues. The creditworthiness of a bond or an issuer is defined as the ability to pay the promised payment on time. There is no precise definition of the credit measure. The measure is not related only to the possible dollar amount of loss. The issuer may delay a payment by six months or may default on the entire principal. These rating agencies do not provide the public with their precise methodologies in evaluating creditworthiness, since the rating process is only partially quantitative. It also depends on the analysts' views on the management style and less tangible attributes.

Two major rating agencies are Standard and Poor's Corporation (S&P) and Moody's Investors Services, Inc. (Moody's). Their rating systems range from AAA to D (S&P) and Aaa to C (Moody's), in a way that is akin to grades for university students, except there are no Fs. Today, few corporations have the highest rating (AAA or Aaa). Most bonds (measured in dollar amount) at issuance carry a rating of A or AA. For example, in November 2001, 20.3% of the bonds sold were rated AA, and 59.1% were rated A. The remaining issues were rated lower. The WMT bond carries a Moody's rating of Aa2 and an S&P of AA.

Bonds with ratings below BBB (S&P) or Baa (Moody's) are considered *high-yield or junk bonds*. These bonds are considered risky in terms of default. Bonds with ratings equal to or above BBB and Baa are called *investment grade*. The distinction can be important. Many pension funds and other asset managements are not allowed to hold junk bonds in their portfolios. A firm with a rating below investment grade cannot access a large portion of potential investors. Thus, ratings are important to corporate financial management.

The default risk of bonds with the same issuer may be different, and the bonds can have different ratings. One main reason is that bonds may have different priority rules. The bond covenants state the obligations of the corporation to the investors. Among these obligations is the responsibility of the corporation to pay interest in a timely fashion and to keep its corporate status high. The covenant also indicates under what conditions the firm will declare bankruptcy. A number of conditions may trigger bankruptcy. For example, the cross-default clause stipulates that the bond is in default if any other bond of the firm is in default. Some clauses specify courses of action that are contingent on the values of standardized financial ratios. For instance, a clause may give investors the right to prepayment of principal if the debt ratio exceeds a stated limit. If the firm cannot raise the funds to pay the principal, then the bond is in default.

At default, under Chapter 11, the firm is protected by the bankruptcy court. The bond trustees will be responsible for proposing a reorganization plan. Not all bonds are treated alike, because there are priority rules. Senior debentures will receive the promised payment first before the junior debt holders. Equity holders are the last to receive any payments. When such a rule is strictly followed, we say that the *absolute priority rule* is followed. That means the payments to different classes of bondholders, junior or senior debts, strictly follow the specifications in the bond covenants.

However, the absolute priority rule is not strictly followed in practice. The reorganization under the bankruptcy law allows for renegotiation among the bondholders and shareholders that seeks to maximize the values to the claimants. Sometimes the firm's value depends on the management in place, and the debt holders are better served if the management (who may own part of the equity) remains in the firm. As a result, the absolute priority rule is adjusted for this purpose. This is referred to as *strategic debt servicing* to underscore how debt holders accept an immediate loss by giving up a portion of the firm to the equity holders in exchange for the longer-term gain. The gain is realized when the management succeeds in increasing the firm's value.

The bond rating is important to bond valuation. A number of studies have provided us with an overview of the behavior of these ratings. Altman and Kao (1992) show that the ratings are serially correlated; a downrating is more likely to be followed by another downrating. Therefore, rating changes are not random walks, where the rating change depends on the firm's recent rating history. Furthermore, the probabilities of an upgrade or downgrade, called *rating transitions*, vary significantly over time. Modeling the changes of rating is quite difficult. Unlike market prices, ratings do not change in real time, continually adjusting to the market conditions. Ratings are derived, for the most part, from historical information. Hite and Warga (1997) show that rating changes by agencies often lag behind market information, as in bond prices and stock prices. And Ederington et al. (1987) also find that credit rating changes lag market pricing.

## 6.3  OPTION-ADJUSTED SPREAD

The final part of the valuation of a corporate bond is tying the credit premiums, liquidity premiums, and the provision values together.

Now we apply the bond model to determine the theoretical bond price. *Option-adjusted spread* (OAS) is the constant spread (in basis points) that we add to the spot curve such that when we apply the bond model based on the spot curve to the OAS, we have the theoretical price or the observed price. OAS is therefore the spread that provides the annual excess returns from the spot curve to compensate for the credit premium and the liquidity premium. The spread is option-adjusted such that we can isolate the values of the call and sinking fund provisions. The bond model incorporates the rational pricing of the interest rate option embedded in the bond. The average OAS of the comparable bonds may provide an indication of the appropriate OAS of the bond we are valuing. Using this average OAS, we can then use the bond model to value the bond.

There are many corporate bonds without embedded options. In those cases, by definition the OAS is the spread added to the spot curve in determining the present value of the promised payments of the bond.

As discussed before, corporate bonds can be classified under one of the following major sectors: utilities, transportation, financial, and industrial. Each sector's bonds possess different characteristics because each sector has different motives for issuing debt. Utility companies, for example, issue bonds to support power plants. Since the plants represent long-term assets, bonds of utility companies tend to have very long maturities. An AAA-rated bond in one sector may provide a higher yield than another sector's AAA bond, given the same coupon, maturity, and provisions. This difference is attributable to unique, nonfinancial risk factors such as political or environmental issues (see figure 6.3).

Let us assume that the yield spreads approximate the option-adjusted spreads for the purpose of this discussion. In recent years, most bonds have not had embedded options, and therefore this assumption should be quite reasonable. According to figure 6.3, we can make the following observations. The option-adjusted spreads depend on the bond rating, the sector, and the maturity. More specifically, the spread increases with maturity. This may suggest that the likelihood of default increases with maturity

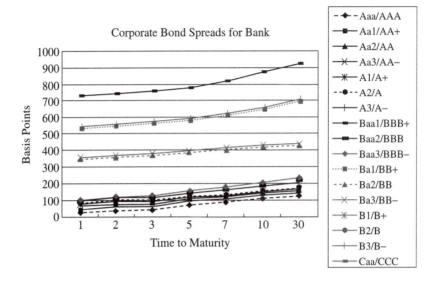

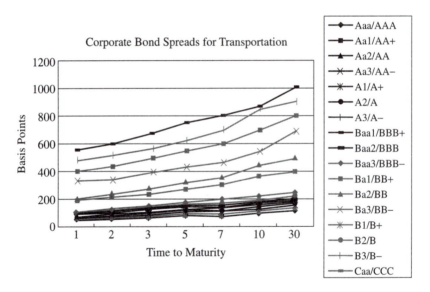

**Figure 6.3** Yield spreads of the corporate sectors, June 21, 2002. This figure depicts the yield spreads between corporate bonds and Treasury bonds with comparable maturities. The yield spreads are plotted as functions of the maturity for different ratings, grouped under different sectors: bank, transportation, utility, industrial, and financials. The results show that the spread increases with maturity and the spread between two consecutive notches widens with the decrease in rating. Bonds with the same rating but in different sectors may have different yield spreads. This is true for all sectors. Source: http//:www.bondsonline.com/asp/corp/spreadfin.html.

or the marketability falls with longer maturity. Of course, one expects the spread to increase with a lower rating. But the spread between two rating notches accelerates as the rating falls. This observation suggests that bond pricing related to credit risk is

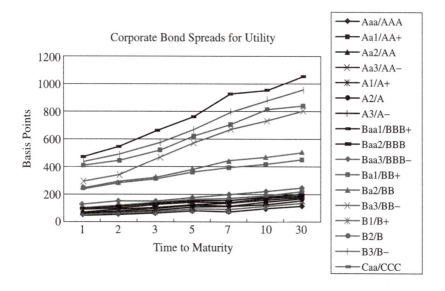

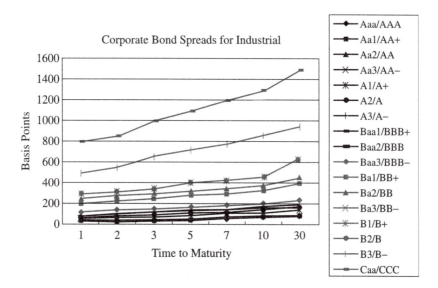

**Figure 6.3** (cont.)

not directly proportional to credit risk measures, such as debt ratios, profitability, and liquidity ratios.

With lower-rated bonds, the credit spread falls with longer maturity, in contrast to investment grade bonds, which are not shown in figure 6.3. The difference between lower-rated bonds and investment grade bonds is the promised payments versus the expected payments. For lower-rated bonds, investors do not expect to receive the promised coupons and principals, because the firm is likely to default on the promised payment— to such an extent that using the spread as an approximation is too crude to be useful.

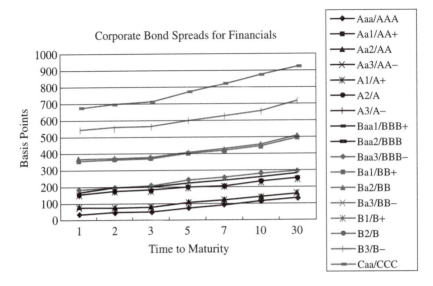

**Figure 6.3** (cont.)

For example, consider a zero-coupon low-rated bond. The investors do not expect to receive the full promised principal of the bond. Assume that they expect to receive only 50% of the principal when the bond matures. Then the bond price is determined by discounting $50 at the Treasury bond rate plus a risk premium. We assume that the yield curve is flat at 6% and the risk premium is 2%. The yield to maturity of the bond would assume the principal payment to be par, $100. The yield to maturity is the discount rate for $100 that equals the market price. The ten-year and twenty-year low-rated bond prices are $23.16 and $10.73, respectively. Furthermore, the yield to maturity is 15.75% for the ten-year bond and 11.81% for the twenty-year bond. This simple numerical example shows that the yield to maturity falls with longer maturity.

Sarig and Warga (1989) studied the term structure of yield spread over three credit ratings—BBB, BB, and B/C. To isolate the credit risks from other factors, they considered only zero-coupon issues without any other provisions, such as callability, coupons, and sinking funds. Their results were interesting: BBB spreads were upward-sloping and the B/C bonds were downward-sloping.

The credit spread is also related to the shape of the yield curve. This is often attributed to the close relationship between the pricing of credit risk and the health of the economy. In credit risk analysis, the most important systematic risk, one that affects a large segment of bonds, is the impact of a recession on the firm's ability to service the debt.

These spreads change, depending on the market supply and demand. During major economic events, such as the Asian crisis of 1997, the Russian economic crisis of 1998, or the tragedy of September 11, 2001, many investors seek to hold liquid and safe bonds such as Treasury securities. As a result, many investors sell corporate bonds and buy government bonds. This phenomenon, called *flight to quality*, leads to an increase in yield spreads. Is the increase in spread a result of increased default premium, risk premium for default, or liquidity premium? Unfortunately, there is no simple answer to this question.

The uncertain changes in these spreads are called *basis risks,* referring to the changes of the relationships across sectors of asset classes. For example, the uncertainty of the spread between the utility sector and the industrial sector of the same rating is called the basis risk between the two sectors.

The basis risks of bonds having different ratings are positively correlated. When the spread of AAA to the Treasury curve widens, the spread of AA to the Treasury curve is also likely to widen. This suggests that the market assigns a credit risk premium that has two components: the expected losses from default and the risk premium for default. For this reason, when the market becomes more risk-averse with respect to the credit risk, corporate bonds will trade with a wider spread.

## 6.4   VALUATION OF CALLABLE BONDS

Consider a flat spot yield curve at 6.5%. Assume that the bond has an annual coupon payment of 7% and a maturity of six years.

### Valuation of a Bond with No Embedded Options

The bond with a principal of $100 has an annual coupon payment of $7. Needless to say, the payment is $107 on the maturity date, which falls in the sixth year. The spot yield curve is flat at 6.5%. The bond value is therefore the present value of the coupon up to year 6, and the principal in year 6.

$$Bond\ Price = \left( \sum_{n=1}^{6} 7e^{-0.065 \cdot n} \right) + 100 \cdot e^{-0.065 \times 6} = 101.366 \qquad (6.2)$$

### Valuation of a Callable Bond

Continuing with the above example, let us now assume that the bond has a call schedule with an immediately callable call price of $106, and the call price linearly declines to $100 for the last year. Therefore, the call price schedule is $106 at year 0, 105 at year 1, ..., $100 at maturity. For illustration purposes, we use the Ho-Lee one-factor model. Let us assume that the volatility is 15%, and the yield curve is flat at 6.5%. Therefore, the normal volatility $\sigma$ is $0.15 \times 0.065$. Let the discount function be denoted by $P(T) = e^{-0.065T}$. The binomial annual discount rate $P(n, i, 1)$ is given below.

$$P(n, i, 1) = \frac{2P(n+1)}{P(n)} \frac{\delta^{n-i}}{(1+\delta^n)}$$

$$\delta = \exp\{-2 \times 0.15 \times 0.065\} = 0.980689$$

For example, when the time period is 3 and the state is 3, $P(3, 3, 1)$ can be obtained by $2 \times \frac{e^{-0.065 \times 4}}{e^{-0.065 \times 3}} \times \frac{0.980688^{3-3}}{(1+0.980688^3)}$, which is 0.96447 in figure 6.4.

Now we conduct the backward substitution procedure for the straight coupon bond. At maturity, the value is $107. The resulting lattice is given in figure 6.5.

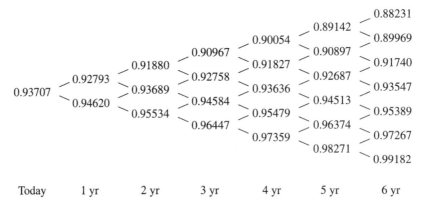

**Figure 6.4** Lattice of one-year pure discount bond prices. Each node denotes a one-year pure discount bond price. The one-year pure discount bond prices follow an arbitrage-free process. We have used the Ho-Lee model to generate the one-year pure discount bond prices. $P(n, i, 1)$ denotes a one-period discount bond price at time $n$ and state $i$. At the initial node, $P(0, 0, 1)$ is $e^{-0.065} = 0.93707$.

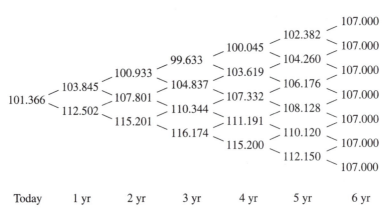

**Figure 6.5** Lattice of the coupon bond price. Each node denotes the coupon bond prices. The annual coupon rate is 7% and the maturity date is year 6. The cash flow of each node at year 6 is $107 (= principal + annual coupon payment). By backward substitution from the maturity date to the initial node, we can calculate the coupon bond price of 101.366, which is identical to the bond price in equation (6.2). When the time period is 5 and the state is 5, 102.382 at period 5 can be obtained by $(107.0 \times 0.5 + 107.0 \times 0.5) \times 0.89142 + 7.0$, where 0.89142 is the one-period discount bond price at that node.

Note that the arbitrage-free interest rate model ensures that the bond price determined by the backward substitution on the arbitrage-free rate movement model is the same as that determined by using the bond model. Now we apply the backward substitution procedure to determine the callable bond price. In this case, we conduct the backward substitution from the bond maturity date. At each step, we compare the bond price with the call price, and determine the value at each node by the following equation. (See figure 6.6.)

bond price $(n, i) =$

$$Min\left[\text{call price}, (0.5 \times \text{bond price } (n+1, i+1) + 0.5 \times \right.$$
$$\left.\text{bond price } (n+1, i)) \times P(n, i, 1)\right] + \text{coupon}$$

## Calculation of a Static Spread and an Option-Adjusted Spread

We assume that the callable bond has credit risk and marketability risk. The bond price is assumed to be \$99.5, which is less than the callable bond price shown in figure 6.6. The promised cash flows and the option-adjusted cash flows from the callable bond are given in figure 6.7. Since the callable bond pays a yearly coupon payment of \$7 and the principal at maturity, the cash flow at each node before maturity is \$7 and the cash flows at each state of the maturity date are \$107. The state-dependent cash flows are determined according to when the call decision is made by the issuing company. Now, we search for an additional spread (OAS) to the one-year period rate given by figure 6.4 such that the theoretical bond price equals the observed bond price of \$99.5. Assume an initial OAS of 50 basis points (bp). Using the backward substitution method and noting the nodes where the call option is exercised, we can determine the call boundary where the firm pays the call price, as depicted in figure 6.7, and the bond price at time 0. Now search for the OAS such that the bond price is 99.5. The OAS is then determined. This procedure affects the call boundary. The calculated static spread is 36.42 bp and the option-adjusted spread is 16.54 bp. The static spread can be calculated by assuming that the cash flow of the callable bond is risk-free and seeking the spread to back out the price. When the option-adjusted spread is 16.54 bp, we have the call boundary shown in figure 6.7.

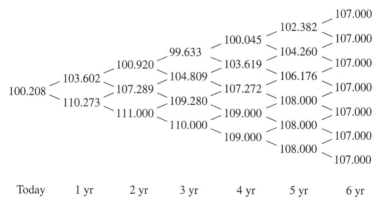

Figure 6.6 A callable bond price lattice. Each node denotes the callable bond price. The call price is \$106 at the initial node, and it linearly declines to \$100 for the maturity year. When we conduct the backward substitution, we compare the bond price from the backward substitution with the call price and replace the bond price with the call price if the bond price exceeds the call price. When the time period is 5 and the state 5, 102.382 is obtained by $Min[95.382, 101.0] + 7.0$ where 95.382 is the backward-substituted bond value at the corresponding node in figure 6.5 and 7.0 is an annual coupon payment.

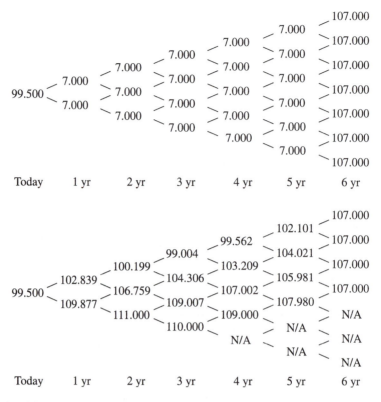

**Figure 6.7** The callable bond promised cash flows and option-adjusted cash flows. The upper lattice shows the promised cash flows and the lower lattice represents the state-dependent cash flows on the binomial lattice for the callable bond. The call boundary will be changed, depending on the discount curve. We depict the call boundary when the discount curve is flat at 6.6654% in the lower lattice. Even though the promised cash flows can be shown on a time line, we show them on the binomial lattice for comparison purposes.

## 6.5 VALUATION OF SINKING FUND BONDS

### Valuation of a Sinking Fund Bond with No Market Purchase Option and No Call Provision

Let us now consider the bond with a sinking fund schedule retiring $10 every year, starting the fourth year. Then the principal repayment and interest schedules are given as shown below.

| Year | 0 | 1 | 2 | 3 | 4 | 5 | 6 |
|---|---|---|---|---|---|---|---|
| Principal to be retired each year | 0 | 0 | 0 | 0 | 10 | 10 | 80 |
| Outstanding amount at the beginning of each year | 100 | 100 | 100 | 100 | 100 | 90 | 80 |
| Remaining principal at the end of each year | 100 | 100 | 100 | 100 | 90 | 80 | 0 |
| Interests | | $100 \times 0.07$ | $100 \times 0.07$ | $100 \times 0.07$ | $100 \times 0.07$ | $90 \times 0.07$ | $80 \times 0.07$ |

The interests are calculated by multiplying the remaining principal by the coupon rate, which is the interest earned over the period on the remaining principal. The bond value is discounting this cash flow, which is the principal payments plus the interest, at the discount rate of 6.5%. The resulting bond value is 101.307.

$$7e^{-0.065} + 7e^{-0.065\times2} + 7e^{-0.065\times3} + 17e^{-0.065\times4} + 16.3e^{-0.065\times5} + 85.6e^{-0.065\times6}$$

$$= 101.307$$

## Valuation of a Sinking Fund Bond with Delivery Option

We use the binomial lattice of interest rates above. Now we consider the terminal condition of the bond at maturity. The value of the bond is $80 \times 1.07$. Now we start the backward substitution. When we retire the $10 face value, we use the market purchase price when the bond price is below par or exercise the sinking fund call at par when the market bond price is above the par price. The *par price* here refers to the principal remaining at the time and not to 100, although by market convention, par is often denoted by 100, to mean 100% of the remaining principal. The lattice of the bond value is given in figure 6.8.

## Valuation of a Double-up Sinking Fund

In this example, we consider a sinking fund bond with a double-up option. We have four cases, depending on when the firm will exercise the double-up option. The four cases are shown in figure 6.9.

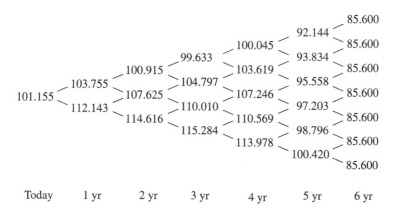

**Figure 6.8** Lattice of the sinking fund bond. The nodes represent the sinking fund bond prices. The sinking fund schedule is that the issuing firm will retire $10 for year 4 and year 5, respectively. Therefore the remaining principal at the maturity year (year 6) is $80. When we conduct the backward substitution, we apply the delivery option to see whether the issuing company buys the bonds at the market price or calls the bonds at par to fulfill the sinking fund obligation. $92.144 at year 5 can be obtained by $Min\left[85.6 \times 0.89142 \times \frac{9}{8}, 85.6 \times 0.89142 + 10\right] + 90 \times 0.07$. The first term in the brackets refers to buying the bonds at the market price, and the second term represents calling the bonds at par to fulfill the sinking fund obligation. The company will choose the lesser of the two terms to maximize the firm's value. Since the outstanding principal between year 4 and year 5 is $90, we multiply the coupon rate by $90 to calculate the coupon payment. For other years, except for the sinking fund operation years, the coupon payment is $7.

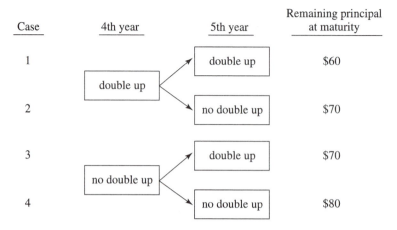

| Case | 4th year | 5th year | Remaining principal at maturity |
|------|----------|----------|--------------------------------|
| 1 | double up | double up | $60 |
| 2 | | no double up | $70 |
| 3 | no double up | double up | $70 |
| 4 | | no double up | $80 |

**Figure 6.9** The double-up sinking fund principal process.

For cases 1 and 2, at the end of the fourth year the firm exercises the double-up option on the first sinking fund, and therefore at the beginning of the fifth year the remaining principal is $80. Since the firm has one more double-up option at the fifth year, the remaining principal at maturity is $60 when the firm exercises the double-up option or $70 when the firm does not. Now we construct the backward substitution procedure for these two cases and evaluate the bond with the double-up sinking fund provision. Specifically, we consider the minimum value of the two alternatives for the delivery option for each state in the world. Using minimum values, we can conduct the backward substitution to the end of the fourth year. The outstanding amount at the beginning of each year in case 1 and case 2 is [100, 100, 100, 100, 80, 60] and [100, 100, 100, 100, 80, 70], respectively. We can determine the outstanding amount at the beginning of each year in cases 3 and 4 in the same way. The binomial lattices for each case are given in figure 6.10.

Let us denote the entries in each lattice by $B^j(n, i)$, where $j$ denotes the $j$th case, $n$ is the period, and $i$ is the state. Now we can decide on the optimal double-up option exercise rule at the end of year 5 by comparing the bond value at each node for the end of year 5. We first consider the case where we elect a double-up option at the end of year 4, using cases 1 and 2. We do so by specifying the bond value for the end of year 5 to be

$$B^{1,2}(5, i) = Min\left[B^1(5, i), B^2(5, i)\right] \text{ for each } i = 0, 1, 2, 3, 4, 5$$

We then roll back the bond value $B^{1,2}(5, i)$ by one year, to the end of year 4. The value at each node for the end of year 4 is denoted by $B^{1,2}(4, i)$.

Similarly, we consider the double-up option decision at the end of year 5 conditional on the no double-up option decision made at the end of year 4, using cases 3 and 4. Once again, we take the minimum of the bond values at each node, in cases 3 and 4, at the end of year 5.

$$B^{3,4}(5, i) = Min\left[B^3(5, i), B^4(5, i)\right] \text{ for each } i = 0, 1, 2, 3, 4, 5$$

Using these optimized numbers, we roll back the bond value $B^{3,4}(5, i)$ by one year, to the end of year 4. The value at each node is denoted by $B^{3,4}(4, i)$.

The appropriate value under the optimal decision at the end of year 4 is taking the minimum of the value of the bonds,

$$B(4, i) = Min\left[B^{1,2}(4, i), B^{3,4}(4, i)\right] \text{ for each } i = 0, 1, 2, 3, 4$$

This approach enables us to specify whether the firm should double up the payment at each node. Now we can roll back the bond value, adjusted for the coupon payments, from the fourth year to the initial date. (See figure 6.11.)

Case 1. Elect to double up at the end of the 4th and 5th years

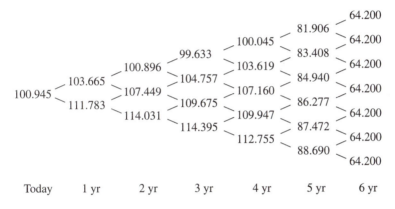

Case 2. Elect to double up at the end of the 4th year and not the 5th year

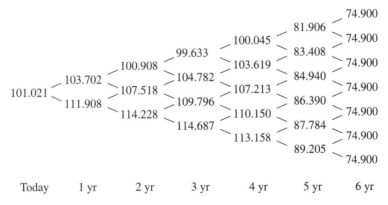

Figure 6.10 The double-up sinking fund. The company with the double-up sinking fund has an option to double the sinking fund retirement amount. Therefore, it can retire up to 20 at the sinking fund operation years, which are years 4 and 5. Since the company has 2 sinking fund operation years, there are 4 cases. Each panel in the figure shows four corresponding cases. For example, the outstanding amounts at the beginning of each year in case 4 are $100, $100, $100, $100, $90, and $80. Once we determine the outstanding amount at the beginning of each year, we can apply the method to determine the bond value with a sinking fund provision in figure 6.8.

Case 3. Elect not to double up in the 4th year but double up in the 5th year

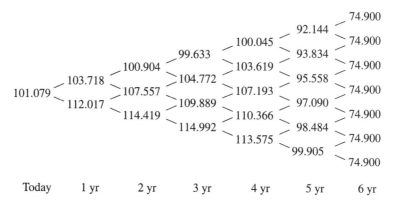

| Today | 1 yr | 2 yr | 3 yr | 4 yr | 5 yr | 6 yr |

Case 4. Elect not to double up in both the 4th and 5th year

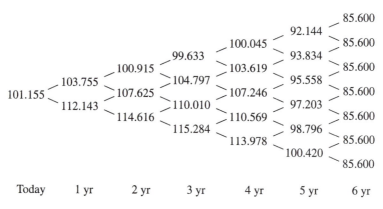

| Today | 1 yr | 2 yr | 3 yr | 4 yr | 5 yr | 6 yr |

**Figure 6.10** (cont.)

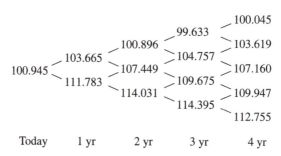

| Today | 1 yr | 2 yr | 3 yr | 4 yr |

**Figure 6.11** Lattice of the bond prices from the end of the fourth year to the starting date. The company decides on the optimal double-up exercise rule by comparing 4 different cases. For example, 112.755 at period 4 is obtained by taking the minimum values among the four cases. That is, *Min*[112.755, 113.158, 113.575, 113.978], where the numbers in the brackets are from the four cases in figure 6.10.

# EXCEL MODEL EXERCISES

## E6.1   CALLABLE BONDS

### Definitions

The parameters in determining the interest rate model are given in the Ho-Lee model. The call schedule is a series of the call prices of the bond on the call dates at which the issuer has the right to call the bonds.

### Description of the Model

The model assumes that the callable bond is priced as a bond with the embedded interest rate option. The initial spot yield curve may not be the risk-free rate or the time value of money. The spot curve may represent the appropriate discount rate for the corresponding option-free bond.

### Numerical Example

Consider a five-year-maturity bond with a call schedule starting with the first call price of $106. The call schedule linearly declines to 100 in four years. The bond coupon rate is 4.5% (annual compounding), and the spot curve is also 4.5% (continuous compounding). The bond price is 99.3775. Since the bond price without the call provisions is 99.5501, the embedded call option value is 0.1726. See figure E6.1.

### Applications

1. The model determines the callable bond value.
2. The model determines the embedded call option value.
3. Given the bond price, the model can determine the option-adjusted spread of the bond.

### Case: Funding Working Capital with Debt

Lee Saiyin was the CFO of a medium-size retailing company whose annual profit just reached $100 million this year. With him in the meeting were Tatenda Shumba, the treasurer, and Muskova Kolamski, the risk manager. The head of financial reporting and the quantitative analyst who had experience with the capital markets were also present. It was at the beginning of the year 2000. The economy was strong and the sales had accelerated. The marketing group had urged the company to mount an advertising campaign and expand the distributions to capture the growing market. The risk manager and the treasurer strongly disagreed on using the working capital. They argued that the use of the working capital at this point was simply reckless. Tatenda summarized the problem in her memo. "The economic boom has been going for several years now. What if the bubble bursts? Our sales would be down and so would our free cash flow. In the same scenario, our working capital would dry up. How could we remain liquid?"

Saiyin called the meeting to come to a conclusion on the matter. He said: "Our potential clients are there ready to knock down our doors for more products. We need

| Inputs | | | | | | |
|---|---|---|---|---|---|---|
| Year | 0 | 1 | 2 | 3 | 4 | 5 |
| Initial yield curve (continuous compounding) | 0.045 | 0.045 | 0.045 | 0.045 | 0.045 | 0.045 |
| Initial discount function p(n) | 1 | 0.956 | 0.91393 | 0.87372 | 0.83527 | 0.798516 |
| Forward curve | 0.045 | 0.045 | 0.045 | 0.045 | 0.045 | 0.045 |
| Lognormal spot volatility ($\sigma^s$) | 0 | 0.1 | 0.095 | 0.09 | 0.085 | 0.08 |
| Lognormal forward volatility ($\sigma^f$) | 0 | 0.1 | 0.09 | 0.08 | 0.07 | 0.06 |
| The number of partitions (m) | 1 | $f(n)\cdot\sigma^f(n+1)=(n+1)\cdot r(n+1)\cdot\sigma^s(n+1)-n\cdot r(n)\cdot\sigma^s(n)$ | | | | |
| Time to maturity (T) at each node | 1 | | | | | |
| Forward price | 0.9560 | 0.9560 | 0.9560 | 0.9560 | 0.9560 | 0.9560 |
| Delta ($\delta$) | 1 | 0.99104 | 0.99193 | 0.99283 | 0.99372 | 0.994615 |
| | | | | | | |
| Face value | 100 | | | | | |
| Call schedule | | 106 | 104 | 102 | 100 | |
| Coupon rate (annual compounding) | 0.045 | | | | | |
| Bond maturity | 5 | | | | | |

| Outputs | | | | | | |
|---|---|---|---|---|---|---|
| | | | | | | 104.5 |
| | | | | | 103.142 | 104.5 |
| | | | | 102.332 | 103.765 | 104.5 |
| | | | 102.155 | 103.635 | 104.392 | 104.5 |
| | | 102.637 | 104.082 | 104.704 | 104.5 | 104.5 |
| Callable bond price | 99.3775 | 105.266 | 105.781 | 105.48 | 104.5 | 104.5 |
| Year | 0 | 1 | 2 | 3 | 4 | 5 |
| | | | | | | |
| Embedded option value | 0.1726 | | | | | |

| Interim Calculations | | | | | | |
|---|---|---|---|---|---|---|
| | | | | | | 104.5 |
| | | | | | 103.142 | 104.5 |
| | | | | 102.332 | 103.765 | 104.5 |
| | | | 102.155 | 103.635 | 104.392 | 104.5 |
| | | 102.694 | 104.202 | 104.955 | 105.024 | 104.5 |
| Fixed coupon bond price | 99.5501 | 105.57 | 106.294 | 106.293 | 105.659 | 104.5 |
| Year | 0 | 1 | 2 | 3 | 4 | 5 |

**Figure E6.1**

to tell them that we have what they want. It just seems that the money is well spent in marketing. Tatenda, aren't you a bit pessimistic? Besides, what is the probability that your scenario will happen? We are breaking new profit records this year." Muskova interjected: "I agree with Tatenda. With the bubble burst, we will have a recession. This recession can last for three years. My quant has done the calculation suggesting that our liquidity will be really squeezed in this scenario. I would say Tatenda's scenario has a good chance of happening."

Tatenda now provided her proposal. "If you really want to use our working capital now, we should then consider issuing a seven-year bond to raise the cash. We have calculated the financing amount needed, such that we would still be solvent in a terrible scenario if a recession were to occur in the next two years." "The problem is that the cost of funding the bond would hurt our earnings. I have to work out which group has to be charged for the cost." Tatenda replied: "This is the cost borne by the headquarters and not the operating units, no?" "Not really; we are using the working capital to support their sales, so it is part of their costs. But that is a separate issue. Let us come back to this bond issuance."

They fell in silence as the CFO was thinking more deeply about the problem. "Tatenda, this is not making sense to me." Tatenda looked taken aback. "You are worried about a recession coming. But if it comes, the interest rates would fall. Then we are locked into the high funding costs for the next seven years. This is not making sense." "We did propose to issue a callable bond. With this funding, if the interest rates fall, we can always buy back our obligations at par." "Don't we have to pay for this option?" "Yes. The market prices these bonds as hedging costs. They say that the option can be priced by an arbitrage-free interest rate model. In an upward-sloping yield curve regime, the call option is priced quite low. The option does not add significantly to our funding costs."

Saiyin then looked around and asked everyone to voice his/her opinion. He wanted everyone to decide, stating clearly "yes" or "no" to the proposal with a reason. All agreed to the proposal. The CFO then concluded, saying he would think about it and would bounce the idea off the CEO. If everyone agreed, he would meet with the investment bankers. He saw no problem in placing the bonds, but he was thinking about the funding cost.

*The seven-year borrowing rate was significantly higher than the interests that he would get from his investments of the working capital because of the upward-sloping yield curve. It is a cost from the accounting sense. But is it a "cost" from the economic sense? How will the proposed funding affect the future financial statements? How should the company charge the funding costs to the operating departments, not to mention taking the call premium into account? Saiyin was sure that the CEO would ask these questions, and for this reason he was going to draft a summary as a memo to be submitted to the final decision maker.*

## Exercises and Answers

1. Given the above numerical example, suppose that the spot curve rate has shifted to 4.6%. What is the callable bond price?
   *Answer:* The callable bond price is 98.9448, which is lower than 99.3775 in the numerical example because of the increase in the interest rates. See figure E6.2.
2. Using the above result, determine the effective duration of the bond.
   *Answer:* The effective duration is 4.3541 (= (99.3775 − 98.9448)/(99.3775(0.046 − 0.045))). If we use numerical analysis to calculate the effective duration for the callable bond, it is 4.3640. See figure E6.3.

| Outputs | | | | | | |
|---|---|---|---|---|---|---|
| | | | | | | 104.5 |
| | | | | | 103.015 | 104.5 |
| | | | | 102.098 | 103.652 | 104.5 |
| | | | 101.829 | 103.426 | 104.292 | 104.5 |
| | | 102.248 | 103.816 | 104.563 | 104.5 | 104.5 |
| Callable bond price | 98.9448 | 104.957 | 105.593 | 105.403 | 104.5 | 104.5 |
| Year | 0 | 1 | 2 | 3 | 4 | 5 |

Figure E6.2

| Δ Spot yield (shift amount) | | -0.001 | 0 | 0.001 | | |
|---|---|---|---|---|---|---|
| Bond price | | 99.8122 | 99.3775 | 98.9448 | | |
| | | Use "data-table" to calculate the bond price for each shifted amount. | | | | |
| | | | | | | |
| Effective duration of bond | 4.3640 | =-(P(r+Δ)-P(r-Δ))/(2ΔP(r)) | | | | |

**Figure E6.3**

| Embedded option value | 0.1726 | | | | | |
|---|---|---|---|---|---|---|
| | | | | | | |
| Δ Spot yield (shift amount) | | -0.001 | 0 | 0.001 | | |
| Embedded option value | | 0.19556 | 0.17257 | 0.14976 | | |
| | | Use "data-table" to calculate the bond price for each shifted amount. | | | | |
| | | | | | | |
| Effective duration of embedded option | 132.68 | =-(P(r+Δ)-P(r-Δ))/(2ΔP(r)) | | | | |

**Figure E6.4**

| Outputs | | | | | | |
|---|---|---|---|---|---|---|
| | | | | | | 104.5 |
| | | | | | 103.031 | 104.5 |
| | | | | 102.127 | 103.666 | 104.5 |
| | | | 101.871 | 103.453 | 104.305 | 104.5 |
| | | 102.298 | 103.85 | 104.581 | 104.5 | 104.5 |
| Callable bond price | 99 | 104.997 | 105.617 | 105.413 | 104.5 | 104.5 |
| Year | 0 | 1 | 2 | 3 | 4 | 5 |
| | | | | | | |
| (market value - estimate)² | 8.1E-28 | | | | | |
| | | This is a target cell for solver to calculate the option-adjusted spread. | | | | |
| OAS | 0.00087 | | | | | |

**Figure E6.5**

3. Using the results of questions 1 and 2, what is the effective duration of the embedded option?

   *Answer:* The embedded option value in the numerical example is 0.1726 (= 99.5501 − 99.3775). If we shift the interest rate by a small amount, the embedded option value changes to 0.19556 and 0.14976, depending on the direction of the interest rate change. The effective duration of the embedded option value is 132.68. See figure E6.4.

4. Using the numerical example above, suppose that the bond price is 99.00. What is the option-adjusted spread?

   *Answer:* The option-adjusted spread is 0.00087. See figure E6.5.

5. Use the numerical example above, but now assume that the first call price is 100, and the call schedule is constant till maturity. What is the embedded option value?

   *Answer:* The embedded option value is 0.5608. See figure E6.6.

6. Use the assumption in question 5, but assume now the first call date is at the end of the second year. What is the embedded option value?

   *Answer:* The embedded option value is 0.5112. See figure E6.7.

| Outputs | | | | | | |
|---|---|---|---|---|---|---|
| | | | | | | 104.5 |
| | | | | | 103.142 | 104.5 |
| | | | | 102.332 | 103.765 | 104.5 |
| | | | 102.155 | 103.635 | 104.392 | 104.5 |
| | | 102.591 | 103.985 | 104.5 | 104.5 | 104.5 |
| Callable bond price | 98.9892 | 104.5 | 104.5 | 104.5 | 104.5 | 104.5 |
| Year | 0 | 1 | 2 | 3 | 4 | 5 |
| | | | | | | |
| Embedded option value | 0.5608 | | | | | |

Figure E6.6

| Outputs | | | | | | |
|---|---|---|---|---|---|---|
| | | | | | | 104.5 |
| | | | | | 103.142 | 104.5 |
| | | | | 102.332 | 103.765 | 104.5 |
| | | | 102.155 | 103.635 | 104.392 | 104.5 |
| | | 102.591 | 103.985 | 104.5 | 104.5 | 104.5 |
| Callable bond price | 99.0389 | 104.604 | 104.5 | 104.5 | 104.5 | 104.5 |
| Year | 0 | 1 | 2 | 3 | 4 | 5 |
| | | | | | | |
| Embedded option value | 0.5112 | | | | | |

Figure E6.7

## Further Exercises

1. A firm issues a bond with the call provision to have more flexibility in borrowing terms, in that the firm can call the bond, which is not possible for a straight bond. In a similar way, an individual can borrow from a bank with a prepayment option. The individual wants to borrow $100 for ten years with the prepayment option. The current interest rate is 10%. He will pay back the money in equal installments for ten years. How much does he pay back every year? What is the prepayment option value? At year 5, the market interest rate drops to 7%. Therefore, he can make a new loan at 7% interest rate. How much can he save for the five years by exercising his prepayment option? To do that, we should determine the remaining balance at year 5. *Answer:* He pays back $16.6378 ($= \frac{100}{\text{PVAF}}$, where $\text{PVAF} = \sum_{i=1}^{10} e^{-0.1i}$) every year and the prepayment option value is $2.56517 ($= 100 - 97.4348$, where 97.4348 is the loan value with the prepayment option). The remaining balance at year 5 after the fifth payment has been made is $68.7924. If the interest rate drops to 7%, the monthly equal payment is $15.7487. Therefore, he can save $0.8891 every month for the remaining five months.

2. Consider a five-year maturity bond with a call schedule starting with the first call price 104.5 at year 1. The call schedule linearly declines to 100 in four years. The bond coupon rate is 4.5% (annual compounding), and the spot curve is also 4.5%

(continuous compounding). Calculate the callable bond price and the call provision value. Given that the bond price is 97, calculate the option-adjusted spread.
*Answer:* The callable bond price is 99.3775, and the call provision value is 0.1726. Given that the callable bond price is 97, the OAS is 55.5 basis points.

## E6.2   SINKING FUND BONDS

### Definitions

The parameters for the interest rate models are explained in the Ho-Lee model. The principal retired is the schedule of the par amount of the bond that the issuer has to retire for the trustee of the bond. The delivery option of the sinking fund bond offers the issuer an option to retire the bond via the open market purchase or the calling of the bonds at par.

### Description of the Model

The sinking fund bond model assumes that the sinking fund bond is an interest rate contingent claim, whereby the issuer uses the delivery option to minimize the bond value by exercising the option optimally.

### Numerical Example

Consider a bond with a maturity of six years at coupon rate 7%. The sinking fund schedule requires the issuers to retire 10% of the bond in years 4 and 5, with the remainder of the bond at maturity. For example, at the beginning of year 4, the outstanding amount is 100. However, since the principal to be retired during year 4 is 10, the remaining principal at the end of year 4 is 90. The yield curve is 6.5% flat, with a constant term structure of volatility of 15%. The bond price is 101.155. See figure E6.8.

### Applications

1. The model values a sinking fund bond.
2. Given the bond price, the model can determine the option-adjusted spread (OAS) of the bond.

### Case: Securitization and the Asset-Backed Securities

Prairie Machine Corporation sells agricultural equipment to farming communities. It has a broad range of products including engines, tractors, and other specialty products. Because of the seasonal aspects of agricultural businesses, where its clients tend to have incomes after harvests, Prairie has a financial company to facilitate the purchase of the equipment. The subsidiary is called Prairie Financial.

Prairie Financial purchases the equipment from Prairie Machine and then leases the equipment to the client. Therefore, Prairie Financial is the leasor and the customer is the leasee. Further, the lease payments would best fit the cash flow needs of the customers mainly receiving the lease payments after the harvests. Meanwhile, Prairie

| Inputs | | | | | | | |
|---|---|---|---|---|---|---|---|
| Year | 0 | 1 | 2 | 3 | 4 | 5 | 6 |
| Initial yield curve (continuous compounding) | 0.065 | 0.065 | 0.065 | 0.065 | 0.065 | 0.065 | 0.065 |
| Initial discount function p(n) | 1.0000 | 0.9371 | 0.8781 | 0.8228 | 0.7711 | 0.7225 | 0.6771 |
| Forward curve | 0.065 | 0.065 | 0.065 | 0.065 | 0.065 | 0.065 | 0.065 |
| Lognormal spot volatility ($\sigma^S$) | 0 | 0.15 | 0.15 | 0.15 | 0.15 | 0.15 | 0.15 |
| Lognormal forward volatility ($\sigma^f$) | 0 | 0.15 | 0.15 | 0.15 | 0.15 | 0.15 | 0.15 |
| The number of partitions (m) | 1 | $f(n)\cdot\sigma^f(n+1)=(n+1)\cdot r(n+1)\cdot\sigma^s(n+1)-n\cdot r(n)\cdot\sigma^s(n)$ | | | | | |
| Time to maturity (T) at each node | 1 | | | | | | |
| Forward price | 0.9371 | 0.9371 | 0.9371 | 0.9371 | 0.9371 | 0.9371 | 0.9371 |
| Delta ($\delta$) | 1 | 0.98069 | 0.98069 | 0.98069 | 0.98069 | 0.980689 | 0.980689 |
| Face value | 100 | | | | | | |
| Coupon rate (annual compounding) | 0.07 | | | | | | |
| Bond maturity | 6 | | | | | | |
| | | | | | | | |
| Principal to be retired at the end of each year | | | | | 10 | 10 | 80 |
| Outstanding amount at the beginning of year | 100 | 100 | 100 | 100 | 100 | 90 | 80 |
| Remaining principal at the end of each year | | 100 | 100 | 100 | 90 | 80 | 0 |
| Coupon | 0.0 | 7.0 | 7.0 | 7.0 | 7.0 | 6.3 | 5.6 |
| Debt CF | 0.0 | 7.0 | 7.0 | 7.0 | 17.0 | 16.3 | 85.6 |
| Year | 0 | 1 | 2 | 3 | 4 | 5 | 6 |

| Outputs | | | | | | | |
|---|---|---|---|---|---|---|---|
| | | | | | | | 85.600 |
| | | | | | | 92.144 | 85.600 |
| | | | | | 100.045 | 93.834 | 85.600 |
| | | | | 99.633 | 103.619 | 95.558 | 85.600 |
| | | | 100.915 | 104.797 | 107.246 | 97.203 | 85.600 |
| | | 103.755 | 107.625 | 110.010 | 110.569 | 98.796 | 85.600 |
| Sinking fund bond with delivery option | 101.155 | 112.143 | 114.616 | 115.284 | 113.978 | 100.420 | 85.600 |
| Year | 0 | 1 | 2 | 3 | 4 | 5 | 6 |

**Figure E6.8**

Financial has to raise significant capital to purchase the equipment. For this purpose, the financial company enters into a pass-through program. The process begins with a working capital. Prairie Financial uses the working capital to buy the equipment. Over a period of about three months, Prairie Financial would build up a portfolio of these leases. Then this portfolio is securitized into a bond. The bond will have a schedule of principals that will pay down over time. The scheduled payments would match the lease payments from the portfolio. By selling this bond, Prairie Financial would receive the capital that would replenish the working capital that has been drawn down in building the portfolio of leases. This process will repeat again. Prairie Financial will guarantee the payments to the bondholders if the leasees default on the lease payments. In other words, the financial company takes on all default risk of the leasees. An investment bank in the region underwrites the bonds. The bank will meet with pension funds and other institutional investors to buy a portion of the bonds when they come out in the market.

Prairie Financial is the issuer of the bonds. The rating of the bond is investment grade because the bonds are backed by the leases and further guaranteed by Prairie Financial, which in turn is guaranteed by Prairie Machines.

"What is the maturity of the bond?" asked Simba Moyo, a pension fund manager. "The maturity is five years, but the weighted average life is only two years. This is because of the scheduled paydown of the principals. In some sense, the bond is a sinking fund bond." "The duration of the bond is not related to the bond maturity then," Simba commented, and continued with his thought, "since we must know the scheduled payments of the principals." After some thought, Simba asked: "Does Prairie Financial provide mortgages to its customers and securitize the mortgages to sell to us too, like what other firms do with the whole loans?" "Not yet," the investment banker replied. "Remember, these bonds are much simpler to analyze than those whole loans because there is no early prepayment option in these leases. And therefore there are no embedded options in these bonds. Unlike the whole loans." Simba said that he would first understand the duration of the bonds so that he can manage them relative to his pension liabilities and that he would use the OAS analysis to see if the bond can offer enough returns for his purpose.

*Simba wants to add this bond type to his portfolio, but he should first evaluate the credit risk, interest rate risk, and the returns of the bonds. What factors should he consider? How does he evaluate the appropriateness of the bond to his portfolio? Why would such a bond be attractive to him?*

## Exercises and Answers

1. Using the numerical example above, determine the effective duration of the bond.
   *Answer:* The effective duration is the bond price sensitivity with respect to a small change in the interest rate. $P(r + \Delta)$ and $P(r - \Delta)$ are the bond prices when we have a flat yield curve at $r + \Delta$ and $r - \Delta$, respectively. Delta ($\Delta$) is a small change in the interest rate. The effective duration of the sinking bond can be calculated and it is 4.9912. See figure E6.9.

2. Given that the bond price is 100. What is the option-adjusted spread of the bond?
   *Answer:* The option-adjusted spread is a spread added to the risk-free rate, which makes the price of the sinking fund bond equal to the market price. To calculate the OAS, we first assume a certain OAS, and given the OAS, we calculate the price of the sinking fund bond. Once we calculate it, we compare it with the market price. If the price of the sinking fund bond is not equal to the market price, we keep changing the OAS until the calculated price of the sinking fund bond is equal to the market price. The option-adjusted spread is 22.9 basis points. See figure E6.10.

3. Use the numerical example above, but suppose that the sinking fund schedule is changed to paying down 40% in year 4 and again in year 5, leaving 20% to be paid at maturity. What is the bond price assuming no option-adjusted spread?
   *Answer:* Since the bond in question 3 has a shorter weighted average life than that of question 1, and the coupon rate is higher than the market interest rate, the bond price in question 3 is lower than the bond price in the numerical example. See figure E6.11.

| Outputs | | | | | | |
|---|---|---|---|---|---|---|
| Δ Spot yield (shift amount) | | -0.0001 | 0 | 0.0001 | | |
| Bond price | | 101.206 | 101.155 | 101.105 | | |
| | | Use "data-table" to calculate the bond price for each shifted amount. | | | | |
| | | | | | | |
| Effective duration (numerical value) | 4.9912 | =-(P(r+Δ)-P(r-Δ))/(2ΔP(r)) | | | | |

**Figure E6.9**

## Outputs

| | | | | | | | | 85.600 |
|---|---|---|---|---|---|---|---|---|
| | | | | | | | 91.793 | 85.600 |
| | | | | | | 99.376 | 93.536 | 85.600 |
| | | | | | 98.762 | 103.051 | 95.315 | 85.600 |
| | | | | 99.906 | 104.080 | 106.827 | 97.038 | 85.600 |
| | | | 102.655 | 106.807 | 109.473 | 110.283 | 98.685 | 85.600 |
| Sinking fund bond with delivery option | 100.000 | 111.267 | 114.013 | 114.922 | 113.803 | 100.365 | 85.600 |
| Year | 0 | 1 | 2 | 3 | 4 | 5 | 6 |

| (market value - estimate)$^2$ | 2E-28 | |
|---|---|---|
| | This is a target cell for solver to calculate the option-adjusted spread. | |
| OAS | 0.00229 | |

Figure E6.10

## Inputs

| | Year | 0 | 1 | 2 | 3 | 4 | 5 | 6 |
|---|---|---|---|---|---|---|---|---|
| | Initial yield curve (continuous compounding) | 0.065 | 0.065 | 0.065 | 0.065 | 0.065 | 0.065 | 0.065 |
| | Option-adjusted spread | 0 | | | | | | |
| | Initial yield curve + OAS | 0.065 | 0.065 | 0.065 | 0.065 | 0.065 | 0.065 | 0.065 |
| | Initial discount function p(n) | 1.0000 | 0.9371 | 0.8781 | 0.8228 | 0.7711 | 0.7225 | 0.6771 |
| | Forward curve | 0.065 | 0.065 | 0.065 | 0.065 | 0.065 | 0.065 | 0.065 |
| | Lognormal spot volatility ($\sigma^S$) | 0 | 0.15 | 0.15 | 0.15 | 0.15 | 0.15 | 0.15 |
| | Lognormal forward volatility ($\sigma^f$) | 0 | 0.15 | 0.15 | 0.15 | 0.15 | 0.15 | 0.15 |
| | The number of partitions (m) | 1 | $f(n)\cdot\sigma^f(n+1)=(n+1)\cdot r(n+1)\cdot\sigma^S(n+1)-n\cdot r(n)\cdot\sigma^S(n)$ | | | | | |
| | Time to maturity (T) at each node | 1 | | | | | | |
| | Forward price | 0.9371 | 0.9371 | 0.9371 | 0.9371 | 0.9371 | 0.9371 | 0.9371 |
| | Delta ($\delta$) | 1 | 0.98069 | 0.98069 | 0.98069 | 0.98069 | 0.980689 | 0.980689 |
| | Face value | 100 | | | | | | |
| | Coupon rate (annual compounding) | 0.07 | | | | | | |
| | Bond maturity | 6 | | | | | | |
| | Sinking fund bond price (market value) | 100 | | | | | | |
| | | | | | | | | |
| | Principal to be retired at the end of each year | | | | | 40 | 40 | 20 |
| | Outstanding amount at the beginning of year | 100 | 100 | 100 | 100 | 100 | 60 | 20 |
| | Remaining principal at the end of each year | | 100 | 100 | 100 | 60 | 20 | 0 |
| | Coupon | 0.0 | 7.0 | 7.0 | 7.0 | 7.0 | 4.2 | 1.4 |
| | Debt CF | 0.0 | 7.0 | 7.0 | 7.0 | 47.0 | 44.2 | 21.4 |
| | Year | 0 | 1 | 2 | 3 | 4 | 5 | 6 |

## Outputs

| | | | | | | | | 21.400 |
|---|---|---|---|---|---|---|---|---|
| | | | | | | | 61.429 | 21.400 |
| | | | | | | 100.045 | 62.556 | 21.400 |
| | | | | | 99.633 | 103.619 | 63.705 | 21.400 |
| | | | | 100.858 | 104.674 | 106.980 | 64.426 | 21.400 |
| | | | 103.483 | 107.095 | 109.001 | 108.703 | 64.824 | 21.400 |
| Sinking fund bond with delivery option | 100.521 | 111.061 | 112.860 | 112.616 | 110.310 | 65.230 | 21.400 |
| Year | 0 | 1 | 2 | 3 | 4 | 5 | 6 |

Figure E6.11

| Outputs | | | | | | | | |
|---|---|---|---|---|---|---|---|---|
| | | | | | | | | 21.400 |
| | | | | | | | 61.429 | 21.400 |
| | | | | | | 100.045 | 62.556 | 21.400 |
| | | | | | 99.633 | 103.619 | 63.705 | 21.400 |
| | | | | 100.858 | 104.674 | 106.980 | 64.426 | 21.400 |
| | | | 103.483 | 107.095 | 109.001 | 108.703 | 64.824 | 21.400 |
| Sinking fund bond with delivery option | 100.521 | 111.061 | 112.860 | 112.616 | 110.310 | 65.230 | 21.400 |
| Year | 0 | 1 | 2 | 3 | 4 | 5 | 6 |
| | | | | | | | | 21.400 |
| | | | | | | | 63.276 | 21.400 |
| | | | | | | 104.152 | 63.652 | 21.400 |
| | | | | | 102.414 | 105.626 | 64.035 | 21.400 |
| | | | | 102.598 | 105.680 | 107.142 | 64.426 | 21.400 |
| | | | 104.526 | 107.602 | 109.078 | 108.703 | 64.824 | 21.400 |
| Sinking fund bond without option provision | 101.130 | 111.318 | 112.896 | 112.616 | 110.310 | 65.230 | 21.400 |
| Year | 0 | 1 | 2 | 3 | 4 | 5 | 6 |
| Delivery option value | 0.609 | | | | | | |

**Figure E6.12**

4. Explain the factors leading to the change in the bond price in question 3 compared to the bond price of the numerical example.

   *Answer:* The price of the sinking fund bond depends on the interest rate, coupon rate, maturity, and the sinking fund schedule. When the coupon rate is above the current interest rate, the shorter the weighted average life is, the lower is the bond price.

5. Assume that there is no delivery option. Then the sinking bond becomes a "serial bond." Calculate the serial bond price and then determine the delivery option value. See figure E6.12.

   *Answer:* If we do not have a delivery option in the sinking fund provision, the bond with a sinking fund provision becomes a serial bond. The price of the serial bond is the present value of the future cash flow, which is predetermined by the cash flow schedule.

## Further Exercises

1. Consider a bond with a maturity of six years at coupon rate 7%. The sinking fund schedule requires the issuers to retire 10% of the bond in years 3, 4, and 5, with the remainder of the bond at maturity. The yield curve is 6.5% flat, with a constant term structure of volatility of 15%. Calculate the sinking fund bond price. Based on the sinking fund bond price, calculate the sinking fund provision value and the delivery option value.

   *Answer:* The sinking fund bond price with the delivery option is 100.953. The sinking fund bond price without the delivery option is 101.245. The corresponding straight bond price is 101.366. Therefore, the sinking fund provision value is 0.413 (= 101.366 − 100.953). Finally, the delivery option value is 0.293 (= 101.245 − 100.953).

2. In question 1, given that the bond price is 100, calculate the option-adjusted spread.
   *Answer:* The OAS is 0.00193.

## Note

1. According to Bond Market Association, *Research Quarterly*, May 2002.

## Bibliography

Altman, E. 1968. Financial ratios, discriminant analysis and the prediction of corporate bankruptcy. *Journal of Finance*, 23, 589–609.

Altman, E., and D. L. Kao. 1992a. Rating drift in high yield bonds. *Journal of Fixed Income*, March, 15–20.

Altman, E., and D. L. Kao. 1992b. The implications of corporate bond rating drift. *Financial Analysts Journal*, May/June, 64–75.

Brennan, M. J., and E. S. Schwartz. 1977. Savings bonds, retractable bonds and callable bonds. *Journal of Financial Economics*, 5, 67–88.

Courtadon, G. 1982. The pricing of options on default-free bonds. *Journal of Financial and Quantitative Analysis*, 17 (1), 75–100.

Duffee, G. R. 1998. The relation between Treasury yields and corporate bond yield spreads. *Journal of Finance*, 53 (6), 2225–2241.

Ederington, L., J. Yawitz, and B. Roberts. 1987. The informational content of bond ratings. *Journal of Financial Research*, 10 (3), 211–226.

Elton, E., M. Gruber, D. Agrawal, and C. Mann. 2001. Explaining the rate spread on corporate bonds. *Journal of Finance*, 56 (1), 247–278.

Harrison, M. J., and D. M. Kreps. 1979. Martingales and arbitrage in multi-period securities markets. *Journal of Economic Theory*, 20, 381–408.

Hite, G., and A. Warga. 1997. The effect of bond rating changes on bond price performance. *Financial Analysts Journal*, 53 (3), 35–51.

Ho, T. S. Y. 1990. *Strategic Fixed-Income Investment.* Homewood, IL: Dow Jones-Irwin.

Ho, T. S. Y. 1994. *Fixed-Income Investment, Resecent Research.* Burr Ridge, IL: Irwin Professional Publishing.

Ho, T. S. Y., and R. F. Singer. 1984. The value of corporate debt with a sinking-fund provision. *Journal of Business*, 57(3), 315–336.

Ho, T. S. Y. 1992. Key rate durations: Measures of interest rate risks. *Journal of Fixed Income*, 2 (2), 19–44.

Ingersol, J., Jr. 1977. An examination of corporate call policies on convertible securities. *Journal of Finance*, 32, 463–478.

Jarrow, R. 2002. *Modelling Fixed Income Securities and Interest Rate Options*, 2nd ed., Stanford, CA: Stanford University Press.

Kliger, D., and O. Sarig. 2000. The information value of bond ratings. *Journal of Finance*, 55 (6), 2879–2902.

Leland, H. E. 1994. Corporate debt value, bond covenants, and optimal capital structure. *Journal of Finance*, 49, 1213–1252.

Litterman, R., and T. Iben. 1991. Corporate bond valuation and the term structure of credit spread. *Journal of Portfolio Management*, Spring, 52–64.

Nunn, K. P., Jr., J. Hill, and T. Schneeweis. 1986. Corporate bond price data sources and return/risk measurement. *Journal of Financial and Quantitative Analysis*, 21 (2), 197–208.

Reitano, R. 1996. Non-parallel yield curve shifts and stochastic immunization. *Journal of Portfolio Management*, Winter, 71–78.

Rendleman, R. J., Jr., and B. J. Bartter. 1980. The pricing of options on debt securities. *Journal of Financial and Quantitative Analysis*, 15 (1), 11–24.

Sarig, O., and A. Warga. 1989. Bond price data and bond market liquidity. *Journal of Financial and Quantitative Analysis*, 24 (3), 367–378.

Sarig, O., and A. Warga. 1989. The risk structure of interest rates: Some empirical estimates. *Journal of Finance*, 44 (5), 1351–1360.

# 7

# Corporate Bonds: High-Yield Bonds

igh-yield bonds are bonds that have significant default risks. These bonds are necessarily complex to value because their values must depend on the profitability of the issuer of the bond as well as the present value of the expected cash flows. Indeed, high-yield bonds combine the complexity of valuing the equities and bonds. This chapter will discuss some of the approaches to deal with this problem.

## 7.1 AN EXAMPLE OF A HIGH-YIELD BOND

Let us consider a high-yield bond of McLeodUSA, Inc., quoted in NASDAQ National Market System as MCLDQ. McLeodUSA provides communication services, including local services in the Southwest, Northwest, and Rocky Mountain states, and long-distance and data services nationwide. On December 3, 2001, the company filed a prenegotiated plan of reorganization through a Chapter 11 bankruptcy petition. On February 11, 2002, the stock was traded at 0.15.

Let us use September 20, 2001, as our evaluation date. We begin the analysis with the quarterly balance sheet, which is summarized by the following major items:

*Balance Sheet ($billion)*

| | | | |
|---|---|---|---|
| Current assets | 0.4 | Current liabilities | 0.7 |
| Net fixed assets | 2.7 | Long-term debt | 3.7 |
| Net goodwill | 1.1 | Others | 0.2 |
| Others | 0.6 | Equity | 0.2 |
| Total assets | 4.8 | Total liabilities and equity | 4.8 |

On a book value basis, the firm has a minimal equity of $200 million to support the debt of $3.7 billion. Furthermore, a significant part of the total asset is a net goodwill of $1.1 billion, as a result of its acquisitions. Therefore there are not enough tangible and liquid assets to support the debt.

The business model of the communication company is not generating enough cash flows to support the operating costs, and is certainly not sufficient to support the interest costs. The income statement below shows that the company was incurring significant losses. (EBT is earnings before tax.)

*Income Statement ($billion)*

| | |
|---|---|
| Revenue | 0.450 |
| Gross profit | 0.179 |
| Operating income | (3.082) |
| EBT | (3.108) |
| Net income | (3.108) |

We now turn our attention from the analysis of the financial statements to the debt structure. The above analysis clearly shows that the firm has significant credit risk. Its credit risk leads to the evaluation of the potential loss of the bond values, which is the default risk of each bond in the debt structure. In order to analyze the default risk, we need to begin with a description of the debt structure. To value the default risk of a high-yield bond, we must value the bond not in isolation, but within the context of all the firm's financial obligations. The debt structure is summarized in tables 7.1 and 7.2.

**Table 7.1**  Debt Structure of McLeodUSA

| Issuer | McLeodUSA 07-1 | McLeodUSA 07-2 | McLeodUSA 08-1 | McLeodUSA 08-2 |
|---|---|---|---|---|
| Coupon rate | 10.50 | 9.25 | 8.38 | 12.00 |
| Coupon type | STEP CPN[1] | Fixed | Fixed | Fixed |
| Maturity | 20070301 | 20070715 | 20080315 | 20080715 |
| Rating | CCC1 | CCC1 | CCC1 | CCC1 |
| Frequency | 2 | 2 | 2 | 2 |
| Maturity type | CALLABLE | CALLABLE | CALLABLE | CALLABLE |
| Outstanding[2] | 500,000.00 | 225,000.00 | 300,000.00 | 150,000.0 |

| Issuer | McLeodUSA 08-3 | McLeodUSA 09-1 | McLeodUSA 09-2 | McLeodUSA 09-3 |
|---|---|---|---|---|
| Coupon rate | 9.50 | 11.38 | 8.13 | 11.50 |
| Coupon type | Fixed | Fixed | Fixed | Fixed |
| Maturity | 20081101 | 20090101 | 20090215 | 20090501 |
| Rating | CCC1 | CCC1 | CCC1 | CCC1 |
| Frequency | 2 | 2 | 2 | 2 |
| Maturity type | CALLABLE | NORMAL | CALLABLE | CALLABLE |
| Outstanding[2] | 300,000.00 | 750,000.00 | 500,000.00 | 210,000.00 |

[1]Step-up coupon.

[2]Outstanding amount.

**Table 7.2**  Call Schedule of the Corporate Debt Securities

| McLeodUSA 07-1 | | McLeodUSA 07-2 | | McLeodUSA 08-1 | | McLeodUSA 08-2 | |
|---|---|---|---|---|---|---|---|
| Call Date | Call Price | Call Date | Call Price | Call Date | Call Price | Call Date | Call Price |
| 20020301 | 105.250 | 20020715 | 104.625 | 20030315 | 104.188 | 20030715 | 106.000 |
| 20030301 | 103.500 | 20030715 | 103.083 | 20040315 | 102.792 | 20040715 | 104.000 |
| 20040301 | 101.750 | 20040715 | 101.542 | 20050315 | 101.396 | 20050715 | 102.000 |
| 20050301 | 100.000 | 20050715 | 100.000 | 20060315 | 100.000 | 20060715 | 100.000 |

| McLeodUSA 08-3 | | McLeodUSA 09-1 | | McLeodUSA 09-2 | | McLeodUSA 09-3 | |
|---|---|---|---|---|---|---|---|
| Call Date | Call Price | Call Date | Call Price | Call Date | Call Price | Call Date | Call Price |
| 20031101 | 106.750 | N/A | N/A | 20040215 | 104.063 | 20040501 | 105.750 |
| 20041101 | 105.400 | N/A | N/A | 20050215 | 102.708 | 20050501 | 103.834 |
| 20051101 | 104.050 | N/A | N/A | 20060215 | 101.354 | 20060501 | 101.917 |
| 20061101 | 102.700 | N/A | N/A | 20070215 | 100.000 | 20070501 | 100.000 |
| 20071101 | 101.350 | N/A | N/A | | | | |

The summary shows that there are eight bonds in the structure. The column heads in table 7.1 present the identifiers of the bonds. The first row presents the coupon rates. The second row shows that all the bonds have a fixed coupon rate except 07-1, which has step-up coupons. The third row presents the exact maturity dates. The numbers show that the maturities vary over a relatively tight maturity spectrum from 2007 to 2009. All the bonds were rated CCC1 at the time. All the bonds have the same semiannual interest payment frequency and are callable (make whole call) except for 09-1. The total bond face value is $2.935 billion in table 7.1. The debt structure shows that all the bonds have the same priority (belong to the same class).

The debt structure provides us with some insight into the credit risk of the firm and the valuation of the bonds. No bond in the debt structure will mature within 12 months. The default of the firm in the next 12 months will not be triggered by any of the bond's maturing, but may be triggered by the drain of cash in operating costs or the coupon payments of the bonds. The bank loans also may trigger default. But the presence of these bonds may exhaust any debt capacity of the firm, and may even restrict the firm's access to equity external funding in the capital market.

The income statement and balance sheet describing the size of the debt in par value and annual income alone cannot properly determine the credit risk of a firm. Such information only suggests that at the liquidation of the firm, the bonds may suffer significant loss in principals, and the firm's internal cash flow is not sufficient to support the operating costs. But the firm may have the potential to be very profitable in the future. For this reason, the firm may have access to the capital market for equity or debt funding, and as a result the probability of defaulting on the existing bonds may be low. To evaluate the firm's ability to use external financing to manage its credit risk, we now turn our attention to its market total capitalization.

A firm's market total capitalization, in academic literature, is usually called the *firm value*, denoted by $V$. The value represents the market valuation of the firm as a going concern. On the one hand, it is the present value of the free cash flows of the firm. On the other hand, it is the value of all the claims on the firm. In the case of McLeodUSA, there are only two claims, the stockholders and the bondholders. The claims of the stockholders are *capitalization*, the product of the stock price and the number of shares outstanding (denoted by $S$). The claim of the debts is the market value of the debt (denoted by $D$). By definition of market valuation, the present value of the free cash flows of the firm must be equal to all the claims on the firm's value.

$$V = S + D \qquad (7.1)$$

Now, let us evaluate the credit risk of McLeodUSA as a going concern. On June 1, 2001, the stock was traded at $5.22. The number of shares outstanding was 611,990,000. Therefore the capitalization was $3.195 billion. The eight bond prices and the respective outstanding par amounts (given in parentheses) are 65.99 ($500 million), 70.6 ($225 million), 64.75 ($300 million), 101.56 ($150 million), 67.5 ($300 million), 74.75 ($750 milion), 64.8 ($500 million), and 74.5 ($210 million). The market value of debt is $2.079 billion. The firm value, the sum of the capitalization and the debt value, is $5.274 billion. Thus the present value of all the free cash flows generated by McLeodUSA to determine the firm value is only $5.274 billion. Since market total capitalization depends on the market price of risk on the firm's future profits, it has a high volatility. The probability that the value will fall below the par value (or the face value) of the bonds, $2.935 billion, over a short horizon (say one year) can be very high. Therefore, the credit risk of the firm is high.

The discussion above provides us with an overview of the credit analysis of a firm, starting from the financial statements, to the terms and conditions of the debt structure, and then to the market valuation of the firm as a going concern. The example also illustrates the challenges in developing a valuation model for high-yield bonds.

You can assume that a valuation model of high-yield bonds must be an extension of the model for investment grade bonds because as credit risk decreases, high-yield bonds have the same ratings as investment grade bonds. However, the high-yield bond cannot be an interest rate contingent claim, whereas the investment grade bond can be the interest rate contingent claim. The high-yield bond must depend on the debt structure, the business risk, and all the issues that we have discussed above. This chapter will present some of the models that deal with these challenges.

The example also illustrates the many possible applications of a high-yield bond valuation model. A high-yield bond market tends to be less liquid than the investment grade bond market because of the bonds' higher credit risk. The quoted bond prices are often indications of the bond value. In these cases, the quoted prices cannot be used for larger transaction sizes and may not even reflect the equilibrium price, which may be established when there is a larger transaction volume. A valuation model can provide a systematic approach to determine the fair value of the bonds, for the purpose of managing the risk of a bond portfolio, marking to market of a high-yield bond portfolio, and many other practical applications of bond portfolio management.

## 7.2 INSTITUTIONAL FRAMEWORK OF BANKRUPTCY AND BANKRUPTCY PROCEEDINGS

We begin with an overview of the institutional framework of bankruptcy and bankruptcy proceedings. The bankruptcy framework describes the principles behind the rules of bankruptcy, and the proceedings show the actual functions of the bankruptcy. Bankruptcy determines the payments to each of the bondholders, the shareholders, and other claimants of the firm's assets or future earnings. Therefore, it is the logical starting point to understand the valuation of a high-yield bond.

### A Bond Indenture

Corporations tend to issue a number of debts, which may be publicly sold and/or privately placed. The portfolio of debt of the corporation is called the *debt structure*. It may consist of bank notes, private loans, and public debts. The portfolio may have long-term bonds and short-term bonds, and each of the bonds may have its own provisions and covenants. Therefore there may be several classes of creditors: secured and unsecured (*secured creditors* have the debt secured by some assets of the firm), and junior and senior (the *senior creditors* have higher priority to the claims than the junior creditors).

Bankruptcies are often triggered by the failure to meet the obligations of any bond in the debt structure. These triggers are specified in the bond contract, called the *indenture*, agreed upon between the bondholders and the shareholders. More specifically, the indenture has two separate agreements. The first part, called the *covenant*, states the obligations of the borrower. A violation of the covenant triggers default. The second part explains what happens in the event of default.

While the shareholders and bondholders can negotiate the agreement in any form, the bond indentures tend to converge on some industry standards. These standards follow a certain format and language for ease of interpretation of the intent and implementation of the agreements. These standards are called *boilerplate*. Some of the standard terms are described below.

The covenant addresses the main concerns of bondholders. It explains the bondholders' privileges and restrictions of their rights. Bondholders want to ensure that equity holders remain as junior claimants to the firm's assets by limiting the shareholders' cash dividends and to prevent the firm's assets from being passed to any classes subordinate to the senior bondholders. They also want to keep down the number of claimants in their class or senior to their class in the future, so that the risk of the bond is not adversely affected—the increase of such claimants would lead to a higher probability of default. Consequently, these claimants will either share the firm's assets with them or have a higher priority in their claims to the firm's assets.

Any substantial breach of the covenants will lead to default. As a result, the *acceleration clause* requires the firm to pay not just the coupon but the principal. The *cross default* on a bond states that the bond is in default if the firm defaults on any bond in the debt structure. The cross-default clause accelerates the other debts' payments (e.g., the principals and unpaid coupons).

The second part of the indenture describes the implication of default. The bonds in the capital structure may be of several classes. Some are more senior than others, as specified in the bond covenants. Each bond class has a representative for all the bondholders, called the *trustee*. The trustee oversees the agreement made between the borrowers and lenders and is also responsible for exerting the rights of the bondholders in the event of default. The rights may vary according to the priority rules specified in the indenture.

The absolute priority rules specify the order of payment in the event of bankruptcy. Senior debt holders have the right to receive their payments before junior debt holders. These rules are usually applied when a firm files for Chapter 13, the liquidation of a firm, where the firm's assets are sold and distributed to all the claimants. The equity holders decide whether or not they want to liquidate the firm.

## Default Proceedings

In the event of default, equity holders can choose not to liquidate. If a firm's value is based on marketable assets, it may plan to pursue a liquidation of all the assets and, in practice, the absolute priority rule would be carried out. However, if the firm's value depends on the management and relationships with clients, it would not make sense to liquidate. For example, liquidating a consulting company would yield little value to the bondholders. It is important for the management team (who often hold shares) to remain in order to maintain the firm's value.

There are other alternative actions a firm can take in the event of default. Equity holders can seek protection under the bankruptcy court procedure. Or they can initiate an out-of-court settlement. In this case, even if there is a settlement, the equity holders may still petition for Chapter 11 protection for a court approval of such a plan.

Chapter 11 provides protection of the firm's assets and its ability to function as a going concern while reorganizing its capital structure. The bankruptcy proceeding under Chapter 11 is a negotiation based on a certain framework. A bankruptcy court does not dictate a solution, nor does a bond indenture have any written or prespecified solution. Chapter 11 offers legal protection for a firm in default to have the opportunity to reorganize so that the firm can emerge from the bankruptcy proceeding as a viable, going concern while satisfying all the claimants in the event of default. However, bankruptcy proceedings can be complicated, involving negotiations that seek to maximize the firm's value.

## The Reorganization Plan

The bankruptcy court oversees the management of the firm. Under its protection, the management of the firm will continue to function as a going concern. The bankruptcy court also oversees the reorganization plan. Usually the senior debt holders will present the plan. The reorganization becomes a negotiating process. Its end result is to propose a reorganization plan that can gain the approval of all the claimants, including the equity holders and the bankruptcy court.

The principle behind the plan should be that the firm can function without envisioning another bankruptcy. The plan has to be timely to minimize bankruptcy costs, ensuring that the management will avoid making highly risky investments with negative net present values, hoping to avoid losing all the equity value. The bankruptcy court needs to approve the plan that the classes agree on. More important, it needs the firm to be viable as a going concern. The court seeks to lower the probability of the firm's declaring bankruptcy in the near future.

In the event of reorganization, the senior debt holders play an important role. They are often responsible for proposing a reorganization plan. A reorganization does not necessarily result in following the provisions as strictly stated in the priority rules. Senior debt holders have the most right to be paid in full. In fact, equity holders may retain a portion of their equity and not give all the shares to the bondholders. In such a case, the bondholders may realize a higher return than what they would be able to receive under liquidation. Senior debt holders would receive less to ensure that the firm's value is maximized by taking into consideration the preservation of the management or seeking better management, maintaining the client base, and the tax implications.

The plan may propose the deferment of the senior debt payments, or permit satisfying the claims by paying with securities other than cash: subordinated debt, preferred shares, or common shares. The plan must be accepted by all the impaired classes, and the votes within each class have to be accepted by half of the votes represented by a two-thirds majority of debt value. Finally, the court has to approve the plan.

When the classes cannot agree on a plan, the court can designate a class to be "not in good faith" because it is not exerting its best effort to support a reorganization plan that is considered workable by the court. For this reason, the court can "cram down" on the dissenting minority, in essence overruling their disagreement.

If the negotiations fail (that is, an agreement cannot be reached to the satisfaction of either party), the final option is to convert from a Chapter 11 filing to a Chapter 13 liquidation of the company.

Since the reorganization plan is about "who will get what," it clearly affects the valuation of a high-yield bond. The plan affects the bond values in two ways: the value of the firm after reorganization and the negotiating positions of each class of creditors. If the plan leads to a higher valuation of the firm, then the holders of high-yield bonds will likely receive more for their claims. After all, the payments to the bondholders must come from the valuation of the reorganized firm. If the bondholders are in a stronger position to negotiate, the bond value can be enhanced. For example, if the firm value is based more on assets with marketability and less on management know-how, the bondholders have a stronger negotiating position against the management team. These two aspects are not independent of each other; they are related because the firm value and the source of the value affect the negotiations.

At bankruptcy, there are other claimants to the firm value. According to the priority rules, taxes owed to the government have the first claim. Then the wages and benefits of the workers have the second claim, which has a higher priority than the debt holders. The benefits to the employees can trigger the default of the firm. The mechanism of the trigger works as follows. When the pension fund is underfunded beyond a limit, the firm is obligated to inject more funding. When the firm fails to inject the funds, the pension liability can force to the firm to declare bankruptcy.

The *Pension Benefits Guarantee Corporation* (*PBGC*) is a federal government agency that insures private defined benefit pension plans. It can protect the pension liability by making the firm meet the obligations. It can also take over the pension plan and assume fiduciary duties. This decision depends on the negotiating positions of the firm and PBGC. Every firm in the plan has to pay insurance premiums to PBGC.

## 7.3   THE FISHER MODEL

All corporate bonds have credit risks. The distinction between the high-yield bonds and the investment grade bonds is based on their exposure levels to the default risk. To formulate a model of credit risk, we will begin with the investment grade bonds. As we discussed in the context of WMT 8.25, the size of the amount outstanding may affect the yield spread. Fisher (1959) provides some indications of the determinants of the yield spreads. The precise specification of the model can be updated because the debt market has changed beyond recognition since the 1960s. However, the basic idea provides important insights.

The model uses historical data and estimates the important factors that determine the bond yields. Both the independent and the dependent variables are expressed in natural log, where the dependent variable is the yield spread (the yield of the bond net the yield of the Treasury bond with a similar maturity). The independent variables are earnings variability, $X_1$, time without default, $X_2$, equity/debt ratio, $X_3$, and market value of debt, $X_4$.

$X_1$ = the ratio of standard deviation of the firm's net income to the average net income

$X_2$ = the number of years that the firm has been operating without a default

$X_3$ = the capitalization (market value of equity) to the par value of all the firm's debts

$X_4$ = the market value of the bond as a proxy for the marketability of the bond issue

$$\text{Yield spread} = 0.987 + 0.307X_1 - 0.253X_2 - 0.537X_3 - 0.275X_4 \qquad (7.2)$$

The coefficients of the model are estimated from the historical data. The model shows that the earnings variability adversely affects the bond value; a 1% increase in earnings variability would lead to a 0.307% increase in the yield spread. Similarly, other variables can be explained intuitively.

The model is useful to gain insight into the determinants of the bond yield spreads. It is also simple to derive and is intuitive in its explanation. Furthermore, it can provide us with a foundation from which to probe deeper into the valuation of a bond with credit risks. It can prompt us to further question the specifications of the valuation, leading us to a more comprehensive view of the model. For example, how should the probability of default be explicitly reflected in the valuation model? The next model provides a solution.

## 7.4   AN ACTUARIAL MODEL

A *default premium* is defined as the difference between the promised yield and the expected yield. Consider a bond maturing in a year with a promised payment of $100, but the expected payment is only $50. Assume the market is willing to pay $50 for the bond (in order to keep the arithmetic simple). This assumption is of course unrealistic, because the bond should be priced below the expected value for the time value of money, if not for risk premium. The *promised yield* is 100% and the expected yield is 0. The promised yield is the yield based on the promised coupon and principal payments. But as a result of default, the expected payments of the bonds may be less than the promised amount.

To begin the investigation of default experiences, we first describe the mortality of individuals in actuarial sciences. Mortality is analogous to a firm's default. For a given population, we first group the population by cohorts: female, male, smokers, nonsmokers. Then we collect the death experiences of the population. From the experiences, we can calculate the conditional probability of death and survival rate for each cohort of each age group. This compilation is called the *mortality table*. From it we can derive the risk of selling insurance to an individual.

The *actuarial approach* to default, proposed by Pye (1974), follows a similar argument. Of course, we have to stretch our imagination to think of a person as a bond or vice versa, since such an idea sounds preposterous. With a person, there is a biological factor; most mortality tables cease at age 100. Firms have no biological termination date, even if investors have an investment horizon of less than ten years for most practical purposes. The actuarial approach to bond valuation is not to model a bond as an individual, but to borrow the methodology of using historical data to help us forecast the future and price the default premium. The focus is on the methodology and not on the modeling or the assumptions of the model.

Here, we present a model similar to Pye's. The model assumes that the marginal probability of default each year is constant, $p_d$. In the event of default, the bondholders realize a proportion of the face value, $\lambda$, the recovery ratio. If there is no default, the bondholders receive the risk-free rate $r_f$ plus the default premium $\pi$. Since we want to relate the expected returns of bonds to the probability of default, we will first derive a model that assumes that the investors are risk-neutral and we do not have any risk premium. This way, the default premium is simply the expected loss of the bond due to default. We have

$$\frac{1}{1 + r_f + \pi} = \frac{p_d \cdot \lambda + (1 - p_d)}{1 + r_f} \tag{7.3}$$

By rearranging the terms, we have

$$\frac{1}{1 + r_f + \pi} = \frac{1 - (1 - \lambda) \cdot p_d}{1 + r_f} \tag{7.4}$$

Therefore, we have

$$1 + \frac{\pi}{(1 + r_f)} = \frac{1}{1 - (1 - \lambda) \cdot p_d} \tag{7.5}$$

To further simplify, we have

$$\pi = \frac{(1 + r_f) \cdot (1 - \lambda) \cdot p_d}{1 - (1 - \lambda) \cdot p_d} \tag{7.6}$$

This elegant model shows more precisely how the increase in probability of default or a lower recovery ratio would lead to higher default premium.

In comparison to the Fisher model, it is important to note that the Pye model focuses on the default premium. The observed yield spread, according to Fisher model, is also determined by the marketability and the investors' risk aversion. The actuarial model provides deeper insight into a component of the yield spread, and such insights can be very useful in deciding how reasonable the observed market option-adjusted spreads are. The Fisher model and the Pye model offer a baseline to measure whether the market is overestimating or underestimating the credit risks based on the observed level of the option-adjusted spreads.

## 7.5   HISTORICAL EXPERIENCE AND ESTIMATION OF THE PARAMETERS OF DEFAULT MODELS

### Default Rate and Mortality Rate

The actuarial model suggests that we need to estimate the probability of default and the recovery rate of a bond. One approach to determine the probability of default is to follow the methodology used in measuring the mortality rate of a person.

The most basic element of a mortality table is the death rate, measured by the number of deaths per 1,000 population. The first question we confront with bonds is how to measure the default rate. Unlike a person, where death is well defined, it is less clear how to measure bond default as an event. Should default (1) measure the proportion of the number of defaults (as events) at the end of the period against the total number of firms at the beginning of the period? Or (2) should it measure the face value of defaults in relation to the total amount of face value at the beginning of the period? For the measure of default rate, we have two possibilities.

If approach (1) is used, the default rate is influenced by many small debts. If approach (2) is used, the default rate is influenced by the experiences of large debt issues. Therefore the choice between the two approaches depends on the application. If the purpose of the model is to determine the likelihood of default of a sample of bonds, then approach (1) is preferred because the sample is based upon a cross section of firms and not biased by the large historical default cases. If the purpose of the model is to measure the default by the dollar amount of a bond portfolio that has a spectrum of bonds, including those of large corporations, approach (2) would be more applicable.

## Default Table

For the mortality table, we have the cumulative probability of default or the conditional probabilities. Cumulative probability measures the probability of a bond's surviving for a certain number of years. Given the cumulative probability, we can calculate the conditional probabilities, showing that likelihood of a default in one year is conditional on the firm surviving a certain number of years. These studies use extensive historical data and follow the "life cycle" of the bond from the day of issuance.

The time-series data (historical default data of the bonds outstanding in the market) are relatively short—because many bonds do not go into default—when compared with the mortality table. These default tables lack the extensive data that mortality tables have to support the results.

Similar to mortality tables, which group the subjects into categories by sex and habits, default tables group bond categories by the sectors of the markets (e.g., utilities, industrial, financial, and others). In addition, default tables can categorize bonds by their credit rating, which is similar to the measures of health levels in mortality tables.

The default table provides the probability of default as a function of the age of the bond and the bond rating at its issuance. It is comparable to a mortality table, although they have distinctive differences. They are both used to determine the probability of future experiences: default and death.

## Recovery Rates by Industry

The other estimate needed for the actuarial model is the *recovery ratio* or *recovery rate*. The recovery ratio is defined as the proportion of the amount received by the creditor emerging from bankruptcy to the par amount. The empirical results show that the recovery rate can vary significantly from one bond to another. As expected, the senior debt holders can receive more than the junior debt holders because they have higher priority claims to the firm's assets.

There are many measures of the recovery rate. We can observe it directly, since it is reported in bankruptcies. But this observation will be based on book value. For example, according to a workout plan, the bondholders may surrender $x\%$ of their claims. Then $(1 - x)$ is the recovery ratio and is based on the par value of the bonds. In order to measure value based on market valuation, some research suggests using trading prices one month after default as the recovery rate. The assumption behind this approach is that the value of the debt after the bankruptcy is the market-determined recovery to the creditor emerging from bankruptcy. Using a one-month lag enables the market to determine the equilibrium price such that the price is not affected by frictions in the market mechanism. For example, the illiquidity of trading of the bonds immediately after bankruptcy may lead to market quotes not reflecting the true market supply of and demand for the bond.

Altman and Kishore (1996) used twenty-five years of defaults in the United States to determine the recovery ratio to be 40% on average. The senior debt recovers 45% of the face value, while the junior debt recovers only 30%.[1] That means in the event of default that senior debt holders may lose about 55% of the par value, while the junior debt holders may lose over 70%. As the model indicates, these losses are not equal to some gains by other claimants. These losses mean that the firm value can no longer cover 100% of the original investments by the bondholders. In practice, the investors who provided the capital infusion for the reorganization of the firm may end up holding the majority of the firm's value as their condition for supplying the new capital.

The recovery ratio is shown to be related to the state of the economy. In particular, the recovery ratio is low at times of high GDP growth rate. One may argue that the debt holders are more willing to recover less in order to expedite the default procedure in a robust economy. The sooner the firm in default becomes operational, the higher the likelihood that it can repay the outstanding debt. Firms like utilities, with more stable income and tangible assets backing the long-term debt, tend to have higher recovery ratios.

There are many other factors affecting the recovery ratio, such as the direct bankruptcy costs. The higher the direct bankruptcy costs, the less the firm value can be allocated for the recovery. Warner (1977) reports that the direct cost of bankruptcy is 5% of the firm's value. Altman and Spivack (1983) estimated that the cost be 2–15%. Alderson and Betker (1995) show that the cost of reorganization is 13–62%, including indirect costs such as the loss of clients, termination of potentially profitable business, failing to exploit profitable new business opportunities because of the oversight of the bankruptcy court, and losing valuable human resources as some employees may leave the company. This shows that the direct cost alone has a large variation in its estimates, and the estimate of the indirect costs has even a wider margin for error.

Another important factor affecting the recovery ratio is the deviation from the absolute priority rule. When a significant portion of the value of the firm is required to pay for the management or new capital infusion, there is much less for the outstanding bondholders.

The last main reason for the variations of the recovery ratio is the specification of the bond covenant. The recovery rate should depend on how the covenant triggers default. Most trustees of the bonds do not declare the firm in default until it cannot meet its obligations. Also, they do not declare the firm in default based on forecasts of its ability to repay. For this reason, when a firm defaults, the recovery ratio depends on what is left for the bondholders at the time. We will revisit this view later, in the description of structural models. For the time being, let us assume that when the firm defaults, the bondholders recover a portion of the face value.

## Credit Risk Migration

The determination of credit risk migration depends on the use of historical data. Using historical data, we can also determine the probability of the rating's migration from one rating to the other. Using historical data this way is analogous to determining the likelihood of a person's health improving or deteriorating in one year. This is called the *transition matrix*. (See table 7.3.)

Consider the cell on the first row and the third column. The value 0.68 means that there is a probability of 0.68% that an AAA bond may lower the rating to A by the end of the year. Other entries of the matrix are defined similarly.

The example shows that the likelihood of a high-rating bond falling several notches down in one year is possible but not probable. The matrix is not symmetrical. That means that the likelihood of downgrading is not the same as that of upgrading.

The usefulness of the transition matrix is that if we perform a matrix multiplication of itself, the resulting matrix is the transition matrix for a two-year period. Another matrix multiplication would be for three years, and so on. Therefore, specifying a transition matrix over a period enables us to specify the transition matrix that can estimate a bond's rating shift over any time horizon. (See table 7.4.)

**Table 7.3** Transition Matrix

| Initial Rating | AAA | AA | A | BBB | BB | B | CCC | Default |
|---|---|---|---|---|---|---|---|---|
| AAA | 90.81 | 8.33 | 0.68 | 0.06 | 0.12 | 0.000 | 0.000 | 0.000 |
| AA | 0.70 | 90.65 | 7.79 | 0.64 | 0.06 | 0.14 | 0.02 | 0.00 |
| A | 0.09 | 2.27 | 91.05 | 5.52 | 0.74 | 0.26 | 0.01 | 0.06 |
| BBB | 0.02 | 0.33 | 5.95 | 86.93 | 5.30 | 1.17 | 0.12 | 0.18 |
| BB | 0.03 | 0.14 | 0.67 | 7.73 | 80.53 | 8.84 | 1.00 | 1.06 |
| B | 0.00 | 0.11 | 0.24 | 0.43 | 6.48 | 83.46 | 4.07 | 5.20 |
| CCC | 0.22 | 0.00 | 0.22 | 1.30 | 2.38 | 11.24 | 64.86 | 19.79 |
| Default | 0.00 | 0.00 | 0.00 | 0.00 | 0.00 | 0.00 | 0.00 | 100.00 |

Source: Standard and Poor's Credit Week, April 15, 1996.

**Table 7.4** Transition Matrix over One, Two, and Three Periods

Assume that the one-period transition matrix for AAA, AA, and others is

$$\Xi = \begin{bmatrix} 0.9081 & 0.0833 & 0.0086 \\ 0.0070 & 0.9065 & 0.0865 \\ 0.0849 & 0.0102 & 0.9049 \end{bmatrix}$$

Two-period transition matrix

$$\Xi\Xi = \begin{bmatrix} 0.825959 & 0.151244 & 0.022797 \\ 0.020050 & 0.823208 & 0.156746 \\ 0.153995 & 0.025548 & 0.820456 \end{bmatrix}$$

Three-period transition matrix

$$\Xi\Xi\Xi = \begin{bmatrix} 0.753047 & 0.206317 & 0.040815 \\ 0.037274 & 0.749506 & 0.213220 \\ 0.209679 & 0.044356 & 0.745968 \end{bmatrix}$$

We have modified the transition matrix to generate a multiperiod transition matrix. First, we derived a simplified one-period transition matrix from the original transition matrix. We chose AAA and AA, and put other ratings into the Others category. The probability of other ratings would be 1 − Prob(AAA) − Prob(AA). Once we have the 3 × 3 simplified one-period transition matrix, we can calculate the two-period transition matrix by squaring the one-period transition matrix. We can calculate the three-period transition matrix by multiplying the one-period transition matrix by the two-period transition matrix. 0.825959 at the northwest corner of the two-period transition matrix represents that AAA firms will remain in the same AAA category in two years with the probability of 82.5959%. The other numbers can be interpreted in similar ways.

For illustration purposes, we derived a simplified one-period transition matrix from the original transition matrix. We chose AAA and AA and put other ratings into the Others category. The probability of other ratings would be $1 - \text{Prob}(AAA) - \text{Prob}(AA)$. Once we have the $3 \times 3$ simplified one-period transition matrix, we can calculate the two-period transition matrix by squaring the one-period transition matrix. We can calculate the three-period transition matrix by multiplying the one-period transition matrix by the two-period transition matrix. 0.825959 at the northwest corner of the two-period transition matrix represents that AAA firms will remain in the same category in two years with the probability of 82.5959 percent. The other numbers can be interpreted in similar ways.

Underlying this property is the assumption that the one-period transition matrix is Markov, meaning that the matrix measures the probability of future rating changes, and these probabilities have no memories independent of the rating of the bonds' previous years. This property is not supported by the empirical observations of Altman and Kao (1992). But the use of the transition matrix can be a practical approximation.

## 7.6   THE REDUCED-FORM MODELS

Based on the historical estimates of the probability of default and the recovery ratio, we can now formulate valuation models that extend from the Pye (actuarial) model. To begin, the Pye model is static. Given the probabilities, we can calculate the expected values. The model does not specify any stochastic process, which enables us to measure the risk and returns over a time horizon.

The Jarrow-Turnbull model (1995) assumes that default is an event. The mathematical formulation used to study default as an event is similar to that which is used to study the durability of a lightbulb. The lightbulb has a finite life. The death of a lightbulb is an event. Measurements can be made to determine the average life span of a lightbulb, but the event can occur at any time. The mathematical model for such a stochastic process is called Poisson jumps. Jarrow and Turnbull use Poisson jumps to develop the model of the behavior of a bond, assuming risk-neutral pricing.

The model can be expressed quite simply as

$$B(t, T) = P(t, T)\left[(1 - p_d(t, T)) + p_d(t, T)\lambda\right] \tag{7.7}$$

By rearranging, we derive

$$B(t, T) = P(t, T) - P(t, T)(1 - \lambda)p_d(t, T) \tag{7.8}$$

where $B(t, T)$ and $P(t, T)$ are the bond values at time $t$ and with maturity $T$, with default risk and without default risk, respectively. $p_d(t, T)$ is the probability of default at time $t$ for a bond with maturity $T$, and $\lambda$ is the recovery rate.

The usefulness of the model clearly lies in its simplicity, making full use of the historical estimates of the recovery ratios and probability of default. The mathematics of the Poisson process is then used to determine the bond value distribution and the bond returns process. The simplicity enables us to understand the implications of the default risks and the losses from default on the bond valuation.

The Jarrow-Lando-Turnbull model (JLT, 1997) incorporates the transition matrix into the bond valuation model. The idea is the same as the Jarrow-Turnbull model in modeling default as an event, but instead of using a mathematical description of the likelihood of a default, the JLT model uses the transition matrix to solve for the default event. This extension enables us to view the transition of the rating changes as a process that leads to default. In doing so, we can make use of the additional information of the estimation of the credit transition matrices and provide additional information on the bond value via the bond rating changes. Specifically, the rating transition matrix can be used in two ways. For a given bond of a certain rating, we can determine the probability of reaching rating D (default) in one year. Once we square the one-period transition matrix, we can determine the probability of default in two years. If we continue this process, we can determine all the conditional probabilities of default over the life of the bond.

Another approach is to use the transition matrices to determine the probability distribution of the ratings of a bond with a certain initial rating. By noting the option-adjusted spread for each rating group, we can then calculate the bond value over the time horizon for the given attained rating. Therefore, we have a distribution of the bond values. This approach enables us to determine the risk of the bond over a horizon. This method is then used to calculate the bond value at risk (VaR).

The Duffie-Singleton model (1999) extends the JLT model to incorporate stochastic spreads. This model further assumes that the market price of risk of default also changes stochastically. Therefore, instead of discounting the uncertain bond payments (as a result of default) at a risk-free rate, the Duffie-Singleton model assumes this discount rate is also stochastic. This extension can incorporate all the uncertain factors that drive the risk of a bond with credit risks.

Thus far, we can see that the models find their roots in the actuarial models, driven by the parameters estimated from historical data. However, the use of financial theory, like option pricing and capital structure models, is limited. The models are not used in any direct and important way. The default is exogenously specified, and the firm's uncertain value follows a specified process. Default is reduced to an event determined by a process without any agents' optimal decisions, providing a simple modeling approach to default, but perhaps unable to capture some of the economics of default in depicting the agents' optimal decisions.

The Ericsson-Reneby (2002) model incorporates firm risk more explicitly than the models described thus far. It considers the equity of a firm as a knockout option on the firm's value. The underlying asset of the knockout option is the value of the firm. The debt is then the firm's value net of the equity. Or the debt can be the knock-in option. In previous models, there is no default trigger point. The Ericsson-Reneby model assumes that the bond covenant has an explicit default trigger point, driven by the risk of the firm's value, and that there is a specified default trigger value or strike price of the knockout options. Whenever the firm's value falls below the default trigger value, the equity holders will be given a call option on the firm's value at the expiration with the strike price of the face value of the debt. The use of the default trigger point leads to the possibility of the firm's defaulting before the maturity of the bonds.

These models are called *reduced-form models* because they relate the bond value to historical estimates and do not depend on detailed information on the firm: its capital structure, the bond covenants, size of issues, and so on. They do not endogenize the recovery rate but use the historical estimates as given. They are driven by historical data and therefore cannot distinguish one firm from another. The strengths of these models are in their simplicity and tractability. We can use historical data to price the bonds, but the simplicity comes with a cost. Much of the information on the firm is not incorporated in the valuation. These methods are useful for pricing default risks when there is not very much information on the firm, or when there is a large portfolio analysis where a relatively rough estimate of the value of each bond is sufficient.

## 7.7  THE STRUCTURAL MODELS

In contrast to the reduced-form model, the *structural model* is concerned with relating the bond value to the firm's business risk and its capital and debt structures, at the time of evaluating the bond. Structural models provide a detailed financial modeling of credit risks of a debt, spelling out more precisely the determinants of its value or of the recovery ratios and probability of defaults.

The Merton model (1974) provides the foundation of this approach. It applies the Black-Scholes model to corporate bond pricing. Beyond the perfect capital market assumption, valuing the corporate debt with credit risk requires further assumptions on the corporation's financial policy. This approach does not require the investors to know the profitability of the firm and its market-expected rate of return; we need to know only the firm's value. Using a relative valuation approach, the firm's profitability and other attributes are captured by the firm's value.

The following assumptions are made:

1. There is no interest rate risk, with a constant risk-free rate of $r$. We will see that this assumption can be relaxed in a straightforward manner.
2. The firm's value $V$ follows a lognormal process with an annualized volatility $\sigma_V$, for simplicity in an arbitrage-free binomial lattice, with $m$ steps per year.
3. The firm pays a dividend at a portion of its firm value.
4. The debt structure is a zero-coupon bond with maturity $T$, and therefore the number of steps of the lattice is $n = T \times m$, where $m$ is the number of steps per year.
5. Default is reorganization, not liquidation. At default, the bondholders take over the firm from the equity holder.
6. The firm is in default when the equity value is 0.
7. The bondholders take over the firm with no bankruptcy costs.
8. The firm value is independent of the capital structure and financial policies. Therefore, the firm value can be kept independent from the default and bond valuation (according to the Miller-Modigliani theory).

The Merton model asserts that the equity holder has the option to own the firm where the exercise price $F$ is the face value at time $T$. Then, following the notations of chapter 2, we have

Cox-Ross-Rubinstein model:

$$S = \frac{1}{e^{rT}} \sum_{i=0}^{n} Max \left[ Vu^i d^{n-i} - F, 0 \right] \binom{n}{i} p^i (1-p)^{n-i} \tag{7.9}$$

$$u = \exp\left\{ \sigma \sqrt{\frac{1}{m}} \right\}, d = \frac{1}{u}, p = \frac{\exp[\frac{r}{m}] - d}{u - d}$$

$S$ is the capitalization of the firm or the shareholders' value, and $V$ is the firm value. $F$ is the face value of the debt. The bond value $D$ is the firm value net of the capitalization value, that is,

$$D = V - S \qquad (7.10)$$

The crux of the model assumptions is a perfect capital market. The firm value can be assumed to follow a lognormal stochastic process, and its value is not affected by the level of debt. All financial claims on the firm, such as stocks and bonds, are contingent claims on the firm value.

The model suggests that the stock of the levered firm should behave like a stock option, and the bond is a portfolio of longing a risk-free bond and shorting a put option. Using the contingent claim valuation approach, the model can determine the appropriate discount rate for the credit risk, using the valuation of the firm. Specifically, a bond is viewed as

$$\text{defaultable bond} = \text{risk-free bond} - \text{put option on the firm} \qquad (7.11)$$

Since this is a contingent claim valuation model, the valuation approach depends on the price and not on the discount rate. Instead of focusing on the appropriate yield spread, we now turn to the valuation of the put option.

Another important departure from the other models is that the recovery rate is stochastic and endogenized. We can no longer assume that the recovery rate is a historical observation that can be applied to all the bonds in a certain group. The recovery ratio in a structural model is uncertain, depending on the outcome. According to the Merton model, the recovery ratio is the firm's value at default on the day of the maturity of the bond. More precisely, when the firm's value is below the bond face value on the maturity date, the debt holders receive only the remaining firm value, which is uncertain at any time before the maturity date. The recovery rate for each industry must depend on the debt structure of its sector.

Given the model assumptions and the mechanism used to describe the valuation of an option, the valuation of a bond according to the Merton model is straightforward. We can use the backward substitution approach on a binomial lattice. This approach enables us to incorporate other bond features, such as the call and sinking fund provisions, into the model. The structural model proposes that a bond is holding a short position in a put option. This approach enables us to value many items on the balance sheet and on corporate securities. An important contribution of the structural model is its ability to integrate the firm's risk to the bond valuation, and solve for the default trigger points using the option pricing theory. Much subsequent research has sought to exploit this insight.

The Black-Cox model uses the Merton model to study the valuation of junior and senior debts according to the absolute priority rule. They wanted to study the allocation of risk among the classes of bonds. In order to do so, they had to view all the classes of claims as options on the firm value with different payments at maturity. The risk-neutral pricing approach (or the relative valuation approach) enabled them to solve for the appropriate value of each claim on the firm value, relative to the firm value. If the discounted cash flow method is used, we will have to calculate the expected payment for each claimant and determine the appropriate discount rate for each claim, given its risks. Without a framework to determine the relationship between the risk and the market risk premium, we cannot evaluate the allocation of risk and value to all the claimants to the firm value. This is exactly what a relative valuation framework seeks to accomplish.

There are many extensions of the models. Most of these models introduce stochastic interest rates. These extensions are motivated by the empirical evidence demonstrating that the shapes of the yield curve and interest rate levels are important factors relating to the number of defaults.

For example, Shimko et al. (1993) developed a model with stochastic interest rates using the Vasicek (1977) normal interest rate model in specifying the short-term interest rates. The credit spreads of the bonds can be derived from the model, and they found that the credit spreads increase with the interest rate volatility, as well as when there is a correlation between the interest rate risks and the firm value risk. This model result can be explained intuitively. When there is interest rate risk, especially when the interest rate risk is positively correlated with the firm value risk, the defaultable bond's embedded option value will increase, leading to a higher credit spread.

These models assume that default occurs only when the firm cannot meet its debt obligations. Since these models also assume that debt is a zero-coupon bond with only one payment, then the firm can default at only one time—bond maturity. This requirement is unpleasant because many defaults do not happen only at the maturities of the bonds. Often the bondholders are protected by *safety covenants* written in the bond indenture. These safety covenants protect the bondholders for the life of the bond by conditions that trigger the firm to accelerate the principal payments to the bondholders. For example, some of the firm's financial ratios cannot fall below certain criteria—for instance, the debt ratio cannot exceed a certain level or the market capitalization cannot be lower than some number. The following models assume a default trigger barrier where the firms default whenever they hit the barrier. The Longstaff-Schwartz model (1995, p. 792, assumption 4) allows the firm to default whenever its value falls below a barrier $K(t)$. This approach combines the Merton model with the default trigger approach. This way, they could use the estimated recovery ratio and did not have to assume default is triggered at maturity and there is no default before maturity.

Saá-Requejo and Santa-Clara (1999) allow for stochastic strike price $X$, and Briys and de Varenne (1997) allow the barrier to be related to the market value of debt. In a way, these models are similar to the reduced-form model of Ericsson and Reneby, in that the default condition is almost specified by the model, particularly the barrier $K(t)$, and less by the debt structure of the firm, the interactions of the shareholders' optimal strategy in declaring default, and the bondholders' ability to protect their investments.

Therefore, these models consider a defaultable bond to be a portfolio of risk-free bonds net of a barrier option.

$$\text{defaultable bond} = \text{risk-free bond} - \text{barrier option}$$

By contrast, the Kim-Ramaswamy-Sundaresan model (1993) allows for stochastic interest rates, and the bondholders get a portion of the face value at default. The bankruptcy condition is based on the lack of cash flow to meet obligations. They define the default trigger point as a net cash flow at the boundary, when the firm cannot pay the interest and dividend. Their assumption is motivated by the observed default experience and tends to be triggered by the lack of cash flow to meet the debt obligations.

Specifically, they assume that at default, the bondholders receive $Min[\delta(t), B_t, V^*]$, where $B_t$ is the value of an otherwise identical bond, $V^*$ is the value of the firm at the time of default, and it is specified by a lognormal binomial lattice of a firm value $V(n, i)$ for time $n$ and state $i$, and $\delta(t)$ is a discount of the risk-free bond value. The most important contribution of the model is the use of the free cash flows of the firm. The model assumes that the free cash flow generated by the firm at each node is a constant fraction of the firm value. Therefore, the free cash flow $f(n, i)$ is given by

$$f(n, i) = \beta \cdot V(n, i) \text{ where } \beta \text{ is a constant}$$

The default trigger is specified by $f(n, i) < c(n, i)$, where $c(n, i)$ is the coupon payment on the debt at time $n$ and state $i$. Therefore the cash flow to the bondholders at each time and state (each node point on the lattice) is defined. Using the backward substitution approach and the risk-neutral probability, we can determine the bond value. Since the recovery rate depends on the negotiation in default, debt holders should not receive the full amount. Leland (1994) develops a model that seeks to determine the default boundary $X(V < X)$ by incorporating the negotiation model to solve for the optimal decision of the shareholders in declaring bankruptcy.

As we have seen in earlier chapters, integrating interest rate risks to the stock risk in a binomial lattice is fairly straightforward. Most of these models seek to analyze the bond behavior under interest rate risks not by simulations but by analytical solutions. Therefore, they need to simplify the interest rate process so that they can determine tractable solutions to the problems. Thus they tend to use normal interest rate models.

For some of the models, the link between the firm's capital structure and the risk of the bond default is the measure of the likelihood of a knockout event as the firm's value reaches the default trigger boundary. The link is rather tenuous, and the distinction between the structural model and the reduced-form models becomes blurred. The following models are more consistent with the spirit of a structural model. They do not assume a default trigger barrier and a recovery ratio.

## 7.8  VALUATION OF A DEBT PACKAGE USING A COMPOUND OPTION MODEL

Geske (1977) and Geske and Johnson (1984) show that the equity of a firm with a coupon-paying bond or a bond with a sinking fund is a compound option. In order to analyze the risk of a bond, we have to value the debt package first. Because of the cross-default clause, any bond risk has to be considered within the context of the debt package.

The description of all the bonds, their covenants, their provisions, and their maturities, is called a debt structure. The argument shows that in order to understand the default risk of a bond, we need to know the entire debt structure. This is clear from the default process and the prevalent use of the cross-default clause in the bond covenant. From the bond package, we can determine the promised cash flows of the entire debt structure, including the coupon payments.

When the firm is obligated to pay the first payment of the debt, which may be the coupon, the principal, or both, we assume that the firm cannot sell its capital assets or use its liquid financial assets to meet the obligation. Instead, the firm must go to the capital market to raise either equity or debt to finance the payments. When the firm uses capital to finance the first payment, the ability to raise the needed amount has to depend on the total debt outstanding. If the present value of debt outstanding plus the first payment is higher than the firm value, then the equity holder will declare the firm in default. The shareholders will not be able to raise the capital via equity market or to refinance the payment with another debt. This argument applies to the following payment and to all subsequent payments. As a result, the equity is a compound option on the firm value. Each bond payment, coupon or principal, is the strike price of a call option to buy another option.

When an equity is viewed as a compound option, the firm can default before the maturity and the default is triggered by a cash obligation, similar to the Kim-Ramaswamy-Sundaresan model. But the firm value can exceed (and usually does exceed) the cash requirement in the compound option model. The firm declares default because the remaining debt forbids it to raise more capital to meet the immediate obligations. This is an important distinction because the compound option approach in fact models the recovery ratio by showing how the design of the debt structure—the payment schedules—affects the probability of default and the recovery ratio. More important, the model closely resembles the way firms generally declare defaults.

By way of contrast, a model using knockout options relies on bonds having protective covenants, which require the firm to declare default as soon as some market value measure (for example, capitalization value) falls below some book value. Such bond covenants do not seem to be widely used or enforced.

## Valuing a Debt Within a Debt Structure

Ho and Singer (1982) extend the concept of the structural model of a bond to a package of bonds where the implications of the absolute priority rules are analyzed. The relative values of the junior and senior debt are affected by three confounding factors: priority rules, the term structure of credit risk, and the coupon level.

To study the impact of the debt structure on the bond valuation, Ho and Singer retain all the assumptions made in the Merton model, except that they modify the assumption on the debt structure. The assumptions made about the debt structure are the following:

1. The debt structure has two zero-coupon bonds: a long-term bond with maturity $T_L$ and face value $F_L$, and a short-term bond with maturity $T_s$ and face value $F_s$.
2. The bond covenant specifies that the senior debt has the absolute priority to take over the firm's assets or value at the time of default. And there are two possible cases: (a) The long-term debt is senior to the short-term debt and (b) the short-term debt is senior to the long term-debt.

When bonds are in the same class in the capital structure, at bankruptcy they are paid according to their proportion of face value. However, when the absolute priority rule applies, the credit risks for the senior debt holders and the junior debt holders are different, and risk is further complicated by their maturities.

Under the absolute priority rule, the senior debt valuation would consider both the junior debt and the equity as one class. The presence of junior debt should not affect the senior debt value. Thus, the value of the senior debt can be valued as "debt" and the package of the junior debt and equity can be considered "equity." We can then apply the compound option model to determine the debt and equity values of the firm, and the senior debt value can be determined

Specifically, let us consider the case where the long-term debt is senior to the short-term debt. In this case, the long-term debt valuation can ignore the presence of the short-term debt because, from the perspective of the long-term debt holders, the junior debt holders and the equity holders belong to the same class of claimants in the event of default—both junior to them. For this reason, the long-term debt value is given by using equations (7.9) and (7.10):

$D$ (senior long-term) $=$

$$V - \frac{1}{e^{r \cdot T_L}} \sum_{i=0}^{T_L} Max \left[ V u^i d^{T_L-i} - F_L, 0 \right] \binom{T_L}{i} p^i (1-p)^{T_L-i} \qquad (7.12)$$

To determine the junior debt value, we consider the package of the senior debt and junior debt as "debt" and the equity as "equity" in the compound option model. This valuation enables us to determine the value of the portfolio of senior and junior debt. Then the junior debt can be valued as the debt package value net of the senior debt value.

Specifically, in this case, first we need to determine the value of the debt package, using Geske's compound option model. At time $T_S$ and state $k$, the capitalization value (the shareholders' value) before the short-term debt payment is given by (see figure 7.1)

$$S_k^* = \frac{1}{e^{r \cdot (T_L - T_S)}} \sum_{i=k}^{k+(T_L-T_S)} Max \left[ V u^i d^{T_L-i} - F_L, 0 \right] \binom{T_L}{i} p^i (1-p)^{T_L-i} \qquad (7.13)$$

The firm will default if the capitalization is negative after paying for the short-term debt face value. Therefore the shareholders' value should be

$$S_k = Max \left[ S_k^* - F_S, 0 \right] \qquad (7.14)$$

Given this terminal condition for the shareholders' value and using the backward substitution, we can determine the shareholders' value, $S$, given by

$$S = \frac{1}{e^{r \cdot T_S}} \sum_{k=0}^{T_S} S_k \binom{T_S}{i} p^k (1-p)^{T_S-k} \qquad (7.15)$$

Therefore the value of the debt package is

$$D \text{ (debt package)} = V - S \qquad (7.16)$$

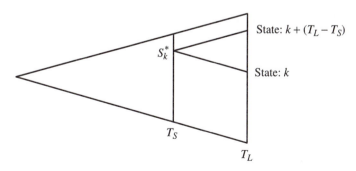

**Figure 7.1** The capitalization value at state $k$ and time $T_S$. $T_L$ is a maturity date of the senior long-term bond. $T_S$ is a maturity date of the junior short-term bond. $S_k^*$ is the stock value at $T_S$ after the stockholders exercise their option at $T_L$. Therefore $S_k^*$ is the expected value over the terminal conditions from state $k$ to state $k + (T_L - T_S)$ at $T_L$, discounted at the risk-free rate for the period between $T_L$ and $T_S$.

But the debt package value must be the sum of the senior and junior debt. Therefore, the junior short-term debt is given by

$$D\ (junior\ short\ term) = D\ (debt\ package) - D\ (senior\ long\text{-}term) \qquad (7.17)$$

To understand the impact of these factors on the bond value, let us consider the case when we have junior short-term debt and senior long-term debt. For illustrative purposes, let us assume that there are priority rules in the McLeodUSA bonds. This assumption is made for illustrative purposes—the actual bonds do not have such priority rules. We then study the bond values as the firm value increases from 0 to a high value of $3 billion. Let us consider three segments in this spectrum of the firm values. (See figure 7.2.)

When the firm value is low relative to the face value of the debt, the default risk is significant. The senior debt must have a lower risk than the junior debt. When the firm value increases, the probability of default of the short-term debt decreases faster than that of the long-term debt. The short-term debt being senior to the long-term debt, the default risk of the short-term debt is allocated to the long-term debt. When the value of the firm becomes high, the long-term debt increases its value more rapidly.

By this argument, we can see that if the long-term debt is junior to the short-term debt, then the long-term bond should always have a higher risk than the short-term bond. On the other hand, if the long-term bond is senior to the short-term bond, then the risk allocation between the long-term bond and short-term bond is more complicated.

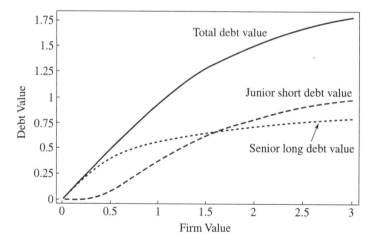

**Figure 7.2** Profile of short-term junior and long-term senior debt. The total face values of the long-term bonds and the short-term bonds are 1.175 and 0.781, respectively. We assume that the junior short bonds have a time to maturity of 9, 13.5, 21.5, and 25.5 months, and the senior long bonds have a time to maturity of 89, 91, 92.5, and 95 months. We assume the time to maturities of the bonds as above in order to have a big gap between two maturities for illustration purposes. One interesting result of the simulation is that when the firm value increases from 0 to 0.2, the senior debt takes most of the increase. The junior debt has a positive gamma and then a negative gamma as the firm value increases.

The complication arises because default risk increases with the term to maturity. But when the long-term debt is senior to the short-term debt, part of the default risk is allocated to the short-term debt. The short-term debt may have significant default risk when the firm value is low, as depicted in figure 7.2, for the firm value less than 0.2. As the firm value increases, the short-term debt value increases slowly relative to the senior long-term debt, as depicted by the firm value ranging from 0.2 to 1 in figure 7.2. Only when the firm value becomes high does the short-term debt value increase rapidly.

Most corporations have a debt structure in which the short-term debts have priority over the long-term debt. Bank loans and other short-term financing are usually secured, while the debentures tend to be longer terms with lower priority. In the presence of a large amount of debentures outstanding relative to its value, the firm may not be able to roll over bank loans or other short-term financing even though its total capitalization value exceeds the immediate obligation payments. This is because the firm will default if its value net of the long-term debt value is less than the immediate obligated payments. In other words, the first option of a compound option may expire out of the money. This is the evidence of the validity of the use of compound options to value the debt in order to capture the impact of long-term bonds on the short-term financing capacity of a firm.

However, long-term debt can be senior to short-term debt. In section 7.2, we described the rule at the bankruptcy court. In this rule, the pension liability has a higher priority than the debt of the firm. Since the pension liability has much longer maturity, the debts should be considered junior obligations to the pension liabilities. Also, the fixed cost of an ongoing concern can be viewed as a perpetual senior debt. With a significant presence of fixed costs, both the bonds, which are junior to the fixed costs, and the equity can be greatly affected. In this case, the debt has positive gamma that turns into negative gamma as the firm's value increases.

# EXCEL MODEL EXERCISES

## E7.1   CREDIT DEFAULT SWAP

### Definitions

The face value of the bond is the principal payment of the bond obligation of the firm. The firm value is the sum of the equity and bond values of the firm. The credit default swap (CDS) notional amount is the payment of the CDS in the event of a default. The premium of the CDS is the annual payment for the tenor of the swap. There are other payment arrangements in CDS. We have chosen the simplest one (though less common) for illustration.

### Description of the Model

The model is a binomial lattice model of the Merton model in pricing a corporate bond. In a perfect capital market framework, the equity of the firm with a coupon bond is considered a compound option. The credit default swap specifies the payments at each node point on the lattice.

| Inputs | | | | |
|---|---|---|---|---|
| Face value of bond | 100 | | | |
| Bond maturity | 10 | | | |
| Coupon rate | 0.08 | Coupons are paid annually. | | |
| Firm value | 300 | | | |
| Firm volatility | 0.4 | | | |
| Risk-free rate | 0.06 | | | |
| Swap termination (year) | 10 | Swap termination year ≤ 10 | | |
| Amount | 5 | | | |
| | | | | |
| Upward jump size | 1.4918 | | | |
| p | 0.4766 | | | |
| 1-p | 0.5234 | | | |
| Outputs | | | | |
| | | | | |
| Swap termination (year) | | | 5 | 10 |
| Annual premium of CDS | 0.125337 | 0.0706 | 0.1253 | |
| Premium is defined as the annual payment for the CDS for the tenor of the swap. | | | | |

**Figure E7.1**

## Numerical Example

Let the firm value be $300 million with a volatility of 40%. Suppose that the firm has only one debt, ten-year maturity with an 8% coupon rate and par $100 million. The credit default swap pays $5 million in the event of a default. Then the ten-year- and five-year-tenor swaps have premiums of $0.1253 million and $0.0706 million respectively. See figure E7.1.

## Application

The model values the credit default swap (CDS).

## Case: Credit Derivatives, Insurance Premiums, and Callable Bonds

Ho Sangbin was the portfolio manager of a pension fund. Credit risk was always a great concern to pension fund managers. The corporate accounts that provided him the funds to manage required all corporate papers in the portfolio to be investment grade. But if there were downgrades, he may be forced to sell the bonds at a discounted price because of the market illiquidity. Therefore, he was always concerned about evaluating the risks. An analyst and the sales representative from the sell-side firm that trades with Sangbin came by to discuss some ideas on managing the credit risk exposure in his portfolio. The topic of the meeting was around credit default swap.

"Sangbin, we have looked at your portfolio." "John, I am sure you have. You sold me some of those bonds. What can you do for me?" "I know you are worried about your credit risk exposure. I got Mandisa here to explain our product CDS." "Well, Mandisa, you know my problem, right? When any one of my bonds becomes a fallen angel, I have to sell it. When I book the loss, they scream at me or fire me. So what can you do for me?"

Mandisa pulled out the colorful charts and explained that a CDS was like an insurance for Sangbin. He paid an insurance premium to her firm. Whenever there was a default event, Sangbin would exchange the bond for the principal in cash with her firm. Given this insurance, there was no need for Sangbin to sell his fallen angels. "This is really simple. Just like the way we buy life insurance—pay your premiums until you die. If you do not die over the term of the contract, you just pay your insurance and are glad that you are alive." "Mandisa, when did you become an insurance agent?" Everyone chuckled.

"Well there is one problem." "Which is?" "What keeps me awake these days is the looming recession. This cycle of strong economic performance will run out of steam. Then we may go into a long recession." Sangbin paused to sip his tea and continued. "If a bond becomes a fallen angel or a firm goes default, I will get shouted at. But in a recession, if a number of my bonds have problems, I will get hell. A recession is what keeps me awake at night." "I do not understand. You can have insurance for all your bonds. We handle your entire portfolio."

"But this is not what I mean. In a recession, many of my bonds may get into trouble, and you give me the principals. But with a recession, interest rates tend also to be very low. Now I have to reinvest my money at low interest rates. Basically, I have a prepayment arrangement with you as in the mortgage market. In this CDS, I have sold some interest rate option to you."

The sales representative looked really puzzled. "Sangbin, we are not talking about callable bonds here, are we? We are not talking about mortgages here either."

Sangbin said: "I know. My life insurance is not related to interest rate level because I do not think I die when interest rates are low. But the CDS pays me in all likelihood in a low interest rate regime. You pay me cash at the time when interest rates are low. That is my problem." Mandisa calmly said: "John, I understand you. You have 'sold' an interest rate option to us as they do in mortgages. But we also reflect that in your insurance premium—I mean the CDS payment. The CDS payments are lowered for the embedded option value." "Then I will have to check that with our in-house model to measure the discount," said Sangbin as he was concluding the meeting. "How do we price our CDS with embedded interest rate option?" the sales representative asked Mandisa quietly as they walked out.

*"John, I will explain that to you when we get back to the office. I will start with an interest rate model, and I will show you what happens to Sangbin's portfolio when we have a recession. OK?" "Sure. No math though. I just need to know the basic idea and why our CDS is related to mortgages and callable bonds." "I know."*

## Exercises and Answers

1. Given the above numerical example assumptions, what is the premium of a CDS if the swap amount is $1? (Hint: use an arbitrage argument to determine the value without using the model.)

   *Answer:* Since the premium of the ten-year CDS, which pays $5 million in the event of a default, is 0.1253, the premium of the ten-year CDS, which pays $1 million,

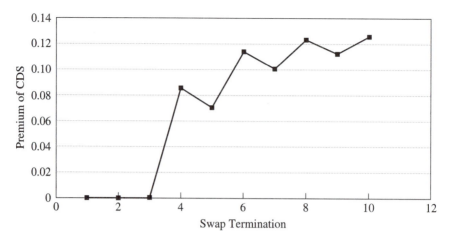

**Figure E7.2**

should be one-fifth of 0.1253. Otherwise we have an arbitrage opportunity. For example, if the price is less than one-fifth of 0.1253, we can buy five units of the CDS to have the same cash flow at the default with less price.

2. What is the premium of the CDS for a nine-year tenor?
   *Answer:* The premium of the CDS for a nine-year tenor is 0.112671. The premium of the CDS increases as the swap tenor lengthens. See figure E7.2.

3. Use the binomial lattice framework to value the coupon bond described in the numerical example. Determine the amount of the risk-free bond and the risky bond that a trader would use to dynamically hedge the ten-year-tenor CDS.
   *Answer:* We calculate the amount of the risk-free bond and the risky bond to duplicate CDS; see figure E7.3. For example, if we long 0.0904028 risk-free bonds and short 0.090099 risky bonds at the initial node, we can duplicate the CDS value at the upward state and the downward state of year 1. However, since the self-financing condition does not satisfy the above CDS lattice, we can say that we cannot duplicate the CDS with the risk-free bonds and the risky bonds.

## Further Exercises

1. Let the firm value be $300 million with a volatility of 30%. Suppose that the firm has only one debt, ten-year maturity with an 8% coupon rate and par $100 million. The CDS pays $5 million in the event of a default. Note that we assume the volatility of 40% in the numerical example. We have the same input data as the numerical example except for the volatility. Calculate the premiums of the ten-year- and five-year-tenor swaps. Interpret how the volatility decrease affects the premiums.
   *Answer:* See figures E7.4 and E7.5.

2. In question 1, we calculate the ten-year and five-year swaps. Calculate the premiums of the nine-year and seven-year CDS to see the effect of the tenor on CDS pricing.
   *Answer:* See figure E7.6.

$$\beta = (CDS_u - CDS_d)/(DB_u - DB_d)$$

| Time | 0 | 1 | 2 | 3 | 4 | 5 | 6 | 7 | 8 | 9 | 10 |
|---|---|---|---|---|---|---|---|---|---|---|---|
| | | | | | | | | | N/A | N/A | |
| | | | | | | | | N/A | N/A | N/A | |
| | | | | | | N/A | N/A | N/A | N/A | N/A | |
| | | | | | N/A | N/A | N/A | N/A | N/A | N/A | |
| | | | | -0.105416 | -0.105416 | -0.105416 | -0.105416 | -0.105416 | -0.105416 | -0.105416 | |
| | | | -0.101223 | -0.100682 | -0.099981 | -0.099037 | -0.097695 | -0.095639 | -0.055185 | 0 | |
| | | -0.096052 | -0.094794 | -0.093176 | -0.091037 | -0.08811 | -0.046862 | 0 | 0 | 0 | |
| | -0.090099 | -0.088095 | -0.085606 | -0.082492 | -0.042355 | 0 | 0 | 0 | 0 | 0 | |

$$\alpha = (CDS_d \cdot DB_u - CDS_u \cdot DB_d)/((DB_u - DB_d) \cdot CB_u)$$

| Time | 0 | 1 | 2 | 3 | 4 | 5 | 6 | 7 | 8 | 9 | 10 |
|---|---|---|---|---|---|---|---|---|---|---|---|
| | | | | | | | | | N/A | N/A | |
| | | | | | | | | N/A | N/A | N/A | |
| | | | | | | N/A | N/A | N/A | N/A | N/A | |
| | | | | | N/A | N/A | N/A | N/A | N/A | N/A | |
| | | | | 0.1054162 | 0.1054162 | 0.1054162 | 0.1054162 | 0.1054162 | 0.1054162 | 0.1054162 | |
| | | | 0.101235 | 0.1007099 | 0.1000464 | 0.0991935 | 0.0980842 | 0.0966512 | 0.0658908 | 0.0462963 | |
| | | 0.0961339 | 0.0949699 | 0.0935571 | 0.0918667 | 0.0899391 | 0.0608987 | 0.0447761 | 0.0455014 | 0.0462963 | |
| | 0.0904028 | 0.0886973 | 0.0867982 | 0.0848347 | 0.0577165 | 0.0435047 | 0.0441127 | 0.0447761 | 0.0455014 | 0.0462963 | |

$$CDS = \alpha CB_u + \beta DB_u$$

| Time | 0 | 1 | 2 | 3 | 4 | 5 | 6 | 7 | 8 | 9 | 10 |
|---|---|---|---|---|---|---|---|---|---|---|---|
| | | | | | | | | | N/A | N/A | |
| | | | | | | | | N/A | N/A | N/A | |
| | | | | | | N/A | N/A | N/A | N/A | N/A | |
| | | | | | N/A | N/A | N/A | N/A | N/A | N/A | |
| | | | | 3.4142799 | 4.2356189 | 5.0650184 | 5.0698828 | 5.0751897 | 5.0809921 | 5.0873515 | |
| | | | 2.2572101 | 1.273031 | 2.0675435 | 3.2750901 | 4.1607184 | 4.1607184 | 5.0809921 | 5.0873515 | |
| | | 1.4592554 | 0.767766 | 0.3099393 | 0.5617548 | 1.0041934 | 1.7635677 | 3.0251737 | 4.0153385 | 5.0873515 | |
| | 0.9224899 | 0.4550714 | 0.169122 | 0.0357894 | 0.0724792 | 0.1467821 | 0.2972572 | 0.6019935 | 1.2191333 | 2.4689404 | |

Figure E7.3

| Outputs | | | |
|---|---|---|---|
| Swap termination (year) | | 5 | 10 |
| Annual premium of CDS | 0.059185 | 0.0210 | 0.0592 |

Figure E7.4

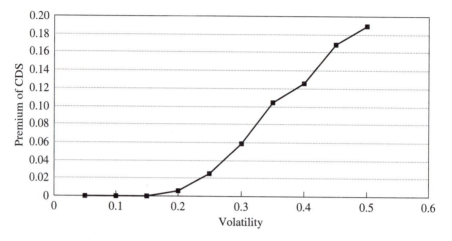

Figure E7.5

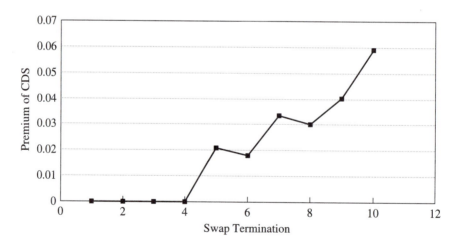

Figure E7.6

# E7.2   HO-SINGER MODEL

## Definitions

The absolute priority rule states that the senior debt holder has the right to the firm value over the junior debt holders. Therefore, from the senior debt holder's point of view, the junior debt holders belong to the same class as the stockholders in the bankruptcy proceedings.

The debt cash flow is the sum of the principal and the coupons over the life of the bond. These are the promised payments, and they are not the expected cash flows because of default risks.

## Description of the Model

The Ho-Singer model is a bond valuation model in a senior and junior debt structure. The model is an extension of the Geske model for a firm with a debt structure that views the equity as a compound option on the firm value. The model is based on a binomial lattice framework, assuming a perfect capital market with no arbitrage opportunity at each node point.

The senior debt valuation is based on a bond valuation, with the junior debt and the equity considered as the same priority class. The junior debt is determined as the debt package value net of the senior debt value.

## Numerical Example

Consider a firm with a value of $30 million. The firm risk is 30% and the risk-free rate is 6%. The firm has two coupon bonds in its debt structure. The senior debt has a face value of $20 million with maturity of eight years. The junior debt has a face value of $10 million maturing in six years. Both bonds have a 10% coupon. See figure E7.7.

The capitalization of the firm is $3.1124 million. The junior debt value is $5.239 million and the senior debt value is $21.6487 million. Note that the junior debt is valued at a discount from its face value, while the senior debt is valued at a premium.

That means that the yield of the junior debt is higher than 10%, while the senior debt yield is below 10%. This shows the transfer of wealth from junior debt holders to the senior debt holder by the absolute priority rule. This example illustrates the complexity of the valuation of junior short-term debt. In general, when the firm value is above the promised payment, the short-term debt is less risky, but when the firm value is below the promised payment, the junior short-term debt bears much of the default risks.

| Inputs | | | | | | | | |
|---|---|---|---|---|---|---|---|---|
| Future debt cash flow ($million) | | | | | | | | |
| 0 yr | 1 yr | 2 yr | 3 yr | 4 yr | 5 yr | 6 yr | 7 yr | 8 yr |
| 0 | 3 | 3 | 3 | 3 | 3 | 13 | 2 | 22 |
| Senior debt | | | | | | | | |
| 0 | 2 | 2 | 2 | 2 | 2 | 2 | 2 | 22 |
| Junior debt | | | | | | | | |
| 0 | 1 | 1 | 1 | 1 | 1 | 11 | 0 | 0 |

| | | | |
|---|---|---|---|
| Risk-free rate (r) | 0.06 | | |
| Time to maturity (T) | 8 | | |
| The number of periods (n) | 8 | dt=T/n | |
| Firm volatility ($\sigma_v$) | 0.3 | | |
| Firm value | 30 | | |

| Outputs | | | | |
|---|---|---|---|---|
| Firm value | Stock value | Debt value | Junior | Senior |
| 30 | 3.1123584 | 26.887642 | 5.2389778 | 21.648664 |

**Figure E7.7**

## Applications

1. The model values a bond within a debt package, which may be complicated.
2. The model can be extended to value a bond package within the business model of a firm.
3. The model analyzes the risks of the capitalization of a firm. In the capital market, the model is a tool to structure the "capital structure arbitrage."

## Case: Reorganization and Debt Restructuring

The room was full—more than ten people in a small conference room. The air was thick with suspense, and the mood was somber. As a result of unanticipated significant losses in the investments, the state examiners had called a meeting to deal with Sunset Insurance's insolvency. The insurance company's assets could no longer support the insurance liabilities. Sunset was a mutual life company with no access to the equity market. The co-insurance that the state offered to support any insolvent insurance company was not adequate to cover Sunset's liability this time. The examiners were meeting with the management of the company, the creditors, and investment bankers to seek a solution to meet the obligations of the insurer—payments to the policyholders.

The state examiner began: "We just cannot roll over and declare bankruptcy and liquidate everything in insurance. We have obligations to individuals whose retirement funds are with us." "If we can sell off all the assets, can we cover the insurance obligations?" asked the investment banker. "Our investment value has plummeted over 20%. There is just no way the assets can take over the liabilities," the CEO replied. "Now, the insurance obligation is senior to the debt. I am asking whether the assets can cover the insurance liabilities, ignoring other obligations to creditors." "I know. Our assets are not there."

The state examiner caught the investment banker's attention and said: "I think Yangtze Life is willing to take over Sunset's liabilities at a price. How should we do this?"

"Sunset has the franchise value. There is value as a going concern. It just has a significant liquidity problem now. Yangtze can provide capital infusion to alleviate the liquidity problem, and in exchange Sunset gives up market share," the CEO proposed.

"I do not think Yangtze will go for it though. At least, it is not going to be simple," the investment banker responded. "If there is no capital infusion, the debt has little or no value, and the policyholders will lose part of the face value. With the capital infusion, Yangtze has to assume all the obligations. The franchise value cannot cover the cost of capital infusion that would be able to support all the obligations." "This is the wealth transfer issue," added the examiner. "Yangtze's investments are transferred to the debt holders and the policyholders, and this wealth transfer is significant enough that the franchise value cannot cover the costs for Yangtze. I know that. We went through this last time in another case." "Look, this is all a matter of negotiation. We creditors are familiar with these work-out scenarios. If Yangtze is willing to take over the obligations, we are willing to extend the maturity. But what do they do about the policies?" The examiner replied: "Yangtze can assume the insurance obligations, but the policyholders may have to receive a lower return on their policies. However, we do want to make sure that they do not lose their principal."

The investment banker added: "For sure, the debt holders will bear much of the loss relative to the policyholders because they are in the junior class. The priority rule in fact is clearly stated and implemented in practice, more so for the insurance industry." "I know. It is really hard to price the risk when we lend money to insurance businesses. We need to understand the implications of priorities more clearly."

*The investment banker proceeded to draw up a diagram representing all the stakeholders in the reorganization. He then drew the arrows showing the wealth transfer from one stakeholder to another under a particular reorganization proposal. The purpose of this representation was to analyze the fairness and the appropriateness of the deal structure. "Let our team come up with a plan, and we will all meet again next week. Is this OK?" he said.*

## Exercises and Answers

1. To isolate the effect of the risk-free rate in the analysis, let us assume the risk-free rate to be zero. Determine the junior debt and the senior debt value.

   *Answer:* If we assume the zero interest rate, we do not have to discount to get present value. Therefore, we have the zero interest assumption for simplicity. To evaluate the senior debt, we treat the junior debt as if it were the stockholders, because from the senior debt holders' point of view, the stockholders and the junior debt holders are residual claimants after the senior debt holders. The senior debt holders have the priority over the firm value over the junior debt holders and the stockholders. To price the senior debt, we consider only the promised payments of the senior debt holders as the exercise prices of the compound options. The next step is to calculate the debt package value, which is a combined value of the senior debt with the junior debt. Note that the equity value is a compound call option on the firm value. We use the promised payments of the debt package as the exercise prices of the compound options and determine the equity value. The debt package value is the firm value net of the equity value. The junior debt value is the difference between the debt package and the senior debt. See figure E7.8.

| Inputs | | | | | | | | | |
|---|---|---|---|---|---|---|---|---|---|
| Future debt cash flow ($billion) | | | | | | | | | |
| 0 yr | 1 yr | 2 yr | 3 yr | 4 yr | 5 yr | 6 yr | 7 yr | 8 yr | |
| 0 | 3 | 3 | 3 | 3 | 3 | 13 | 2 | 22 | |
| Senior debt | | | | | | | | | |
| 0 | 2 | 2 | 2 | 2 | 2 | 2 | 2 | 22 | |
| Junior debt | | | | | | | | | |
| 0 | 1 | 1 | 1 | 1 | 1 | 11 | 0 | 0 | |

| | | | | |
|---|---|---|---|---|
| Risk-free rate (r) | 0.00 | | | |
| Time to maturity (T) | 8 | | | |
| The number of periods (n) | 8 | dt=T/n | | |
| Firm volatility ($\sigma_v$) | 0.3 | | | |
| Firm value | 30 | | | |

| Outputs | | | | | |
|---|---|---|---|---|---|
| | Firm value | Stock value | Debt value | Junior | Senior |
| | 30 | 0.7303957 | 29.269604 | 3.1184318 | 26.151172 |

Figure E7.8

| Junior debt face | 0 | 3 | 6 | 9 | 12 | 15 | 18 | 21 | 24 | 27 | 30 |
|---|---|---|---|---|---|---|---|---|---|---|---|
| Capitalization | 0.599721 | 0.601425 | 0.656698 | 0.711971 | 0.767244 | 0.822517 | 0.87779 | 0.933063 | 0.988337 | 1.04361 | 1.098883 |
| Junior debt value | 0 | 0.634905 | 1.520878 | 2.685243 | 4.106034 | 6.464804 | 9.733445 | 13.71544 | 18.40023 | 23.56325 | 28.90112 |
| Senior debt value | 29.40028 | 28.76367 | 27.82242 | 26.60279 | 25.12672 | 22.71268 | 19.3888 | 15.3515 | 10.61143 | 5.393141 | 0 |

**Figure E7.9**

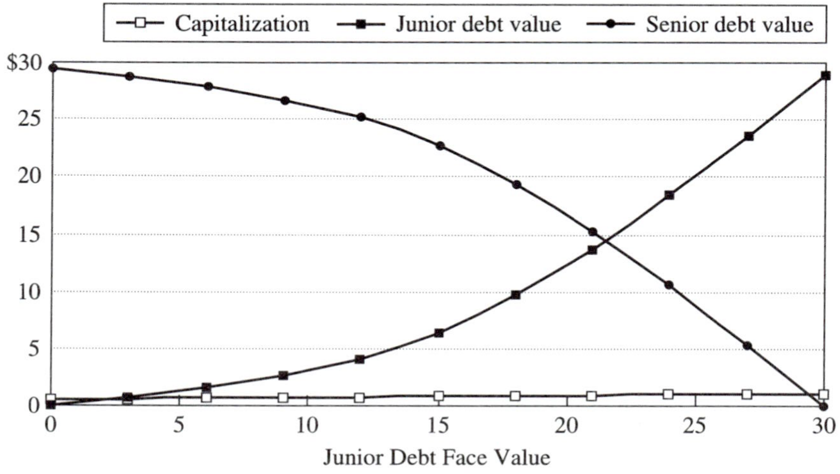

**Figure E7.10**

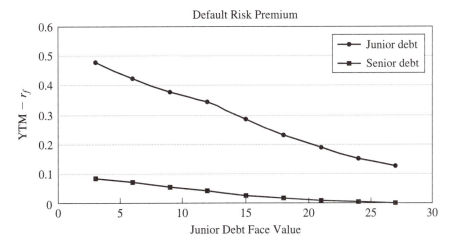

Figure E7.11

2. Construct the table of the capitalization value, the junior debt, and senior debt as the junior debt face value changes from zero to $30 million, while keeping the total face value of the debt package to be $30 million.

   *Answer:* As the junior debt face value gets larger, the stock value also increases accordingly, because we decrease the senior debt face value so that the total package face value is held constant; see figure E7.9. When the junior debt face is $0 (or $30 million), the senior debt face is $30 million (or $0), because the face value of the debt package is the same for each case. Since the junior debt matures earlier than the senior debt, the stock value when there is only the senior debt is less than the stock value when there is only the junior debt. From figure E7.10, we can determine the face value level of the junior debt or the senior debt, which makes the two debt values equal.

3. Plot the default risk premium of the bonds in yields (the yield to maturity of the bond net of the yield of the risk-free bond) as the face value of the short-term debt increases.

   *Answer:* The risk premium of the senior debt decreases as the face value of the junior debt (the short-term debt) increases, because the senior debt becomes safer due to the declining amount of the senior debt. The junior debt also becomes safer as the outstanding amount of the senior debt decreases. See figure E7.11.

## Further Exercises

1. When we assume that the senior debt and the junior debt have the same maturity, such as eight years, repeat question 2 to draw the chart of the capitalization value, the junior debt, and senior debt as the junior debt value changes from zero to $30 million.

   *Answer:* See figure E7.12.

2. When we assume that the senior debt and the junior debt have the same maturity, such as eight years, repeat question 3.

   *Answer:* See figure E7.13.

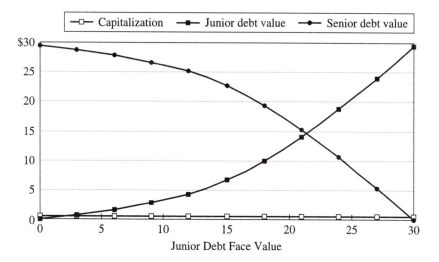

Figure E7.12

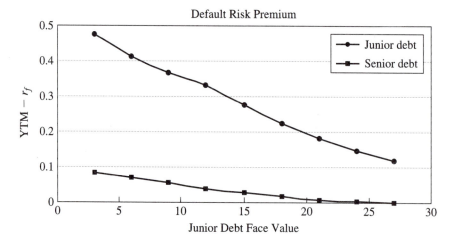

Figure E7.13

## Note

1. We might question why the senior debt does not recover in full when the junior debt recovers. One reason is that the priority rule is not followed. Another reason is that this is an average. Some junior debt may lose everything and some receive the full par amount.

## Bibliography

Alderson, M., and B. Betker. 1995. Liquidation costs and capital structure. *Journal of Financial Economics*, 39 (1), 45–69.

Altman, E. I. 1984. A further empirical investigation of the bankruptcy cost question. *Journal of Finance*, 39 (4), 1067–1090.

Altman, E. I. 1987. The anatomy of the high-yield bond market. *Financial Analysts Journal*, 43 (4), 12–25.

Altman, E. I. 1989. Measuring corporate bond mortality and performance. *Journal of Finance*, 44, 909–922.

Altman, E. I., and D. L. Kao. 1992. The implications of corporate bonds ratings drift. *Financial Analysts Journal,* 48 (3), 65–75.

Altman, E. I., and V. Kishore. 1996. Almost everything you wanted to know about recoveries on defaulted bonds. *Financial Analysts Journal*, November–December, 57–64.

Altman, E. I., and J. Spivack. 1983. Predicting bankruptcy: The value line relative financial strength system vs. the zeta bankruptcy classification approach. *Financial Analysts Journal*, 39 (6), 60–67.

Anderson, R., and S. Sundaresan. 2000. A comparative study of structural models of corporate bond yields: An exploratory investigation. *Journal of Banking and Finance*, 24, 255–269.

Asquith, P., R. Gertner, and D. Scharfstein. 1994. Anatomy of financial distress: An examination of junk-bond issuers. *Quarterly Journal of Economics*, 109 (3), 625–657.

Barnhill, T., Jr., M. Barnhill, F. L. Joutz, and W. F. Maxwell. 2000. Factors affecting the yields on noninvestment grade bond indices: A cointegration analysis. *Journal of Empirical Finance*, 7 (1), 57–86.

Black, F., and J. Cox. 1976. Valuing corporate securities: Some effects of bond indenture provisions. *Journal of Finance*, 31, 351–367.

Briys, E., and F. de Varenne. 1997. Valuing risky fixed rate debt: An extension. *Journal of Financial and Quantitative Analysis*, 32 (2), 239–248.

Brown, K. C., and D. J. Smith. 1993. Default risk and innovations in the design of interest rate swaps. *Financial Management*, 22 (2), 94–105.

Chance, D. M. 1990. Default risk and the duration of zero-coupon bonds. *Journal of Finance*, 45, 265–274.

Das, S., and R. Sundaram. 1999. A discrete-time approach to arbitrage-free pricing of credit derivatives. *Management Science*, 46 (1), 46–63.

Duffie, D., and K. J. Singleton. 1999. Modeling term structures of defaultable bonds. *Review of Financial Studies*, 12, 687–720.

Elton, E., M. Gruber, D. Agrawal, and C. Mann. 2001. Explaining the rate spread on corporate bonds. *Journal of Finance*, 56 (1), 247–277.

Ericsson, J., and J. Reneby. 1998. A framework for valuing corporate securities. *Applied Mathematical Finance*, 5 (3), 143–163.

Ericsson, J., and J. Reneby. 2002. Estimating structural bond pricing model. Working paper, McGill University.

Fisher, L. 1959. Determinants of risk premiums of corporate bonds. *Journal of Political Economy*, 67 (3), 217–237.

Fons, J. S. 1987. The default premium and corporate bond experience. *Journal of Finance*, 42 (1), 81–97.

Geske, R. 1977. The valuation of corporate liabilities as compound options. *Journal of Financial and Quantitative Analysis*, 12, 541–552.

Geske, R., and H. Johnson. 1984. The valuation of corporate liabilities as compound options: A correction. *Journal of Financial and Quantitative Analysis*, 19, 231–232.

Helwege, J. 1999. How long do junk bonds spend in default? *Journal of Finance* 54 (1), 341–357.

Helwege, J., and Christopher M. Turner. 1999. The slope of the credit yield curve for speculative-grade issuers. *Journal of Finance*, 54 (5), 1869–1884.

Ho, T., and R. Singer. 1982. Bond indenture provisions and the risk of corporate debt. *Journal of Finance*, 41, 375–406.

Jarrow, R., D. Lando, and S. Turnbull. 1997. A Markov model for the term structure of credit spreads. *Review of Financial Studies*, 10, 481–523.

Jarrow, R., and S. M. Turnbull. 1995. Pricing derivatives on financial securities subject to credit risk. *Journal of Finance*, 50, 53–86.

Jones, E. P., S. P. Mason, and E. Rosenfeld. 1984. Contingent claims analysis of corporate capital structures: An empirical investigation. *Journal of Finance*, 39, 611–625.

Kim, I. J., K. Ramaswamy, and S. Sundaresan. 1993. Does default risk in coupons affect the valuation of corporate bonds? *Financial Management*, 22, 117–131.

Leland, H. 1994. Corporate debt value, bond covenants, and optimal capital structure. *Journal of Finance*, 49, 1213–1252.

Leland, H., and K. Toft. 1996. Optimal capital structure, endogenous bankruptcy, and the term structure of credit spreads. *Journal of Finance*, 51, 987–1019.

Longstaff, F. A., and E. M. Schwartz. 1995. A simple approach to valuing risky fixed and floating rate debt. *Journal of Finance*, 50 (3), 789–819.

Merton, R. C. 1974. On the pricing of corporate debt: The risk structure of interest rates. *Journal of Finance*, 29, 449–470.

Pye, G. 1974. Gauging the default premium. *Financial Analysts Journal*, 30 (1), 49–69.

Rocardo, J. R. 1998. Default risk, yield spreads, and time to maturity. *Journal of Financial and Quantitative Analysis*, 23 (1), 111–117.

Saá-Requejo, J., and P. Santa-Clara. 1999. Bond pricing with default risk. Working paper, University of California at Los Angeles.

Schonbucher, P. J. 1997. Term structure modelling of defaultable bonds. Working paper, London School of Economics.

Shimko, D., N. Tejima, and D. Deventer. 1993. The pricing of risky debt when interest rates are stochastic. *Journal of Fixed Income*, 3 (2), 58–65.

Skinner, F. S. 1994. A trinomial model of bonds with default risk. *Financial Analysts Journal*, March–April, 73–78.

Sorensen, E. H., and T. F. Bollier. 1994. Pricing swap default risk. *Financial Analysts Journal*, May–June, 23–33.

Vasicek, O. 1977. An equilibrium characterization of the term structure. *Journal of Financial Economics* 5, 177–188.

Warner, J. B. 1977. Bankruptcy costs: Some evidence. *Journal of Finance*, 32 (2), 337–347.

Zhou, C. 1997. *A Jump-Diffusion Approach to Modeling Credit Risk and Valuing Defaultable Securities*. Finance and Economics Discussion Series. Washington, DC: Federal Reserve Board.

# 8

# Other Bonds: Convertible Bonds, MBS, CMO

F inance is a social science and not a natural science. Financial securities are designed and created to serve the needs of the marketplace. For this reason, there are many types of bonds. An effort to categorize all bond types and provide the algorithms to value all the bonds would be a futile effort. Instead, having a general methodology to value a broad range of securities is the key to understanding our financial markets. To illustrate this concept of applying a general method to specific bond types, this chapter will describe how we value some of the bonds that have not yet been discussed in the previous chapters.

## 8.1 DESCRIPTION OF A CONVERTIBLE BOND

Corporations raise capital through the sale of equities and bonds. They also raise capital through a hybrid security of stocks and bonds called *convertible bonds*. Often, a convertible bond is described as a bond with a warrant, a long-dated call option that is issued by a company on its own stock, attached. While the statement is fairly true, taking this claim at face value can be misleading. This section will explain how some of the bond provisions affect the bond value in such a way that a convertible bond cannot be viewed as a bond with an attached warrant.

### Overview

The convertible bond market is an important segment of the fixed-income sector. A convertible bond is a bond with an embedded call option on the company's stock. It offers the holder the option to convert the bond into a specific number of shares of the firm, usually at any time up to the maturity of the bond.

Typically, the face value of the bond is assumed to be 1,000. The *conversion ratio, CR*, is the number of shares that the face value of the bond can convert into. The *conversion price, CP*, is the stock price, at which the converted equity holding equals the par value of the bond. That is,

$$CP \cdot CR = 1,000 \tag{8.1}$$

The *parity, CV* (the *conversion value*), is the value of the bond at the face value if the bondholder decides to convert. It is equivalent to the equity worth of the convertible bond. Therefore the parity is the product of the conversion ratio and the stock price, $S$:

$$CV = CR \cdot S \tag{8.2}$$

The *investment value* of the bond is the value of the bond, ignoring the possibility of converting it to equity. The investment value is therefore the underlying bond value, which is the present value of the bond cash flow (coupon and principal) adjusted for the credit risk, the sinking fund provision, and other bond-related issues.

The conversion is an addition to the other features of corporate bonds that are briefly restated below:

1. the call provision that allows the firm to buy back bonds at prespecified prices
2. the sinking fund requirement that obligates the firm to redeem the bonds over a period of time
3. the put option that gives the investor the right to sell the bonds back to the firm at predetermined prices

As we have explained, these features often dramatically affect the behavior and value of a bond. Although similar to nonconvertible corporate bonds, convertible bonds represent a spectrum of vastly different securities. Because convertibles are hybrids of bonds and stocks, they must inherit all the complexities of the underlying instruments and behave in an often complicated fashion as a mix of two securities. While convertible securities may offer many opportunities for investing and for formulating portfolio strategies, they are also relatively complicated to analyze. Thus, the purpose of this chapter is to provide a basic framework for analyzing these securities, given their diverse characteristics. This section offers an analytical framework that will enable bond issuers and investors to deal with these difficulties in a systematic fashion.

## Basic Framework

This section will describe the basic assumptions of the model. The approach we will take here is the standard framework for studying securities pricing. Since our concern is to derive the fair value of a convertible bond, we will need to consider the determining factors of the bond price in a specific way. We will take the perfect capital market assumption.

We will ignore all types of transaction costs: the commissions, the bid-ask spreads, the issuance costs, and all the explicit costs. In essence, we want to determine the bond price if the market is functioning perfectly (i.e., the fair value).

These assumptions will enable us to focus our discussion on the options aspect of the pricing problem. We will ignore issues such as tax implications of the convertible, marketability of the issues, and corporate strategies. While we recognize that these issues are important to bond pricing, they are beyond the scope of this chapter.

## An Illustrative Example

There are many terms and notations used to describe a convertible bond. We will discuss them by examining a particular bond.

Amazon.com is an E-commerce/products company based in Seattle. On January 15, 2002, Amazon 4.75 (coupon rate) of maturity 2009 was trading at 507.556 (yield = 12.92). The Moody rating was Caa2. The par amount was 1,000, the conversion ratio, 12.816, and the conversion price, 78.027. The stock was trading at 10.240. The parity was 131.236. The bond was callable at 103.325 in 2002, declining to par on maturity.

The market capitalization was \$3,810.470 million. The debt structure had two private placements and three convertible bonds. Three of them were

| Coupon | Maturity | Amount ($million) | Type |
|--------|----------|-------------------|------|
| 10 | 5/1/08 | 264 | callable |
| 4.75 | 2/1/09 | 1249.81 | convertible |
| 6.875 | 2/16/10 | 690 | convertible |

## Valuation of a Convertible Bond

A convertible bond is similar to a corporate bond in that it has a maturity, coupon payments, and face value. We can use the investment grade corporate bond model with the spot yield curve to value a convertible bond.

The example illustrates several important aspects of a convertible bond differing from a corporate bond in their valuation. First, the latent warrant on the bond offers equity returns to the investor while the downside is protected by the face value of the bond. Second, the call provision that leads to the forced conversion of the bond reduces the interest payout by the firm. Unlike the call provision of a corporate bond, the optimal call must be exercised taking stock volatility into account. Third, many convertible bonds in the United States do not have high creditworthiness. Credit risks have to be taken into account. Finally, when the convertible bond issue is relatively large compared to the firm size, the effect of dilution has to be taken into account. Even though these aspects are important to a convertible bond, there are other features peculiar to particular convertible bonds. Understanding how these features are valued provides us with a methodology to value many bond types. We will discuss each of these aspects.

## Latent Warrant

A warrant is a long-dated call option on a stock. A convertible bond can be thought of as a straight bond that has a coupon and principal with a warrant that expires at the bond's maturity. The exercise price of the warrant is the principal value of the convertible bond. This warrant embedded in a convertible bond is called a *latent warrant*. If the stock price rises above the principal at the bond's maturity, the convertible bond holder will exercise the warrant to convert the bond into stock. If the stock falls below the principal amount at the bond's maturity, the convertible bond holder will let the warrant expire worthless and receives the principal payment.

The latent warrant is an American call option on a stock that may pay a dividend. But typically, even if the firm pays the dividend, it is less than the interest from the bond. There is no incentive for the convertible bond holder to convert, exchanging the bond for stock at any time, even if the latent warrant is very much in the money, because convertible bond value always exceeds the conversion value. For the same reason, if the stock does not pay a dividend, there is no early exercise of an American call option. The latent warrant is indeed a long-dated call option. (See figures 8.1–8.3.)

# 8.2   CALL PROVISION AND FORCED CONVERSION

Similar to the call provision of a corporate bond, the optimal exercise of the call option depends on the stock level and the time to expiration—much like an American call. The main difference is that at any given time the convertible bond depends not only on the interest rate level but also on the stock price level because it is a hybrid of a bond and a

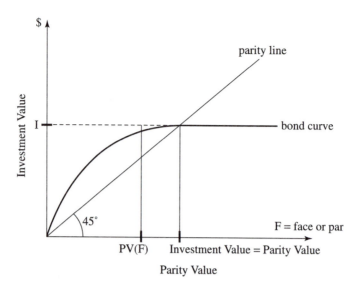

**Figure 8.1** Bond curve and parity line. The bond curve depicts the behavior of a bond. The 45° line through the origin is called the parity line. It represents the convertible bond value at the instant the bond is converted to equity (conversion value). Since we can decompose the convertible bond value into the bond value and the latent warrant, the bond value converges to the risk-free bond as stock prices increase. On the 45° line, the investment value is equal to the parity value.

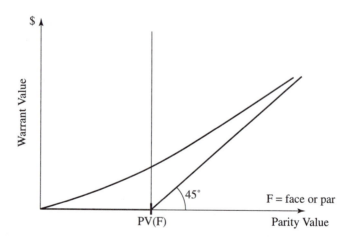

**Figure 8.2** Warrant curve. Standard option theory shows that the minimum warrant value is the 45° line that intersects the x-axis at the present value of the exercise price (the present value of the par value, in our case). Given this argument, we can sketch the warrant curve. Since a warrant is a call option with a strike price of face value, we see that the warrant diagram looks like the call option on a stock.

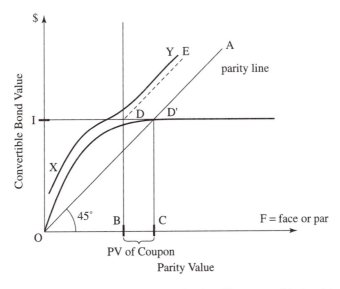

**Figure 8.3** Composition of the convertible bond value. The convertible bond is the sum of the bond curve and the warrant curve. Here it is represented where the curve XY represents the convertible bond value. The line OA is the parity line. However, when the parity value is high, the convertible bond value does not converge to the parity line. Instead, it converges to the parallel line DE. The distance of point D from the y-axis (it is the same as OB) is the present value of the face value of the bond. Since the bond value, or the investment value, is the sum of the present value of the face value and the coupon value, it follows that the distance between the parity value and the line DE is the present value of the coupon.

stock. When the firm calls the convertible bond, the bondholders may choose to convert the bonds to equity instead of surrendering them for the cash payment at the call price. The value of the bond at the time of converting to shares is called the conversion value.

In valuing the convertible bond, we may use the binomial lattice. Given the terminal condition, when we roll back on the binomial lattice, the firm will call the convertible bond whenever its price is above the call price.

However, the convertible bond price when the bond is called is not necessarily the call price. The bond value is the maximum of the call price and the conversion value. Interest rates may have fallen to the extent that it is advantageous for the firm to call the bond to refinance at lower interest rates. When the bondholders are expected not to convert the bonds to equity and receive the call price, the bond will be valued at the call price. However, in the event the stock has risen to the extent that when a firm calls the bond, the bondholders will prefer to convert the bonds to stocks and not surrender the bonds at the call price, then the bond will trade at the conversion value. In this case, we say that the firm seeks to effect a *forced conversion*, forcing the bondholders to convert the convertible bond to stock by calling the bond. The investors will not surrender the bond at the call price because the conversion is more advantageous to them.

There is an additional minor adjustment to the model to take into account. It pertains to the desire of the firm's management to be sure that the bondholders convert the bonds to equity without having a chance to choose surrendering the bond at the call price. When they choose surrendering the bond at the call price, the firm must raise cash to pay the call price. However, if they convert to equity, the firm does not have to be prepared to raise cash. Whether the investors choose surrendering or not depends on how the stock price behaves during the period between the announcement date and the effective call date. When the conversion value is less than the call price on the effective call date, the investors choose surrendering the bond at the call price. Even though the call announcement is made by the firm when the conversion value is greater than the call price, the firm cannot be sure that the conversion value will still be greater than the call price on the effective call date. Therefore, the call should be made when the convertible bond price is above an effective call price—when the effective call price exceeds the call price by an amount equaling, for example, one standard deviation of the stock price volatility. The spread between the effective call price and the stated call price depends on the trade-off between the likelihood that the stock will fall to a level at which the bondholders will surrender the bonds instead of converting them into stock during the period between the announcement date and the effective call date, and the cost of delay in a forced conversion.

$$\text{effective call} = \text{call price} + \text{factor}$$

Suppose the stated call price is 104 percent. Let us define the *critical parity value* to be the parity value at which the firm will optimally exercise the forced conversion. At this critical parity value, the cash value to retire the debt via the call is \$1,040 ($= 104$ percent of 1,000 par). The convertible bond is forced to convert, and therefore its value equals the conversion value. Assume that the stock volatility is 35% annually. The time period between the conversion decision made by the investors and the announcement of the calling of the bond by the issuer is typically 30 days (one month). Therefore, the stock

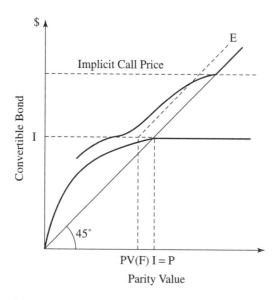

**Figure 8.4** Effect of the implicit call price. Here, we see that the convertible bond value must be capped by the implicit call price. As the parity value rises, the convertible bond value rises in step. But as the convertible bond value approaches the implicit call price, the market will anticipate the firm's calling the bond, and the bondholders will convert the bonds to the parity value.

volatility over one month is $0.35/\sqrt{12}$. Suppose that the firm's financial management requires at least one standard deviation for the stock price to be above the stock price that defines the cash value to retire the debt via the call (i.e., $1,040); then the increase in the parity value (or the stock price, since the parity value is proportional to the stock price) required above $1,040 is $105.078 (= $(0.35/\sqrt{12}) \times$ 1,040). The effective call is the call decision that is triggered by this higher parity value. The factor is $105.078 (= $(0.35/\sqrt{12}) \times$ 1,040) (see figure 8.4).

The determination of the factor and the effective call price is considered a behavioral model, because the derivation of the model is not based on a precise optimization of economic gains by the financial management of the firm. We have not taken into consideration the transaction costs for the firm to prepare to pay the investors cash or new shares, or any other economic reasons for the firm's delay in exercising the option explicitly to solve for the effective call. A factor is simply proposed to reflect the "inefficiency" for the firm in exercising the option, and the model proposes that the inefficiency depends on the stock price volatility.

## 8.3  CREDIT RISK

To incorporate the credit risk, we use the firm value, and not the stock value, as the underlying risk source, following the approach of the Merton structural model for credit risk. At the terminal date, the convertible bond value is given by $Max$[conversion value, $Min$[the principal, firm value]]. $Min$[the principal, firm value] is supposed to take care of credit risk for pricing purposes.

The firm may default at any time. It defaults when the convertible bond value exceeds the firm value, which means the firm's liability is higher than its value. At default, we assume that the convertible bond holders take over the ownership of the firm, and the convertible bond price is then the firm value.

If the firm does not default on the bond, it may call the bond when the convertible bond price exceeds the effective call price. The value of the convertible bond price at the time of call is $Max$ [conversion value, call price].

$$\text{bond price} = Max[\text{conversion value, call price}]$$

## 8.4  MORTGAGE-BACKED SECURITIES (PASS-THROUGH CERTIFICATES)

The mortgage-backed securities market is a significant segment of U.S. fixed-income markets. *Mortgage-backed securities* are securities backed by a pool of individual home mortgages. A *mortgage pool* is a portfolio of mortgages collected under certain guidelines. The pool is put into a trust, and bonds are issued as claims against the portfolio. These bonds are referred to as *pass-throughs*, in that they simply pass the interest and principal collected from all the mortgagors and pass them to the bondholders on a pro rata basis. That is, the bond represents a percent of the original pool, and the interest and principal that the bondholder receives each month will be based on that percentage.

The mortgage-backed securities market is broad and diverse, with many variations. This chapter will focus only on the basic valuation principles of these securities. We will not dwell on the complex and intricate bond arithmetic, such as calculations of yields, prepayment speeds, and day count conventions. We emphasize two aspects of the market: (1) embedded options in these securities and (2) different bond types that can be derived from these mortgage-backed pass-throughs. For this reason, the pass-throughs and all the bonds derived from them are often generically called derivatives.

## Agency and Nonagency Deals

The Government National Mortgage Association (GNMA), the Federal National Mortgage Association (FNMA), and the Federal Home Loan Mortgage Corporation (FHLMC) are three major government agencies that are responsible for providing mortgages to homeowners. The mortgage pass-throughs that originate from these government agencies are called *agency deals*. The mortgage pass-throughs that originate from private corporations are called *whole loans*.

The GNMA mortgage-backed securities program has over $600 billion of securities outstanding. These securities are backed by mortgage loans and mortgage-backed securities themselves. The process of originating a GNMA pool (or a GNMA pass-through) begins with a mortgage bank, which acts as a dealer taking principal risks. That means they do not just act as a broker. They buy mortgages and sell out of the position at an uncertain price. They assemble the mortgages (usually under certain guidelines) from banks or financial companies that provide mortgages to homeowners. When the pool reaches a certain size, say $500 million, the bankers structure the pool as a trust. The trust will then pass to GNMA for insurance (which will be elaborated later). After GNMA's approval, the pool is sold to investment banks. The investment banks in turn sell shares of the pool to investors through their distributive networks. Investors may be portfolio managers, insurance companies, and other financial institutions.

Now we follow through this process from the payment point of view. The payment begins with a homeowner, the mortgagor. The mortgagor pays the bank, the lender of the mortgage (the mortgagee), the monthly interest payment and the scheduled principal paydown. The mortgagee takes a portion of the interest payment (not principal) as a servicing fee. At this point, the bank is not really the lender. The bank is acting as servicer (or intermediary), collecting the payments and keeping track of all the paperwork. The net payment goes to GNMA. GNMA also takes a portion of the interest (not principal) as insurance and passes the rest of the amount to trusts. Then the trusts distribute the payments to all the investors (see figure 8.5).

What happens to the insurance? U.S. mortgages allow mortgagors to prepay the mortgage in part or in whole at any time, at par. There is usually no penalty for mortgagors to prepay. In this case, the total amount, including the entire principal, will be passed to the investors. For that month, the investors will note that more principal has been paid down. This paydown of principal is measured by a factor (the proportion of the principal remaining to the original face value). At issuance, the factor is 1, and it decreases over time to 0, when all the mortgagors retire their debts. When many mortgagors pay down the principals in one particular month, the factor will fall faster. However, when a mortgagor defaults and cannot make the monthly payment, the missing payment affects the investors' returns on their investments. That is, the investors are subject to the credit risks of the mortgagors. To eliminate this risk, GNMA steps in. Using its insurance pool, the funds collected from the insurance fees taken from the payments,

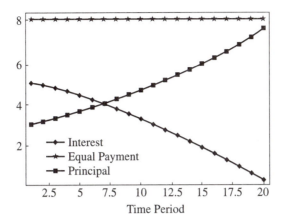

**Figure 8.5** Level payments on mortgage loans. This figure shows how the interest payments and the principal payments behave over the life of the loan when the loan is paid in equal installments. To this end, we assume a flat 10% yield curve and 10% annual interest. The interest is paid semi-annually. The term of the loan is 10 years and the principal is $100. The level payment is 8.02426.

GNMA makes whole that monthly payment, paying the investors the promised interest and principal in full. If the mortgagor defaults on the payment, GNMA will pay the entire principal amount. The investor will receive the paydown as if the mortgagor had prepaid. The investor cannot distinguish whether the paydown is a result of a prepayment by a mortgagor or a make whole by GNMA. There is no reason for the investor to care. In essence, GNMA steps into this process as a guarantor of the creditworthiness of mortgagors to the investors.

Are agency pass-throughs safe from credit risk? There are two layers of insurance. First, GNMA capital is supporting the credit risk. Second, GNMA as a corporation has the full backing of the U.S. government. The security of the GNMA corporation compared with Treasury bonds is a matter of some legal discussions, but certainly the general understanding is that the corporation is sufficiently safe. For this reason, agency deals are often sold as being "as safe as U.S. government securities."

## 8.5 PREPAYMENT MODEL AND VALUATION

"Safety" has to be properly defined. In credit analysis, safety applies to the loss of principal and interest. However, when mortgagors do not prepay according to the payment schedule, there is a risk, or uncertainty, of the cash flow of the mortgage pass-through. Some of that risk is almost inconsequential, but some is significant.

When a mortgagor sells a home because of job relocation or has an urge to be rid of all debt, the mortgage may be prepaid. There are many mortgages in a pool, and on average there is always a certain level of prepayment. This average is quite stable because of the diversification effect if we assume that all mortgagors act quite independently of each other in their prepayment, selling their houses, reducing their debt, and other reasons. When the pool is large, we can estimate the proportion of mortgagors who will prepay each month. We can determine the historical monthly prepayment as a portion of the face value outstanding for each pool. In this empirical investigation, we can take into account geographic distribution, coupon distribution, and other attributes of the mortgages.

Now consider a mortgage pool of thirty-year fixed-rate mortgages. When the interest rate falls significantly, and particularly when talk shows and newspapers suggest that the time is ripe for refinancing—prepay the entire mortgage and take another mortgage with a lower rate—many mortgagors will prepay. As a result, the investors will have to reinvest the payments in lower interest rates, resulting in a loss of interest that they would have received if the mortgagors had not refinanced.

The crux of the argument is that mortgagors have a call option on the mortgages, similar to a callable corporate bond where the issuer (the borrower) can call back the bond and terminate the agreement. On mortgages, the mortgagor (the borrower) can call the mortgage at par (with no call premium) at any time. On the flip side, we can see that the investor has sold a call option. This option clearly has value to the mortgagors and costs to the investors. The investors demand a higher coupon rate (or interest costs) to compensate for the options that they have offered to the mortgagors for such pass-through securities.

From the above discussion, the principle behind valuing a mortgage pass-through is related to the valuation of a call option. But we cannot directly apply the callable corporate bond procedure because for a corporate bond, the financial manager usually is "rational," focusing only on the maximization of wealth. Rational behavior is used here in the context of financial theory. All agents are rational when they always seek the highest returns among all the investment alternatives.

But mortgagors have many motives for prepayment other than refinancing; they are not seeking only to maximize their wealth. To determine the value of the embedded call option in mortgages, we need to model the behavior of the mortgagor. This model is commonly called the *prepayment model*. Prepayment models are estimated from historical data of mortgagors' prepayment behavior. Some of the factors that are commonly cited as the main reasons for the prepayment are the following:

1. Seasonality—There are more prepayments in late spring because there are more home sales; families usually want to settle into a new home during the summer, before school starts.
2. Seasoning and aging—There is usually very little prepayment with a new mortgage pool. The prepayment speed gradually increases for two years. Conversely, for an aged pool, there are very few prepayments because the remaining mortgagors tend not to move.
3. Interest spread between the new mortgage rate and the mortgagor's present mortgage rate—When the new mortgage rate is lower than the mortgage rate of the pool, particularly when the rate has fallen over 200 basis points, the mortgagors will likely refinance.
4. Burnout—A pool that has gone through a low interest rate period is more likely to have less prepayment risk than a pool that has not gone through such a period. Mortgagors who are alert and ready to refinance their mortgages are not likely to remain in this pool because they have prepaid already. This pool is called *burnout*.
5. Slope of the yield curve—Historical data show that the slope of the yield curve is a factor in deciding refinancing behavior. This observation may be explained by the mortgagors' alternatives in refinancing. They can refinance at an adjustable rate with interest costs based on the short-term rate. When the yield curve is upward-sloping, they may refinance their fixed-rate mortages with adjustable-rate mortgages, leading to an increase in refinancing.

Using historical data, the prepayment model can be specified. Given the prepayment model, we can determine the cash flows of the pass-through under different scenarios. The mortgage pass-through model is then specified.

The prepayment model is a behavioral model in that we use historical experiences to hypothesize how mortgagors behave. The model does not solve for mortgagors' optimal prepayment decisions from economic principles. Instead, the prepayment model assumes that mortgagors are "myopic," in that they make their prepayment decisions without simulating the future outcomes or conducting dynamic optimization strategies that take future uncertainties and optimal decisions into account (e.g., the Bellman solution). They simply follow some rules based on the prevailing economic realities.

The prepayment model is important in valuing mortgage-backed securities because it specifies the value of the embedded option in mortgage-backed securities. The prepayment model captures the mortgagors' behavior.

First consider a homeowner's mortgage. The mortgagor can refinance when the interest rates fall to a level that enables him to refinance optimally or to retire the debt at the par price, since there is no prepayment premium. In this case, a mortgage is similar to the callable corporate bond. For a mortgage, the borrower (the mortgagor) has the option to retire the debt at par. For this reason, we can express the mortgage as a combination of an option-free bond and an embedded option, as we have done for the callable corporate bond.

$$\text{Mortgage} = \text{option-free bond} - \text{a bond call option}$$

For mortgage-backed securities where we have a portfolio of mortgages, the embedded options can be viewed slightly differently. A higher prepayment rate, associated with falling interest rates (called prepayment risk to the investors), is detrimental to the investors. This cost to investors is equivalent to their holding a short position in an interest rate floor. In other words, when the interest rate falls, mortgagors can save the difference between the lower interest rate and the fixed mortgage rate by prepaying the mortgage, which is tantamount to holding the interest rate floor. Conversely, a lower prepayment rate is related to rising interest rates (called extension risk to the investors). This delay of prepayment also is detrimental to the investors, because they cannot reinvest the prepayment that they would receive at a higher market interest rates. The extension risk results in the investment being locked into fixed-interest payments lower than the market reinvestment rate for a longer period of time. The investors have a short position of a cap whereby they will sustain a loss when interest rates rise, particularly beyond a certain rate. The reason for this is that the mortgagors will not pay interest rates higher than the fixed mortgage interest rates. This can be summarized by the following equation.

$$\text{Mortgage-backed securities} = \text{option-free bond} - \text{a floor} - \text{a cap}$$

The above discussion suggests that we can be slightly more specific about bond options. To capture both the extension risk and the prepayment risk, the investors have in fact sold both caps and floors to the mortgagors. As interest rates continue to fall or rise, the impact of the extension risk and prepayment risk on the bond value begins to lessen, and the burnout effect starts to affect the bond behavior. For this reason, we can think of the mortgage-backed securities as having sold a cap but bought back a more out-of-the money cap. These options replicate the impact of extension risk on the mortgages. Also, the mortgage-backed securities have sold a floor but bought back a more out-of-the-money floor. These options replicate the impact of prepayment risks on the mortgages. The result is summarized below:

Mortgage-backed securities

= option-free bond − a floor + out-of-the-money floor

− a cap + out-of-the-money cap

## PSA Methods and Embedded Options

In the previous chapters, we have extensively discussed the yield to maturity of a bond because the measure is used widely in fixed-income markets, despite its many defects in properly measuring the returns of a bond. For a bond with a coupon rate and maturity, the yield to maturity can be calculated as the internal rate of return of the coupon and principal cash flows.

For mortgage-backed securities, there are two aspects that we need to address before an internal rate of return concept can be used. First, the principal of the mortgage is amortized over the life of the obligation, such that the cash flow of the mortgage interest and the principal payments together is level over time. The yield of the mortgage should therefore be the internal rates of return of the cash flow. This aspect of the mortgage does not pose any problem to the definition of a yield. After all, it is the same as that of a sinking fund bond in the corporate bond market, where bonds are required to be retired over time according to a specified schedule on a pro rata basis. Obviously, a mortgage amortizes the principal over a payment schedule.

The second aspect, however, is more complicated and the discussion is more involved. In the United States, since there is no penalty for prepayment, the prepayment risk can be significant. The average life of mortgage-backed securities is shortened by the prepayments. In the early years after mortgage-backed securities were introduced to the market, research found two empirical facts regarding the prepayment behavior. First, the prepayments tended to be a proportion of the remaining principals outstanding. Second, there was little prepayment when the mortgage was taken down recently. Mortgagors tend not to refinance in the early years of their mortgages. Both observations seem reasonable. Prepayments should be related to the size of the mortgage pool; when a pool size increases, more mortgages are expected to be prepaid. Also, if you consider all the expenses that are needed to take down a mortgage, the likelihood of an immediate prepayment should be low. The Public Securities Association (PSA) determined a convention whose results are summarized by a PSA formula. A mortgage-backed pool that has a 100 PSA means that the prepayment speed, defined as the annual principal amount prepaid divided by the amount outstanding at the beginning of the period, increases linearly to 6% in 30 months and stays constant for the remaining life of the pool. (See figure 8.6.)

If a mortgage pool has a higher prepayment speed, say twice that of the 100 PSA pool, then it is said to have a 200 PSA. In general, a mortgage pool speed is measured as a percent of the 100 PSA. For any mortgage pool, if the mortgage prepayment speed is quoted, the yield of the projected cash flow can be calculated from a given price. This yield measure is called the *static yield* because we assume that the prepayment experience will be that of the quoted prepayment speed.

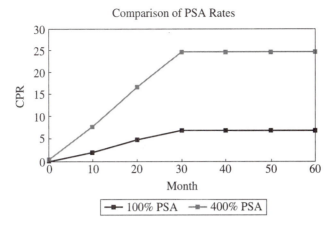

**Figure 8.6** PSA rates. Prepayment rates are commonly expressed in three different ways: SMM, CPR, and PSA. Single monthly mortality (SMM) is a prepayment rate that measures the percentage of dollars prepaid in any month, expressed as a percentage of the expected mortgage balance. SMM is expressed mathematically by the following equation: SMM = 100 × [(Scheduled Balance − Actual Balance)/(Scheduled Balance)]. The conditional prepayment rate (CPR) is a percentage prepayment rate that relates the percentage of the outstanding balance prepaid on an annual basis. CPR is expressed mathematically as CPR = 100 × (1 − (1 − SMM/100)$^{12}$). Finally, PSA is a market convention adopted by the Public Securities Association in the mid-1980s in which prepayment rates, expressed in CPR, are assumed to follow a standard path over time. A 100% PSA curve implies that the prepayment rate starts at 0.2% in the first month and then rises by 0.2% in each month until month 30, when it levels out at 6%.

There are some interesting characteristics of the static yields. They have to be quoted along with the PSA assumption. The yield is based on the speed assumption of the trader. Also, one expects that the static yield has a different value than the yield of the Treasury bond with a comparable weighted average life. There are several reasons for this difference, even though GNMA and other government agency pools have few, if any, credit risks. One reason is that the projected cash flows of a mortgage pool and the Treasury bonds are very different, even if they have a similar weighted average life. The cash flow pattern of a mortgage pool must take into account the principal amortization and the PSA speed. Another reason is that the static approach of PSA cannot capture the embedded option value. Since the embedded option is detrimental to the investors, in that the mortgage falls in value when the interest rate rises or falls, it should lead to a higher yield of the bond. The final related reason is the model risk of the mortgage pool. The prepayment behavior is assumed in the model, and therefore there are some model risks involved. As a result, the arbitrage relationship between the Treasury bond market and the mortgage market is not perfect, resulting in basis risks (changes in the relationship due to fluctuations in the option-adjusted spread) between the two markets.

The bond arithmetic gives a precise bond price for a given PSA and yield. When a bond manager evaluates a particular mortgage pool, he takes its coupon rate, the age of the pool, the factor indicating how much the pool has been paid down, and types of mortgages into account, and decides on the speed of prepayment and the appropriate yield for the bond. Using the PSA and the yield of the bond, the bond manager can then decide on the price. In this sense, PSA may be viewed as a valuation model. But there are of course many limitations to this approach. More appropriately, PSA should be viewed only as a market convention, a common measure of prepayment speed for the market. A financial model should capture the prepayment behavior more precisely.

## Monte Carlo Simulations

To value mortgage-backed securities with embedded options appropriately, one popular approach is to use Monte Carlo simulations. We have shown that the value of a bond can be determined as the average of the present value of the cash flows along the interest rate paths, for all the possible interest rate paths in the binomial lattice. In other words, if we can enumerate all the possible scenario interest rate paths, and determine the bond cash flows for each path, then the average of the present values of these cash flows (the average of the pathwise values) is the bond price.

Given a particular scenario and prepayment model, we can determine the cash flows of the mortgages. Once again, this is bond arithmetic. At each point in time along the interest rate scenario, the mortgage terms and conditions determine the interest and the principal the investor should receive.

However, enumerating all the possible interest rate paths is problematic. There are just too many possible paths. A random sampling of these scenarios can provide one solution. But these scenarios do not have to be selected purely at random. There is much research conducted on the subject of finding intelligent ways to select a sample. However, we are not concerned with this issue here, even though it is certainly important in financial engineering.

Another approach in valuing a mortgage pool is to recognize any mortgage pool as a portfolio of mortgages. We have discussed the valuation of a mortgage where a mortgagor exercises the call option optimally. The approach can treat a mortgage like a callable bond. The mortgagor considers the final payment of the mortgage at the maturity date as if there were no prepayment. Then, using the backward substitution approach, the mortgagor determines the optimal exercise decision in calling the mortgage at par. When the mortgage reaches the initial date in the backward substitution procedure, the value determined is the value of the mortgage when the mortgagor's prepayment decision is optimal. We call this a *high prepayment efficiency*.

However, not all mortgagors exercise their options efficiently. We can assume that there is a distribution of mortgagors with a varying degree of implicit transaction costs involved in prepayments. We can assume some mortgagors will prepay irrespective of the interest rate level. Then a mortgage pool is a portfolio of all such mortgages. The precise distribution of these mortgagors has to be estimated from historical data or implied from market prices.

Using either the Monte Carlo simulation model or viewing a mortgage pool as a portfolio of mortgages, along with the prepayment model and the arbitrage-free interest rate model, we have completed the description of valuation models for mortgage-backed securities. Similar to the discussion of corporate bonds, for a particular mortgage pool, given the price, we can determine the spread off the Treasury spot curve such that the mortgage pool value (as determined by the valuation model) equals the quoted price of the mortgage pool. This spread is the option-adjusted spread for the mortgage pool. A corporate bond, which may have a call provision or a sinking fund provision, is quite different from a mortgage pool in terms of cash flow characteristics and embedded options. But the option-adjusted spread has isolated all these features in its valuation, and thus we can compare the corporate bond and mortgage-backed securities using the option-adjusted spread. This is something that a static yield of a mortgage pool cannot provide.

# 8.6  COLLATERALIZED MORTGAGE OBLIGATIONS (CMOs)

The financial innovation of pass-through securities has had a tremendous impact on the financial market. The introduction of these securities has benefited homeowners in their access to capital because mortgagors can access the capital market for the mortgages via the pass-throughs. This innovation was followed by another development that dramatically changed the financial markets in the following years, collateralized mortgage obligations (CMOs).

Individual mortgages are used in a trust to create pass-throughs. Investment banks assemble a portfolio of mortgage pass-through pools, which are the assets of a trust. The claims on these assets are CMOs, which are backed by pass-throughs. The main innovative feature of pass-through securities is that they generate different classes of claims. The advantages of segmenting a bond into different classes will be discussed below. These classes are called *tranches*, a French word for slice.

Different packaging of these tranches creates different CMOs. There is no limit to the number of designs of the deals. The design is driven by market demands because the cost of producing different designs is relatively small. However, there is still a need for some standardization for marketability. Some of the more common structures are discussed below.

## Interest Only and Principal Only (IO/PO)

The interest only (IO) and principal only (PO) are tranches of a mortgage pool. The IO investor will receive only monthly interests of the mortgage pass-through. The PO investor will receive only the principal of the pass-through monthly.

A mortgagor pays down the principal slowly at the beginning and accelerates the paydown in the latter years. For this reason, much of the scheduled principal payment is deferred until years later and the PO that pays the principal payments to the investor has a longer weighted average life. Conversely, since the early payments of a mortgage consist mostly of interest, and the IO pays the interest portions of the mortgage payments to the investors, the IO has a shorter weighted average life. In separating the pass-through into two classes—the PO and IO polarize the weighted average lives of the CMO bonds—investors are given more choices to fit their needs. IO and PO also have significant embedded options, which lengthen the PO duration and shorten the IO duration.

Consider an extreme scenario when all mortgagors prepay. PO investors would receive all the payments in full immediately, and that would be a windfall to them. On the other hand, the IO value becomes 0, since there is no interest to be paid in the future. In another scenario, if all the mortgagors decide never to prepay, then the IO investors will enjoy their interest payments for a much longer time while the PO payments will be deferred for many years.

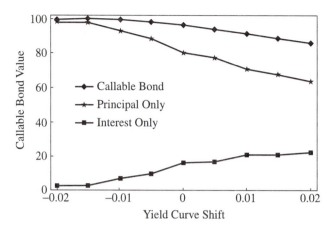

**Figure 8.7** Callable bond, principal only, and interest only. This figure shows the performance profiles of a callable bond, a principal-only bond (PO), and an interest-only bond (IO) for illustration purposes. The PO and IO receive the principal and the interests of the callable bond, respectively. We choose the callable bond rather than mortgage-backed securities (MBS) as an underlying bond of PO and IO, because the callable bond has characteristics similar to MBS. The initial term structure is 4% flat. The term structure has been shifted by 50 basis points to show how those bonds are behaving as interest rates increase. We can see that the IO increases as the interest rate goes up, in contrast to the PO. Needless to say, the sum of PO and IO is the callable bond.

When IO and PO stand alone, each become riskier than when they are combined. When they combine and make whole the pass-through, their individual risks are mitigated. Moreover, the risks are initiated from the call option embedded in the pass-through. That means IO and PO have significant options. PO has an embedded call option (in a long position). The option increases the price and hence lowers the yield. IO has an embedded short call option, lowering the price and increasing the yield.

When IO and PO are recombined, we can construct the mortgage-backed bond. Hence, the following arbitrage condition must hold (see figure 8.7):

$$MBS = IO + PO$$

The above result shows that the principal-only bond has a higher and positive duration, with a more negatively sloped performance profile. The interest-only bond has a negative duration with a positively sloped performance profile. For the interest-only bond, when the interest rate falls, the bond value falls, unlike a Treasury bond or any typical corporate bond.

## Sequential Structure

The classic vanilla structure enables investors to buy bonds with the weighted average life that they prefer. It is a five-tranche deal, and each tranche has its own embedded options. These tranches are labeled A, B, C, D, and Z. Each tranche is structured to look like a vanilla corporate bond, with a fixed coupon rate and a sinking fund schedule. A, B, C, and D all have sinking funds and fixed coupon payments. Z is an accrual bond with no coupon payments, and its interest is accrued. Therefore, each bond has its own coupon and its principal repayment schedule, a sinking fund schedule.

Each bond is paid down by a priority rule. Every month, the interests and principals from the mortgage pass-throughs are used to pay down the scheduled payments of all the bonds, their coupon and principal. If the prepayments are much faster than anticipated, bond A's principal will be paid down first. After bond A is paid down entirely, bond B stands next in line to absorb all the early payments. Bond C is next in line, and so on.

If the prepayment is slower than anticipated, then all the bonds' interests will be paid first. The principal paydown will be deferred, but bond A's principal will always be paid down before B, and B before C, and so on. Z will be paid down when all other bonds have been paid down.

Finally, there is the residual bond. A residual bond is the remaining cash flow from the mortgage pass-through bonds in a trust. For example, a CMO is a trust certificate. That means the CMO bonds are usually overcollateralized and it is expected that, when all the CMO bonds are paid down, there will still be some mortgage pass-through bonds left in the trust. The residual bonds are the residual cash flows. The residual bond-holders are in fact the shareholders of the trust and receive the remaining assets in the trust after all the liabilities have been paid down.

## Planned Amortization Class (PAC)

We have discussed that agency mortgage-backed securities have negligible default risks but may have significant prepayment risks. Can we design a CMO such that one bond class can also have negligible prepayment risk? Yes. This class of bonds is called the *planned amortization class* (PAC).

PAC bonds have a planned amortization schedule stating precisely the principals that will be paid down over a period of time. The proportion of PAC bonds to the entire package of mortgage-backed bonds varies significantly. Let us assume that the proportion is 30%. The other tranches, the non-PAC bonds, in the deal are called *supporting tranches*. Bonds are designated PAC or non-PAC in the structuring of a CMO. The design is often driven by the supply and demand of the marketplace for the type of bonds that need to be created.

When the prepayment speed is faster than expected, the supporting tranches' principals will be paid down before the PAC bonds. If the prepayment speed slows down, then the supporting tranches will not be paid down and are deferred to allow the principals of the PAC bonds to be paid down according to the plan. In other words, supporting tranches are used to ensure that PAC bonds are not affected by uncertain prepayments.

## Other CMO Bonds

With the innovation of CMO tranches, the designs of the bonds are unlimited. The basic idea is to use mortgage pass-through bonds and rearrange the cash flows so that each cash flow is directed to a different class of buyers.

For example, buyers such as banks want to hold floating-rate instruments in their portfolio because their liabilities tend to be of short duration. One can even generate floating-rate notes out of a portfolio of fixed-rate mortgage-backed securities. The approach is to first determine an amortization schedule of the principal of the floating-rate tranche. Then we determine the floating-rate index, say 1-month LIBOR plus 20 basis points. This index determines the interst payments of the tranche. Clearly, we cannot be obligated to pay the interests at any rate level because the bonds are supported by the fixed-rate bonds. If the 1-month LIBOR becomes very high, the total interest payments may exceed the interest incomes of the fixed-rate collateral bonds. Therefore, these bonds have caps and floors on the interest rates in their terms and conditions. Also, these floating-rate bonds must have companion bonds, so that the floating-rate bonds together with the companion bonds become the mortgage-backed pass-through.

In structuring a floating-rate bond inside a pass-through, we must have a companion bond that neutralizes the floating-rate risk of the bond. This companion bond is called the inverse floater. When the interest rate (LIBOR in this case) rises, the inverse floater has a formula of a form $(a^* - r)$ such that the bond pays a lower interest rate, where $a^*$ is a constant number decided in the structuring of the deal and $r$ is the specified interest rate (e.g., 3-month LIBOR). Conversely, when the interest rate falls, inverse floaters will pay higher interest rates. An inverse floater bond and a floating-rate bond become a fixed-rate bond. Inverse floaters have very interesting properties. When interest rates fall, fixed-rate bonds rise in value because the discount rates on their fixed-interest payments are lowered. For inverse floaters, their interest payments actually increase in this scenario, and therefore their values should rise even faster. This means that they have a high duration and positive convexity. Inverse floaters are useful for asset managers to capture the falling-rate scenario.

## The Cow Graph

It can be confusing to study collateralized mortgage obligations since there are many financial innovations that create different bond types. Further, one has to ask how these innovations enhance the economy, especially when we take all the structuring fees and bond sales commissions into account. What is the business purpose of creating these bonds?

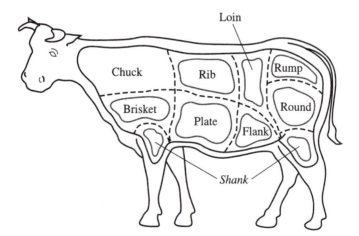

**Figure 8.8** The cow graph. We can think of many examples in the real world where the sum of the parts is more valuable than the whole. Consider stripping, a process to create synthetic zero-coupon bonds by decomposing a coupon bond, because the coupon bond is a portfolio of zero-coupon bonds. Since people prefer a zero-coupon bond to a coupon bond, stripping the coupon bond into zero-coupon bonds is profitable. The same argument is applicable to the cow diagram.

Consider going to a steak restaurant. A restaurant in New York City would typically charge $35 for a 14-ounce steak. If we go to a cattle auction, we would find that $900 can buy an 1,100-pound beef cow. One has to be struck by the spread between the source of meat and the end product served in the restaurant.

Let us now go to a butcher shop. You will often see a "cow graph" on the wall, with white lines on the black hide identifying the parts of the cow: flank steak, rump roast, brisket, standing rib, and so on. Customers buy the cuts they want. The sum of the cost of the parts is much more than the cost of the individual animal. Customers prefer to pay higher prices because they get what they need. (See figure 8.8.)

Mortgage-backed securities provide the sources of cash flows for financial engineers to rearrange assets and resell the final products to the customers. In rearranging the cash flows, we can reallocate the embedded options or create embedded options to fit the needs of the portfolio managers. The growth of collateralized mortgage obligations markets and related markets, such as the asset-backed securities market and whole loan markets, show the importance of the role of the butcher shops in delivering the appropriate products to the end customers.

## 8.7   OTHER BONDS

### Dual-Currency Bonds

This bond pays interests in one currency and principal in another. For example, a dual-currency bond may pay coupon in yen and the principal in U.S. dollars. It can be driven by the tax code and accounting of some countries, depending on their treatment of the bond book value and income (whether the exchange rate is based on the historical book value or marking to market to the changing level of the exchange rate). Indexed currency option notes allow issuers to pay reduced principal at maturity if the specified foreign currency appreciates sufficiently relative to the domestic currency. (See figure 8.9.)

### Floating-Rate Note

The floating-rate note is a note that pays interest reset at regular intervals. The vanilla floating-rate note's interest rate is adjusted to the market rate, say LIBOR, plus a margin, say 50 basis points. In so doing, the floating-rate note should always be traded close to par at all the reset dates. Such may not be the case if the liquidity spread widens or the rating of the issuer changes. In these cases, the floating-rate bonds may trade at a discount, even at the reset dates.

However, the interest rate reset does not need to be the prevailing market rate with the same term. There are several variations.

1. The reset rate is based on a term other than the reset period. A monthly reset floating rate can be paid over a one-year rate.
2. The rate can be a formula depending on a floating-rate index. The index can be a swap rate of a particular tenor.
3. The formula may be *inverse floating*, meaning that if the market rate goes up, the interest rate falls.

Rating-sensitive notes are floating-rate notes in which a floating rate resets with a spread off LIBOR, but the spread depends on the rating.

An oil-interest indexed dual-currency bond is a bond with the principal indexed to the yen and the semiannual coupon payment indexed to crude oil (e.g., *Max*[$34, two barrels of crude oil]). The maturity of the bond is five years. The cash flow of the bond is

||

This bond can be decomposed into three parts: a straight bond, ten call options on two barrels of crude oil, and a five-year forward contract with the forward price of 140 ¥/$.

Buying a straight bond

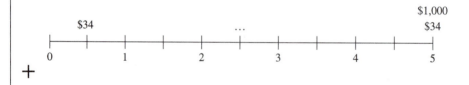

+

Buying ten call options on two barrels of crude oil

+

Buying a five-year currency forward contract with the forward price of 140 ¥/$

Money unit = $; underlying asset = ¥

**Figure 8.9** Oil-interest indexed dual-currency bond.

## Spread-Protected Debt Securities and Credit-Sensitive Bonds

*Spread-protected debt securities* can be redeemed on a specified date prior to maturity, at the option of the holders. The redemption price is equal to the present value of the remaining promised payment discounted at a rate equal to a specified Treasury benchmark yield plus a fixed spread. This feature offers protection to the investor against a possible deteriorating of the creditworthiness of the bond. When the bond has a higher default risk, the investors can exercise the option to ensure that they receive a payment with a credit spread no wider than that specified in the provision.

A *credit-sensitive bond* is a bond with the coupon rate related to the bond rating. The issuers show their confidence in their firm by issuing these bonds, which have a coupon rate that is not fixed until the maturity of the bond, but depends on the bond rating. As the bond rating falls, the coupon rate will increase by a prespecified schedule. When these bonds were first issued, the design was motivated by market demand. The investors had concerns about the issuer's credit and wanted to be compensated if the rating fell. However, if the firm's financial health deteriorates, credit-sensitive bonds add more financial pressure for the firm.

These two bond types are related to the credit risk of the issuer. Modeling credit risk is complex, to say the least, and these bonds are also difficult to model. Their valuation must be related to the operations and profitability of the issuers. Therefore, to better understand the valuation of these bonds, we cannot simply view them as another type of market security, but as securities tied to corporate finance.

# EXCEL MODEL EXERCISES

## E8.1   CONVERTIBLE BONDS

### Definitions

The maturity and the coupon rate of the convertible bond are self-explanatory. The conversion price (CP) is the stock price at which the conversion ratio times the conversion price is equal to the par value of the bond. The conversion ratio (CR) is the number of shares into which the face value of the convertible bond can convert, given the current stock price. Therefore, we have that $CP \cdot CR = 1,000$.

### Description of the Model

The holder of a convertible bond has the right to convert the bond into a predetermined number of shares of common stocks. The convertible bond is a hybrid of a bond and a stock.

### Numerical Example

Consider a ten-year-maturity convertible bond with a coupon rate of 15%. The convertible bond is assumed a straight bond for simplicity. The convertible bond could have a call provision, a sinking fund provision, and a put provision. The yield curve is flat at 15% for simplicity. See figure E8.1.

| Inputs | |
| --- | --- |
| Bond maturity (year) | 10 |
| Coupon rate | 0.15 |
| Conversion price | $20 |
| Par value | $1,000 |
| Convertible bond price | $1,124 |
| Common stock price | $21 |
| Dividend per share | $1 |
| Flat yield curve | 0.15 |
| Credit spread | 0.01 |
| **Outputs** | |
| Conversion ratio | 50.00 |
| Conversion value (parity) | $1,050.00 |
| Investment value | $920.59 |

Figure E8.1

The holder of exchangeable bonds has the right to exchange the bonds for the common stocks of a firm other than the issuer of the bonds. The conversion ratio is 50 and the conversion value (parity) is $1,050, which is the value of the convertible bond if it is converted immediately. The investment value is the value of the convertible bond when we ignore the possibility of converting it to the equity. Therefore, the investment value is the underlying bond value, which is the present value of the bond cash flow adjusted for the credit risk.

The minimum price of the convertible bond is the greater of its conversion value or its investment value.

## Applications

1. The model determines the convertible bond value.
2. The model determines the convertible bond value with other features rather than the convertible provision such as the call and put provisions.
3. The model can disaggregate the convertible bond value into several components such as the investment value or the value of the conversion provision.

## Case: Hedging a Convertible Bond Issue

Hans Stephano greeted Giovani Fun with deference. Giovani was the founder of Fun with Funds (FF), a highly successful fund of funds that was holding more than twenty hedge funds in the portfolio, diversifying their risks for the investors of FF. Giovani was considering replacing some bond funds by some convertible hedge funds, like the fund that Hans was managing. He wanted to take more equity risks, at the expense of credit risks.

"Giovani, thank you for seeing us." "Hans, thank you for finding time to see me," Giovani replied cheerfully. "Look, this hedge fund world never fails to surprise me.

Why they call themselves 'hedge fund,' I know not. Most of the time, they don't seem to hedge anything." "They have the license to take short positions—I guess that would qualify these funds to be called 'hedged.'" "Hans, I just saw this fund," Giovani started laughing. "They told me that they have seven hedge strategies that together would give investors 20% annual returns with a Sharpe ratio of 4. (Sharpe ratio is the excess return to the standard deviation of the returns)." Giovani continued to laugh.

"They then showed me one of their strategies called TIPS" (Treasury inflation protection securities, which have their coupon rate linked to the inflation rate). "That strategy consists of holding six TIPS bonds, and so I asked: 'Where is the hedge?' The guy said, looking really puzzled, 'We are hedging against inflation. That is our strategy!'" Giovani laughed heartily, so much so that Hans had to join him laughing. "Well, they get their stable high returns anyway. That counts," Hans concluded.

"No, that is not all. Then that guy continued to brag about his performance. He then told me that, last quarter, his investor called him and said: 'Your fund is making too much money.' So he asked: 'Is that a problem to you?' His investor said: 'Yes. My board has many bean counters. When they see too many beans, they become convinced that you are taking too much risk or stealing. After all, the market is supposed to be efficient, right?'" Giovani could not continue because he was laughing too much. "Hedge fund is so much fun." Giovani caught his breath and then continued: "The guy then said: 'OK, I will lose some money for you for the rest of the quarter then.'"

They paused. Then Giovani looked serious again. "So, tell me how you get your returns." "As you know, we are a convertible arbitrage shop. All the principals here were arbitrage traders in convertibles previously from Pac Atlantic Securities. We look for special situations." Hans now lowered his voice, underscoring the seriousness of the business. "For example, we now look at Monobio Technologies." "What, Mono Tech? That is in distress, isn't it?" "But that is where the opportunities are. This issue, which we call Peace, has a special feature. This issue is basically a note maturing in five years paying 7% coupon. Period. That is it. The wrinkle is that the holder of the bond has to buy one share of the stock at $30 for each $100 bond by the end of next year." "So, this Peace thing is a bond with a forward contract on a share." Giovani was making sure that he understood the terms. "That is right. But, if the firm goes default, there would be no shares to buy, and then the forward contract is nullified. The bond would get the recovery amount, and there would be no obligation to buy the stock. The bond is totally mispriced. People do not understand the recovery part and the nullification of the forward contract. The market price of Peace has mispriced the digital option, even though the closing price of the stock is only $3."

"So what do you do?" "Mr. Fun, of course, we buy loads of them." "How do you arbitrage this?" "We short the three-year Treasuries." "That is it?" "Why do more? Mona Lisa's smile is great, but you do not need to put another smile on her face, do you?"

*"I just do not see the arbitrage and the hedge in these strategies. In fact, I am not even sure that the Peace thing is a convertible bond. Let me analyze this Peace when I get back to the office."* Giovani was shaking his head and saying to himself, *"This is no fun. Digital?"*

## Exercises and Answers

1. In figure 8.1 (bond curve and parity line), the x-axis and the y-axis represent the parity value and the investment value, respectively. Explain why the bond value is a curve rather than a horizon line.

*Answer:* Since many convertible bonds in the United States do not have high credit-worthiness, we should assume that the convertible bonds are risky bonds. Therefore, when the parity value is low (i.e., the firm value is low), the investment value is low accordingly. When the investment value does not depend on the firm's default risk, the investment value should be a horizontal line.

To incorporate the credit risk, we use the firm value rather than the stock value as the underlying risk source to evaluate the convertible bond.

2. In figure 8.2 (warrant curve), the warrant value converges to the 45° line originating from the present value of the face value at the x-axis. Explain why?

*Answer:* We know that the European call option on a stock converges to a 45° line originating from the present value of an exercise price at the x-axis as the stock price is getting larger. Here, the warrant is a long-dated American option. However, when the dividend on a stock is lower than the coupon payment of the convertible bond, there is no value to the early exercise. Therefore, we can now simply focus our attention on what the investors optimally do at maturity.

3. In figure 8.3 (composition of the convertible bond value), the curve XY represents the convertible bond value. The line OA is the parity line. However, when the parity line is high, the convertible bond value does not converge to the parity line. Instead the convertible bond value converges to the parallel line of DE. The distance of point D from the y-axis is the present value of the face value. Explain why. What is the minimum value of the convertible bond value in figure 8.3?

*Answer:* As we have explained in question 2, the latent warrant value converges to the present value of the face value.

The minimum value of the convertible bond is the curve ODA in figure 8.3. The difference between the curve XY and the curve ODA is the latent warrant value in figure 8.2.

### Further Exercises

1. Repeat the numerical example assuming that the conversion price (CP) is $25 and the common strock price is $22.
*Answer:* The conversion ratio is 40, the conversion value is $880, and the investment value is $920.59.
2. Repeat numerical example assuming that the conversion price (CP) is $25, the common stock price is $22, and the yield curve is flat at 16%.
*Answer:* The conversion ratio is 40, the conversion value is $880, and the investment value is $873.63.

## E8.2   MORTGAGE-BACKED SECURITIES (LEVEL PAYMENT, PSA, IO & PO)

### Definitions

Mortgage-backed securities are securities backed by a pool of individual home mortgages. A mortgage pool is a portfolio of mortgages collected under certain guidelines. The pool is put into a trust, and bonds are issued as claims against the portfolio. These bonds are referred to as pass-throughs, in that they simply pass the interest and principal collected from all the mortgagors and pass them to the bondholders on a pro rata basis.

## Description of the Model

The model uses a behavioral model of prepayments. The value is derived from Monte Carlo simulations and the pathwise values of cash flows of the bond.

## Numerical Example

The spot curve is flat at 10%. The loan principal is $100, and the annual interest rate on the loan is 10%. The loan term is ten years. See figure E8.2.

Consider a ten-year-maturity loan with a 10% annual interest. The interest will be paid semiannually. What is the level payment? How will the interest and the principal portion change over the life of the loan? The level payment is $8.02426. The interest portion is decreasing from $5 at year 1. However, the principal portion is increasing from $3.02426 at year 1.

## Applications

1. The model determines the payments of the mortgage-backed securities at each period.
2. The IO & PO model evaluates a security called the interest only and principal only.

## Case: Pricing a Guaranteed Investment Contract and the Profit Spread

Bombay Financial International exploited a niche in the marketplace. Over the years, the firm had developed close relationships with a network of manufacturing companies, which had grown significantly in recently years. Bombay would sell these firms

| Inputs | | | | | |
|---|---|---|---|---|---|
| | Spot curve (%) | | 10% | | |
| | Annual interest payment (%) | | 10% | | |
| | The term of loan (year) | | 10 | | |
| | The principal ($) | | 100 | | |
| **Outputs** | | | | | |
| Period | | 1 | 2 | 3 | 4 |
| Cash flow | | 5 | 5 | 5 | 5 |
| PV of each period | | 4.76190 | 4.53515 | 4.31919 | 4.11351 |
| Level payment | 8.02426 | | | | |
| PV of loan | | 100 | 96.97574 | 93.80027 | 90.46602 |
| Interest | | 5.00000 | 4.84879 | 4.69001 | 4.52330 |
| Principal | | 3.02426 | 3.17547 | 3.33425 | 3.50096 |
| | | 8.02426 | 8.02426 | 8.02426 | 8.02426 |

Figure E8.2

investment vehicles for the pension funds, cash management, and other financial instruments for their retained earnings. One product was particularly popular, called guaranteed investment contract (GIC).

Typically, their GIC was a three-year contract with a face value of $5 million. The manufacturing firm would buy a GIC from Bombay at a discount of the face value, called the price, and then receive the face value at the termination date. "Basically, a zero-coupon bond," as Morihito Hashimoto, the CEO of Bombay, would say.

Morihito's business model was quite simple, as he explained: "I told my salespeople to look for clients, then come back and see our investment guys. The yield of the GIC, and that is the return to our clients, has to be less than our investment returns. Now, my investment manager must, I mean must, assign certain assets to back the GIC that is to be sold. The spread between the asset returns and the returns of the GIC to our clients is our gross profit." He spoke with an air of a commander in chief. "If the gross profit spread is negative, we just do not sell. Nil. I am telling you, Bombay did not grow so phenomenally without a sound philosophy."

"That is exactly right, boss. This idea sounds simple and it works. Just incredible." Amazonia Brazilia concurred. "I just sold a GIC to a client at a 7%. Our client could not find any paper that would give them 6%. Our GIC is really selling well. They just grabbed our stuff." "Amazonia, you know you have to back your GICs with higher-yielding assets." "Sure, boss, I check with our investment people every time. This is how it works. Recently, they can find these STRIPS IOs with average life about three years, matching our GIC, and the yield of these bonds are about 9%. These are great rates, full 500 basis points above Treasuries."

"Explain to me about this STRIPS IO?" "These are Fannie Mae STRIPS, for example, backed by thirty-year FNMA 8% mortgages. They have 175 PSA. As I said, they have weighted average life of three years. Priced at around 37.5 recently. We get the interests of these mortgages but do not get the principals, as the mortgagors pay their interests and principals to the banks."

"Amazonia, there is something I am missing here. If the mortgagors prepay, we would lose our payments. Am I right?" "Yes. I guess. But boss, you are living in a hypothetical world now. The mortgagors do not really call up each other to prepay altogether you know." "Tell me, if interest rates fall, does the price of the IO fall because the prepayment risks go up?" "Yep. We do see the price change. But we really do not care because we are not buying or selling. We hold the bond till maturity and we really do not care about the market price. You want it that way, right?"

"Just a minute, that would mean that our duration of the IO is negative and not three years," Morihito raised his voice a bit to show his concern. "You lose me there, boss. Our weighted average life takes the prepayment into account. Therefore our Macauley duration is three years. Why is it negative?"

Without answering Amazonia's question, Morihito continued his thought. "And the loss would increase as the rate falls farther, a negative convexity." Amazonia was staring at his boss at a loss. "That means, we sold a bunch of options in our IOs. And no wonder, we get such a high yield for our investments."

"Boss, can you go a bit slower." "Amazonia, you made a blunder. Our asset duration is nowhere matching our GICs. Our asset returns cannot cover our GIC cost of funding. We are digging a deep hole here!" Morihito began to raise his voice as many thoughts of risks went through his mind. "Boss, we are just following your philosophy," Amazonia murmured.

*Morihito did not hear anything other than his own voice: "What should I do now? How should I change my philosophy? How can I get my staff to understand basic stuff?"*

## Exercises and Answers

1. We assume that the bond principal is $100 and the annual coupon payment is 4.5%. The call price is $100. Calculate the callable bond price, the interest only, and the principal only. Confirm that the sum of the interest only and the principal only is equal to the callable bond price.
   *Answer:* The callable bond price is $98.989, the principal only is $87.985, and the interest only is $11.004. The sum of the interest only and the principal only is 98.989, which is the callable bond price. See figure E8.3.
2. Repeat question 1 when we assume that the yield curve makes an upward movement by 0.1%. Based on the results, calculate the effective duration of the callable bond, the principal only, and the interest only.
   *Answer:* The effective duration of the callable bond, the principal only, and the interest only are 3.118, 48.200, and −357.334, respectively. Since the effective duration of the interest only is −357.334, we expect that the interest-only price increases whenever the interest increases, which is opposite to the ordinary interest-sensitive securities like the callable bond or the principal only. See figure E8.4.
3. Prepayment rates are commonly expressed in three different ways. Given the scheduled balance and the actual balance, calculate the single monthly mortality (SMM) and the conditional prepayment rate (CPR). The monthly scheduled balance is 100 and the monthly actual balance is 90.
   *Answer:* The SMM is 10 and the CPR is 71.757. The PSA diagram is given in figure E8.5.

| Outputs | | | | | | |
|---|---|---|---|---|---|---|
| | | | | | | 100.000 |
| | | | | | 94.394 | 100.000 |
| | | | | 89.547 | 94.990 | 100.000 |
| | | | 85.490 | 90.764 | 95.591 | 100.000 |
| | | 84.069 | 91.182 | 100.000 | 100.000 | 100.000 |
| Principal only | 87.985 | 100.000 | 100.000 | 100.000 | 100.000 | 100.000 |
| Year | 0 | 1 | 2 | 3 | 4 | 5 |
| | | | | | | 4.500 |
| | | | | | 8.748 | 4.500 |
| | | | | 12.785 | 8.775 | 4.500 |
| | | | 16.664 | 12.871 | 8.802 | 4.500 |
| | | 18.522 | 12.803 | 4.500 | 4.500 | 4.500 |
| Interest only | 11.004 | 4.500 | 4.500 | 4.500 | 4.500 | 4.500 |
| Year | 0 | 1 | 2 | 3 | 4 | 5 |
| IO + PO = callable bond | 98.989 | | | | | |

**Figure E8.3**

## Outputs

| | | 0 | 1 | 2 | 3 | 4 | 5 |
|---|---|---|---|---|---|---|---|
| | | | | | | | 100.000 |
| | | | | | | 94.273 | 100.000 |
| | | | | | 89.328 | 94.882 | 100.000 |
| | | | | 85.193 | 90.569 | 95.495 | 100.000 |
| | | | 83.747 | 90.997 | 100.000 | 100.000 | 100.000 |
| Principal only | | 83.744 | 91.625 | 100.000 | 100.000 | 100.000 | 100.000 |
| Year | | 0 | 1 | 2 | 3 | 4 | 5 |
| | | | | | | | 4.500 |
| | | | | | | 8.742 | 4.500 |
| | | | | | 12.770 | 8.770 | 4.500 |
| | | | | 16.636 | 12.857 | 8.797 | 4.500 |
| | | | 18.486 | 12.788 | 4.500 | 4.500 | 4.500 |
| Interest only | | 14.937 | 12.793 | 4.500 | 4.500 | 4.500 | 4.500 |
| Year | | 0 | 1 | 2 | 3 | 4 | 5 |
| Effective duration of the callable bond | | 3.118 | | | | | |
| Effective duration of the principal only | | 48.200 | | | | | |
| Effective duration of the interest only | | -357.334 | | | | | |
| IO + PO = callable bond | | 98.681 | | | | | |

Figure E8.4

## Inputs

### Input Data

| | | | | |
|---|---|---|---|---|
| Scheduled balance ($) | 100 | <= | Monthly | |
| Actual balance ($) | 90 | <= | Monthly | |

### Output Data

| | |
|---|---|
| SMM | 10 |
| CPR | 71.757 |

| PSA | 0.20% | 0 | 10 | 20 | 30 | 40 | 50 | 60 |
|---|---|---|---|---|---|---|---|---|
| | 100% | 0.02 | 0.02 | 0.04 | 0.06 | 0.06 | 0.06 | 0.06 |
| | 150% | 0.02 | 0.03 | 0.06 | 0.09 | 0.09 | 0.09 | 0.09 |
| | 200% | 0.02 | 0.04 | 0.08 | 0.12 | 0.12 | 0.12 | 0.12 |
| | 400% | 0.02 | 0.08 | 0.16 | 0.24 | 0.24 | 0.24 | 0.24 |

Figure E8.5

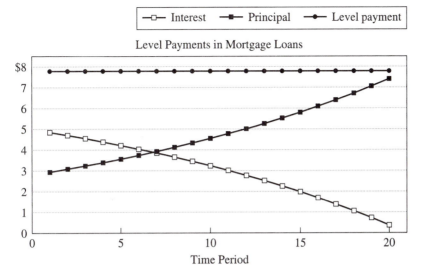

Figure E8.6

## Further Exercises

1. When the yield curve makes an upward movement by 1%, repeat the numerical example.
   *Answer:* The level payment is $7.77947. See figure E8.6.
2. When we change the call price to $103 and the annual coupon rate to 5.5% in question 1, calculate the callable bond price, the interest only, and the principal only.
   *Answer:* The callable bond price is $103.122. The principal only is $88.549, and the interest only is $14.574.

### Bibliography

Brennan, M. J., and E. S. Schwartz. 1977. Convertible bonds: Valuation and optimal strategies for call and conversion. *Journal of Finance*, 32 (5), 1699–1715.

Davidson, A. S., T. S. Y. Ho, and Y. C. Lim. 1994. *Collateralized Mortgage Obligations*. Chicago: Probus.

Fabozzi, F., ed. 1997. *Advances in Fixed Income Valuation Modeling and Risk Management*. New Hope, PA: Wiley.

Ingersoll, J. E. 1977. An examination of corporate call policies on convertible securities. *Journal of Finance*, 32 (2), 463–478.

Kang, J. K., and Y. W. Lee. 1986. The pricing of convertible debt offerings. *Journal of Financial Economics*, 41, 231–248.

Lavely, J. A. 1971. Comparative usage of bond-warrant and convertible bond issues. *Journal of Finance*, 26 (3), 796–797.

Mayers, D. 1998. Why firms issue convertible bonds: The matching of financial and real investment options. *Journal of Financial Economics*, 47 (1), 83–102.

Schwarz, E. S., and W. N. Torous. 1992. Prepayment, default, and the valuation of mortgage pass-through securities. *Journal of Business*, 65 (2), 221–239.

Tsiveriotis, K., and C. Fernandes. 1998. Valuing convertible bonds with credit risk. *Journal of Fixed Income*, September, 95–102.

# Index

Note: Page numbers followed by an "f" refer to figures, page numbers followed by an "n" refer to notes, and page numbers followed by a "t" refer to tables.

Absolute priority rule, 228
Absorption barrier, 89
ABSs. *See* Asset-backed securities
Acceleration clause, 256
Accumulators, 225
Actuarial models, 259–64
Agency deals, 294
Amazon.com case study, 288
American options, 90–94, 97–103
    comparative statics for, 120–21
    Cox-Ross-Rubinstein model for, 51, 97
    dividends and, 79, 90–91
    European options vs., 66–67, 90–92, 94f, 101–2
    exchange trade of, 30–31
    put-call parity and, 66–67, 92, 99
    risk-free rate and, 103, 104f
    warrants and, 289, 310
American Stock Exchange, 31
Amortization schedule, swap market, 128
Arbitrage
    American options and, 91, 97
    Black-Scholes model and, 42, 184
    call option price and, 91
    capital and, 132
    CAPM and, 9
    compound options and, 104
    credit default premium and, 275–76
    digital options and, 110
    dynamic hedging and, 37
    interest rates and, 183–89
    law of one price and, 132–33
    market efficiency and, 132
    probability distribution and, 37
    put-call parity and, 33
    risk-neutral options and, 42, 184
    STRIPS program and, 127
    tranches and, 302
    Treasury securities and, 127
Arbitrage-free model. *See* Ho-Lee model
Asset-backed securities (ABSs), 221, 246–48
Asset liability committee case study, 169–70
"At make whole" call option, 222–23
"At the money," 30
Attrition rate, 98

Backward substitution method, 40, 41f, 44
Balance sheet, 252, 254
Bankruptcy, 228, 255–58
    in Kim-Ramaswamy-Sundaresan model, 268
    in Leland model, 269

McLeodUSA case study, 252–55
    recovery ratio and, 262
Barbell position, 147–49
Barrier options, 87–90
Basis points. *See* Price value of a basis point
Basis risks, 233, 299
Bellman optimization concept, 91, 94, 297
Benchmark bonds, 192
Bermuda option, 90, 95f
Beta, 7–9, 15
Bid-ask spreads, 33, 74, 209
Bills, Treasury. *See* Treasury bills
Binary option, 85–86, 110–15
Binomial lattice, 34–36
    backward substitution method and, 40, 41f
    market, 45–46, 80–83
    pathwise methodology in, 43–44
    risk-neutral, 42–43, 45–46, 80–83
Black-Cox model, 267
Black model, 208–11
Black-Scholes model, 34, 37–40
    arbitrage and, 42, 184
    for comparative statics, 115–16, 118–21
    Cox-Ingersoll-Ross model vs., 182
    Cox-Ross-Rubinstein model vs., 37, 51
    Excel exercises for, 70–76
    Ho-Lee model and, 183–84
    Merton model and, 266
    risk-neutral probability and, 42–43
    for swap market, 117
    Vasicek model vs., 182
    volatility and, 50, 64
Boilerplate, 256
Bond factor, 223
Bond model, 133, 134–35
Bonds
    binomial lattice for, 233, 234f
    consol, 123, 125
    convertible, 287–93, 307–10
    credit-sensitive, 307
    debentures, 221–24, 273
    definition of, 123
    equipment, 221
    in index portfolio, 149
    investment-grade, 222, 228
    issue size, 222
    medium-term notes, 221
    municipal, 127
    perpetual, 123, 125
    public, 221
    residual, 303
    retirement of, pro rata, 223
    serial, 250

*See also* Corporate bonds; Discount bonds; High-yield bonds; Mortgages; Pass-through certificates; Treasury bonds; Zero-coupon bonds
Boundary conditions, 87–90
British Bankers Association, 125
Briys–de Varenne model, 268
Bullet payment, 128, 133
Burnout, 296, 297

Call options
    accumulators and, 225
    American vs. European, 66–67, 90–92, 101–2
    "at make whole" provision, 222–23
    Bellman optimization concept, 91, 94
    binomial lattice for, 34–36, 41f
    in Black model, 208–11
    in Black-Scholes model, 42–43, 70–71, 73–75
    bond price and, 224–26, 233–36, 241–46
    boundary conditions on, 87–90
    closed-form solution for, 120
    comparative statics for, 48f, 77–78, 118–21
    compound option vs., 106–8
    in convertible bonds, 287–93
    convexity and, 192
    in corporate bonds, 222–26, 233–36
    coupons and, 222–23
    covered, 48–49, 77
    in Cox-Ingersoll-Ross model, 195, 197
    in Cox-Ross-Rubinstein model, 38–40, 42–43, 51, 97
    in debentures, 222
    definition of, 29, 97
    digital options and, 85–86, 112–15
    in discrete time option pricing model, 42–43
    dividends and, 64, 73–75, 77, 79, 90–91
    duration and, 189–91, 243–44, 313
    dynamic hedging and, 36–37
    in Ericsson-Reneby model, 265
    Excel exercises for, 51–64, 70–79, 97–102, 241–46
    exchange trade of, 30–31
    face value and, 222
    hedge funds and, 117–18
    hedge ratio and, 48f, 54–56, 77–78, 118–21
    installment payments on, 95–96, 108–10
    interest rates and, 225, 289, 291

intrinsic value of, 30–31
key rate and, 189–91
market binomial lattice and, 83
McLeodUSA case study, 253
Microsoft case study, 31
on mortgages, 296–300, 313–15
option-adjusted spread and, 235–36
parity and, 292–93
payoff diagram for, 30
performance profile for, 46f, 48f, 88f, 92f, 302f
profit diagram for, 77
put-call parity and, 31–33, 64–70, 92, 99
recession and, 241–43
returns and risk in, 30
risk-free rate and, 60, 103, 104f, 211
risk-neutral binomial lattice and, 83
risk-neutral probability and, 42–43
schedules for, 126, 222
sinking fund provision vs., 226
stock price and, 30, 46f, 91–92
straddle strategy for, 49
strike price and, 29–31, 91–92
STRIPS and, 98–99
in swap market case study, 117
time values and, 31t
tranches and, 302f, 313–15
in Treasury securities, 126
Vasicek model for, 200, 202
volatility and, 54, 103, 211
yield and, 222–26, 229–33, 243
zero-coupon bonds and, 189–91, 195, 197
See also Warrants
Capital
arbitrage and, 132
debt structure and, 220, 241–43, 269
pass-through case study, 247–48
REITs and, 23
Capital Asset Pricing model (CAPM), 5–9, 15–22
Capital gains, 123, 133f, 142
Capitalization
absolute priority rule and, 283, 284f
in compound option model, 271
in Cox-Ross-Rubinstein model, 266–67
debt structure and, 219, 273
default risk and, 271
definition of, 7, 254
firm value and, 254
in Fisher model, 258
in Ho-Singer model, 280, 283
in Merton model, 266–67
stock price and, 7, 254
Capital market line (CML), 5–6, 17–18, 20f, 21
CAPM. See Capital Asset Pricing model
Cash flow
bond price and, 143
"call at make whole" provision and, 222
definition of, 123
discount function and, 133–34
firm value and, 254
floating rate and, 170–71
forwards and futures and, 136t
in Ho-Singer model, 279
in Kim-Ramaswamy-Sundaresan model, 268–69
law of one price and, 133
in Monte Carlo simulations, 300
mortgages and, 299
pass-through certificates and, 221
serial bonds and, 250

sinking fund provision and, 223, 250
yield to maturity and, 143
in zero-coupon case study, 134–35
Cash market, 135
CBs. See Convertible bonds
Certificate of Deposit (CD), 64, 165, 169–70
Chapter 11, filing of, 228, 255–58
Chapter 13, filing of, 256, 257
Cheap securities, 21, 127, 132
Chicago Board of Trade, 31
CIR. See Cox-Ingersoll-Ross model
Clean price, 123–24
Closed-end funds, 9, 11
CML. See Capital market line
CMOs. See Collateralized mortgage obligations
Collateralized mortgage obligations (CMOs), 301–5
Commercial paper rate, 64, 125
Company reorganization case study, 280–81
Complete market, 133
Compounding frequency, 160
Compound options, 95–96, 104–8, 269–73, 278–84
Concavity, 192
Concentration risk, 220
Conditional prepayment rate (CPR), 299f, 313
Confirm sheet, 128
Consol bonds, 123, 125
Convertible bonds (CBs), 287–93, 307–10
Convexity, 145–48, 167–68, 192
Corporate bonds
binomial lattice for, 233, 234f
definition of, 127
issue size, 222
payment schedules for, 221–22
types of, 221
See also High-yield bonds; Pass-through certificates
Correlation coefficient, 14f, 15
Correlation matrix, 178t
Coupons
acceleration clause and, 256
accrued interest and, 123–24
bankruptcy and, 256
binomial lattice and, 233, 234f
call options and, 222–23
capital gains and, 123
compound options and, 96, 105, 269
credit risk ratings and, 307
debt structure and, 253–54, 269–70
definition of, 123
discount function and, 134
duration and, 153–55
fixed rate and, 128, 221
floating rate and, 128
forwards/futures and, 136t, 157–58, 160
inflation rate and, 126, 309
invoice price and, 124
in Kim-Ramaswamy-Sundaresan model, 269
market interest rate and, 124
mortgages and, 296
perpetual bonds and, 125
principal and, 123, 221
pro rata bond retirement and, 223
quoted price and, 123–24
sinking fund provision and, 223, 237, 248–50
in swap market, 127–28, 214–17
tax and, 123
TIPS and, 309

tranches and, 302–3
Treasury securities and, 125–26
Wal-Mart case study, 219–22
yield and, 124–25, 259
See also Zero-coupon bonds
Covariance/variance, 3–4, 7, 9f, 13–15, 17–18
Covenants
bankruptcy and, 228, 256
in Ericsson-Reneby model, 265
knockout option and, 270
recovery ratio and, 262
safety, 268
Covered call option, 48–49, 77
Cow graph, 304–5
Cox-Ingersoll-Ross (CIR) model, 181–82, 192–97
Cox-Ross-Rubinstein (CRR) model
for American options, 51, 97
Black-Scholes model vs., 37, 51
call options in, 38–40, 42–43, 51
capitalization in, 266–67
dividends and, 51
Excel exercises for, 51, 61, 97
face value in, 266
firm value in, 266–67
Merton model and, 266
for put-call parity, 64–65
put options in, 51
risk-neutral probability and, 42, 43t
volatility and, 38, 51, 61
yield and, 51
CPR. See Conditional prepayment rate
Credit default, 273–78
Creditors
bankruptcy and, 255–58
in Black-Cox model, 267
classification of, 255
recovery rates of, 261–62
reorganization plan and, 257–58
strategic debt servicing and, 228
See also Absolute priority rule
Credit risk ratings
actuarial model for, 259–64
bond price and, 227–29
components in, 233
for convertible bonds, 289, 293, 310
for corporate bonds, 227–29
coupons and, 307
debt structure and, 253–54
default risk and, 261
in Fisher model, 258–59, 260
interest rates and, 268
McLeodUSA case study, 253–55
in Merton model, 266–67
option-adjusted spread and, 229–33, 260
recession and, 232
reduced-form models for, 264–66
sectors and, 220, 229–32
spread-protected debt securities and, 307
structural models for, 266–69
term structure and, 232, 270
transition matrix for, 262–65
yield and, 229–32
Credit-sensitive bonds, 307
Critical parity value, 292
Cross default, 228, 256, 269
CRR model. See Cox-Ross-Rubinstein model
Currency exchange rates, 305

Debentures, 221–24, 273
Debt structure
bank loans and, 273
bankruptcy and, 228
capital and, 220, 241–43, 269

Debt structure (*continued*)
capitalization and, 219, 273
compound options and, 269–73
corporate bonds and, 220, 222, 228, 229–32
coupons and, 253–54, 269–70
credit risk ratings and, 253–54
debentures and, 273
default and, 260, 269
definition of, 255, 269
firm value and, 269–70
in Ho-Singer model, 270–71
McLeodUSA case study, 253–54
in Merton model, 266
option-adjusted spread and, 229–32
pension funds and, 273
principal and, 269–70
sectors and, 220, 229
sinking fund provision and, 222
Default premium, 259–60
Default risk
actuarial models for, 259–64
bank loans and, 254
bankruptcy and, 228, 255–57
in Black-Cox model, 267
in Bond model, 133
capitalization and, 271
in CDs, 64
commercial paper rate and, 64
credit risk ratings and, 261
debt structure and, 260, 269
in Duffie-Singleton model, 265
in Ericsson-Reneby model, 265, 268
firm value and, 272–73
in Fisher model, 258–59, 260
of high-yield bonds, 228, 260–61
interest rate and, 267–69
in Jarrow-Lando-Turnbull model, 264–65
in Jarrow-Turnbull model, 264
in Kim-Ramaswamy-Sundaresan model, 268–69
knockout option and, 265, 269
in Leland model, 269
in Longstaff-Schwartz model, 268
McLeodUSA case study, 253
in Merton model, 266–67
mortgages and, 294–95
pass-through certificates and, 247
reduced-form models for, 264–66
sectors and, 261
sinking fund provision and, 224
strike price and, 268
in STRIPS, 127
structural models for, 266–69
swap rates and, 128, 168, 213
transition matrix for, 262–65
in Treasury securities, 64, 127
yield and, 267–68
Delta
call options and, 48f, 77–78, 118–21
in Cox-Ross-Rubinstein model, 38–39
definition of, 34, 46–47, 115
digital options and, 85
of straddle strategy, 49, 50f
volatility and, 54, 185–86, 203, 208
*See also* Hedge ratio
Derivatives, 294. *See also* Pass-through certificates
Digital options, 85–87, 110–15
Dilution, 289
Dirty price. *See* Invoice price
Disclosure requirements, 221
Discount, trading at, 124
Discount bonds, 127, 133, 185–88, 233, 234f
Discount factor, 185–88

Discount function
arbitrage-free models and, 184–88
in Black model, 209
bond price and, 133–34, 185–88
bullet payment and, 133
cash flow and, 133–34
in corporate bonds, 233
coupons and, 134
definition of, 133, 155
face value of, 127
forwards/futures and, 137, 140, 156
interest rate and, 187–88
principal and, 134
STRIPS and, 133
swap market and, 133
yield and, 134, 184
for zero-coupon bonds, 185–88
Discount rate
in arbitrage-free models, 186
for bullet payment, 128
"call at make whole" provision and, 222–23
in corporate bonds, 233
for digital options, 87f
dividends and, 10, 22–23
in Duffie-Singleton model, 265
from Federal Reserve banks, 125
fixed-rate bond and, 304
floating rate and, 170
interest rates and, 180, 186–88
in Merton model, 267
for money markets, 125
option-adjusted spread and, 232
in put-call parity, 32–33
in risk premium, 1
systematic risk and, 3, 9
Discount window, 130
Discrete time option pricing model. *See* Cox-Ross-Rubinstein model
Diversification
concentration risk and, 220
definition of, 1, 11
pension fund case study, 12–13
of stock portfolios, 2–5, 11–15, 17–18
Dividend Discount model, 9–11, 22–26
Dividends
American option and, 79, 90–91
in Black-Scholes model, 70, 73–75
call options and, 64, 73–75, 77, 79, 91
comparative statics and, 115, 116f
in Cox-Ross-Rubinstein model, 51
discount rate and, 10, 22–23
earnings and, 10, 23
Excel exercises for, 22–26
firm value and, 266
in Merton model, 266
payout ratio for, 10, 23
plowback ratio for, 23–25
put-call parity and, 66, 68–69
PVGO and, 25–26
rate of return and, 10, 22–26
REITs and, 23–24
risk-free rate and, 22
warrants and, 289, 310
yield and, 115–17, 119f
Dollar duration, 142–43, 147, 160–68
Double-up option, 226–27, 237–40
Dow Jones Industrial Average Call and Put, 31
Down parameter, 35f, 38–39, 41f, 42–43, 45, 54, 87
Drift
definition of, 80
interest rates and, 177, 180
market price of risk and, 182
risk-neutral probability and, 43, 45

stock price and, 175–76
in Treasury securities, 180
Dual-currency bonds, 305, 306f
Duffie-Singleton model, 265
Duplicating portfolio. *See* Levered portfolio
Duration
bond price and, 141–47, 153–55
call options and, 189–91, 243–44, 313
capital gains and, 142
CDs and, 169–70
of convertible bonds, 310
convexity and, 146
coupons and, 153–55
definition of, 140–41
dollar, 142–43, 147, 160–68
Excel exercises for, 149–55
in hedging case study, 169–70
interest rates and, 141–47, 151–53, 164–68, 189–92, 302, 313
Macauley, 142
modified, 143
performance profile and, 147
principal and, 151
put option and, 189–91
sinking fund provision and, 248
spot rates and, 141–42
tranches and, 302, 313
value at risk and, 151
yield and, 141–45, 150–55, 165–68, 189–92
zero-coupon bond and, 141–42, 145, 150–53, 189–90
*See also* Key rate
Dynamic hedging
arbitrage and, 37
binomial lattice for, 36–37
Black model and, 210–11
call options and, 36–37
comparative statics for, 116
credit default premium and, 276
definition of, 36–37, 47
duration and, 165
interest rates and, 189–90, 192
option premiums and, 36–37
price value of a basis point and, 165
risk-free rate and, 36–37
stock price and, 36–37
in swap market case study, 117–18

Earnings, 10, 23–24, 258–59
Efficient frontier, 5–6, 17–18
Efficient market hypothesis, 36
Efficient portfolios, 5, 17
Embedded options, 29
Employee options, 97–103, 112–13
Equilibrium, 9, 10, 16, 21–22
Equilibrium models, 180–82, 193–202
Equipment bonds, 221
Equity, 23–24
Equity options
Bermuda provision and, 90, 95f
comparative statics for, 46–48, 115–16, 118–21
dynamic hedging and, 36–37, 42, 47
implied volatility in, 49–50, 64, 75–76
put-call parity and, 31–33
straddle strategy for, 49, 50f, 77
terminology of, 29–30
trading of, 30–31, 48–49
volatility in, 30, 46
*See also* Black-Scholes model; Cox-Ross-Rubinstein model
Ericsson-Reneby model, 265, 268
European options
American options vs., 66–67, 90–92, 94f, 101–2

digital option, 85–86, 112–15
pathwise value and, 43–44
*See also* Call options; Put options
Excel exercises
for absolute priority rule, 278–84
for American option, 97–103
for Black-Scholes model, 70–76
for call options, 51–64, 70–79, 97–102, 241–46
for CAPM, 15–22
for comparative statics, 115–16, 118–21
for compound options, 104–8, 278–84
for convertible bonds, 307–10
for Cox-Ingersoll-Ross model, 192–97
for Cox-Ross-Rubinstein model, 51, 61, 97
for credit default swap, 273–78
for digital option, 110–15
for diversification, 11–15
for dividends, 22–26
for dollar duration, 160–68
for duration, 149–55, 160–68
for forward contracts, 156–60
for "Greeks," 115–16, 118–21
for Ho-Lee model, 203–8, 241–50
for Ho-Singer model, 278–84
for installment option, 108–10
for market binomial lattices, 80–83
for mortgages, 310–15
for option-adjusted spread, 244, 248, 250
for put-call parity, 64–70
for put option, 99–103
for risk-neutral binomial lattices, 80–83
for sinking fund provision, 246–50
for swap market, 168–73
for Treasury bills, 61–64, 79
for Vasicek model, 198–202
Exchange-traded funds, 11
Exchange-traded options, 30–31
Executive option case study, 111–15
Exercise price. *See* Strike price
Exotic options
compound, 95–96, 104–8, 269–73, 278–84
definition of, 85
digital, 85–87, 110–15
*See also* American options
Expectation hypothesis, 131, 137–38, 182
Extension risk, 297

Face value
in actuarial default model, 259–60
call price and, 222
in Cox-Ross-Rubinstein model, 266
definition of, 123
of discount function, 127
firm value vs., 273
in Merton model, 266
parity and, 310
*See also* Principal
Factor, bond, 223
Fannie Mae, 294, 312
Federal Home Loan Mortgage Corporation (FHLMC), 294
Federal National Mortgage Association (FNMA), 294, 312
Federal Reserve banks, 125
Fees, fund, 11
FHLMC. *See* Federal Home Loan Mortgage Corporation
Financial sector, 230f

Firm value
absolute priority rule and, 273
in Black-Cox model, 267
capitalization and, 254
cash flow and, 254
comparative statics for, 273
in compound option model, 270
conversion value and, 293
in Cox-Ross-Rubinstein model, 266–67
debt structure and, 269–70
default risk and, 272–73
definition of, 254
dividends and, 266
face value vs., 273
in Ho-Singer model, 270–71
interest rates and, 268
in Kim-Ramaswamy-Sundaresan model, 268–69
in Merton model, 266–67
parity and, 310
recovery ratio and, 262
Fisher model, 130, 258–59, 260
Fixed-income securities
definition of, 123
discount bonds and, 133
forward rate and, 137
market for, 219, 220f
Fixed rate
coupons and, 128, 221
definition of, 128
hedging case study, 165
in swaps, 128, 168, 170–71
Fixed-rate bond
corporate bond case study, 221
discount rate and, 304
interest rates and, 304
inverse floaters and, 304
in swaps, 117
Fixed-rate loans, 169–70
Flight to quality, 232
Floating rate
cash flow and, 170–71
coupons and, 128
definition of, 128, 221
discount rate and, 170
interest rates and, 128, 168
inverse formula for, 305
reset dates for, 221, 305
in swaps, 128, 168, 170–73, 216
yield and, 172–73
Floating-rate note
CMOs and, 303–4
definition of, 305
interest rates and, 117, 128, 190, 303–5
inverse floater for, 304
key rate and, 190
reset dates for, 221, 305
in swaps, 117, 305
FNMA. *See* Federal National Mortgage Association
Forced conversion, 291
Forward contracts
in Black model, 208–9
bond price and, 135–40, 155–58
cash flow and, 136t
coupons and, 136t, 157–58, 160
definition of, 135
discount function and, 137, 140, 156
Excel exercises for, 156–60
expectation hypothesis and, 137–38
fixed-income securities and, 137
in Ho-Lee model, 203, 208
interest rates and, 135–40, 157–58, 203, 208
law of one price and, 136
in money markets, 139–40

par for, 160
pricing of, 135–40, 155–58
principal and, 136t
risk-neutral rate and, 206
spot rate and, 137–40, 156–60
STRIPS and, 158
swaps and, 214–16
Treasury securities and, 135
yield and, 136–40, 156–60
zero-coupon bonds and, 138–39, 155–56, 158
Funds, closed-end, 9, 11
Futures
bond price and, 135–40, 155–58
cash flow and, 136t
coupons and, 136t, 157–58, 160
definition of, 135
interest rates and, 135–40, 157–58, 203, 208
law of one price and, 136
in money markets, 139–40
par for, 160
pricing of, 135–37
principal and, 136t
STRIPS and, 158
swaps and, 214–16
Treasury securities and, 135
yield and, 136–40, 156–60
zero-coupon bonds and, 138–39

Gamma
call options and, 118–21
definition of, 47, 115
digital options and, 85, 86–87
firm value and, 273
of straddle strategy, 49, 50f
theta and, 49
vega and, 49
volatility and, 47
GDP. *See* Gross domestic product
Geske model, 104, 269, 271, 279
GIC. *See* Guaranteed investment contract
GNMA. *See* Government National Mortgage Association
Government National Mortgage Association (GNMA), 294–95
"Greeks"
beta, 7–9, 15
definition of, 46–48, 115
Excel exercises for, 115–16, 118–21
modeling of, 115–16, 118–21
omega, 115, 118, 119f
rho, 60, 115, 118, 119f
straddle strategy and, 49
theta, 48–49, 85, 115, 118–21
vega, 47–49, 50f, 115, 118–21
*See also* Delta; Gamma
Gross domestic product (GDP), 262
Guaranteed investment contract (GIC), 312

Hedge funds
call options and, 117–18
convertible bond case study, 308–9
put options and, 71
quarterly earnings case study, 16–17
Hedge ratio
binomial lattice and, 54
Black model and, 210–11
bond options and, 189–90, 192, 210–11
call option and, 54–56, 77–78
definition of, 34
interest rate and, 189–90, 192
key rate and, 189–90
in levered portfolio, 55
stock price and, 54
use of, 47

Hedge ratio (*continued*)
  volatility and, 54
  zero-coupon bonds and, 189–90
  *See also* Delta
Hedging case study, 165, 169–70
High prepayment efficiency, 300
High-yield bonds
  bankruptcy and, 255–58
  "call at make whole" provision and, 222
  default risk of, 228, 260–61
  definition of, 228
  McLeodUSA case study, 252–55
Ho-Lee model
  Black-Scholes model and, 183–84
  bond price in, 233–35
  Excel exercises for, 203–8, 241–50
  forward contracts in, 203, 208
  interest rates in, 183–89, 203–8
  mean reversion process in, 186
  option-adjusted spread in, 241
  standard deviation in, 185–87
  volatility in, 183, 185–88, 203
  yield in, 183–86, 203
Ho-Singer model, 270–73, 278–84

Implied volatility, 49–50, 64, 75–76
Incentive options, 112–13
Income statement, 252, 254
Income tax, 123
Indenture, 228, 255–57
Indexed currency option notes, 305
Index fund, 7
Index portfolio, 149
Industrial sector, 229, 231f
Inflation rate
  coupons and, 126, 309
  interest rate and, 130, 180
  principal and, 126
  in recession, 130
  Treasury securities and, 126, 309
  yield and, 130–31
Initial public offering (IPO) case study, 111–15
Installment option, 95–96, 108–10
Interest-only tranch, 301–2, 313–15
Interest payments, 127, 221
Interest rates
  absolute priority rule and, 281
  arbitrage-free model for, 183–89, 203–8
  in Black model, 208–11
  in Black-Scholes model, 182–84
  bond price and, 146–47, 167–68, 175–89, 185–88, 206–7
  call option and, 225, 289, 291
  compound options and, 108f
  continuously vs. yearly compounding, 214
  convexity and, 145–47, 167–68, 192
  correlation matrix of, 178t
  in Cox-Ingersoll-Ross model, 181, 193–97
  in Cox-Ross-Rubinstein model, 38
  credit risk ratings and, 268
  default risk and, 267–69
  digital options and, 114
  discount bond, 185–88
  discount factor and, 187
  discount function and, 187–88
  discount rate and, 180, 186–88
  drift and, 177, 180
  dual-currency bonds and, 305
  duration and, 141–47, 151–53, 164–68, 189–92, 302, 313
  dynamic hedging and, 189–90, 192
  equilibrium models for, 180–82, 193–97
  expectation hypothesis for, 131, 182

firm value and, 268
Fisher equation for, 130
fixed-rate bond and, 304
floating rate and, 117, 128, 168, 190, 303–5
forwards/futures and, 135–40, 157–58, 203, 208
hedge ratio and, 189–90, 192
in Ho-Lee model, 183–89, 203–8
inflation rate and, 130, 180
inverse floaters and, 304
key rate and, 143–45, 189–92
in Kim-Ramaswamy-Sundaresan model, 268
lognormal distribution of, 177–79
long-run vs. long-term, 181
mean reversion of, 180
in Merton model, 266
in Monte Carlo simulations, 300
mortgages and, 296–301
movement of, 175–80
nominal, 130, 180
"no refunding restriction" and, 226
normal distribution of, 177–79
pass-through certificates and, 221
pension fund case study, 199–200
performance profile and, 147
prepayment options and, 245
price value of a basis point and, 164–68
put-call parity and, 67–68
quoted price and, 124
real rate and, 130
in recession, 130
resetting of, 221, 305
risk-neutral probability and, 184, 187–88, 206
sectors and, 220
sinking fund provision and, 226–27, 236–37
standard deviation for, 179, 185–87
strike price and, 187–88
swap market and, 168
term structure and, 181
tranches and, 301–4
in Vasicek model, 181–82, 184, 195–96, 198–202, 268
volatility and, 177–80, 185–88, 268
Wal-Mart case study, 220–22
yield and, 175–86, 195, 196–97, 201, 224–25
zero-coupon bonds and, 185–90, 205–7
  *See also* Risk-free rate; Term premium
"In the money," 30
Intrinsic value, 30–31, 79
Inverse floaters, 304
Inverse formula, 305
Investment-grade bonds, 222, 228
Investment value, 288, 290f, 291f, 308, 309–10
Invoice price, 124
IPO. *See* Initial public offering case study
Issue size, 222

Jarrow-Lando-Turnbull model, 264–65
Jarrow-Turnbull model, 264
Junk bonds. *See* High-yield bonds

Key rate, 143–45, 148, 150, 189–92
Kim-Ramaswamy-Sundaresan model, 268–69
Knock-in option, 88–90, 265
Knockout option
  covenants and, 270
  default risk and, 265, 269

definition of, 87–90
in Ericsson-Reneby model, 265
performance profile for, 88f

Latent warrant, 289
Law of one price, 133–36, 156–57
LEAPs. *See* Long-term equity anticipation securities
Leland model, 269
Levered portfolio, 38, 40, 55, 145
LIBOR. *See* London Interbank Offered Rate
Life insurance, 132, 280–81
Liquidity premium, 132, 182
Loans, bank
  in debt structure, 273
  default risk and, 254
  prepayment options and, 245
Local expectation hypothesis, 137
Lognormal distribution
  in Black model, 208
  in Black-Scholes model, 72
  definition of, 2
  of interest rates, 177–79
  of mean, 2f
  normal distribution and, 26–27n2, 72–73
  risk-neutral probability and, 43
  skew of, 72
  of stock prices, 2–3, 72
London Interbank Offered Rate (LIBOR), 117, 125
Long-run interest rate, 181
Longstaff-Schwartz model, 268
Long-term equity anticipation securities (LEAPs), 31
Long-term interest rate, 181, 193–94, 198

Macauley duration, 142
"Make whole" provision, 222
Margin, buying at
  in Cox-Ross-Rubinstein model, 38
  definition of, 6
  key rate and, 190
  put-call parity and, 32f
  security market line and, 9f, 19f
Market binomial lattice, 45–46, 80–83
Market efficiency, 132
Market interest rate, 124
Market-observed spot curve, 127
Market portfolio, 7–8, 20
Market price of risk, 182, 265
Market probability, 34–35, 45–46, 80
Market risk, 3–4, 7–9, 15, 20
Market total capitalization, 254
Markov property, 36, 264
Markowitz model, 3, 5
Matrix pricing, 224
Maturity, 123
McLeodUSA case study, 252–55, 272–73
Mean, 2f, 35–36, 44, 175
Mean reversion process, 180, 181, 186, 193, 198
Medium-term notes, 221
Merton model, 266–67, 270, 273–74
Microsoft case studies, 31, 67, 74–76
Miller-Modigliani Theory, 266
Modified duration, 143
Money markets, 125, 127, 139–40
Monte Carlo simulations, 300
Moody's Investors Services, 228
Mortality, 259, 299f
Mortgages
  accrued interest and, 221
  basis risks in, 299
  call options in, 296–300, 313–15
  cash flow in, 299

CMOs and, 301–5
coupons and, 296
default risk and, 294–95
definition of, 127, 221, 293
Excel exercises for, 310–15
government programs for, 294–95
interest rates and, 296–301
Monte Carlo simulations for, 300
option-adjusted spread and, 299–301
prepayment options and, 294–301
price value of a basis point, 296
principal in, 293–95, 298–301
PSA formula for, 298–300
servicing fees for, 294
Treasury bonds and, 299
yield and, 296–302, 313–15
Municipal bonds, 127
Mutual funds, 9, 11

NASDAQ index (QQQ), 11
NASDAQ-100 Index Tracking Stock, 31
National Association of Securities Dealers Automated Quotation. *See* NASDAQ index; NASDAQ-100 Index Tracking Stock
Nearby contracts, 30
New York Stock Exchange, 127
Nodes, 34
"No free lunch," 133f
Nominal interest rates, 130, 180
Nominal yield, 129
"No refunding restriction," 226
Normal distribution
definition of, 2
of interest rates, 177–79
lognormal distribution and, 26–27n2, 72–73
of mean, 2f, 175
standard deviation of, 175
of stock prices, 2–3, 72, 175–76
Normative theory, 3
Notational amount, 128
principal, 168
Notes
medium-term, 221
*See* Floating-rate note; Treasury notes
"Not in good faith" class, 257

OAS. *See* Option-adjusted spread
Oil-interest indexed dual-currency bonds, 306f
Omega, 115, 118, 119f
One-factor model, 182
"On-the-run" issues, 126, 129, 143–44
Open interest, 30
Open market operations, 130
Option-adjusted spread (OAS)
basis risks in, 233
binomial lattice for, 235–36
call options and, 235–36
credit risk ratings and, 229–33, 260
debt structure and, 229–32
definition of, 229
discount rate and, 232
Excel exercises for, 244, 248, 250
in Ho-Lee model, 241
in Jarrow-Lando-Turnbull model, 265
mortgages and, 299–301
price value of a basis point and, 230–32, 235–36
risk-free rate and, 248
risk premium and, 232
sectors and, 229–33
sinking fund provision and, 248, 250

term structure and, 232
yield and, 229–33
zero-coupon bond and, 232
Option contract, 30, 169
Option exercise, 98
Option premiums
backward substitution method for, 40
binomial lattice and, 34–36
Black-Scholes model for, 34, 37–40
comparative statics for, 46–49, 60, 77–78, 85, 115–16, 118–21
Cox-Ross-Rubinstein model for, 37–40
definition of, 30
dynamic hedging and, 36–37
implied volatility and, 64
intrinsic value and, 79
pathwise value and, 44
put-call parity and, 31–33
Rendleman-Bartter model for, 37–40
risk-neutral probability and, 42–43
stock price and, 30, 91–92
strike price and, 29–31, 91–92
Oracle case studies, 61–64, 79
OTC. *See* Over-the-counter bond market
"Out of the money," 30
Overnight repurchase rate, 125
Over-the-counter (OTC) bond market, 127

PAC. *See* Planned amortization class
Par
definition of, 124
dollar duration and, 165–67
forwards and futures, 160
sinking fund provision and, 237
in swaps, 128, 214–17
in Treasury securities, 126
yield and, 129, 155
Parity, 287, 290f, 291f, 292–93, 307–10
Passive management, 149
Pass-through certificates
capital and, 247–48
cash flow and, 221
CMOs and, 301–5
corporate bond case study, 221
default risk and, 247
definition of, 127, 293
interest rates and, 221
principal and, 221
sinking fund provision and, 246–48
trusts and, 221
*See also* Mortgages
Path, 43–44, 88–89
Payoff diagram, 30, 32, 38–44
Payout ratio, 10, 23
PBGC. *See* Pension Benefits Guarantee Corporation
Pension Benefits Guarantee Corporation (PBGC), 258
Pension fund
bankruptcy and, 258
credit default swap case study, 274–75
debt structure and, 273
diversification and, 11–13
interest rate case study, 199–200
recession impact on, 275
Perfect capital market, 3
Perpetual bonds, 123, 125
Perpetual cash flow, 25–26
Planned amortization class (PAC), 303
Plowback ratio, 23–25
PO. *See* Principle-only tranch

Poisson jumps, 264
Portfolio risk, 13
Preferred habitat, 132, 182
Premium, trading at, 124–25
Prepayment, 245, 294–301, 303, 313
Prescriptive theory, 3
Present value annuity factors (PVAF), 245
Present value factor, 40
Present value of growth opportunities (PVGO), 25–26
Price, bond, 233
arbitrage-free models for, 185–88, 206–7, 233–50
arbitrage-opportunity model for, 132–35
binomial lattice for, 233, 234f
for conversion, 287
discrete time pricing model for, 208–11
equilibrium models for, 180–82, 192–97
invoice, 124
law of one price and, 132–35, 156–57
market price of risk and, 182, 265
matrix pricing and, 224
one-factor models for, 181–82, 184, 198–202
quoted, 123–24
reduced-form models for, 264–66
relative-pricing model for, 190
structural models for, 266–73, 278–84
valuation vs., 224–29
*See also* Price value of a basis point
Price, option. *See* Option premiums
Price, stock
binomial lattice for, 34–36
in Black-Scholes model, 70
in CAPM, 7
comparative statics for, 46–49, 60, 115, 118–21
Markov property and, 36
probability distribution of, 2–3, 72, 175–76
standard deviation and, 175
*See also* Strike price
Price value of a basis point
definition of, 142
dollar duration and, 142, 164–68
dynamic hedging and, 165
interest rates and, 164–68
key rate and, 145
mortgages and, 296
option-adjusted spread and, 230–32, 235–36
swap market and, 165
yield and, 142, 224–25, 230–32, 235–36
Prime rate, 125
Principal
acceleration clause and, 256
bankruptcy and, 228, 256
bond factor and, 223
coupons and, 123, 221
currency exchange rates and, 305
debt structure and, 269–70
definition of, 123
discount function and, 134
dual-currency bonds and, 305
duration and, 151
forward/futures and, 136t
inflation rate and, 126
invoice price and, 124
in mortgages, 293–95, 298–301
notational amount and, 168
PAC and, 303
pass-through certificates and, 221

Principal (*continued*)
 pro rata bond retirement and, 223
 sinking fund provision and, 223,
  297
 in swap market, 128, 168
 tax and, 123
 tranches and, 301–3
 Wal-Mart case study, 219–21
 warrants and, 289
 yield and, 124, 166, 259
Principal-only (PO) tranch, 301–2,
 313–15
Probability distribution
 definition of, 2
 standard deviation and, 2f
 *See also* Lognormal distribution;
  Normal distribution
Profit and interest rate options case
 study, 203–5
Profit diagram, 77
Project financing case study, 105–6
Promised yield, 259
Proprietary trading case study, 65–68,
 209–10
Protective put option, 77
PSA. *See* Public Securities Association
Public bonds, 221
Public Securities Association (PSA),
 298–300, 313
Put-call parity, 31–33, 64–70, 92, 99,
 210
Put options
 American vs. European, 66–67, 92,
  94f, 101
 binomial lattice for, 93f, 95f
 in Black model, 208–11
 in Black-Scholes model, 70–71
 boundary conditions on, 87–90
 in convertible bonds, 288
 convexity and, 192
 in Cox-Ross-Rubinstein model,
  51
 definition of, 29
 digital options and, 115
 duration and, 189–91
 Excel exercises for, 99–103
 hedging and, 71
 intrinsic value of, 30–31
 key rate and, 189–91
 in Merton model, 267
 Microsoft case study, 31
 payoff diagram for, 30
 performance profile for, 47f, 88f,
  93f
 profit diagram for, 77
 put-call parity and, 31–33, 64–70
 risk-free rate and, 103
 stock price and, 47f
 straddle strategy for, 49
 strike price in, 29–31, 92
 in swap market case study, 118
 swaption and, 217
 zero-coupon bonds and, 103,
  189–91
PVAF. *See* Present value annuity
 factors
PVGO. *See* Present value of growth
 opportunities
Pye model, 259–60, 264

QQQ. *See* NASDAQ index
Quarterly earnings case study, 16–17
Quoted price, 123–24

Rate of return on equity (ROE), 24
Ratings, credit risk. *See* Credit risk
 ratings
Rating transitions, 229
Ratio, conversion, 287, 307–8

Real Estate Investment Trust (REIT),
 23–24
Real rate, 130
Recession
 call options and, 241–43
 credit default swap case study, 275
 credit risk ratings and, 232
 inflation rate in, 130
 interest rate in, 130
 pension funds and, 275
Recombining Tree model, 34
Recovery ratio, 259–62, 264, 267, 270
Reduced-form models, 264–66
REIT. *See* Real Estate Investment
 Trust
Relative pricing model, 190
Rendleman-Bartter model, 37. *See also*
 Cox-Ross-Rubinstein model
Reorganization plan, 257–58, 262
Replicating portfolio. *See* Levered
 portfolio
Repo rate, 125
Reset dates, 221, 305
Residual bond, 303
Residual risk, 3, 14
Retention option, 95–96, 105
Retirement funds case study, 280–81.
 *See also* Pension fund
Returns
 from cheap securities, 21, 127, 132
 correlation coefficient and, 14f, 15
 definition of, 2
 from rich securities, 21, 132
 systematic risk and, 3, 7–9
 term premium and, 182
 volatility and, 14f, 46
 *See also* Dividends; Drift
Rho, 60, 115, 118, 119f
Rich securities, 21, 132
Risk-averse lattice, 45–46, 83n3. *See
 also* Market binomial lattice
Risk-free rate
 in actuarial model, 259–60
 American options and, 103, 104f
 binomial lattice for, 35f, 41f
 in Black model, 208
 in Black-Scholes model, 70
 borrowing at, 6
 call option and, 60, 103, 104f, 211
 in CAPM, 5–6, 8, 15–17
 comparative statics for, 60, 115
 compound options and, 106
 in Cox-Ross-Rubinstein model,
  38–40
 digital options and, 112, 114, 115f
 dividends and, 22
 in dynamic hedging, 36–37
 in Merton model, 266
 option-adjusted spread and, 248
 path and, 43–44
 put-call parity and, 32–33, 67–68
 put option and, 103
 risk premium and, 8
 security market line and, 9f, 19f, 20
 swaption and, 217
 volatility and, 112
Risk-neutral binomial lattice, 35f, 41f,
 80–83, 87f
Risk-neutral probability, 39–45, 184,
 187–88, 206
Risk premium
 absolute priority rule and, 283, 284f
 in discount rate, 1
 diversification and, 4–5
 in market portfolio, 8
 option-adjusted spread and, 232
 risk-free rate and, 8
 standard deviation and, 4
 volatility and, 46

ROE. *See* Rate of return on equity
Rolling back method, 89

S&P. *See* Standard and Poor's 500
Saá-Requejo and Santa-Clara model,
 268
Safety covenants, 268
SEC. *See* Securities and Exchange
 Commission
Sectors, 220, 229–33, 261
Secured creditors, 255
Securities and Exchange Commission
 (SEC), 221
Security market line (SML), 7–8, 9f,
 19f, 20–21
Self-financing portfolio, 56
Separate Trading of Registered
 Interest and Principal of
 Securities (STRIPS)
 American options and, 98–99
 bond options and, 175–76, 180–82
 bonds and, 126–28, 133, 135, 158
 equity options and, 67, 74
Separation Theorem, 6, 17
Serial bond, 250
Servicing fees, 294
Sharpe model, 5–9, 15–22
Sharpe ratio, 309
Shimko model, 268
Short-term interest rate, 181, 193–95,
 198–202
Single monthly mortality, 299f, 313
Sinking fund provision
 asset-backed security case study,
  246–48
 call options and, 226
 cash flow and, 223, 250
 compound options and, 269
 conversion and, 288
 coupons and, 223, 237, 248–50
 debentures and, 223–24
 debt structure and, 222
 default risk and, 224
 definition of, 222, 223–24
 double-up option in, 226, 237–40
 duration and, 248
 Excel exercises for, 246–50
 interest rates and, 226–27, 236–37
 option-adjusted spread and, 248,
  250
 pass-through case study, 246–48
 principal and, 223, 297
 serial bonds and, 250
 tranches and, 302–3
 trusts and, 223–24
 yield and, 226
SML. *See* Security market line
Spot curve. *See* Yield
Spreads
 bid-ask, 33, 74, 209
 in Duffie-Singleton model, 265
 in Fisher model, 258–59, 260
 matrix pricing and, 224
 spread-protected debt securities,
  307
 static, 235–36, 298–99
 yield, 224–25, 229–33, 235–36,
  258–60
 *See also* Option-adjusted spread
SPY. *See* Standard and Poor's stock
 index
Standard and Poor's 500 (S&P), 7–8,
 11, 68, 72–73, 116–17
Standard and Poor's rating agency, 228
Standard and Poor's stock index
 (SPY), 11
Standard deviation
 in arbitrage-free models, 185–87
 capital market line and, 5–6

comparative statics and, 48
correlation coefficient and, 15
definition of, 1
diversification and, 3–4, 11–12, 15
in Fisher model, 258
in Ho-Lee model, 185–87
interest rates and, 179, 185–87
market price of risk and, 182
of normal distribution, 175
probability distribution and, 2f
risk-neutral probability and, 43
risk premium and, 4
stock price and, 35, 175
volatility and, 30, 46
Static hedging strategy, 33
Static spread, 235–36, 298–99
Step-up coupon, 253t
Stock movement model, 175
Stocks
    closed-end funds and, 9, 11
    comparative statics for, 7–9, 15
    convertible bonds and, 287–93,
        307–10
    correlation coefficient for, 14f, 15
    probability distribution of, 2–3, 72
    weight of, 4, 7, 15, 18
Straddle strategy, 49, 50f, 77
Strangle strategy, 77
Strategic debt servicing, 228
Strike price
    in American options, 91–92
    in Black model, 208–9
    in Black-Scholes model, 70
    in call options, 29–31, 48, 91–92,
        289
    in covered call options, 48
    in Cox-Ross-Rubinstein model, 38,
        40
    default risk and, 268
    in digital option, 85
    in Ericsson-Reneby model, 265
    interest rate and, 187–88
    in Merton model, 266–67
    in put-call parity, 31–32
    in put option, 29–31, 92
    in retention option, 95
    risk-neutral probability and, 43
    in swaption model, 212, 214–15
    of warrants, 289
Stripping, 304f
STRIPS. See Separate Trading of
    Registered Interest and Principal
    of Securities
Structural models, 266–69
Swap market
    amortization schedule in, 128
    basis points and, 165
    Black-Scholes model for, 117
    bullet payments in, 128, 133
    call options in, 117
    case study on, 116–17
    CDs and, 165
    coupons in, 127–28, 214–17
    default risk and, 128, 168, 213,
        273–78
    definition of, 127–28, 168
    discount function and, 133
    dynamic hedging and, 117–18
    Excel exercises for, 168–73
    fixed-rate bonds in, 117, 128, 168,
        170–71
    floating-rate notes in, 117, 128,
        168, 170–73, 216, 305
    forwards and futures on, 214–16
    interest rates and, 168, 194
    key rate and, 145
    LIBOR and, 117
    principal in, 128, 168
    put option in, 118

swaption model for, 169, 212–17
vanilla, 128, 168
yield for, 130
zero-coupon bond case study, 118
Swaption model, 169, 212–17
Systematic risk, 3–4, 7–9, 15, 20

Tangent portfolio, 5–7, 17
Tax, 123, 258
Tenor, 128, 171–72
Terminal conditions, 30
Term premium, 132, 181, 182, 184
Term sheet case study, 116–17
Term structure
    Cox-Ingersoll-Ross model and,
        196–97
    credit risk ratings and, 232, 270
    of interest rates, 181
    liquidity premium and, 132, 182
    option-adjusted spread and, 232
    term premium and, 182
    Vasicek model and, 201
    of volatilities, 179–80
Theta, 48–49, 85, 115, 118–21
TIPS. See Treasury inflation protection
    securities
Tranches, 301–4, 313–15
Transaction costs, 11, 288
Transfer pricing rate, 169–70
Transition matrix, 262–65
Transportation sector, 230f
Treasury bills, 61–64, 79, 125, 127
Treasury bonds
    benchmarking of, 192
    call options in, 126
    definition of, 126–27
    drift and, 180
    in index portfolio, 149
    inflation rate and, 126
    key rate and, 143–44
    liquidity premium and, 132
    matrix pricing and, 224
    mortgages and, 299
    PSA and, 299
    yield spreads and, 224
Treasury inflation protection securities
    (TIPS), 126, 309
Treasury notes, 125–26
Treasury securities
    benchmarking of, 192
    call options in, 126
    coupons for, 125–26
    default risk in, 64, 127
    definition of, 125, 126–27
    discount bonds and, 127
    drift and, 180
    flight to quality and, 232
    forwards and futures, 135
    in index portfolio, 149
    inflation rate and, 126
    interest payments for, 127
    key rate and, 143–44
    liquidity premium and, 132
    matrix pricing and, 224
    mortgages and, 299
    overnight repurchase rate for, 125
    passive management of, 149
    PSA and, 299
    spot curve for, 128–30
    trading of, 127
    yield of, 126, 128–30, 132, 224
    See also Separate Trading of
        Registered Interest and Principal
        of Securities; Treasury bills;
        Treasury bonds; Treasury notes
True lattice, 83n3. See also Market
    binomial lattice
Trusts
    bankruptcy and, 256

CMO bonds in, 303
    definition of, 221
    mortgage pools in, 293–94
    pass-through certificates and, 221
    sinking fund provision and, 223–24

Unsystematic risk, 3, 14
Up parameter, 35f, 38–39, 41f, 42–43,
    45, 54, 87f
Up-tick rule, 75
Utility sector, 220, 229, 231f, 262

Valuation, definition of, 225
Value at risk, bond, 151, 265
Vanilla swap, 128, 168
Vasicek model, 181–82, 184, 195–96,
    198–202, 268
Vega, 47–49, 50f, 115, 118–21
Vested period, 98
Volatility
    American options and, 103
    in arbitrage-free models, 185–88
    in binomial lattice, 41f
    in Black model, 208–11
    in Black-Scholes model, 50, 64,
        75–76
    call option and, 54, 103, 211
    comparative statics for, 47, 54, 115,
        185–86, 203, 208
    compound options and, 106, 107f
    conversion value and, 292–93
    correlation coefficient and, 14f
    in Cox-Ingersoll-Ross model, 181,
        193
    in Cox-Ross-Rubinstein model, 38,
        51, 61
    credit default premium and, 276
    definition of, 30
    digital options and, 112
    hedge ratio and, 54
    historical vs. implied, 75
    in Ho-Lee model, 183, 185–88,
        203
    implied, 49–50, 64, 75–76
    interest rates and, 177–80, 185–88,
        268
    market price of risk and, 182
    in Merton model, 266
    Microsoft case study, 75–76
    rate of return and, 14f, 46
    risk-free rate and, 112
    risk-neutral probability and, 43
    risk premiums and, 46
    standard deviation and, 30, 46
    stock price and, 175–76
    straddle strategy for, 49
    swaption and, 213
    of term structure, 179–80
    time-dependent, 61
    in Vasicek model, 181, 198
    zero-coupon bonds and, 179

Wal-Mart case study, 219–24, 228
Warrants, 78, 287, 289, 290f, 291f,
    310
Wealth management case study, 52–54
Whole loans, 294

Yield
    absolute priority rule and, 283, 284f
    arbitrage-free models for, 183–89
    barbell position and, 148–49
    basis points and, 142, 224–25,
        235–36
    bullet payment and, 128
    call options and, 222–26, 229–33,
        243
    cash flow and, 143
    comparative statics for, 60

Yield (*continued*)
  compounding frequency and, 160
  convexity and, 145–46
  coupons and, 124–25, 259
  Cox-Ingersoll-Ross model for, 181,
    182, 196–97
  Cox-Ross-Rubinstein model and,
    51
  credit risk ratings and, 229–32
  default and, 259, 267–68
  definition of, 124
  discount function and, 134, 184
  dividends and, 115, 116f, 119f
  dollar duration and, 165–68
  duration and, 141–45, 150–55,
    165–68, 189–92
  equilibrium models for, 180–82
  expectation hypothesis and, 131,
    137–38
  in Fisher model, 258–59
  flight to quality and, 232
  floating rate and, 172–73
  forwards and futures, 136–40,
    156–60
  graphing of, 131f, 175
  Ho-Lee model and, 183–86, 203
  inflation rate and, 130–31
  interest rates and, 175–86, 195,
    196–97, 201, 224–25
  invoice price and, 124
  key rate and, 143–45, 150, 189, 192
  liquidity premium and, 132, 182
  market price of risk and, 182
  modified duration and, 143
  in Monte Carlo simulations, 300

  mortgages and, 296–302, 313–15
  nominal, 129
  one-factor movement of, 182
  for "on-the-run" issues, 129, 143–44
  par and, 129, 155
  parity and, 290f, 291f, 309–10
  preferred habitat and, 132
  principal and, 124, 166, 259
  put-call parity and, 67–68
  in recession, 130
  sinking fund provision and, 226
  spreads of, 224–25, 229–33,
    235–36, 258–60
  for STRIPS, 127–28, 175–76
  for swap market, 130
  in swaption model, 214, 216–17
  tranches and, 302, 313
  for Treasury securities, 126, 128–30,
    132
  Vasicek model for, 181–82, 184,
    201
  warrants and, 290f, 291f
  zero-coupon bonds and, 155
  *See also* Option-adjusted spread;
    Returns; Yield to maturity
Yield to call, 225
Yield to maturity
  absolute priority rule and, 283, 284f
  call options and, 224–25
  cash flow and, 143
  coupons and, 124–25
  definition of, 124
  interest rates and, 175–76, 179,
    224–25
  invoice price and, 124

  modified duration and, 143
  option-adjusted spread and, 232
Yield to worst, 225

Zero-coupon bonds
  barbell position and, 148
  in Black model, 208
  call options and, 189–91, 195, 197
  cash flow and, 134–35
  convexity and, 146
  coupon rate and, 135
  definition of, 126
  for discount function, 185–88
  duration and, 141–42, 145, 150–53,
    189–90
  forwards and futures, 138–39,
    155–56, 158
  hedge ratio and, 189–90
  in Ho-Singer model, 270
  interest rates and, 185–90,
    205–7
  key rate and, 145, 189–91
  law of one price and, 135
  in Merton model, 266
  modeling of, 133–35
  option-adjusted spread and, 232
  performance profile for, 147f
  put-call parity and, 64, 69
  put options and, 103, 189–91
  relative pricing model for, 190
  stripping and, 304f
  STRIPS and, 127
  in swap market case study, 118
  volatility and, 179
  yield and, 155